To Susan, Ashley, and Alec
–A.S.

To Amanda, partly for her help and mostly for herself
–M.R.

Contents at a Glance

*T*able of Contents

PART ONE

In Chapter 1, Master the Basic Concepts, we'll introduce beginners to the basic concepts of database management, concentrating on relational databases. In this chapter, we also go through the basic concepts of the dBASE for Windows program, preparing you for rolling up your sleeves and getting to work in Chapter 2.

In Chapter 2, dBASE for Windows in an Evening, we show you how to design a table and enter that design in the Table Structure tool. Then you'll proceed to use the Table Records tool to enter and edit your data. You can also print simple reports directly from the Table Records tool.

Menu choices are indicated by underscoring the hot keys and separating multiple menu choices with a ► symbol. For example, File ► Print... means choose the File option on the main menu. Then, from the pull-down menu, choose the Print... option.

►► *How to Use This Book: Planning for Understanding*

We already know a bit about you, so we feel that some words of advice on working with this book are in order. But let us introduce ourselves, first.

Alan Simpson is a software consultant and prolific author of a variety of books. His dBASE books have been best sellers since 1982. Martin Rinehart is a consultant and author who specializes in dBASE. He is a frequent contributor to *DataBased Advisor, dBASE Advisor, dBASE Informant,* and *Reference dBASE* magazines, as well as the author of three other books on dBASE.

What we know about you is that you have probably looked at a shelf of dBASE books and passed right by the little ones to pick out this oversized work. We know that you are interested in understanding dBASE for Windows, and you aren't about to settle for a superficial, enough-to-get-by approach.

So let us give you some advice. Start with Chapter 1. Find a place where you can really concentrate and time yourself. Then make a plan, setting aside the time that you can afford, to work steadily for an hour each evening, or a half hour every morning, or whatever suits your schedule.

Plan on working steadily, at whatever pace suits you, through Part 1 and Part 2. If you do one chapter a day, that will take a week. If you do one chapter a week, that will take the better part of two months. Whatever way you do it, do it with a plan. Just the first seven chapters will get you to an above average level of productivity with dBASE for Windows.

Then, when you have completed Chapter 7, go to work on your own database problems. Use the rest of the book as you solve the problems that made you decide to turn to a database management system in the first place.

Welcome to *Understanding dBASE 5 for Windows.*

▶▶ W A R N I N G

This is a sample warning note. Don't overlook these warnings!

When there's a way to speed your work or an extra tidbit about how to accomplish something more efficiently, we'll tell you about it in a tip, like the one you see here.

▶▶ T I P

This is a sample tip. Read these for time-savers and other helpful hints.

Occasionally, we'll want to note something that is neither a warning nor a helpful hint. For example, we might supply some additional background material that we find interesting. This type of information is provided in a note.

▶▶ N O T E

This is something we think you may want to note.

▶ Keyboard and Menu Conventions

Arrow keys are shown as ←, ↑, →, and ↓. The Home, End, PgUp, PgDn, Ins, and Del keys are named in the style of the original IBM keyboard. Your keyboard may show the latter four spelled-out as Page Up, Page Down, Insert, and Delete. We call the Enter key *Enter*, although it is labeled *Return* on some keyboards.

Combination keys are labeled by specifying the shifting key (Shift, Ctrl, or Alt), a hyphen, and the other key in the combination. For example, one way to enter Design mode is with Shift-F2, which means to hold down the Shift key and press F2.

Chapter 3 provides critical information about designing a database. The more you know about database work, the more you'll benefit from a careful reading of Chapter 3.

Part 2, Running dBASE for Windows, is four chapters of tutorials. Get in front of your computer and start using dBASE for Windows. We'll dive right into the use of multiple tables in a single database. Before you're finished, you'll have put together a single system with two tables plus forms and reports.

Part 3, Master Classes, is for those who want to get to know the tools thoroughly, leaving no stone unturned, no click unclicked, no menu choice unexamined. You can read it in front of your computer, trying every single feature, or you can skim it while you're waiting for the train, looking for helpful tricks.

Part 4, Programming Basics, should get dog-eared as you tack down corners pointing to useful commands and functions. You'll want to at least skim these chapters to get the most out of Part 5.

Part 5, Working with Forms, should also get dog-eared as you flag the parts that are most useful to you. You can experiment with the items that seem interesting, then return to the reference sections whenever you need specific information.

▶▶ Conventions You'll See in This Book

Throughout this book, you'll see in-text notes, marked by icons in the margin. You'll also see our particular style of referring to keyboard keys and menu selections.

▶ Book Notes

When there's a way to get in trouble, we'll alert you in the form of a warning note, as you see at the top of the next page.

In Part 4, we'll introduce you to the basics of programming. We'll treat dBASE programming at the beginning level. You'll find that as you get into building your own forms, you'll be adding simple programs (often just one line long) to handle the user-interface events, such as button clicks. These chapters serve both as an introduction and as reference. On a quick reading of Chapter 12, for instance, you'll meet all the most commonly used functions in the dBASE language. We don't expect you to memorize the facts you need to supply to calculate a mortgage payment, but we do hope you'll know that there is a function for this, and you'll be able to refer here when you need it.

The final part, Part 5, describes how to design your own data forms to make your database systems efficient and reliable. As you'll see, there are many different types of objects that you can place on a form, such as text, pushbuttons, and entry fields, as well as a substantial number of Windows objects, such as drop-down lists and comboboxes. The chapters in Part 5 provide examples you can work through to see what can be done with these objects. You can decide which are useful for your own systems. Then you can easily find just the details you need in the reference sections at the end of the chapters.

►► *How Do You Read This Book?*

Read Chapter 1 in your favorite easy chair, or on the train as you commute to work. But for Chapter 2 and all of Part 2, you'll need to be in front of your computer, typing and clicking as you go along. Actually, although we strongly recommend a mouse, there is nothing in dBASE for Windows that you can't access from the keyboard, so the clicking is not strictly necessary. But it's very, very helpful.

Chapter 1 is for beginners and those new to dBASE for Windows. It's relatively short, so we suggest you go through it, even if you think you know the basics.

Chapter 2, Use dBASE for Windows in an Evening, is just what it says. If you've never used dBASE, or any database for that matter, go through Chapter 2 thoroughly. By the time you're finished, you'll be able to enter a table definition, enter and edit data, query your data, and print simple reports. If you know a little about dBASE for Windows, skim this chapter quickly, slowing down for new topics.

We don't assume that you're an expert at running database systems. We'll begin at the beginning, starting with how to design your own databases using tables to organize your data. You'll learn to manipulate these tables singly and in combinations as a complete database.

If you do have some experience with database systems, you'll be able to progress through the first chapters more quickly.

The user-interface components of dBASE for Windows are all completely new, since this is the first dBASE to run in a true graphical user interface (GUI) environment. These elements include pull-down menus, dialog boxes, speedbar buttons, and even Speed menus (accessed with a right mouse-click). dBASE for Windows provides several alternative ways to get to the features you need. We'll explain how to use the mouse and keyboard to give commands, and you can pick the methods that suit your own style of working.

►► *What's in This Book?*

The manuals that came with your dBASE for Windows are an excellent source of information, and the on-line help is even more exhaustive. But this book provides all the information you need, organized so that you can learn dBASE for Windows as quickly as possible. In Part 1, you'll get started using dBASE for Windows for practical work in just one evening. The chapters in Part 2 give you more details on each of the key portions of the program.

After you've finished reading and following the examples in Part 2, you'll be able to design multiple-table databases, prepare forms that guide your data entry and editing, build queries that let you view portions of your data, and prepare custom reports from your database. For example, if you can click a pushbutton labeled OK today, before you're finished with Chapter 6, you'll know how to add pushbuttons on your own forms.

Part 3, Master Classes, goes into every area of dBASE for Windows in depth. After you complete Part 2, you'll find that your work directs you into one or more of the topics covered here. Some of you may want to learn more about the data-entry tools, while others will be more interested in sophisticated reporting. The details are here, to be explored as your needs dictate.

▶▶ *Introduction*

Welcome to dBASE for Windows. If you've worked with dBASE IV or an earlier version, or another Xbase system, you'll find dBASE for Windows familiar. Whether or not you know how to use an earlier dBASE version, you'll find that dBASE for Windows is an exciting, powerful, and flexible database system.

The Windows version of dBASE has been reworked and rethought from the ground up. It is an object-oriented and event-driven database management system that lets you create custom applications without any programming. If you can point and click, you can build database systems that meet your needs.

▶▶ *Who Should Read This Book?*

We don't assume that you know an earlier version of dBASE. If you've worked with dBASE before, you'll learn dBASE for Windows that much more quickly. We do assume that you want to master the use of dBASE for Windows, from simple data-entry applications through building sophisticated forms, menus, and reports.

We assume that you already know the basics of operating an industry-standard computer. That includes getting around in DOS and in Microsoft Windows.

We'll stop briefly at the Query Designer tool to ask questions about your data. Then you'll meet the Form Expert, and use it to generate a custom form for your table. Finally, we'll take a quick tour of Crystal Reports, designing and running a simple report.

Chapter 3, Design Your Database, is both the simplest and the most critical chapter in this book. If we needed to apportion the ingredients for successful database systems, we would say good design is three-quarters of the battle, and the other quarter is being proficient with dBASE for Windows. We can't overstate the importance of understanding the material in Chapter 3 as you go forward into the rest of the dBASE for Windows product.

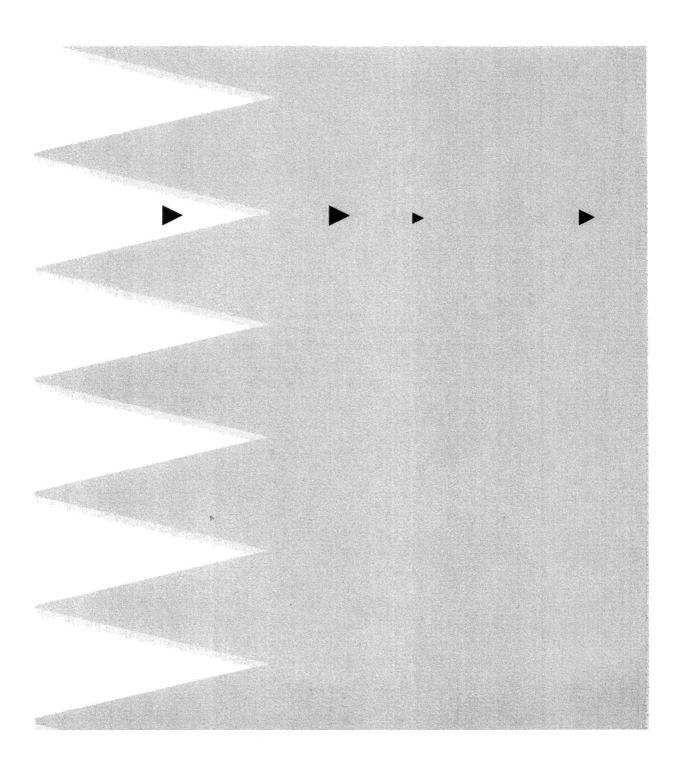

▶ ▶ CHAPTER **1**

Master the Basic
Concepts

——

►► **W**e know that you want to get to your computer and get going. But one of the oldest and wisest pieces of advice ever given to computer programmers also applies to database users. It's this: The first step in building a computer system is to turn your computer off.

And that's just what we're going to do. Before we get started with dBASE for Windows, we'll talk about what you need to know to use a relational database system. This chapter is about the basics. First we'll discuss the fundamentals of databases, and then we'll give you an overview of the components of dBASE for Windows.

►► *Database Basics*

Let's begin with databases in general before we get to relational databases in particular. If you are familiar with databases already, turn ahead a few pages and study Figure 1.2. If it makes perfect sense to you, skip this section. Or read on, and we'll give you a short history and overview of database systems.

► *Database Origins*

In the 1950s, the first computers could only read data one item at a time. Data was stored on punched paper tape, then punched cards used in pre-computer business data processing. Magnetic tape was an early improvement, but the computer still would start reading at the beginning and continue reading one item at a time. This is referred to as *serial* data access. For example, your computer probably has serial ports, which transmit and receive data one bit (an individual 0 or 1) at a time. (Parallel ports handle multiple bits at once.)

In data storage, the alternative to serial storage is random-access storage. Floppy disks, hard disks and CD-ROMs are random-access devices. It was the development of the hard disk that made random-access storage a reality.

Of course, reading "randomly" would not be useful in data processing. *Random access* means that if you have a million items of data on your disk, you can read item 654321 first, item 1 second, and item 999999 third. You don't need to read item 1, then item 2, and so on.

Serial storage limited the computer to processing files. Random-access storage made computerized database systems possible. The fundamental goals of a database system are to record different types of information in sensible groupings and to bring that information together in useful ways on demand.

Let's consider a typical example of a database. You probably have a personal phone list. For some people, you list a single number; for others, you list a home number and a separate work number. This phone list is a data file.

Let's say that you have three people in your list that work for BigCo, which is reached at 555-1234. One problem with a simple data file is that data gets repeated. If BigCo's phone number changes to 123-4567, you have three people whose work number needs changing. Will you remember them all?

With a database system, you don't need to worry about finding repeated items and changing each one. When you enter the data, you can note that each of your three friends works for BigCo. When you need a work number, the computer will look up the person, see that he or she works for BigCo, and then find BigCo's phone number. You'll see how this works in the next chapter, in which we'll implement a database of phone numbers and addresses.

▶ Relational Databases

Strangely, the word *relational*, as applied to databases, has nothing to do with the relationships that a database tracks. For example, one relationship that a database might track is that Fred and Judy both work for BigCo. If the database "knows" this, we can get the correct work number for either Fred or Judy. When BigCo changes its phone number, we'll enter that change as the new number for BigCo. We'll then get the new number if we look up either Fred or Judy's work number. This works because we tell the computer that there is a relationship between BigCo and Fred, and a similar relationship between BigCo and Judy.

But that's not what *relational* means. The term comes from what once was an obscure branch of mathematics: relational algebra and relational calculus. In the mathematics terminology, a *relation* is a table. A *relational database* is simply one that stores its data in tables—familiar rows and columns. Figure 1.1 shows a simple, two-table database.

FIGURE 1.1 ▶

Relational means data in tables

Table Records (PEOPLE.DBF)

Rec	Name	Address	City	ST	ZIP	Employer	Phone
1	Phil Friendly	5 Maple Ave.	Pleasantville	NY	12345	BigCo	(800) 111-1234
2	Adrianne Adamson	10 Oak Dr.	Sun City	CA	55555	Sacred Heart	(800) 123-4567
3	Madilyn Monroe	Sunset Blvd.	Hollywood	CA	5555	Zebra Feed Store	(123) 123-1234
4	Eve Gable	High Rise, # 24J	New York	NY	12345	BigCo	(212) 911-9111
5	Herb Hacker	Orange Grove	MountainView	CA	5555	BigCo	(800) 987-6543
6	Feline Garfield	Studio 4	Century City	CA	5555	Fourth St. Blues	(800) 555-5555
7	Aphonse Brown, Md	12 Main St.	Peoria	IL	12345	Sacred Heart	(555) 444-4444
8	Wilfred Witherspoon	1 Fifth Avenue	New York	NY	10001	BigCo	(212) 999-9999
10	John Smith	747 Plane St.	Chicago	IL	44444	Harry's Hardware	(444) 444-4444

Employers

Rec	Name	Address	City	ST	ZIP	Phone
1	BigCo	1 Main St.	Pleasantville	NY	11111	(800) 111-1111
3	Sacred Heart Hospital	2 Main St.	Pleasantville	NY	12345	(800) 222-2222
4	Harry's Hardware	3 Main St.	Pleasantville	NY	12345	(800) 333-3333
6	Fourth Street Blues and Genes	4 Main St.	Pleasantville	NY	12345	(800) 444-4444
7	Zebra Feed Store	5 Main St.	Pleasantville	NY	12345	(800) 555-5555

Relational theorists have built our databases on a strong, theoretical foundation. In 1969, E. F. Codd, then a scientist at IBM, published the first of many papers on the application of relational mathematics to databases. He showed how joining data from one table to data in another provided a precise description for, getting the BigCo phone number when you want to call Judy at work (as one example).

You can't add and subtract tables, but you can perform other interesting operations on them, such as selecting a set of rows or joining columns from a row in one table with columns from a row in another table.

Although many people are working on different database forms, such as object-oriented databases, the relational database is the most popular choice today.

▶ *Arranging Data in Tables*

Tables are a common structure for arranging data. You decide that you will need data about people, so you create a table to store this data. At the outset, you decide that you will need the person's name, address, phone number, and employer. You put a column into your table for each of these items.

The columns in a relational database are considered fixed; the rows are variable. As you add new people to your table, it gets longer. If you delete people, your table gets shorter, but it retains the same columns.

Of course, as your needs change, you'll add new columns and delete ones that you don't use. And you'll change the column definitions, too. Perhaps you'll find that your Name column just isn't wide enough; or maybe it's too wide, and it would be a lot more convenient if it didn't waste so much space. You can make these adjustments as often as you need, but they will be far less frequent than the routine process of adding and deleting rows.

Each row in a relational database table is called a record. (If you are a relational theorist, you call it a *tuple*, which rhymes with *couple*.) The term *record* was borrowed from record keeping in the early days of computers and has been with us ever since.

In a relational database, the word *field* has two distinct meanings. If you speak of the fields in a table, you are referring to the table's columns. On the other hand, if you speak of the fields in a record, you refer to the individual entries in each column in a particular row.

When that ambiguity might be a problem, we'll be specific about referring to the field's definition or the field's value. For example, our table of people has a Name field. The field might be defined as a character data field, 32 characters wide. The value of the name field in a particular record might be "John Smith."

In dBASE, a field can contain character data, numbers, dates, and other data types. When you define your tables, you'll pick an appropriate type for each field. dBASE will make sure that only the selected type of data is allowed in each field. For example, you can't enter "Smith" into a numeric Weight field.

As you'll see, you can put further restrictions on the values allowed in a field. For example, you could have a rule that the value in the Ship_Date field is a date that doesn't come before the value in the Order_Date field. Restricting the values that get into your table fields helps ensure that you have valid information in your database. (The restrictions we put on the values that can go into a field define what the theorists call the field's *domain*.)

For a quick summary of these terms and concepts, take a look at Figure 1.2. It shows that a relational database is built of tables. The table rows are called records, and the columns are called fields. The field has a definition, and it has values in each record that match its definition.

FIGURE 1.2 ▶

Relational database terms

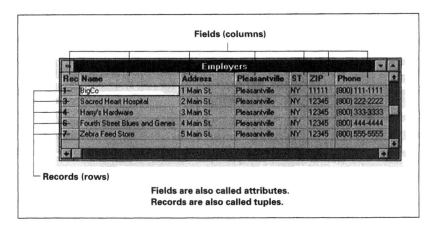

An Overview of dBASE for
===

▶▶ *An Overview of dBASE for Windows*

How does dBASE for Windows work? Any relational database management system (RDBMS) works mostly behind the scenes. Its job is to get data from the keyboard and convert it into appropriate 1s and 0s on disk. Then, on demand, to return these 1s and 0s in the form of text

Master the Basic Concepts

and numbers that are meaningful to us. What we see is the surface through which this data management takes place.

▶ Features of dBASE for Windows

Figure 1.3 shows dBASE for Window's main features. The main window's *client area* is the space between the bar with icons (called the *speedbar*) at the top and the bar with status information (called the *status bar*) at the bottom. In the figure, this area contains the Navigator and Command windows.

FIGURE 1.3 ▶

Main dBASE for Windows features

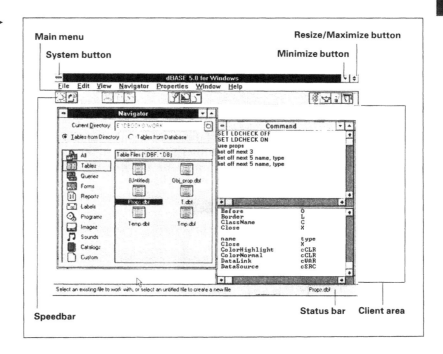

▶ *The Navigator and the Command Windows*

The Navigator and Command windows are the alternate control windows. Both are capable of fully controlling dBASE for Windows. We'll work mostly with the Navigator until we get to the more advanced topics.

As you'll see, as you point and click in the Navigator, your actions are translated into program commands in the Command window. Typing the commands in the Command window achieves exactly the same results as pointing and clicking in the Navigator.

Once you know your way around dBASE for Windows, you may find that some actions are easier to initiate from the Command window. If you are used to the dot prompt in dBASE IV and earlier, the Command window will be an old friend. On the other hand, if you prefer point-and-click actions, you may use the Navigator almost exclusively. Just remember that everything that you can launch in the Navigator can also be launched from the Command window.

▶ *The Top Line*

At the very top of the screen are the standard Windows buttons and the name of the Windows application. In the upper-left is the System button (shown in the margin). Click on the System button to see the standard System menu choices:

Double-clicking on the System button closes dBASE for Windows.

Note that you don't need a mouse (or other pointing device) to use the System menu. From the keyboard, press Alt-spacebar to get to this menu.

▶▶ **T I P**

> As is the case with most Microsoft Windows applications,
> being able to work from the keyboard and with the
> mouse will greatly increase your productivity in dBASE
> for Windows. You will benefit by taking the time to learn
> both the keyboard and mouse actions.

 In the top-right corner of the main window are the Minimize and
Resize/Maximize buttons (shown in the margin). The default startup
size is maximized (full screen). Clicking on the Resize button (double-
headed arrow) reduces the size.

You can drag the sides and corners to change dBASE's window size,
but there's a problem. If you're running dBASE for Windows on a
standard 14-inch monitor, you'll probably want to use 640 × 480 resolution. At higher resolutions, the icons and text become too small to
read. At 640 × 480, you'll want to use most of the screen because
there's a lot to put inside dBASE for Windows' client area.

 ▶▶ **N O T E**

> Your screen resolution is determined by Windows when
> it is started. You can change the resolution through
> the Windows Setup program.

Of course, the higher resolutions are great if you have a 17- or 21-inch
monitor. On a 14-inch monitor, you may go to 800 × 600 resolution after you know dBASE's icons very well.

Under the top line comes the main menu.

▶ *dBASE for Windows Menus*

Most of what you will do in dBASE for Windows is done by clicking on
objects visible in the client area. When you begin with dBASE for Windows, you'll find that you don't use the menus much. As you get to
more advanced uses, however, you'll find that the menus cover a wealth
of operations that are difficult or impossible to find elsewhere.

The File Menu

The main menu starts with the IBM's Common User Access (CUA) standard menus. The File menu is on the left. This menu changes to reflect the active child window (the active window inside dBASE for Windows). For example, if you are working in a data table, it includes options to save your data, print your data, and close the table:

New	▶
Open...	Ctrl+O
Close	Ctrl+F4
Import...	
Exit	
1 TEMP.DBF	
2 PEOPLE.DBF	
3 ORGS.DBF	
4 PEOPLESV.DBF	
5 TEMP.WFM	

With the Navigator or Command window active, the File menu includes options to open tables or import data, as well as to close the active tool. If a child window isn't open, the File menu includes options to open a file or to exit from dBASE for Windows.

The Help Menu

Again conforming to the CUA convention, the Help option is on the far right. A Windows Help menu drops down when you click on Help (or press Alt-H).

Contents	Shift+F1
Search...	
Views and Tools	
Language	
Keyboard	
Experts	▶
Interactive Tutors...	
How to Use Help	
About dBASE 5.0 for Windows...	

As you can see, the Help menu includes the various Help options, plus the About dBASE 5.0 for Windows choice, which displays information about your machine and your version of dBASE for Windows.

The Edit Menu

The Edit menu, with the normal selection of cut, copy, and paste operations, is near the left, next to the File option. It performs the usual functions via the Windows Clipboard:

Undo	Ctrl+Z
Cut	Ctrl+X
Copy	Ctrl+C
Paste	Ctrl+V
Delete	**Del**
Select All	

This menu provides convenient ways to move data or other information around within dBASE for Windows, and between dBASE and other Windows programs.

The Window Menu

The Window menu is near the right, next to the Help option. It lets you cascade or tile your windows, and lists all the windows you have available, as in this example:

Cascade	Shift+F5
Tile Horizontally	
Tile Vertically	Shift+F4
Arrange Icons	
Close All Windows	
√ 1 Navigator	
2 Command	

You can choose any window in the list, and this can be important when the rich collection of tools here encourages you to make quite a mess of your computer's desktop.

The Properties Menu

The Properties option is always just to the left of the Window option. Clicking on it (or pressing Alt-P) pulls down a short menu, which always begins with the Desktop choice:

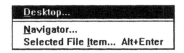

Choosing Desktop brings up a multi-tab form that lets you select your preferences in the following categories:

- Country
- Table
- Data Entry
- Files
- Application
- Programming

In addition to the Desktop properties, the menu includes any other properties relevant to the currently active tool. For example, if the Navigator is selected, a Navigator option is available to set your preferences for the Navigator.

Other Menus

The rest of the menu choices vary, depending on your location in dBASE for Windows. They are always appropriate to the active tool. Figure 1.4 shows menu choices available when the Table Records tool is active. As you'll see in Chapter 2, the Table Records tool is the basic tool for entering and maintaining data.

As you can see, the menu has View and Table choices, along with the standard File, Edit, Properties, Window, and Help options. In this case, the View menu lets you select from different ways to view your data. The Table menu offers a wealth of choices for manipulating your data. It is

FIGURE 1.4

dBASE for Windows browsing a table

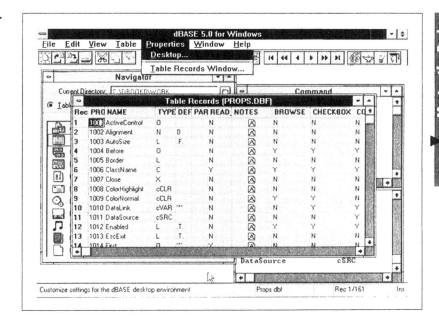

often true that the menu option that matches the active tool's name (Table for the Table Records tool) accesses the key operations for that tool.

▶ Speedbars

Below the menus are the speedbars. Like the menus, they vary with the tool you are using. For example, Figure 1.5 shows the speedbar when the Table Structure tool is active.

These four speedbar buttons appear on the left:

FIGURE 1.5 ▶

Using the Table Structure tool

These buttons are for performing common file and print operations.

To the right of these are the buttons for Clipboard (cut, copy, and paste) operations:

These four buttons appear on the far right:

They provide access to special dBASE for Windows features: the Navigator window, the Command window, Experts, and Tutors.

In between are buttons specific to the tool in use. The run and design icons are available in many places in dBASE for Windows. The run icon is a lightning bolt, and the design icon shows drafting tools:

The three other speedbar buttons for the Table Structure tool look like this:

These allow you to choose one of the standard layouts for your data.

Once you become familiar with dBASE for Windows, you'll find yourself doing a lot of work by simply clicking on the appropriate speedbar choice.

▶ The Status Bar

At the bottom of the dBASE for Windows window is the status bar. This provides information that is continuously changing. For example, as you move your mouse pointer over the speedbar buttons, an explanation of the active button's function appears in the left side of the status bar.

In an Editor, you'll see your current line and column position, a notation regarding whether you're in Insert or Overstrike mode, and other status information.

▶ dBASE for Windows Tools and Experts

Most of dBASE for Windows work is done with tools that Borland provides, or with the tools that you build using the tools that Borland provides. For example, Figure 1.6 shows the Form Designer with its Controls palette of standard and custom form objects.

Everything on a form—an entry field, a list box, a check box, and so on—is an object. In fact, all the dBASE for Windows user interfaces are built from objects. This includes the built-in tools that you see and the forms that you can build.

FIGURE 1.6 ►

The Form Designer's Controls palette

When you build your own forms, you'll start with a Form object. Then you'll add other objects as properties of the Form object. You might add Entryfield, Pushbutton, Listbox, and Radiobutton objects, as well as the other objects you need for a modern Windows interface.

These objects are described by properties which you can examine and change with the Object Properties Inspector (discussed later in this chapter). Properties include data (such as Top, Left, Height, and Width) and code for events (such as OnClick for pushbuttons and OnOpen for forms).

Using the Form Designer, we created the form shown in Figure 1.7. We use this form to access data in our People table. Note that this form would have required expensive, custom programming—many hours worth—just a few years back.

Building a form could still be a time-consuming activity, especially if your database has many fields. This is why we use the built-in Form Expert. For example, we always use this Expert to get an almost instantaneous form, once we've defined the fields in a table.

FIGURE 1.7 ▶

A form for the People table

We built the preliminary version of the form in Figure 1.7 in less than a minute. More exactly, we answered the questions that the Form Expert asked, which took about half a minute, and then it built the form in another few seconds.

It took us about three minutes using the Form Designer to make a handful of changes, such as inserting proper formatting for a North American telephone number.

The components you see here are all objects selected from the Form Designer's Controls palette. If you want a check box, radio button, field, or edit box, you just click on that element in the Controls palette and drop it into place on your form.

Using the Form Expert, you'll be asked some questions about your preferences. As you see in Figure 1.8, the Form Expert wants to know how we want to lay out the form. You answer this question and some others, and the Form Expert builds the form to your specifications.

FIGURE 1.8 ▶

The Form Expert asking which layout we want

If you're not satisfied with the way the form looks, just run the Expert again. You can try a form in two or three ways in minutes. When you get one you like, you can begin to customize it with your favorite objects from the Form Designer's Controls palette. You'll see how the Form Designer and Expert work in the next chapter and get details in Chapter 6.

▶ Design and Run Modes

As you build forms, reports, or other components, you can switch between Design mode and Run mode. In Run mode, you'll actually be using the tool you're creating. This is wonderful for building a form, for example, because you can try it in operation just by clicking on a speed-bar icon.

As you work, you'll click on the design icon (or press Shift-F2) to make improvements in a form, and then click on the run icon (or press F2) to test it. It makes creating reports, forms, and data tables fast and fun.

▶ Speed Menus

As with many Borland products, clicking with the right mouse button brings up a Speed menu. For example, here's the Speed menu for a table in the Navigator:

Navigator Properties...	
Cut	Ctrl+X
Copy	Ctrl+C
Paste	Ctrl+V

You just point at the table and click the right button to see this menu. Then, with one more click, you can choose to look at the table's properties, delete the table, add or edit records, or modify the table's structure.

▶ Object Properties Inspectors

The Object Properties Inspectors are key to much of your work. An Object Properties Inspector maintains an extensive list of properties. For example, Figure 1.9 shows the list for a simple Text object on a form.

As you can see, there's a lot to know about a Text object. dBASE for Windows wants to know what form it's attached to, where the form is located, what font we're using, if we want normal or boldface or italic text, what color to use, and so on.

In fact, in Figure 1.9, we've moved the speedbar to the left of the screen and turned the status bar off to get all the vertical room possible, and we still haven't shown all the text properties. Each entry on the Properties list that has a plus sign (+) next to it is a group entry, contracted to hide its details. The minus sign (–) entries are groups that are expanded to show all their details. For example, in the figure, you can see the position properties, but not the identification properties.

FIGURE 1.9 ▶

Properties of a text object

▶▶▶ **T I P**

You can reposition the speedbar and turn the status bar on and off through the Desktop Properties window. Choose Desktop from the Properties menu, and then click on the Application tab to change the speedbar and status bar settings.

Don't assume that you'll need to make all these decisions for every object you use. Each property has a default, so you can skip almost all of this. However, the default text for your first Text object is *text1*, so you'll need to enter something here. Otherwise, all these controls are here to satisfy your creative urges, not to make you do a lot of work.

▶ *Your Job with dBASE for Windows*

To build a system with dBASE for Windows, you'll start by defining your tables. Then you can use the Query tool to describe how your tables are related. As you'll see when we get there, this is almost no work at all. (For the simplest single-table system, the Query step isn't needed.)

With a query that defines how your tables are related, you can build one or more forms. One form can handle several tables, or you can have a separate form for each table. If you're in a big hurry, you can skip the forms altogether and use dBASE for Windows defaults. But with the Form Expert, creating forms is quick and simple, so you'll probably want to use forms.

Now you have the tools you need to enter, browse through, and edit your data. After you enter some data, you'll go back to the Query tool to define other queries. Queries allow you to select and work with sub-sets of your table. For example, queries let you locate your biggest spending customers and your lowest paid employees.

Finally, you'll use the Crystal Reports report writer to create reports, so you can get your data on paper. Like forms, reports can be created virtually instantaneously with the aid of Experts. Even a complex cross-tab report can be created in minutes. dBASE for Windows provides a rich selection of report tools, so that once you decide to get creative, you have almost unlimited power to produce anything from intelligent form letters to complex catalogs.

For really polished work, you can wrap all your other tools into an application with its own menus, courtesy of the built-in menu maker. If you want to go further, you can begin programming in dBASE's built-in programming language.

▶ ▶ *Summary*

You've learned that a relational database is a database that stores all its data in tables. A table is made up of rows and columns. The columns, called fields, are predefined (by you).

The rows, called records, are what you insert to add data or delete when your data is obsolete. Each record's fields contain values appropriate to the column type: text in the Name field, a date in the Ship_Date field, and so on.

dBASE for Windows provides the underlying database layer that makes a relational database work, but most of what we see is the interface layer that lets us work with our data in our own way.

dBASE for Windows has the features (buttons and menus) common to most Microsoft Windows applications. In its client area, it sports a large number of tools, including Experts that speed you through your work.

At the top level, you can do useful work very quickly with dBASE. As you delve more deeply into each tool, you'll find that there are no serious limits to get in the way of building systems that provide you with powerful, flexible databases.

In Chapter 2, we'll get started on a simple system in just one evening's work. We hope you enjoy it.

If you haven't done so yet, it's time to turn your computer back on!

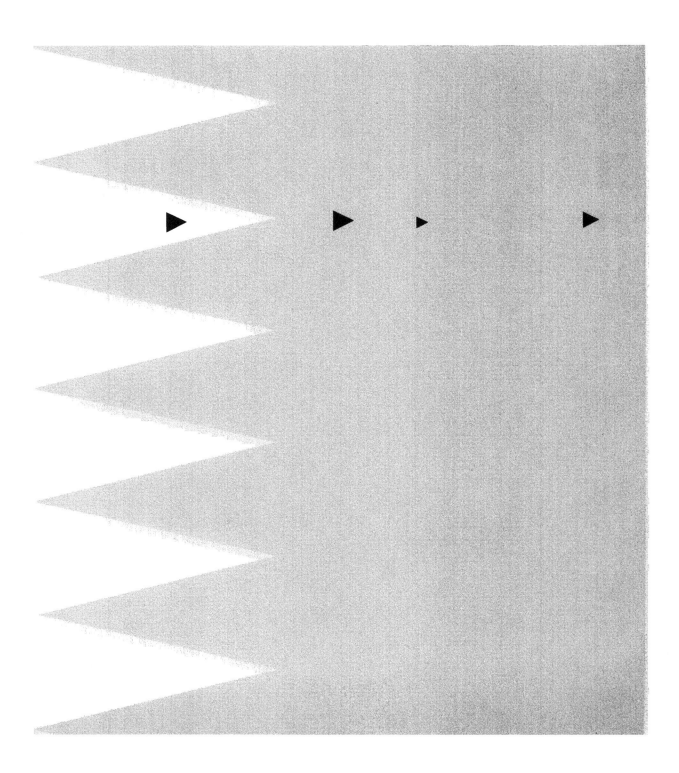

► ► CHAPTER **2**

dBASE for Windows
in an Evening

► ► **I**n this chapter, we'll introduce you to dBASE for Windows and dive right into some useful work. We'll define a data table, enter some data, edit the data, query the table for a summary, and finally write a report. Although you won't become an advanced dBASE for Windows user in a single evening, you'll be able to use many of the program's tools.

This chapter is like the guided tour you might take on your first visit to Paris. From the tour bus, you can learn the general layout of the city—see the Seine, Notre Dame, the Arc de Triomphe, and so on. But to get to know Paris, you need to set off on foot and spend some time in every part of the city. In Part 2 of this book, we'll be touring each section of dBASE for Windows on foot (in detail). For now, we'll just look at the highlights.

And this guided tour has one advantage over any you can find in Paris (or any other city): if you see something interesting, you can stop and poke around. Try some menu choices or click some speedbar buttons. We'll wait patiently until you're ready to get back on the bus.

► ► *You Get Ready to Work*

You'll need three things to be ready to work: basic Microsoft Windows skills, the dBASE for Windows software, and a working directory.

If you're new to Windows, you'll need skills outside the scope of this book. Please don't try to plow forward here, hoping to learn Windows along the way. You'll either get mad at us, or worse, you'll get mad at yourself.

Windows comes with a *Getting Started* manual, and there are lots of books on this subject. Alan might be biased, but we'll still recommend his book, *Windows Running Start* (also from SYBEX). If you do not

have a manual and can't get to a bookstore, press Alt-H (for Help) in
Windows 3.1 and choose the Windows Tutorial from the Help menu.

If you haven't installed dBASE for Windows, you'll need to do that
first. Instructions are in Appendix A. Even if you've already installed
the software, you might want to look at Appendix A. The method we
suggest there is a lot faster than the standard installation procedure.

Those of you who are using dBASE for Windows on a network will
need to ask your network administrator for installation instructions.

If you followed the default installation procedure, dBASE for Windows
is available in a Program Manager group called dBASE for Windows.
The default group looks like the one in Figure 2.1.

FIGURE 2.1 ▶

*The dBASE for Win-
dows group in the
Program Manager*

▶ *Menu Choices and Mouse Clicks*

Throughout this book, we'll frequently tell you to choose something
like the following: Help ▶ Windows Tutorial. This means choose the
Help menu. Then, from the drop-down menu, choose Windows Tutorial. The underscored characters are the ones you press if you're using the keyboard. For this example, you could press F10 (or Alt) to
get to the main menu, and then press H to see the Help menu. In
the Help menu, press W for the Windows Tutorial. Or you could press
Alt-H, to skip over the F10 or Alt step. Of course, mouse clicks work, too.

Windows users usually click their mouse with the index finger. This is the left button if you have a two-button mouse and are right-handed. It's also the left button if you're left-handed and don't reverse the mouse buttons. If you're a lefty who has reversed buttons, you'll need to remember that what we call "left" is really right, and vice-versa.

dBASE for Windows, like many Borland products, also uses the right button. If your mouse cursor is over an object and you click the right button, you typically get a pop-up menu, called the Speed menu. This menu lists the most common operations for that object. For example, if your cursor is over a form in the Navigator, clicking the right mouse button brings up a Speed menu with choices to use the form, delete the form, or modify the form's design.

dBASE for Windows does not use the middle button of three-button mice. dBASE's programming language has support for the middle button, so programmers can build special applications that use the middle button. For our purposes, we assume (as does dBASE for Windows) that you probably have just two buttons on your mouse. If your mouse has only one button, you'll miss the convenience of the Speed menus, but all their functions are available from the other menus and speedbars, too.

▶ We Make a Test Run

Before the first lesson, let's make sure that everything is in working order. In Windows' Program Manager, double-click on the dBASE for Windows icon, shown in Figure 2.1.

After a brief pause, you'll see the dBASE for Windows screen, which should look something like the one shown in Figure 2.2.

You now have dBASE for Windows up and running. Let's say goodbye to it, for now. Click on the System button in the upper-left corner (at the very top) to display the System menu, and then click on Close, or press C, and you are out of the program. Of course, as the menu suggests, you could have pressed Alt-F4 instead of going through the menu.

FIGURE 2.2 ▶

*dBASE for Windows'
Navigator and Com-
mand windows*

▶▶N O T E

**As with all standard Microsoft Windows programs,
you can also double-click on the System button or
choose the eXit option from the Files menu to exit the
application.**

Now, let's reenter dBASE for Windows, with keyboard commands.
Sooner or later, your mouse will break, or you'll be using a mouseless
laptop on a plane trip, or whatever. It pays to know the keyboard
alternatives.

In the Program Manager, press Ctrl-Tab to cycle from one group to
the next. Press Ctrl-Shift-Tab to cycle in the other direction. Don't be
surprised if the "cycle" doesn't make much sense; you could go in a
logical pattern or hop around quite crazily. Stop when you get to the
dBASE for Windows group. In a group, the arrow keys select a program. Use yours to select dBASE for Windows.

With dBASE for Windows selected, you can choose File ➤ Run to start dBASE for Windows (Alt-F then R, or F10, F, and then R). You can also press Enter. Your Enter key may be labeled Return. At any rate, it's located on the right, where an electric typewriter's carriage-return key is found.

Are you back in dBASE for Windows, looking at a screen similar to the one in Figure 2.2? Good. Now press Alt-F4 to exit back to the Program Manager. Throughout the book, we'll repeat a lot of operations with both mouse and keyboard methods, as we just did.

 ►►**T I P**

If you want to be a real WinMeister, get Robert Cowart's *Mastering Windows*, also from SYBEX. See how many times you can get into and out of dBASE for Windows without repeating your keystrokes and mouse clicks.

► Making a Working Directory

You can make your working directory on any hard disk drive (or floppy disk drive, but it will be slow) where you normally store your work. It doesn't need to be on the drive that holds dBASE for Windows.

In this example, we'll show you how to make a \DBWORK directory on the D: drive. If D:\DBWORK is convenient for you, copy us exactly. If you want to put it somewhere else, that's fine, too. Just makeyour own adjustments to these instructions. If you're working on a network and you don't have a local disk, you'll need advice from your network administrator.

Follow these steps to create a working directory:

1. In Windows, run the File Manager (its default location is in the Main group).

2. Choose File ➤ Create Directory ..., and you'll see a dialog box.

3. At the Name prompt, enter **D:\DBWORK**.

4. Press Enter or click on OK. Now your directory is ready.

5. Press Alt-F4 to exit the File Manager.

With your new work directory ready, let's tell dBASE for Windows where we'll be working. Start dBASE for Windows and then choose Properties ➤ Desktop. You'll see the display shown in Figure 2.3.

FIGURE 2.3 ▶

*Country tab, Desktop
Properties dialog box*

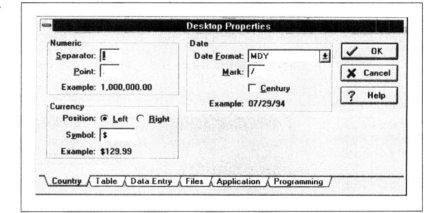

One of the settings that dBASE for Windows remembers between sessions is the last tab you used in the Desktop Properties dialog box. Your dBASE for Windows might open on another tab. If it did, click on the Country tab.

As you can see, the Country tab of the Desktop Properties dialog box gives you choices related to national preferences. dBASE for Windows defaults to local settings in many countries; it has been an international product for many years. If your defaults are not appropriate for your country, you'll want to look at the settings you can choose from here.

Of course, we said that we were going to tell dBASE for Windows where we were working, but we meant where on the disk, not where in the world. Look at the bottom of this dialog box, and you'll see a series of tabs:

Click on these tabs to look at some of the options available to you.

►►**N O T E**

You can change the Desktop Properties tabs using the keyboard, although it's inconvenient. Press the Tab key until your current tab is highlighted, and then use the ← and → keys, followed by Enter, to change tabs. We'll assume you have a mouse for these instructions.

Click on Files to see the dialog box shown in Figure 2.4.

FIGURE 2.4 ►

Files tab, Desktop Properties dialog box

Enter **D:\DBWORK** (or the drive and directory you selected) in the Current Directory box, as you see in Figure 2.4. Then click on OK or press Enter. You'll now be back to the main dBASE for Windows screen, probably showing the Navigator and Command windows. We're ready to begin.

▶▶ *Lesson 1: You Create a Table*

If you aren't in dBASE for Windows, start it now. We'll need the Navigator. If it's not on your screen, choose <u>W</u>indow ➤ <u>1</u> Navigator. The Navigator is shown in Figure 2.5.

FIGURE 2.5 ▶

The Navigator set to \DBWORK

If you weren't able to enter your working directory via the <u>P</u>roperties ➤ <u>D</u>esktop dialog box, you can click on the button to the right of current directory name:

Clicking on this button displays the Choose Directory dialog box. You can select a drive by clicking the down button next to the drive (in the lower-right area of the dialog box) and a directory by clicking on the directory in the left window. Press Enter or click on OK when your directory is set. With that done, let's take a good look at the Navigator.

▶ Navigating with the Navigator

The Navigator can be your main control tool, from which you get around in dBASE for Windows. As you see, the Navigator has entries for all the main dBASE for Windows file categories:

Use the ↑ and ↓ keys to move through these selections. In each case except All, you'll see a single entry, named Untitled. When you select All, you see one Untitled icon for every file type. (We're assuming that you haven't starting adding files to your \DBWORK directory.)

▶▶ T I P

> **The default path is set to the \DBASEWIN\SAMPLES directory. You can leave this setting (Properties\ Desktop, Files tab) but change the current directory in the Navigator to D:\DBWORK. With the Navigator selected, use Properties ➤ Navigator and uncheck the Use Supplemental Search Path option.**

Having just Untitled entries shows that you have switched dBASE for Windows into your new, empty \DBWORK directory. Now let's consider the job at hand.

We want to create a data table to hold a list of people. We're starting with a list of people since almost every system we have ever seen has at least one list of people: employees, customers, sales contacts, or whatever. We're fairly sure that for the work you're doing, you'll want a list of people, too.

▶ Designing Offline

The first step in defining a table doesn't involve your computer. Working in your mind's eye, or on your favorite doodle pad, ask yourself what problem or problems you want your database to solve. Then consider the different types of things you need to have some data about.

Let's assume that one type of thing about which you want data is people. Now, for each type of thing, such as people, consider the detailed data you'll want. Remember that collecting data is expensive. Separate the data you would like to have from the data that you need. When you have a list of the data you really need, you're ready to turn your computer on and start up dBASE for Windows.

 ▶▶ N O T E

> Actually, dBASE's Table Structure tool is flexible and visual. You might want to use it right from the start for designing your tables. But every time you enter a field, think about the expense of collecting and maintaining the data, even if the only expense is your own time.

▶ Using the Table Structure Tool

We've already thought through the data we want in our People table, and we suggest you follow our recommendations for this short course. But as we work, bear in mind that we're using an American address and telephone format. Use fields and field sizes that correspond to your own country. Add a Country field if you'll be keeping track of an international group of people.

You use the Table Structure tool to create a list of the fields in your table. Figure 2.6 shows the field list for our People table. You can make whatever adjustments are necessary for your own data.

FIGURE 2.6

Field definitions for the People table in the Table Structure tool

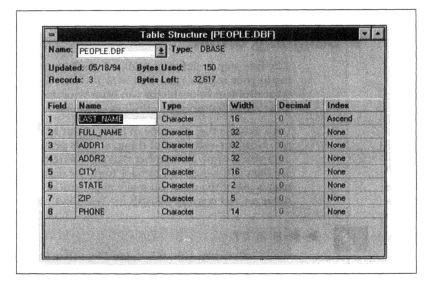

Follow these steps to create a field list:

1. In the Navigator, select Tables. Press Enter, or double-click on Untitled. This brings up the Table Structure tool.

2. Type **LAST_NAME**. Note that you can only have letters, digits, and underscore characters in a field name. No spaces or other punctuation are allowed. Press Tab to move to the next field.

3. All our fields are for Character data, so just press Tab to move from the Type field to the Width field.

4. In the Width field, type **16**. You can also spin this number higher or lower by clicking the mouse on the up or down arrow. Holding the left mouse button down while the cursor is on either of these arrows will spin the number quickly. Press Tab to move to the next field.

5. You skipped right over the Decimal field (since decimal places do not apply to character data). You are now at the Index field. Press Tab again; we won't be using indexes in this chapter.

6. Continue entering the field names and widths shown in Figure 2.6 (with whatever changes are necessary for your own data). You can use the Backspace key to correct typing mistakes. If you don't notice a mistake until you have left a field, you can use Shift-Tab to back up or Tab to move forward. Note that Tab and Shift-Tab won't leave an empty name field. Use the ↑ key to move out of the last, unwanted field name.

7. After you've finished creating the field list, press Ctrl-W (as in Write to disk) to save your table definition. You get the Save Table dialog box.

8. Type **People** in for the name, and then press Enter or click on OK. The extension .DBF is supplied for you. (Without this extension, dBASE wouldn't know that the file was a dBASE table.)

9. Tell the Add or Generate Records dialog box that you're Done.

Before we leave the Table Structure tool to add some data, let's have some fun.

▶ *Rearranging and Deleting Fields*

Use the Navigator to select the People table. Press Shift-F2 or right double-click to return to the Table Structure tool.

Press Tab or press ↓ to get to the last field. Then press ↓ to add a new row. Type a dummy name, like **DUMMY**. Don't bother tabbing out of the Name column.

 Now, with the mouse, move the pointer to the field number (just to the left of the name you just typed). Press and hold down the left button. The mouse pointer turns into a hand (as shown in the margin). This grabs the field. Holding the mouse down, move this field up and down with the mouse. You can drag the field anywhere you like.

Put it into the middle of your table structure and release the mouse button. It drops right in, and the other fields are renumbered appropriately. You can use this technique to add new fields anytime you want. Of course, now you have a field you don't want in the middle of your table structure. Is this a problem? No.

Use the same technique to grab the extra field and drag it to the bottom of the table. With the cursor in the Name column, use Backspace to erase the field name. Then press ↑, and the field is gone.

With this technique, do any serious arranging that you want. When you're satisfied with your table structure (it should look like Figure 2.6, adjusted for your country), choose File ▶ Save. (This is the same as Ctrl-S.)

This time your work was just saved; you didn't see the Save Table dialog box because dBASE for Windows now knows the name of your table.

Exit from the Table Structure tool by pressing Ctrl-F4 or by double-clicking on the Table Structure System button (the button in the Table Structure window, not dBASE's main window System button).

Back in the Navigator, you now see Untitled and People files. You've defined and created your first dBASE for Windows table. Ready for a break?

▶ Leaving Your Work Safely Filed

To take a break, exit from dBASE for Windows. dBASE will remind you if you have any unsaved work. If you exit with a new table structure defined but not saved, for example, dBASE for Windows will give you a chance to save it before exiting. This ensures that all your data is written to files and that the files are properly closed.

Actually, that's not quite true. dBASE has told Windows and DOS about all the data that it wants written and which files to close. But Windows and DOS may still have them open, with data cached for performance reasons. To be sure you work is safely filed, exit from Windows and wait several seconds before turning your computer off.

▶▶ *Lesson 2: You Add and Change Data*

Ready to use the People table? We'll continue to navigate with the Navigator. We'll open the table and work with the Table Records tool to add our data.

▶ *Using the Table Records Tool*

Internally, dBASE for Windows stores your table definitions as a table. This means that the Table Structure tool you used to define your table is just a specialized version of the Table Records tool. So you've already got the basics of entering and changing data.

To get started, if the table isn't already open, follow these steps:

1. Return to the Navigator (if you aren't already there) and select Tables.

2. Tab into your list of tables. It should have Untitled and People. Using the arrow keys, select People and press Enter.

3. Open the table for adding records. Either choose <u>N</u>avigator ➤ <u>A</u>dd Records from the menu, or right-click and choose <u>A</u>dd Records from the Speed menu.

4. You're now looking at the Table Records tool, but it might not look familiar. The Table Structure tool used the Browse Layout view. If your view is not familiar, select <u>V</u>iew ➤ <u>B</u>rowse Layout. Your table should look similar to the one in Figure 2.7.

FIGURE 2.7 ▶

The empty People table in Browse Layout view

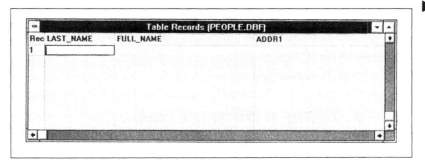

▶ *Entering Some Data*

Enter a few records, using Tab and the other keys and clicks you used in the Table Structure tool. The columns will scroll in the Browse Layout view as you move from one to the next.

Do you feel cramped? Click on the Maximize button in the upper-right corner of the Table Records window. This gives you a little more room, but all the data still doesn't fit inside a single screen.

Here are some ways to speed up your data entry:

● Type as fast as you can. Backspace corrections are easy to make on the fly. You'll make other corrections easily when you proofread your work.

● dBASE for Windows saves your data as you enter it. Starting a new record automatically saves the old one. So just keep going.

● Put the data in whatever order is most convenient. Later, you can use indexes to get the data in alphabetical or any other order you want.

Here are some ways to slow down your data entry:

● Don't look at the column headings. Type the right data into the wrong fields.

● Go so slowly that you never, ever make a mistake.

Here are some ways to make sure that your data is correct:

● Proofread everything carefully.

● Get a second opinion. A co-worker will catch mistakes that you miss.

With these tips in mind, enter several records. Use your own Rolodex or card file.

► Taking a Different Look

Now that you've got some data, let's look at it in different ways.

To see a single record, choose View ➤ Columnar Layout. That's a better view of a single record. While we're checking, try View ➤ Form Layout, too. (This is very different from the great-looking forms we'll create with the Form Designer tool.)

These views are also available directly from the speedbar. Click on each of these three icons to switch to the different views:

When you are comfortable with the different views, return to the Browse Layout view (click on the leftmost of the speedbar view icons or choose <u>V</u>iew ➤ <u>B</u>rowse Layout).

 ▶▶ **N O T E**

> **As you move your mouse pointer through the speedbar buttons, descriptions of the buttons appear on the status bar at the bottom of the window.**

▶ *Customizing the Browse Layout View*

There's an inherent conflict here that no amount of clever programming can get around. If you want to view lots of records, you need a browse-type view. But if you show your records this way, each whole record probably won't fit across the screen. However, dBASE for Windows does what it can to help by letting you adjust field widths manually.

With your mouse in a record, move slowly to the vertical bar between two fields. When you are right on the bar, the cursor shape changes:

This is the field width adjustment cursor shape. Now you can drag to change the field width. Hold the left mouse button down and slide the mouse either left or right. Use this technique to shrink each of your fields.

With the Browse Layout view maximized (press Alt-hyphen ➤ Ma<u>x</u>imize or click on the window's Maximize button), make each column smaller, working from left to right. You should be able to fit most of the record within the width of your screen.

NOTE

Skinny columns don't lose data. The size of the underlying data field isn't changed when you adjust the visible field width.

► Getting Around in the Table

In each of the record layout views, new navigation buttons appear on the speedbar:

These move you one record at a time, one page of data at a time, or to either end of the file, as the icons suggest.

In the Browse Layout view, try these buttons. You'll see that they work just as you think they would in most cases. If you're already on the last record and you click on the right arrow icon, you'll be asked if you want to add more records. Choose No for now.

Click on the speedbar button for the Columnar Layout view (or choose View ► Columnar Layout) and try these buttons again. You should be moving around with ease. You'll see that the same question about adding data appears in the same situation as in the Browse Layout view. You can also test this in the Form Layout view if you like.

► Changing Data

Did you notice that the address of the third person in your table is wrong? (Actually, it's probably just fine, but bear with us for a moment.) If you could get to the address field of the third record, you could fix it.

Here are some ways to get to the field you want to correct:

- In Columnar or Form Layout view, click on the speedbar button for the beginning of file, then click on the speedbar button that moves to the next record, twice. Click on the address field.

- In Columnar or Form Layout view, press Ctrl-PgUp to get to the first record in the table. Then press PgDn twice to get to the third record. Press Tab until you are in the address field.

- In Browse Layout view, click on the page up or page down speedbar buttons to get the data that you want to change on the screen. Then click on the erroneous field. For the third record, of course, click on the speedbar button for the beginning of file.

- In Browse Layout view, use the PgUp or PgDn keys to get the erroneous data on the screen. Then use the ↑ and ↓ keys to change from record to record. Use Tab and Shift-Tab to navigate left and right among the fields.

Whatever method you use to get to the field, you can use the ← and → keys to position your cursor within the field. You can use the Del key to delete characters. The new characters you type will either overstrike existing characters or be inserted in front of the characters that are already there. Pressing Ins toggles between Overstrike and Insert modes. Your current mode is shown in the status bar, in the lower-right corner of the screen.

▶ *Printing the Table*

In Lesson 5 later in this chapter, we'll use the Crystal Reports tool to make a nice-looking report. But in some cases, you may just want dBASE for Windows to print your table quickly, without any work on your part. There are two ways to do this:

- The fourth speedbar icon shows a printer with paper coming out. Click on this icon (shown in the margin) to see the Print Records dialog box.

- Choose File ➤ Print to get to the same dialog box.

To print all the records, click on OK or press Enter in the Print Records dialog box.

When you print your records this way, if your fields don't fit on a single line, dBASE for Windows prints as many pages as required. You can tape the pages together to show the full table. (Perhaps wrapping the records to fit on a single page would have been a better choice; having the program ask would be better still.)

To save all your work (or at least to get close; as we said before, Windows and DOS have something to say about this, too), leave the Table Records tool by any of the standard Windows exits:

- Double-click on the Table Records System button.
- Click on the Table Records System button and choose Close.
- Get to the System menu by pressing Alt-hyphen and choose Close.
- Press Ctrl-F4.

Or you can exit from dBASE for Windows without bothering to first leave the Table Records tool, by any of the following standard exits:

- Double-click on the dBASE for Windows System button.
- Click on the dBASE for Windows System button and choose Close.
- Choose File ➤ Exit.
- Press Alt-F4.

►► *Lesson 3: You Query Your Data*

With only a small amount of data, the ability to do fast queries (find all the people in your list who live in California, for example) is not important. But as the size of your table grows, query time becomes critical. This is one place the Query tools come into play.

But there's another use for the Query Designer and Query Results tools. We think that the use of the name *Query* is misleading. Perhaps the more important use of the Query Designer is to establish different views of your data.

▶ *Using the Query Designer Tool*

For this lesson, let's establish a view of our People table that skips the address information. This will be a handy one when you want to find a phone number. These are the steps to get to the Query Designer to create this view:

1. From the Program Manager, start dBASE for Windows.

2. Open the Navigator (choose <u>W</u>indow ➤ <u>1</u> or click on the compass icon on the speedbar) if it isn't already on your screen.

3. Select Queries (click on it, or tab to the list of file types and use the ↓ key to highlight Queries).

4. Click on Untitled in the file window, or press Tab to enter the file window and press Enter to select Untitled.

5. In the Open Table Required dialog box, choose PEOPLE.DBF and click on OK or press Enter. You are now in the Query Designer, which should look like the window in Figure 2.8.

FIGURE 2.8 ▶

Query Designer with PEOPLE.DBF loaded

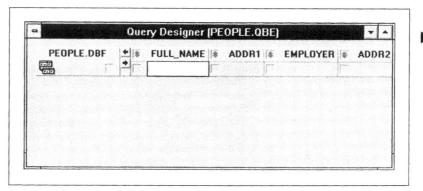

We love the Query Designer, but if you can't make head or tail of it at first, you're not alone. It's powerful and fast once you get used to it, but it's a bit short on description at first.

To begin with, you see a list of fields (as many as will fit), starting with the first one. Begin by clicking on the left and right arrows just to the right of PEOPLE.DBF. These arrows scroll the list of fields, which gives you access to your whole table.

Click on the little check box just to the left of these arrows. If you got the right one, every field in your table is now checked. Click on this box again to remove the check marks from every field.

Creating Views

Now we're ready to create a view.

1. Click on the check box (that's the lower of the two squares in each field, as shown in the margin) in the LAST_NAME field. It is now checked.

2. Using the arrows to shift your columns as needed, click on the check box to select FULL_NAME, CITY, and HOME_PHONE.

3. Click on the lightning icon in the speedbar (shown in the margin) to run this query. You should now be looking at the Query Results Table view, similar to the one in Figure 2.9.

FIGURE 2.9 ►

Query Results for se-lected fields in PEOPLE.DBF

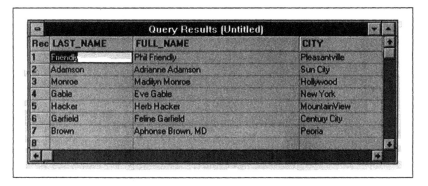

Your query established a view that selected some pertinent fields from PEOPLE.DBF. This view is convenient for searching for home phone numbers. Next, we'll query this view to find all the people in our table who live in New York.

4. To switch back to the Query Designer, click on the drafting tools icon (shown in the margin), to the right of the lightning icon.

Back in the Query Designer, we want to query our PEOPLE.DBF file to find just the people who live in New York. (Pick a city where you have more than one person in your own table.) For this, you can work from the keyboard.

5. Press Tab enough times to get to the CITY field. In the empty box, type = "**New York**". (Use your own city, of course.)

For this query, you type a relational operator first. In this case, the = operator selects values that are equal. You'll meet the other relational operators in Chapter 12. The relational operator is followed by a value or expression. In this case, the value is a character string, which you must enclose in quotation marks in dBASE for Windows.

6. Choose <u>V</u>iew ➤ Query <u>R</u>esults. You'll be looking at just the people who live in New York.

▶▶ **N O T E**

As you see when you do choose <u>V</u>iew ➤ Query <u>R</u>esults, pressing F2 is a shortcut. So, you can use the menu command, the keyboard shortcut, or the speedbar button with the lightning icon to run your queries.

7. If you would like a printed list, click on the printer icon, press Ctrl-P, or choose <u>F</u>ile ➤ <u>P</u>rint. In the last lesson, we'll make a nicer looking report.

▶ *Leaving the Query Designer Tool*

When you exit from the Query Designer, you'll be asked if you want to save your query. Before you do this, remove the city restriction from the table. To do this, follow these steps:

1. Press Shift-F2 (or click on the speedbar button with the drafting tools icon) to switch from Query Results back to the Query Designer.

2. Press Tab until you are in the CITY field.

3. Hold down the Del key until the field is empty.

4. Press Ctrl-F4 to leave the Query Designer. You'll be asked if you want to save the query. Choose Y̲es.

5. In the Save File dialog box, call this query **Phones**. just type it into the file name field. dBASE for Windows will add the extension .QBE.

6. Press Enter or click on OK, and you're back in the Navigator, ready for our next lesson.

▶▶ *Lesson 4: You Create a Custom Form*

dBASE for Windows has a marvelous Form Designer. Working with the Form Expert, you can design a good-looking form for your data entry in a matter of minutes. More important, it is the Form Designer that lets you add rules that reject invalid data. This is a key tool for building database systems.

For this lesson, however, we are going to settle for creating an attractive form. We'll begin by asking the Form Expert to do the bulk of the work for us.

▶ *Using the Form Expert*

The Form Expert will introduce itself every time you create a new form. To get into this Expert, follow these steps:

1. In the Navigator, select Forms. (Click on Forms or press Tab to reach the file type column and then use the ↑ or ↓ key to get there.)

2. In the file list, select Untitled. (Double-click on the Untitled item or press Tab, then Enter.)

3. You are now in the Form Expert. You see a pair of radio buttons that let you choose E̲xpert Assistance or B̲lank Form. The default choice, E̲xpert Assistance, is precisely what we want, so you can proceed. Click on the N̲ext button or press Alt-N.

The Form Expert will now ask you some questions, and then prepare a default form based on those answers. Once it has finished its work, you'll have a preliminary form in the Form Designer, ready for minor touch-up work.

4. You are first asked to choose a file. To get all the fields in the file, choose PEOPLE.DBF. (Type the name in the file name field or double-click on the name.) If you chose PEOPLE.QBE, you would have only those fields that you checked in the Query Designer.

5. Choose <u>N</u>ext to proceed.

6. You are now at the field selection panel, as shown in Figure 2.10.

FIGURE 2.10 ▶

Selecting fields in the Form Expert

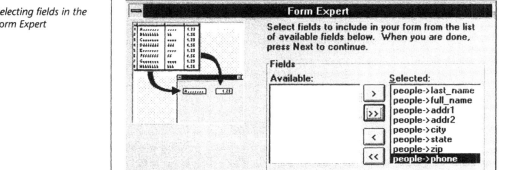

This panel is not as self-explanatory as the others. You run it by clicking the arrow buttons to send fields from the Available box to the Selected box.

7. Click on the **>>** button to select all fields. (The **<<** button deselects all fields; the **>** and **<** buttons move one field at a time in the indicated direction.)

8. Choose Next to proceed. (Next is not enabled if there aren't any fields in the Selected box.)

9. The next panel asks you to choose a layout. The default choice is Columnar Layout, which is usually just right. Just choose Next and proceed.

10. The final panel allows you to select fonts and colors. Choose any that you like. Note that the location of the Next button is now taken by a Build button with a lightning icon. Choose it when you have made your choices.

 ►►TIP

The best-looking forms use color sparingly (unlike the Form Expert defaults!), and we suggest that you adopt this policy. We like black text on a light-gray background, with white entry fields. With these choices, any colored icons or text will really stand out. On the other hand, the default font choices that the Form Expert suggests are good ones. We accept the defaults and use other fonts only for decorative effects.

► Using the Form Designer

You are now in the Form Designer, looking at a setup like the one shown in Figure 2.11. You see the Form Designer in the foreground, with its two related tools: the Object Properties Inspector and the Controls palette.

If you don't have these windows on your screen, choose View ➤ Object Properties. You'll see these choices:

Form Designer Properties...	
Cut	Ctrl+X
Copy	Ctrl+C
Paste	Ctrl+V
✓ Controls	
✓ Object Properties	
Procedures	

FIGURE 2.11 ▶

Form Designer with the People form

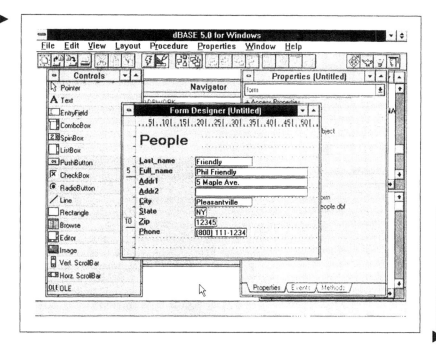

You want Controls and Object Properties checked, and Procedures left unchecked. If this isn't the case, click on the unchecked one(s) to get them checked. Click on Procedures, if it is checked, to get it unchecked. On each click, the named item will be activated (or deactivated). Click on the Form Designer and right-click again to return to the Speed menu.

 ▶▶ **W A R N I N G**

> **The Form Designer is a very graphical tool. It's only barely possible to use a few of its features without a mouse or other pointing device. We recommend that you don't use it if you don't have access to a mouse.**

A Form (we'll capitalize the names of the dBASE for Windows built-in objects and their properties) is an object that contains other objects.

The title *People*, for example, is a Text object. All the Form's objects can be moved and sized in the same way.

Let's start by moving the title Text object over to the center. Position your mouse pointer over the *People* title. Click once, and you'll see a standard selection border surround the object. This forms a rectangle with black squares, called *handles*, at the corners and in the middle of each of the sides, as shown in Figure 2.12.

FIGURE 2.12 ►

Selecting the People
Text object

To move the object, place your mouse pointer within this border and drag the object to the top center of your form. As you drag, the mouse pointer changes into the hand icon you've already seen in the Table Structure tool.

If you drag on any of the black squares that appear around a selected object, you can resize the object, just as you can resize a window.

►►NOTE

Entryfield objects are automatically sized to fit the fields in your database. See Part 5 for details.

Text objects from the Form Expert are often larger than the text they contain. This makes it easy to change to a larger font. It also means that you'll need to reduce some of your Text objects to avoid overlap. The text will be adjusted automatically within the object, as long as it still fits.

▶ *Improving the Form*

Not all of our fields conveniently fit, because we asked the Form Expert to build a Columnar Layout form. (If you try a Form Layout form, you'll find that dBASE's choices for positioning are probably not what you would select.) We can make a better-looking form by first stretching the form itself, and then moving the fields and Text objects around.

Try to make your form look something like the one shown in Figure 2.13.

FIGURE 2.13 ▶

People form with manual changes

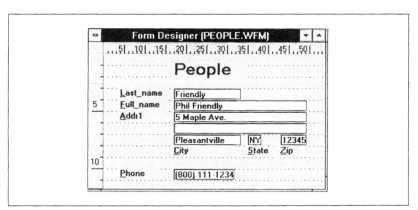

As you work, press Ctrl-S occasionally to save your work. The first time you press Ctrl-S, you'll be asked to choose a file name. Choose People, and your form will be stored as PEOPLE.WFM (Windows ForM). The next time you press Ctrl-S, this file will be resaved under the same name.

> You can use the File ➤ Save As choice to save your form
> under a new name.

▶ Using Your New Form

Like the other dBASE for Windows tools, the Form Designer lets you
alternate between Run and Design modes. Again, as with the other
tools, you can use F2 and Shift-F2, or you can click on the lightning
and design icons on the speedbar.

To use this form, just click on the lightning icon. You're now looking at
your data one record at a time in a good-looking form. You can use the
same buttons as before to navigate in your table and to add new records. These speedbar buttons are the run and design buttons, the record search and record append buttons, and the four navigation buttons:

In a form layout, there are no full page-movement buttons. Each record is a page on the form.

You can alternate between Design and Run modes as often as you wish
to make adjustments to your form. When you're finished, press Ctrl-W
in either mode to return to the Navigator.

> Your latest changes are saved automatically when you
> switch from Design mode to Run mode. You don't need
> to explicitly save your work when changing modes.

▶▶ *Lesson 5: You Write a Report*

We've already seen that it's simple to print your data. But the results don't win any prizes for appearance. For prize-winning, world-class documents, you can use Crystal Reports. Crystal Reports is a third-party reporting program, licensed by Borland for inclusion in dBASE for Windows.

 ▶▶ **N O T E**

> **After licensing Crystal Reports, Borland bought the whole company that made the ReportSmith report writer, which is also a superb reporting program. We expect to see Crystal Reports replaced with ReportSmith in later versions of dBASE for Windows.**

Now let's get started. First, in the Navigator, select Reports and double-click on Untitled. This will launch Crystal Reports, a separate program that runs under Windows, outside dBASE for Windows.

Unless you already have a table open, you'll first see the Open Table Required dialog box, shown in Figure 2.14.

FIGURE 2.14 ▶

Choosing a table for Crystal Reports

Open Table Required
File Name: `*.dbf;*.db;*.qbe`
Directory: d:\dbwork
people.dbf / phones.qbe
d:\ / dbwork
✓ OK / ✗ Cancel / ? Help
File Type: Data (*.DBF;*.DB;*.QBE)
Drives: d: stacvol_000

As Figure 2.14 shows, you can choose either a .DBF or a .QBE file. If you were using Paradox tables, you would have .DB files. If your tables were coming from an SQL database, those tables also would be available.

For this lesson, choose PEOPLE.DBF. After you choose the table, Crystal Reports is launched, and you're faced with the somewhat intimidating screen shown in Figure 2.15.

FIGURE 2.15 ►

Crystal Reports open-ing look

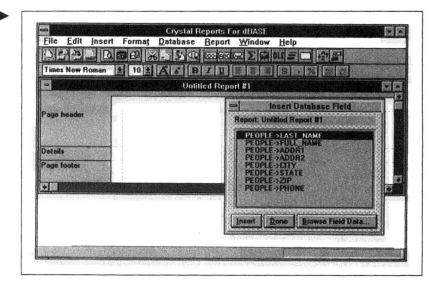

Don't be too worried by what you see here. Crystal Reports is a reasonably friendly, as well as very powerful, reporter. (It was originally marketed as an add-on, so the appearance of sophistication was a selling point.)

► Picking Fields

Your first task is to pick the fields you want. Let's do a simple phone list.

1. Start with the LAST_NAME field. Click on the field in the field list, and your mouse pointer turns into a rectangle. When you move the mouse pointer into the report area, the rectangle expands to reflect the size of the field.

2. Position the LAST_NAME field on the left in the Details band, as shown in Figure 2.16.

FIGURE 2.16 ▶

Putting the LAST_NAME field in the Details band

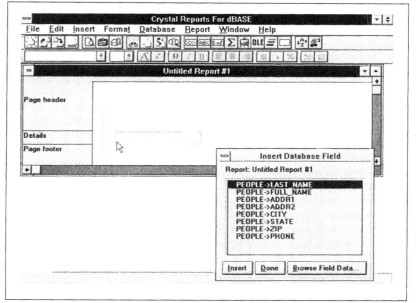

3. When you have the field in place, click the mouse to drop the field. When it drops, you'll see the text *LAST_NAME* hop into the report's Page header area, and the field, also reading *LAST_ NAME*, drop into the Details area. When we begin the report, the Page header area will have the text, and the Details area will have data from our table.

4. Continue by placing the fields PHONE and FULL_NAME in the Details band.

5. Click on the <u>D</u>one pushbutton in the Insert Database Field box. Your screen should look like what you see in Figure 2.17.

FIGURE 2.17 ▶

Fields selected in Crystal Reports

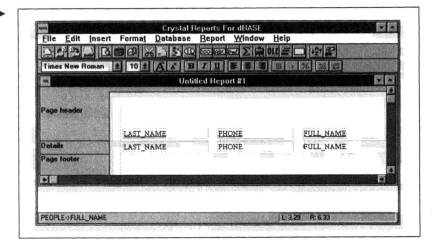

▶ *Adding a Title*

Now that we have some fields, let's add a title.

1. Choose Insert ▶ Text Field … from the menus, or click on the speedbar icon that says ABC (shown in the margin). You'll see a dialog box titled Edit Text Field.

2. Type **Telephone List** in this box, and then click on Accept or press Alt-A.

3. As when you're placing fields, your mouse pointer now turns into a rectangle. Position it in the Page header area of the report, somewhere near the top center. Click to drop the text field.

4. When you drop the text field, it is selected (outlined in yellow) and has resize handles on both ends. Grab one of the handles and drag it until the field is about twice as wide as it was originally. The title text field should look similar to the one shown in Figure 2.18.

Now we're ready to make that field look like a proper title. In the upper-left area of the Crystal Reports window, you'll see two comboboxes. One selects the font (it says Times New Roman, by default); the one to its right selects the point size. The default size is 10 points.

FIGURE 2.18 ▶

The title text field positioned

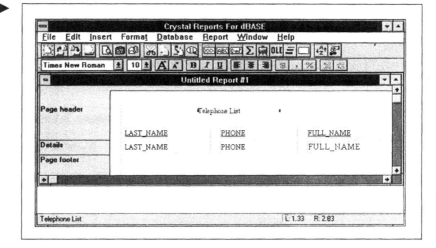

5. Change the point size to something dramatic. We'll use 24 in this lesson.

6. Let's also center the title and use boldface for added emphasis. Click on the speedbar icon with a capital **B** for boldface, and then click on the speedbar icon for centering. These icons (shown in the margin) are in the center of the second speedbar row.

7. Your title should look like the one you see in Figure 2.19. If the title field is not centered above the report, use the mouse to drag it into position, just as you did in the Form Designer. When you drag a field in Crystal Reports, you don't see the mouse pointer turn into the hand icon, but it has the same effect.

FIGURE 2.19 ►

An assertive report heading

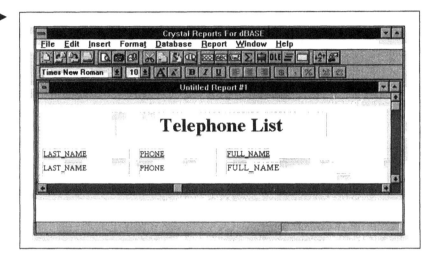

►►**N O T E**

The Crystal Reports speedbar icons in the center of the second row are used to format text. If you use a Microsoft Windows word processor, you're probably using similar buttons. They let you choose boldface, italic, underscored, left-justified, centered, and right-justified formatting.

8. Let's use boldface for our column headings, too. Move the mouse pointer over the LAST_NAME heading and click to select it.

9. Move the mouse pointer to the next column heading, press and hold down the Shift key, then click.

10. Repeat step 9 for the final column. You now have three fields selected.

11. Click on the boldface speedbar icon to convert all three to **boldface.**

Now let's see what our finished product will look like.

▶ Previewing the Report

Before sending the report to the printer, let's look at a sneak preview. Choose File ➤ Print ➤ Window from the menus. This prints the first page of the report in a Preview window. Ours is shown in Figure 2.20.

FIGURE 2.20 ▶

Previewing the report before printing

One of the best features of Crystal Reports is that you can manipulate the items in the Preview window, just as you can while defining the report. For example, you can click on an object and drag it to adjust its position. Select an object or group of objects and change the font or style. This is a wonderful capability for working directly with the report exactly as it will appear when printed.

Have everything looking good? One more item to take care of, and then we'll call it an evening.

▶ Sorting the Data

Our telephone list looks good, but it's not in order. There are lots of ways to keep your data in order in dBASE for Windows. Probably the least frequently used way is to have Crystal Reports do it for you, but right now, that capability is just what we need. Follow these steps:

1. From the menus, choose Report ➤ Record Sort Order .... The dialog box shown in Figure 2.21 appears.

FIGURE 2.21 ▶

Choosing fields for sorting

2. With the LAST_NAME field highlighted in the left rectangle, click on the Add button. It pops over to the right, as in Figure 2.21. We only need to sort on this one field.

3. Below the Sort Fields box, you see that you can choose to sort in ascending or descending order. The ascending order default is just what we want. Click on the OK button and wait patiently for a few seconds.

When your report preview is repainted, it is now in properly sorted order. If you are hooked to a printer, you can go ahead and print the report. Of course, we've just scratched the surface, but you should already have something fairly good looking.

4. Exit from Crystal Reports. (Press Ctrl-F4 or choose File ➤ Exit.)

5. Before closing, Crystal Reports will ask you if you want to save your data in your Untitled report. Choose Yes.

6. Finally, since you haven't chosen a title yet, you'll be asked to select one in the File Save As dialog box. We called ours Phone, and it was saved in PHONE.RPT.

▶▶ *Summary*

Congratulations! You've gone from ground zero through using each of the main tools of dBASE for Windows. You know enough now to go off on your own and use dBASE for Windows for basic database tasks.

You learned that the Navigator and the Command window are complementary control tools. You've used the Navigator in this chapter.

After that, you used the Table Structure tool to define a table. When you were finished, you saw that the Design and Run modes complement each other. You entered Run mode to use your new table definition.

In the Table Records tool, you saw that you can look at your data in Browse, Form, or Columnar Layout view. Using the Browse Layout view, you adjusted your data to fit and then added and edited data.

You used the Query Designer to build a Query view that included only some of your fields. Then you used the Query Designer to select only a portion of your records.

Next, you went into the Form Designer, letting the Form Expert do most of your work in laying out a custom form. You looked at the Object Properties Inspector and the Form Designer's Controls palette. As before, you alternated between Design and Run modes.

Finally, you used Crystal Reports to design and print an attractive, properly sorted report.

Is there anything left? Yes and no. You've met each of the main tools. There are others, such as the Menu Designer, still waiting to be explored.

More important, you've worked with data in a single table. As you'll see in Part 2, the real art of database management comes into play when you draw together data in multiple tables.

Sure, there's lots more, but we're definitely on our way.

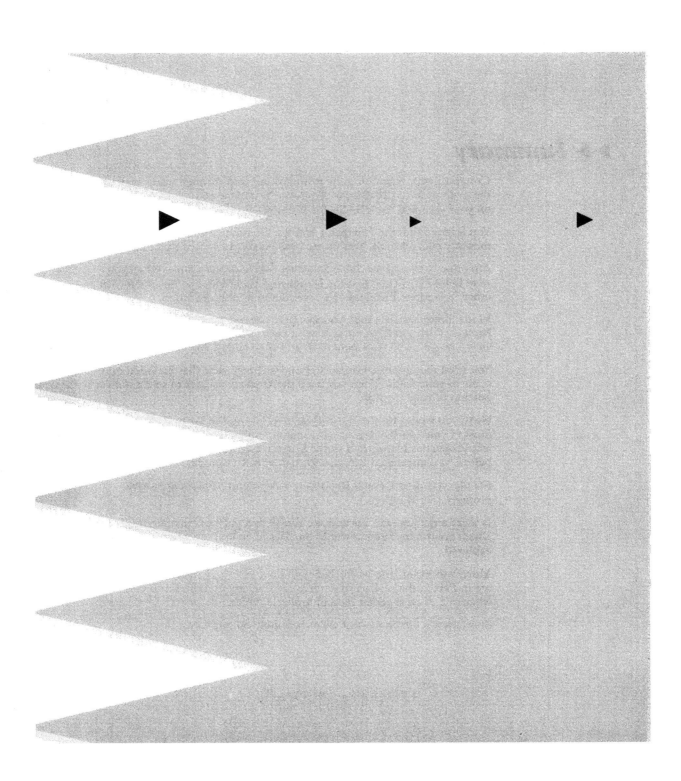

Design Your
Database

___

▶ ▶ **F**or the second and last time, we're going to start with some theory before we dive back into dBASE for Windows. In this chapter, we're going to explain the art of database design.

Of course, we mean the art of relational database design, since dBASE for Windows is built for relational databases. A relational database is a collection of one or more tables of data devoted to a common purpose. The art of database design is the art of using exactly as many tables as you need and filling them with well-chosen fields.

▶ ▶ The Art and Science of Database Design

Nothing else in this book is as important as mastering database design. If you mastered every nook and cranny of dBASE for Windows but couldn't set up good database designs, you wouldn't be able to get good results. You could be able to whip up table structures faster than Julia Child whips up an omelette. You could do three-table queries with as much grace as Michael Jordan doing a lay-up. Your forms could be as elegant as Fred Astaire dancing. It wouldn't matter.

Without a sound database design, the rest of your skills are meaningless. You might as well give Julia Child the basketball.

Without a sound database design, you'll delete one record and others will mysteriously disappear. You'll update one fact, and it will still be wrong on another report. You'll be meticulously careful about entering invoice data, but you'll end up sending an accurate invoice to the wrong customer.

With a sound database design, you can always add another table to your query or improve your forms. Your forms don't need to be elegant; they just need to work for your application.

In this section, we'll discuss the art and science of database design. You'll see that our art builds on the underlying science, as good engineering does in every discipline.

► Bad Database Design

Let's begin with the story of Mack, the owner of Peter Bilt Trucking. Mack owns his own tractor with which he hauls other people's trailers from one depot to another in North America.

Mack paid his accountant $5,000 last year. His accountant, who uses Lotus 1-2-3, assured him that he could save about half his fee if he provided his data in a computerized form that could be read into his spreadsheets.

Mack figured that a laptop and dBASE for Windows together cost less than the annual savings, so he decided to computerize. He followed us through Chapter 2, and decided he could dive right in immediately. The design he came up with is shown in Figure 3.1.

FIGURE 3.1 ►

Mack's table design

Field	Name	Type	Width	Decimal	Index
1	DEPOT_PKUP	Character	32	0	None
2	DATE_PKUP	Date	8	0	None
3	WEIGHT	Numeric	6	0	None
4	DEPOT_DROP	Character	32	0	None
5	DATE_DROP	Date	8	0	None
6	DISTANCE	Numeric	4	0	None
7	INCOME	Numeric	8	2	None
8	FUEL	Numeric	7	2	None
9	OTHER_EXP	Numeric	7	2	None
10	GROSS_PRFT	Numeric	7	2	None

Design Your Database

Mack's depot names are enough for Mack. He knows where each one is. He can give his accountant a list of the couple dozen depots where he picks up and delivers. A better system would include a table that showed the depots, but this solution is fine for a personal database.

But Mack has just reinvented a classic in the history of bad database design. It's in the Distance field. Mack's going to make some pickups south of Los Angeles and drop off just outside New York City. That's about 2800 miles. In New York, Mack might make a pickup heading 250 miles to Boston.

The problem is that the distance from the New York depot to the Boston depot never varies. Mack will be keying this distance into every record for a New York to Boston run. The same applies to every other run. There is just about zero probability that Mack will always enter the same distance for the same run.

Mack is going to start recording data in his table at the start of the year. He'll back up the table at the end of the year, then clear it out to start fresh next year.

When he starts, the database has no idea of the length of the Los Angeles to New York run, nor of the New York to Boston run. By the end of the year, it will probably have several different ideas of the lengths of these runs. Mack should really have another table, like the one shown in Figure 3.2.

FIGURE 3.2 ▶

The Route table Mack needs

Field	Name	Type	Width	Decimal	Index
1	DEPOT_PKUP	Character	32	0	None
2	DEPOT_DROP	Character	32	0	None
3	DISTANCE	Numeric	4	0	None

With this table, Mack would never put the distance data into his individual run records. The length of each run would be entered just once, and that would be it. The table would be there every year.

But there's a complication introduced when Mack does this. To get the distance for a run combined with the other run data (to compute fuel mileage, for example), Mack will need to join this table to his main table. The design shown here doesn't make that easy.

If Mack had read the rest of this chapter, he would see just how easily joining these tables could be accommodated. He would have his two tables and the correct cross-referencing technique, so that joining them would just take a couple simple mouse clicks in the Query Designer.

Let's learn how to do it right.

▶ The Art of Database Design

There's nothing complex about database design. Your grandmother probably said, "A place for everything, and everything in its place." That simple axiom is exactly what we'll be driving at here.

Suppose you work for a company that sells to other companies. One table in your database will probably be for customers. Now let's consider the art.

Suppose our employer is a company with three divisions. One sharpens knives for butchers, the second provides flour for bakers, and the third sells brass to candlestick manufacturers. Clearly, the data needs are very different.

In the knife-sharpening business, we'll need to know how many knives each butcher has, how frequently each type needs sharpening, and so on. The bakery supply business needs to know how much white flour is sold, how much whole wheat flour is sold, and so on. Similarly, the candlestick manufacturing supply business has its own requirements.

So, we'll want three separate tables: one each for butchers, bakers, and candlestick makers. Or will we?

For each customer, regardless of type, there is some basic information we'll want. We need a name, address, phone number, and other identification details. For each customer, we'll have a credit limit, an outstanding balance, and other common accounting information.

Perhaps we need just one table for customers, but with enough fields so that we can accommodate each of the individual types. (For butchers, we'll skip the entry for whole wheat flour, for example.) Perhaps we need three tables: one for each type of customer. Or perhaps we need a single customer table, and then three other tables geared to the specific needs of each type. Any of these ideas might be right. They'll

Design Your Database

each provide a sound database design, within the known limits of the science of database design. Next, we'll consider that science and its relationship to the TED method of database design, which we'll explain later in this chapter.

▶ The Science of Database Design

In this section, we'll introduce the science of database design. If you're totally practical, in a hurry, and want to just get on with it, go ahead and skip this material. You're not going to become a computer scientist by reading this, and we'll necessarily be compressing a large subject into a short space.

In the next section, we'll present a practical, in a hurry, and "let's get on with it" method for designing databases. This section is for those of you who always want to know more about everything and who aren't willing to believe that hurry-up methods are sound unless you've looked at the underlying reasons.

The science of relational database design involves a process called *normalization*. Normal forms, beginning with First Normal Form and ending with Fifth Normal Form, represent progressively better database designs. By "better" we mean less subject to what the scientists call *update anomalies*. For example, in Mack's database (Figure 3.1), deleting a record about an individual run could delete the only record of the distance for a route. Adding a new record may add a duplicated (and not necessarily consistent) distance fact.

First, Second, and Third Normal Forms

If all your data is put into tables, it's in First Normal Form. Since dBASE for Windows defines its data in tables, all .DBF file data is in First Normal Form automatically.

Second and Third Normal Forms define some complex concepts, including functional dependency, full-functional dependency, and transitive dependencies. Fortunately for us, another Normal Form was discovered between the Third and Fourth Normal Forms. This form, called the Boyce-Codd Normal form, lets us skip right over these steps.

Boyce-Codd Normal Form

Until recently, most data analysts struggled with the dependency concepts of Second and Third Normal Forms. Luckily for us, the scientists have proven that a database which is in Boyce-Codd Normal Form is already in Third Normal Form. In fact, it's also been proven that Boyce-Codd Normal Form is superior to Third Normal Form.

A database is in Boyce-Codd Normal Form if it uses only First Normal Form tables and each record in each table has a unique key that identifies each item in the record.

A large body of normalization literature is devoted to the process of selecting record *keys*, which are identifiers that uniquely specify a particular record. These unique identifiers are called *primary* or *candidate* keys. Database scientist Chris Date proposed a system, which we follow here, that greatly simplifies this.

The TED design method, which we'll explain soon, does precisely what Boyce-Codd Normal Form prescribes. It puts data into tables where each record has a unique key that identifies each item in the record.

Higher Normal Forms

The higher Normal Forms include Fourth Normal Form, Projection-Join Normal Form, Domain-Key Normal Form, and Fifth Normal Form. Each eliminates additional possible update anomalies.

Fifth Normal Form was proven to be the highest possible Normal Form. The proponents of Domain-Key Normal Form argue that Fifth Normal is highest in only a limited sense, and that there are entirely different avenues to explore, which may yet yield higher forms.

We think this is true, although the associated mathematics get quite abstract. We're happy to report that designs in Third Normal Form are generally considered adequate for practical software engineering. Our TED system gets to the Boyce-Codd Normal Form, so it is even better.

▶▶ TED Lets You Master Database Design

We use the acronym TED as an *aide memoire* for the three items in our very short list of table types:

- Things
- Events
- Details

These are the three types of tables that together will account for about 90 percent of the tables that you'll see if you spend your entire working life designing databases.

In brief, *Things* are items that you can kick. People, buildings, and products are examples of Things.

Events are not kickable. They happen at a point in time. For example, you sell products to your customers. A patient is admitted to the hospital and assigned a bed.

Details are a necessity of table-based data. If you have more than one of a Thing involved in an Event, you'll need a separate table to record Details. For example, a customer buys several products in one sale. That's one sale Event, but you need a Detail table to keep track of the quantity and price of each Thing purchased.

▶ Things

The easiest way to find out if something in your database is a Thing is to ask if it can be kicked. If the answer is Yes, it's definitely a Thing.

But that's not the real distinguishing characteristic. What really distinguishes Things from other items in our universe is that the Thing is relatively permanent. By relatively permanent, we mean it will have a long duration in the life of your system.

Employees come and go, but they generally are part of your database's universe for a long time once they are hired. The hospital's patients come and go, too, and much more rapidly than employees. Still, you hope that they are still around after getting out of the hospital (when it's time to pay the bill, for instance).

Here are some Things that are quite permanent, but definitely aren't kickable:

- Musical compositions
- Mathematical theorems
- Patents
- Leases
- Philosophical schools of thought

You may have noticed that some of these Things are written on paper. When you design a database, be careful to ignore the pieces of paper and look at the underlying reality. Pythagoras' theorem will be just as true when the last piece of paper on which it was ever written crumbles into dust.

A lease is a contract between parties, which exists in the abstract, even if the paperwork is lost. (Of course, hanging onto the paper can be distinctly helpful if a dispute arises.)

► *Events*

In contrast to a Thing, an Event is instantaneous. It happens at a moment in time. Actually, events are no more instantaneous than Things are permanent. But for the purposes of our database, we can treat them as if they were.

Here are some typical events:

- A customer *purchases* a product
- A patent is *issued*
- A hotel guest *registers*
- An insurance premium is *paid*

You probably see that Events are named by verbs. Things are all nouns. This is another good way of thinking about the items about which you'll be collecting data. Put the nouns in one group and the verbs in another.

Some perfectly useful systems exist without Events. For example, the phone list that we'll be putting together links a set of people (definite Things) to their employers (also Things).

In contrast, Events depend on Things. Let's revisit our list of events, but this time we'll emphasize the Things that participate in each event:

- A *customer* purchases a *product*
- A *patent* is issued (to an *applicant*)
- A *hotel guest* registers
- An insurance (*policy's*) premium is paid (by the *insured*)

Note that sometimes you'll explicitly record the Things that participate in an Event. A *customer* purchasing a *product* is a common example.

Other times, one or more of the Things are implied by your system. For example, if you are keeping a list of patents that your organization has been issued, the applicant is implied—it's your organization.

The same is true of guest registrations at a hotel. If you're creating a registration system for the Regency, each registration by a guest implies that the guest is registering at your hotel. On the other hand, if your system is for a chain of hotels, you'll always include the particular hotel in your registration Event.

Whether the Things are recorded or implied, every Event is an interaction between Things, at a point in time.

▶ Designing with Things and Events

The first step in database design is to make a list of the Things and Events that are important to your system. Remember that collecting data is expensive, even if (or especially if) it's your time at stake. Firmly reject your urge to include "nice to have" Things and Events. Stick to absolutely necessary Things and Events.

Each Thing and Event is a table. Your list of Things and Events is your preliminary overall database design. The first choice is to pick a name. If you're using .DBF or .DB files to store your tables, you're limited to DOS's eight characters. Within that limit, pick the most descriptive name possible.

Then start to work on your field lists. The first field you'll place in each table is an ID field, but postpone that until we begin considering keys.

For each table, carefully list the characteristics that you'll need to record. These are your fields. As you list your fields, note the type and, if necessary, the length and number of decimal places.

  T I P

> **It used to be important to allocate no more space than needed for fields, especially for character fields such as names. With today's disk-compression technology, our fixed-length character fields don't actually take much space if they are mostly blank. So err on the wide side initially.**

You'll see in practice that oversized character fields are a nuisance, even if they don't cost much in disk space. For example, a field that is 40 characters wide takes about half the screen's width in a Browse Layout view in the Table Records tool.

You already know that you can drag the bars dividing fields in the Browse Layout view to reduce space. You can still type to the full width of the field, even with the visible width reduced. Later on, you'll meet more ways for bringing this problem under control. So again, err on the high side for widths, but don't overdo it. You can always add more space or take away space you find you don't need.

In Event tables, we'll have a specific technique for referring to the Things that participate in the Event. For now, just note that you need to know, for example, which patient is being admitted in your Admssion table.

Design Your Database

▶ Details

There's one more letter in TED: D for Details. When you list your Thing and Event characteristics, sometimes you may note that you need to allow for one (or zero) or more of an item. In a sale, for example, a customer will buy one or more products. (Zero products isn't a sale.)

Zero or more also crops up frequently. Your health insurance plan probably wants to know facts about your employees' dependents. Here you must allow for zero or more dependents per employee.

Whenever you have an indefinite number (zero or more, or one or more), you need to create a Detail table. The most typically cited Detail table is the line-item table for a sales system. In this table, you would have one record for each product. It would include a product identifier (we'll get to that soon), the number sold, and the unit price. The record would also include a reference to the sale which it is part of. We'll get to these references soon.

▶ TED in Action

In this section, we'll take a look at a few databases, so you can get an idea of how TED can be applied. First, we're going to sneak ahead and steal from the next section to introduce you to record identifiers. We'll call these *record IDs*, or just *IDs*. We'll put a column in each table for a record ID. We'll name it after the table and append the two letters *ID*. We'll use an underscore character when it fits. Here are typical examples:

Table	ID Field
Sales	SALES_ID
Admsion	ADMSION_ID
Employee	EMPLOYEEID
People	PEOPLE_ID

In the next section, we'll explain exactly how these fields work. For now, the value in an ID field will uniquely identify a record in the table for which it is named. Each record in the Sales table will have a unique SALES_ID value.

Now let's design some tables. First, we'll want a pair of tables to keep track of our contacts and the organizations where they are employed. With these tables, and with all the others, there is really no end to the data which we could collect. People have home phones, car phones, company phones, private lines through the company switchboard, private extensions from the company number, and so on. Here, we'll concentrate on the basics.

  T I P

> **Add fields like a backpacker adds gear to a pack: "When in doubt, leave it out."**

A Phone and Mail List Example

Figure 3.3 shows the structures of two tables in a phone and mail list system. Note that each table starts with an ID field. For cross-referencing people to employers, you simply add the EMPLOYERID field to the People table.

FIGURE 3.3

Structures of People and Employer tables for a phone and mail list system

Table Structure [PEOPLE.DBF]

Name: PEOPLE.DBF Type: DBASE
Updated: 08/14/94 Bytes Used: 158
Records: 11 Bytes Left: 32,609

Field	Name	Type	Width	Decimal
1	PEOPLE_ID	Numeric	4	0
2	LAST_NAME	Character	16	0
3	FULL_NAME	Character	32	0
4	EMPLOYERID	Numeric	4	0
5	ADDR1	Character	32	0
6	ADDR2	Character	32	0
7	CITY	Character	16	0
8	STATE	Character	2	0
9	ZIP	Character	5	0

Table Structure [EMPLOYER.DBF]

me: EMPLOYER.DBF Type: DBASE
dated: 01/08/96 Bytes Used: 143
cords: 9 Bytes Left: 32,624

Id	Name	Type	Width	Decimal
	EMPLOYERID	Numeric	4	0
	NAME	Character	32	0
	ADDRESS1	Character	32	0
	ADDRESS2	Character	32	0
	CITY	Character	16	0
	STATE	Character	2	0
	ZIP	Character	10	0
	PHONE	Character	14	0

Design Your Database

Figure 3.4 shows how a simplified version of this database might look in practice. Although our real ID fields are numeric, in these examples, we'll use names as if they were IDs. You can't do this in practice, but it helps make these examples easy to follow. You'll learn all about this later in this chapter.

FIGURE 3.4 ▶

Some data in the People and Employer tables

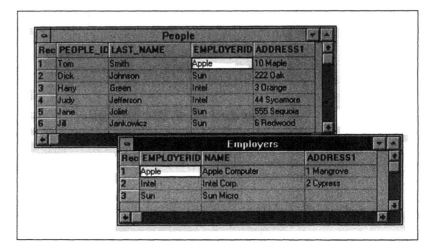

Now let's consider some other examples.

Hotel Guest Registration

Our hotel started with a dozen rooms. The price was moderate, and the service was exceptional. We are now just about ready to open rooms 32 through 56. The old manual system has got to be replaced. Let's think through the Things and Events relevant to a registration system.

The Things are fairly obvious: our guests and the rooms they stay in. There are two significant Events: arrivals and departures. Our first cut is this:

Things:	Guests
	Rooms
Events:	Arrival
	Departure

Now let's sketch in the characteristics of each:

Things:	Guests
	Name
	Address data
	Number in party
	Method of payment
	Special requests?
	Rooms
	Number
	Floor
	Maximum occupants
	Special features?
Events:	Arrival
	Which guest
	Which room
	Date
	Length of stay
	Departure
	Which guest (or room)
	Date

At this point, it's not necessary to spell out exactly which specific fields, such as address data, are required. We generally leave this until we get to the Table Structure tool.

Note that there are "Special requests?" possible for our guests. Impeccable service is what has made our reputation. If Mr. Johnson likes coffee and fresh juice at 6:45 a.m., let's not start forgetting now that we're successful.

The same is true for the rooms. We have "Special features?" that don't lead to easy classification. One room may have especially nice decor, another faces the courtyard and is very quiet, and another has a good view. Wouldn't you want to be asked, "Would you prefer a quiet room on the courtyard or do you want a view?" (The first computer systems forced you to make everything impersonal; today's smart computer systems help you do just the opposite.) Both these items are free-form, so we can use Memo fields to record a sentence or two.

Now let's look at the Events. The departure could note which guest or which room. We could note that Smith has gone. Checking registrations we'll see that Smith was in room 26. Or we could note that the party in room 26 has departed. Checking registration, we'll see that it was Smith.

Either way, our guest is gone, and that room is available. Don't record both! That would be redundant data, and redundant data is bad design. You'll get mistakes soon enough.

There is another possibility. Stare at those two Events for a moment and see if you can simplify the design.

Here's what we would do:

Events: Stay
           Arrival date
           Which guest
           Which room
           Departure date

We'll have a Stay Event. The arrival and departure are characteristics of that Event. That eliminates a table, but fits our data quite naturally.

Finally, we studied our fields for any evidence of a zero or more, or one or more, condition. We don't see any, so we don't need a table for Details.

Now here's our design, in enough detail so that we would be comfortable sitting down with the Table Structure tool, filling in the final details as we go:

Things: Guest

          GUEST_ID

          NAME

          Address data

          PARTY_SIZE

          HOW_PAY

          SPECIAL (memo)

      Room

          ROOM_ID

          FLOOR

          MAX_IN_RM

          SPECIAL (memo)

Events: Stay

          DATE_IN

          GUEST_ID

          ROOM_ID

          DATE_OUT

A common choice in databases is whether we should have just one item, as in DATE_OUT, or an estimate and an actual. Here we chose just one. If we felt it was important to be able to accurately project actual departures based on original estimates, we would keep both.

Note that the room number became the ROOM_ID field. The room number in hotels has always been the sort of unique identifier that we need in our systems. Each number is assigned to exactly one room. No

Design Your Database

two numbers are the same. Since the hotel employees already are familiar with these numbers, we'll retain them.

As a final note, our Stay Event is much less instantaneous than our original Arrival and Departure Events. It still captures the same information, so nothing is lost by simplifying. Always eliminate tables when there is a natural way to do so.

  T I P

> **Never eliminate tables if you have to force the data to fit into the new structure. Always eliminate tables if there is a natural way to simplify.**

This isn't complicated, is it? We're just creating a place for everything, and keeping everything in its place.

A Wholesale Supplier

Let's look at another example of a simplified system for a wholesale supplier of computer software. This is not a trivial database, even though we're eliminating a lot of details.

Our supplier is shipped software by software companies. From its warehouse, our supplier ships software to computer and office supply dealers and to software retailers.

Here's a first cut at Things and Events:

Things:	Software Packages
	Software companies
	Computer dealers
	Office-supply dealers
	Software retailers
Events:	Receiving stock
	Shipping stock

Don't those events remind you of our hotel example. Could we just re-cord the software's "stay" in our warehouse?

No, don't do it. Remember our rule: Only simplify if the result is a natural fit. The product is not a natural guest in our supplier's ware-house. There's a critical difference that would cause all kinds of prob-lems if we ignored this rule.

The difference is that a guest (or party) checks into a hotel and sub-sequently checks out. In a wholesale business, we check our product in by the caseload, and it checks out one or a few units at a time. When we ship two units to a dealer, we might be shipping the last of the case we got last month and the first of the case we got this month.

But let's look at the Things in our rough design. Do we really need to differentiate between computer and office-supply dealers and software retailers? We need the same data for each one, and for purposes of our system, it doesn't really matter which they are. Those three could be put together and all called customers.

We might want to add a field for the customer type, so we can break our sales down into each of these customer categories.

Here's our new version, with the first details filled in:

Things: Product

               PRODUCT_ID

               NAME

               SOFT_CO_ID

               LIST_PRICE

               Other

          Soft_Co

               SOFT_CO_ID

               NAME

               Address and phone

               Other

          Custmer

               CUSTMER_ID

Design Your Database

Type (computer, office, software only)

Address and phone

Credit and balance data

Events: Receive

RECEIVE_ID

SOFT_CO_ID

DATE_RECD

Product(s)

Quantity(s)

Ship

SHIP_ID

CUSTMER_ID

DATE_SHIP

Product(s)

Quantity(s)

Here we meet our first fields calling for one or more entries. In both receiving and shipping, it is likely that multiple units will come and go. So we need to add details.

Here is the new breakdown:

Things: Product

PRODUCT_ID

NAME

SOFT_CO_ID

LIST_PRICE

Other

Soft_Co

SOFT_CO_ID

NAME

Address and phone

Other

Custmer

CUSTMER_ID

Address and phone

Credit and balance data

Events: Receive

RECEIVE_ID

SOFT_CO_ID

DATE_RECD

Ship

SHIP_ID

CUSTMER_ID

DATE_SHIP

Details: Rec_Dtl

REC_DTL_ID

RECEIVE_ID

PRODUCT_ID

QUANTITY

Shp_Dtl

SHP_DTL_ID

SHIP_ID

PRODUCT_ID

QUANTITY

There will be other data, such as for special terms from suppliers or granted to customers. But for this example, we'll skip these to concentrate on the main point.

When we break out a Detail table, we start it with its own ID, as we do every other table. We continue with the ID of the table from which it was broken out. Then we add the repeating item and any data about the repeating item. In this case, the repeater is which product and how many of each.

Figure 3.5 shows an example of the details of a receipt Event. Again, the example uses phony ID values that make it easy to read. In the next section, we'll discuss the real key details.

FIGURE 3.5 ▶

*Details of a receipt
Event*

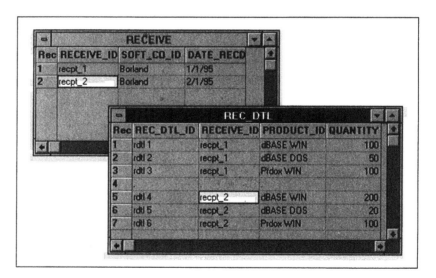

In this example, we received two shipments from Borland. The first was for 100 units each of dBASE for Windows and Paradox for Windows, with 50 units of dBASE for DOS.

For clarity, we've used a blank line in the Rec_Dtl table to separate the details of the first receipt from the second. The second receipt was for 200 units of dBASE for Windows, 20 units of dBASE for DOS, and 100 units of Paradox for Windows.

Figure 3.6 shows a similar example of a shipment. As you can see, the SHIP_ID field in the Detail table lets us tie the individual items back to the Ship table record of which they were parts. The PRODUCT_ID field tells us which product was shipped. Actually, it tells us this by referring back to a record in the Product table, not by using a name as we show here for simplicity's sake. By referring back to a record, we have access to the product's name, shipping weight, list price, discount structure, and whatever other information you stored in the fields.

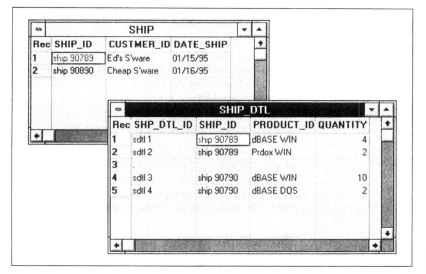

You have seen three examples of how the TED method works to organize your design process. It helps you get a place for everything, and to put everything in its place. Now let's get to the full details about those keys.

Design Your Database

▶▶ *You Master the Keys to Database Integrity*

Database integrity is what the computer scientists call a database with no fundamental flaws. It doesn't happen often, but in this case, the term means just what you might think. The scientists tell us that we want several kinds of integrity.

▶ *Principle Integrity Constraints*

We'll consider four types of integrity that our TED design method and consistent use of keys will maintain for you. The first two are so closely related that we'll consider them together. Don't let the size of the words in this scientific jargon throw you; the concepts are as simple as the words are large.

Entity and Primary Key Integrity

If every record has an ID field, and the value in every ID field is unique within each table, you have entity and primary key integrity. In the TED method, we automatically give each table an ID field, so part one is done. In the work that follows, we'll show you how to be sure that each key is unique. It's really not hard.

Domain Integrity

Domain integrity specifies that each field's value is a legal value for the field. At its simplest, this means that a Date field must contain a valid date (not a number or a name or a bitmap). dBASE for Windows maintains this simple level of domain integrity for you.

For better or worse, the concept of domain integrity is as complex as the data you are modeling. For instance, the domain of values for a salary field would be a range of numbers. Presumably, the exact range would depend on the size of the organization and on the responsibilities of the employee. Without setting any hard rules, you would expect the salary of the CEO of an international bank to be higher than the salary of a clerk in a small hardware store.

dBASE for Windows supports domain integrity rules of arbitrary complexity through its VALID handlers. If the rules can be expressed rigorously (not vaguely, as in the preceding paragraph), they can be programmed and dBASE for Windows will enforce them.

Relational Integrity

Relational integrity, or just RI, is the requirement that every ID value refer to exactly one record. If you have a PRODUCT_ID value in a Ship_Dtl table record, for example, there must be exactly one Product table record identified by this ID. Zero is unacceptable; so is two.

Relational integrity cannot be maintained if you don't have primary key integrity. A product has a unique ID number. Receiving and shipping records record that ID appropriately.

If you added a new product and assigned it a duplicate of that ID number (violating primary key integrity), you would lose your relational integrity. The IDs in the detail table records would ambiguously refer to two different products.

We'll elaborate on this rule when we get to assigning and using IDs. These IDs are called *keys* in the relational literature.

▶ Assigning Unique Keys

All sorts of systems have been used for assigning unique keys. One common system is to pick a large random number (dBASE for Windows has a RANDOM function that will do this). After you pick the number, you search your table to be sure that you haven't already used that number. If the number isn't there, you go ahead and assign it. If it's already in use, you discard it, get another random number, and try again.

This system has problems, which we'll discuss shortly. Fortunately, a much simpler system works: assign the first ID the number 1, the second ID the number 2, and so on.

For an ID field, start by guessing the largest number of records you might ever have in your table. Make the ID field one or two digits wider than necessary for that number. For example, if you think you might have hundreds of people in your phone list, use at least a four-digit ID field.

In practice, we use a little trick that can simplify things. We don't start with 1 as the first ID number. If we have a four-digit ID, we start with 1001. This means that every ID field will be four digits wide. With this method, all sorts of quickly printed lists line up neatly, no matter what software we might be using to read the table.

Another trick we use is to accept some unique keys as IDs. The hotel room numbers in the example in the previous section are one good example. However, before you use such keys, make sure that they are appropriate.

For example, each working American has an assigned tax identification number, called the Social Security number. These are suitable unique identifiers for database work. Actually, they are far too suitable. Privacy legislation restricts the use of these numbers to their intended purpose: providing tax information to the government.

If there are no legal impediments and the IDs are naturally occurring, definitely unique identifiers, go ahead and use them.

It's simple enough to type in a new ID number each time you add a record. It is also error-prone in a high-volume environment. In Chapter 4, we explain a short routine that automatically supplies a new ID for each new record created. For now, you can just type the IDs in.

Do not reuse IDs after records have been deleted. The word we have been using is *unique*. This means forever and permanently unique. If you delete an inactive customer, you don't want to reassign that customer's ID. You might find that you want to reconstruct last year's billing, for example. You won't be able to do it if you have given an old ID to a new customer.

The deleted record problem is the one that causes the random ID system problems we mentioned earlier. Just because an ID is not in the table doesn't mean that it wasn't there at some time in the past.

► *Maintaining Relational Integrity*

The first step in maintaining relational integrity is to maintain entity and primary key integrity. If you assign each record a unique ID as we have discussed, you'll meet these two integrity constraints.

Now we're ready for the three cases where we must consider relational integrity:

- When you add a record
- When you edit a record
- When you delete a record

One-to-Many Relationships

In our phone list system, each employer can have many employees. This is known as a *one-to-many relationship*. One employer can have many employees.

From the opposite perspective, we could say that there is a many-to-one relationship between employees and employers. Many employees work for one employer.

Many-to-many and *one-to-one* relationships are also possible. For example, if your system is keeping track of consultants and their employers, you might have one employer using many consultants, and one consultant working for many employers. If your software company has a product manager for every product, that is a one-to-one relationship.

The way we will most commonly look at relationships is the one-to-many perspective.

Parent and Child Records

A one-to-many relationship is also called a *parent-child relationship*. For instance, in the example of a wholesale supplier database presented earlier in this chapter, we had a Ship table and a Ship_Dtl table. This is a one-to-many relationship: each Ship table record can have many Ship_Dtl records.

We call the Ship record the *parent* of the Ship_Dtl record. Let's reconsider the way we use IDs in a parent-child relationship.

As you can see, the SHIP_ID field is placed in the child record to identify its parent. The SHIP_ID is, by definition, unique for each Ship table record. When we use it in the Ship_Dtl table, we will reuse it once for every child record attached to the parent Ship table record.

Design Your Database

Foreign Keys

When the Ship table record is identified by the SHIP_ID key, the key is called a *primary key*. When the SHIP_ID field is used in a child record to select the parent, it is called a *foreign key*. Those SHIP_ID fields in the Ship_Dtl table are foreign keys. They are sometimes called foreign keys *into* the Ship table.

Other people say that the foreign key *points to* the parent record. This usage bothers the scientists, but we still use it. To give the science its due, remember that the ID doesn't point to a particular place in the parent table. You could shuffle the parent table's records like a deck of playing cards. The foreign key doesn't specify "card 24." It specifies "3 of spades," wherever that might be located.

Relational integrity is all about the maintenance of foreign keys.

Relational Integrity and Adding Records

Let's begin with another look at our phone list system, but this time we'll use real keys as they'll appear in our database. Figure 3.4, shown earlier in this chapter, portrays the system as you might think about it. But the way a database with relational integrity would represent it is shown in Figure 3.7.

FIGURE 3.7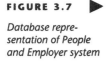

Database representation of People and Employer system

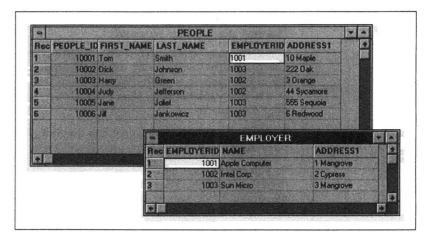

Now let's add a record to the Employer table. This has a primary key and no foreign keys. All we need to do is make sure that our new record uses the next higher key:

Rec	EMPLOYERID	NAME	ADDRESS1
		EMPLOYER	
1	1001	Apple Computer	1 Mangrove
2	1002	Intel Corp.	2 Cypress
3	1003	Sun Micro	3 Mangrove
4	1004	Compaq	4 Live Oak

There are no relational integrity problems, because no other record has an EMPLOYERID of 1004.

Adding a record to the People table has an additional consideration. We'll pick the next higher primary key, but when we pick a foreign key, we must make sure that it exists in the appropriate table. Here we'll add the first employee working for Compaq:

Rec	PEOPLE_ID	FIRST_NAME	LAST_NAME	EMPLOYERID	ADDRESS1
			PEOPLE		
1	10001	Tom	Smith	1001	10 Maple
2	10002	Dick	Johnson	1003	222 Oak
3	10003	Harry	Green	1002	3 Orange
4	10004	Judy	Jefferson	1002	44 Sycamore
5	10005	Jane	Joliet	1003	555 Sequoia
6	10006	Jill	Jankowicz	1003	6 Redwood
7	10007	Fred	Furrier	1004	747 Plane

To maintain relational integrity when you add records, you need to be sure that your primary key is new, and that any foreign keys are *not* new.

When we get to Part 4, you'll see that this can be done by a simple bit of event-handler programming. If you're working on a personal system, use the Navigator to launch your table, and then launch browse views of any tables where you'll pick foreign keys.

Design Your
Database

Relational Integrity and Editing Records

If you assigned a primary key correctly, it should never be changed. Other records may be using the primary key's value as a foreign key. Changing it could "orphan" those child records.

You could, if necessary, carefully change the primary key in the parent record, and then find each child record that was attached and change the children's foreign key values. This would maintain relational integrity.

However, the simple way to maintain integrity is to never change the primary key. When you add records, enter the primary keys, check them carefully, and fix any mistakes. Then go on to the next record; never go back to that primary key.

You can use the Table Records Properties dialog box to make your primary keys Read Only. When you're ready to add records, use this tool to reverse this setting.

You won't often need to edit foreign keys, either. For example, all our Ship_Dtl table records will be permanently attached to their parent Ship table record. One exception is in correcting errors. You may discover that those copies of dBASE for Windows were, in fact, shipped to a different dealer, for example.

In some cases, you'll need to edit foreign keys because facts have changed. For example, we'll need to change a key in our phone list when one of our acquaintances changes jobs.

The rule for changing a foreign key is the same as the rule for adding a new one. You must check that it exists. For example, a correct change for our phone list when Tom leaves Apple and goes to work for Compaq is shown on the next page.

Rec	PEOPLE_ID	FIRST_NAME	LAST_NAME	EMPLOYERID	ADDRESS1
1	10001	Tom	Smith	1004	10 Maple
2	10002	Dick	Johnson	1003	222 Oak
3	10003	Harry	Green	1002	3 Orange
4	10004	Judy	Jefferson	1002	44 Sycamore
5	10005	Jane	Joliet	1003	555 Sequoia
6	10006	Jill	Jankowicz	1003	6 Redwood
7	10007	Fred	Furrier	1004	747 Plane

Just be sure that the new foreign key correctly attaches the child record to another parent record. Again, if you're working from the Navigator, launch the parent table and choose a Browse Layout view.

Relational Integrity and Deleting Records

Deletions follow a very simple rule: never delete a parent record.

Before deleting a record, you must check every table that is a child of that parent. Search the foreign key field for that parent's ID value. If you find one, you cannot delete the parent record.

In relational jargon, we talk about *refuse deletes* and *cascade deletes*. What we just described is the refuse deletes system. Never delete a parent record.

The other alternative does not violate this rule. A cascade deletes system searches for all child records. It deletes every child record. Once all the children are gone, it deletes the parent record.

This is called *cascade* because the child records themselves could be parents of other records. Deleting a child record requires that you repeat the process: find all its children and delete them first. This could proceed down several levels.

For example, in our software distributor system, deleting a customer requires that we delete all Ship table records for that customer. Deleting the Ship table records requires that we delete each Ship_Dtl table record for that shipment.

The cascade deletes method requires a program set up for that purpose. If you think that cascade deletes has the potential for disastrous consequences, you're right. For example, if we cascaded the deletion of an employer in our phone list, all the people employed by that employer would be deleted. Even if the employer went out of business, you probably wouldn't want to lose all the other data about those people.

There is one place where a cascade delete is helpful. If your tables are backed up to suitable permanent storage media (tape, removable disk, or something similar), you may want to delete the records for inactive customers. In this case, a cascade delete would remove all the sales and sales detail records for that customer. This would be appropriate if, for example, all these sales were made last year and last year's books are closed.

▶▶ *Summary*

We've considered the art and science of database design. Ultimately, it is an art, with many "correct" ways to design a database.

The science of database design works through normal forms, beginning with First Normal Form, progressing through Fifth Normal form. Most software engineers consider Third Normal Form adequate. We use the TED method, which is simple and always generates a Boyce-Codd Normal Form design, which is proven to lie between Third and Fourth Normal Forms.

The TED method is to break down your target database into a list of Things (long-duration, often kickable) and Events (instantaneous interactions among Things). For each Thing and Event, you list the important characteristics. For repeating characteristics, you create Detail tables.

We use ID fields for each record. These become our records' primary keys, ensuring entity and primary key integrity.

We assign the first record an integer value that fills its width, such as 1001 for a four-digit field. With each new record, we assign the next integer in sequence: 1002, 1003, and so on. These IDs, or keys, are certain to be unique, which is the main requirement.

We use these ID fields as foreign keys in the *many* part of one-to-many relationships, which are also called *child* records in a parent-child relationship.

We maintain complete referential integrity by always adding new, unique primary keys when we add records and by adding existing foreign keys.

We don't edit the primary keys. Occasionally, we may change an existing foreign key in a child record to "point to" a new parent record.

We don't ever delete parent records if there are child records referring to them.

Design Your Database

PART TWO

dBASE for Windows is one of those products that you can run at a very simple level, as you learned to do in Chapter 2. Here in Part 2, we'll bring you from that beginning up to a strong intermediate level.

In Chapter 4, Manipulating Your Data, we'll cover the use of the Table Records tool in depth. You'll use the Table Utilities for chores such as setting up indexes. dBASE for Windows' indexes allow you to sort your data on various criteria.

In Chapter 5, The Two-Way Query Designer, you'll use the Query Designer to not only query your data, but to organize multiple tables into a database system. The "Two-Way" part of this tool means that it creates programs for you. You can edit these programs directly, or use the Query Designer. You'll discover that the Query Designer writes programs that are consistently error-free, and being able to edit those programs gives you additional power. You can do this type of editing long before you get into even the beginnings of dBASE for Windows programming.

In Chapter 6, Building Forms with the Two-Way Form Designer, you'll use the Form Expert, which we met in Chapter 2. You'll also do your own work with blank forms. You'll use the Menu Designer to create a menu program that will tie together a two-table phone list system, with one table for employees and another for employers. You'll be able to access your tables either individually or in a combined view.

You'll also use the Form Designer to add custom touches, such as Browse and Pushbutton objects. As we do this work, you'll use the Procedure Editor to add programs that run when triggered by user-interface events. (These programs are either one or two lines long—not over the head of even a determined nonprogrammer.)

In Chapter 7, Producing Database Reports, you'll start with a two-table report to tie together your employer and employee data. Beginning with a simple listing, you'll work forward to a sophisticated grouped report, which will include a variety of decorative effects highlighting information.

Before leaving Chapter 7, you'll return to the menu you developed in Chapter 6 and tie in a report as part of your phone list system. We finish the tutorial sections in Part 2 with a discussion of mailing label generation using the Crystal Reports tool.

▶ ▶   CHAPTER **4**

Manipulating
Your Data

———

► ►   ***I**n* this chapter, we'll work on single table operations. To begin, we'll apply what we discussed in Chapter 3 to add an ID (key) field to our People table. We'll have dBASE for Windows fill in every ID in a single stroke. Next, we'll use an index to sort the People table by last name. You'll learn more about using indexes to maintain multiple orders continuously and to permit virtually instantaneous searches for last names or record IDs.

Then we'll go on to take a closer look at searching and modifying our data in bulk operations. Just as the Table Record tool lets us edit individual records, the Table menus let us apply edits across large groups of records.

Finally, we'll cover importing and exporting data from a variety of formats. These operations will give us instant tables, filled from existing sources. Going the other way, they'll instantly fill our spreadsheets and other files with data culled from our tables.

We'll begin by updating our People table to the design standards discussed in Chapter 2.

► ► *Improving the People Table*

For starters, the People table doesn't have the ID field that it will need when we get to the next chapter, where we'll add a related table. For this task, we'll use the Table Structure tool again. We used that tool to create the People table; now we'll use it to improve that table.

▶ *Adding an ID Field to the Structure*

We'll need a field, PEOPLE_ID, to hold identifiers for each record in the table. Adding this field is not difficult. Follow these steps:

1. Launch dBASE for Windows and open the Navigator, if you haven't already done so. Select the D:\DBWORK directory (or whatever directory you're using). This is the way dBASE for Windows will start itself if you haven't done additional work since Chapter 1.

2. Select Tables from the list of file types, and then choose People from the list of tables. (It's the only table if you haven't added more on your own.)

3. Right double-click on People or press Shift-F2 to launch the table in Design mode. You should now be in the Table Structure tool, looking at the structure of your People table, as you see in Figure 4.1.

▶▶ **N O T E**

For every file type in the Navigator list, you can left double-click or press F2 to launch a file in Run mode, or right double-click or press Shift-F2 to launch a file in Design mode.

4. We want to add a new field at the beginning or the table. Be sure the currently highlighted record is the first one, then press Ctrl-N, or choose Structure ➤ Insert Field. This inserts a new record immediately above the previously selected one.

5. Type **PEOPLE_ID** for the field name.

6. Press Tab or Enter to move to the Type field. With the mouse, click on the down arrow and then click on Numeric. From the keyboard, just press N. You can't pull down the list of types from the keyboard—a design oversight. You can use the ↓ and ↑ keys to scroll through the options.

▶▶ **T I P**

Most table operations are quicker from the keyboard. Don't get your hand glued to that mouse.

FIGURE 4.1 ▶

Ready to add a new field to PEOPLE.DBF

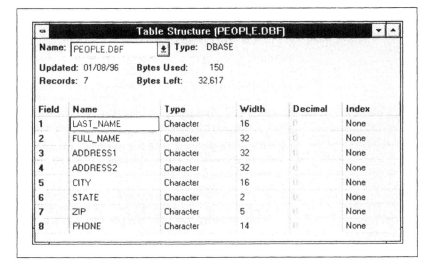

Field	Name	Type	Width	Decimal	Index
1	LAST_NAME	Character	16	0	None
2	FULL_NAME	Character	32	0	None
3	ADDRESS1	Character	32	0	None
4	ADDRESS2	Character	32	0	None
5	CITY	Character	16	0	None
6	STATE	Character	2	0	None
7	ZIP	Character	5	0	None
8	PHONE	Character	14	0	None

Table Structure (PEOPLE.DBF)
Name: PEOPLE.DBF   Type: DBASE
Updated: 01/08/96   Bytes Used: 150
Records: 7   Bytes Left: 32,617

7. Press Tab or Enter to move to the Width field. Enter **4** or higher number. If your personal phone list is not likely to get to 1000, 4 is adequate. If you're a professional in a people field (employment agent, perhaps), you may want to make the field wider.

8. Press Tab or Enter twice to pass over the Decimals field (the default 0 is just what we want) and reach the Index field. Press A for an ascending index.

9. If you haven't already done so, specify A for an ascending index for the LAST_NAME field. Your first two records should specify A, and the rest N (for None). You'll be learning all about indexes later in the chapter.

10. Choose Structure ➤ Manage Indexes ... from the menus. Before you get to the Manage Indexes dialog box, you'll see the Changes Made - Table Structure dialog box. Tell it Yes, you do want to save your changes.

Take a good look at the Manage Indexes dialog box. For the moment, we won't make any selections. Just remember that this dialog box is available from the Table Structure tool. Later in this chapter, we'll use this same dialog box from the Table Records tool (in Run mode). In the future, you'll find it convenient to specify your indexes when you design your tables (from the Table Structure tool).

11. Choose Cancel to exit the Manage Indexes dialog box.

12. To run the new table structure, press F2 or click on the lightning icon on the speedbar. Don't start typing!

▶▶ **W A R N I N G**

If you've been experimenting on your own and you've used the Table Properties dialog box, you've created a custom Fields list. When you change from the Table Structure tool to the Table Records tool, dBASE for Windows ignores previous Fields lists. This means that the next time you browse your table from the Navigator, you won't see the fields you added. To add the new fields to your Fields list, return to the Table Properties tool (choose Properties ➤ Table Records Window ...) and add the new fields.

▶ Letting dBASE Fill in the ID Field

We think you'll be surprised at how easy it is to add the data to our new field. (No, we're not going to type IDs one at a time!)

If you aren't in the Browse Layout view, select it by clicking on its icon on the speedbar or by choosing View ➤ Browse Layout from the menus. Your table should look like the one in Figure 4.2.

Now we want to explain to dBASE that it should put the number 1001 (use more zeros if you have a field wider than four characters) in the first record's PEOPLE_ID field, 1002 in the second, and so on.

The more records you have in the table, the more valuable this technique will be. If you have only a handful of records, just imagine that you've added several hundred and need to fill in all those PEOPLE_ID numbers.

FIGURE 4.2 ▶

*People table, with
blank PEOPLE_ID fields*

Rec	PEOPLE_ID	LAST_NAME	FULL_NAME	ADDR1
1		Friendly	Phil Friendly	5 Maple Ave.
2		Adamson	Adrianne Adamson	10 Oak Dr.
3		Monroe	Madilyn Monroe	Sunset Blvd.
4		Gable	Eve Gable	High Rise, # 2
5		Hacker	Herb Hacker	Orange Grove
6		Garfield	Feline Garfield	Studio 4
7		Brown	Aphonse Brown, MD	12 Main St.
8				

Table Records (PEOPLE.DBF)

This operation, and many others, is available from the Table drop-down menu. Choose the Replace Records ... choice:

Find Records...	**Ctrl+F**
Replace Records...	**Ctrl+R**
Create **Q**uery	
Table Utilities	▶
Add Records	Ctrl+A
Delete Selected Record	Ctrl+U
Lock Selected Record	Ctrl+L
Blank Selected Record	
Go to Record Number...	Ctrl+G
Previous Record	Up Arrow
Next Record	Down Arrow
Pre**v**ious Page	PgUp
Ne**x**t Page	PgDn
To**p** Record	Ctrl+PgUp
Botto**m** Record	Ctrl+PgDn

This brings up the Replace Records dialog box, which lets you search for a value in one field and replace values in a field for every record that matches. In a word processor, this would be the global search and replace function. In a data table, it works with text, numbers, dates, and the other data types.

We want to look for all the PEOPLE_IDs that contain a zero value. Type a **0** in the Find What entry field. Press Tab to reach the Replace With entry field, and type this expression:

recno() + 1000

We'll cover expressions in detail in Chapter 12. For now, we'll jump ahead to explain this one. The RECNO() function (the trailing parentheses identify it as a function) returns the record number. It will be 1 for the first record, 2 for the second, and so on.

dBASE will evaluate the Replace With expression once for every record that matches the Find What expression. In this case, every record will match. On the first record, the expression will evaluate to 1001; at the second record, it will evaluate to 1002, and so on.

Your Replace Records dialog box should look like the one shown in Figure 4.3. From the pushbuttons on the right, choose Replace All. This will fill our PEOPLE_ID fields with exactly the unique key values that we want.

When you're finished, choose Close. When you're asked if you want to keep your changes, respond Yes. Now all the PEOPLE_ID fields in our table are filled in with ascending numbers beginning with 1001. Next, we'll customize our view to match our table.

▶ Customizing the Table Records Tool

Let's make more of the People table visible in a Browse Layout view. Follow these steps:

1. Launch the People table and choose the Browse Layout view.

2. From the Table Records tool, choose Properties ▶ Table Records Window .... This opens the Table Records Properties dialog box.

The default selection is all fields. Let's start by removing the second line of address data. Note that this doesn't change the table or its data; it just controls what fields you'll see in the Table Records tool.

FIGURE 4.3 ►

Filling PEOPLE_IDs with the Replace Records dialog box

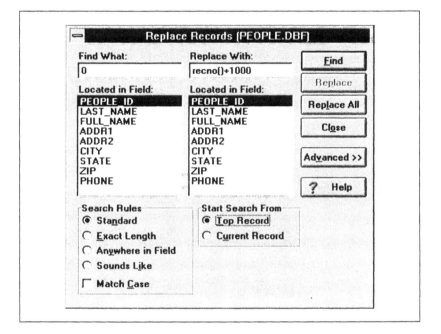

3. Click on the ADDR2 field, or tab to the Selected Fields box and use the ↓ key to select this field.

4. Click on the < pushbutton. This shoots just the selected field back to the Available Fields box, as shown in Figure 4.4.

Now let's customize the other fields. We'll change their width and give the PEOPLE_ID field a shorter name. Remember, these changes affect only the appearance of the table in Browse Layout view.

5. Highlight the PEOPLE_ID field in the Selected Fields box and click on the Properties ... pushbutton at the bottom of the dialog box. You'll see the Field Properties dialog box.

6. In the Heading box, enter **ID**. Use the down arrow for the Width box to change the width to 4. These entries are shown in Figure 4.5.

FIGURE 4.4 ▶

Choosing fields to appear in the Browse Layout view

Manipulating Your Data

7. Choose OK in the Field Properties dialog box, then again in the Table Records Properties dialog box. Now you're back in your Browse Layout view. This should show the PEOPLE_ID field nicely sized and titled ID.

8. Return to the Table Records Properties dialog box. For each of the remaining fields, except the PHONE field, use Properties... to set a width two-thirds or less of the field's actual width. When you're finished, return to your Browse Layout view. Ours is shown in Figure 4.6.

Adjust your view as needed, until you can comfortably view your People table. When you leave the Table Records tool, these settings are stored in a Fields record in your DBASEWIN.INI file. They will be recalled each time you run the Table Records tool for the People table.

FIGURE 4.5 ▶

Setting properties for the PEOPLE_ID field

FIGURE 4.6 ▶

A Browse Layout view with the whole record visible

▶▶ **T I P**

**If you start in Design mode (Table Records Structure
tool) and switch to Run mode, the stored Fields list is
ignored. This lets you see the structure changes you
just made. For a quick look that ignores your Fields list,
launch the Table Records Structure tool before you
switch to Run mode.**

See Chapter 9 for a full explanation of all the features of the Table Records Properties tool.

Let's finish up by putting our people into alphabetical order by last name.

▶ Organizing People Alphabetically

Remember the Manage Indexes dialog box that we looked at, but didn't use, from the Table Structure tool? That's where we're heading next. We wanted to get those IDs in place and have a nice Browse Layout view to see the effects of the indexes.

Launch your People table and choose a Browse Layout view. Choose Tables ➤ Table Utilities from the menus.

Table	Properties	Window	Help
Find Records...	Ctrl+F		
Replace Records...	Ctrl+R		
Create Query			
Table Utilities			

Manage Indexes...	
Reindex	
Close Table	
Close All Tables	
Delete Records...	
Recall Records...	
Pack Records	
Zap Records	
Append Records from File...	
Export Records...	
Sort Records...	
Generate Records...	
Count Records...	
Calculate Records	

As you see, the first choice here is Manage Indexes .... Select that option to get to the Manage Indexes dialog box.

In the Manage Indexes dialog box for the People table, you should see three choices:

- [Natural Order]
- PEOPLE_ID
- LAST_NAME

When you first use the Manage Indexes dialog box, the default index highlighted is Natural Order. Actually, that means no index is in use.

 ▶▶ **N O T E**

> **Natural Order may not be the best choice of words. For us, a phone list is most natural when it's in alphabetic order. Remember that Natural Order really means no index at all. The records are in the order in which they were added to the table.**

Choose the LAST_NAME index, as shown in Figure 4.7. Then click on OK.

FIGURE 4.7 ▶

Choosing the LAST_NAME index for organizing PEOPLE.DBF

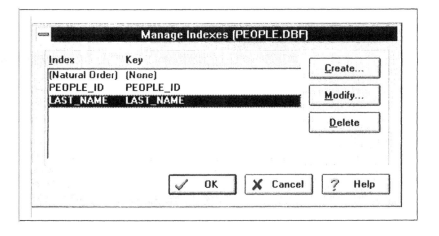

Manipulating
Your Data

When dBASE for Windows redisplays your table, your records will be ordered alphabetically by last name. You might see two problems in this view, depending on your data.

Retrieving Disappearing Records

You may see that you've lost some of your records. Actually, they're not lost at all. When dBASE redisplays your table, it begins its display at record 1. Record 1 is your first physical record, but the index reorders the table. (It doesn't actually sort the records, which we will discuss later in this chapter.) Unless your first record happens to be first in alphabetical order, this will "hide" the records that come before it.

Click on the beginning of file speedbar icon, or press Ctrl-PgUp, and you'll go to the first record in the alphabetic order that your index specifies.

▶▶ **W A R N I N G**

In the first release, there is a bug in the vertical elevator. It may not show you that you're not looking at the top of the Browse Layout view.

True Alphabetic Sorting

If your LAST_NAME fields begin with a capital letter and continue with lowercase letters, your sort will be acceptable. But it isn't a true alphabetic sort; it's an ASCII collating sequence sort.

In the ASCII character set, the capital letters *A* through *Z* come before the lowercase letters *a* through *z*. This means that *Zebra* sorts before *aardvark*.

Later in this chapter, we'll explain the technique for doing a true alphabetic sort. If you have simple LAST_NAME field values, you'll have no problem so far. But consider some of these:

- Zenith will sort before adams.
- LeBeouf will sort before Lebatt.
- LeValley will sort before Leanne.
- DePres will sort before Deparne.

- McPhee will sort before Mcmanus.
- Smith, PID will sort before Smith, PhD.

The default ASCII sort won't be satisfactory in the long run.

Now let's dig into these topics in more detail, starting with sorting.

▶▶ *Putting Your Data in Order*

For most applications, you want your data to appear in a sensible order. The order that makes the most sense is seldom the order in which you enter the data. If you meet a new supplier, named Adams, you'll enter a new record in your phone list. You'll want to see Adams name appear between Adam and Addams when you look at your phone list.

Putting a small table into order is not a problem. But dBASE doesn't handle just small problems. It can handle up to a billion records in a single table. Real tables frequently run into the millions of records.

Sorting a table of 10,000 records takes several seconds. Sorting 100,000 records takes minutes; 1,000,000 records would need hours.

Consider also that many applications require that the data be organized in more than one way. When we look at our lists, alphabetic order often makes sense. When our system wants to relate two records, it will be looking for an ID value, so it needs the table sorted by ID. Often, both needs must be accommodated at the same time.

This is where indexes come in.

▶ *What Is an Index?*

This book has an index. If you need to find information about sorting your data, you could look in the index, find the page number, and then turn to that page. Without the index, you could start reading at page 1 and keep reading until you arrived here. Obviously, indexed access is much more efficient.

Computer indexes serve the same purpose, except that they have record number entries, not book page numbers. Actually, the computer indexes are themselves indexed.

If the computer is looking for the name Smith, it will first look in its index of the last names. That might tell it that the *S* entries start on page 17 of the index. Page 17 might be the place where the *S* entries start, or it might have another index. On page 17, the computer might learn that the *Sm* entries start on page 24.

These indexed indexes are called *B-trees* by computer scientists. For our purposes, we can just call them lightning fast. Borland and its main database rival, Microsoft, compete fiercely in trying to produce ever more effective (fast) indexes.

The exact details of each release's indexes keep changing as Borland keeps discovering more effective indexing techniques. From our perspective, this means that each relase will run more quickly than the last.

On our test machine (a generic 33 MHz 486), finding one entry from 10,000 in a sample PEOPLE.DBF file takes only a small fraction of a second.

▶ Storing Your Indexes

If you use the Table Structure tool and the Manage Indexes dialog box to specify your indexes, dBASE for Windows automatically creates and maintains an index file whose name is the same as your table name, giving it the extension .MDX.

Your Production Index

The .MDX file whose name matches your table's name is called the *production index*. Older versions of dBASE used single index files, with the extension .NDX. The .NDX file stored only one index; the .MDX file can store up to 47 separate indexes.

This means that PEOPLE.MDX can conveniently store all the indexes you'll need for PEOPLE.DBF, for one example.

Your Master Index

When you selected an index other than Natural Order, you were choosing a *master index* for your table. The master index is the index that you're using. As you browse through your data, or scroll through it in any layout, it appears to be ordered by the master index.

You can choose a different master index at any time. This will change the apparent order of the records in your table. In fact, you can launch two or more separate instances of the Table Records tool and set a different master index for each. Figure 4.8 shows two simultaneous views of the People table, set to different indexes.

FIGURE 4.8 ▶

PEOPLE.DBF sorted by the ID and LAST_NAME fields

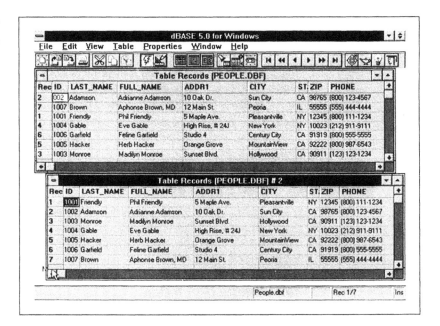

The index that is highlighted in the Manage Indexes dialog box is your master index for the currently active Table Records tool or custom form.

Each index is given a name, called a *tag*, that can be used in the Command window when you open a table. From the Navigator, you can't specify a master index until you have launched a form or a Table tool. dBASE for Windows doesn't record your choice for a master index in DBASEWIN.INI, either. You must reselect the field for indexing each time.

There is a partial solution to this minor problem. If you have only one index as the production index, dBASE will always choose that index as the default master index. With multiple tags, dBASE defaults to the Natural Order choice (no index).

▶ *Managing Your Production Index*

When you choose an ascending or descending index in the Table Structure tool, an appropriate index tag and expression is created in the production index (.MDX) file. After your table is created, you can use the Manage Indexes dialog box to edit, create, and delete indexes.

So far, you've just used your tables and not worried about the possibility that others might want to use them, too. The default access that you've been using is *shared*. Shared access lets others use your tables, and it lets you use a table in several different windows simultaneously. However, some operations don't work if you are sharing access. For these you'll need *exclusive* access.

One operation that requires exclusive access to your table is index manipulation. If you're using the default shared access, dBASE for Windows will point this out and offer to correct the situation for you. Accept its offer of exclusive use if it asks you.

When you first display the Manage Indexes dialog box, the Modify ... and Delete pushbuttons are grayed. (Remember, you can access this dialog box from the Structure menu of the Table Structure tool, or from the Table ▶ Table Utilities menu of the Table Records tool.) These pushbuttons aren't available because the default first index is Natural Order, which is no index at all. If you select an index, the Modify ... and Delete pushbuttons become available.

Modifying an Index

We want to change the index expression to one which will cause the order for the LAST_NAME index to be truly alphabetic, as opposed to being in ASCII collating sequence.

Go ahead and select the LAST_NAME index and click on Modify ... to reach the Modify Index dialog box.

The indexes you created by choosing Ascending or Descending in the Table Structure tool have the simplest possible index expression: just the name of the field. Any dBASE expression, from the simplest to the most complex, can be used.

We'll apply the dBASE UPPER() function to the LAST_NAME field. UPPER() converts all the alphabetic characters in a string to uppercase characters. (It leaves other characters unchanged.) Recall that the problem with the ASCII collating sequence is that A–Z comes before a–z. These are a couple of the problems we cited:

- Zenith will sort before adams.
- LeBeouf will sort before Lebatt.

If you convert all letters to uppercase, then your problem is solved:

- ADAMS sorts before ZENITH.
- LEBATT sorts before LEBEOUF.

To use UPPER(), just use the function name, putting whatever it is to get UPPER()ed inside the parentheses. In this case, it is the LAST_NAME field, so you want the expression to be:

    UPPER(LAST_NAME)

Figure 4.9 shows the correct expression added to the Modify Index dialog box.

 ►►**N O T E**

> **dBASE expressions are not case-sensitive. You can use any combination of uppercase and lowercase letters. By tradition, dBASE's built-in functions, such as UPPER(), are written in all capital letters.**

Enter the expression in the Modify Index dialog box, just as you see it in Figure 4.9, then click on OK. There will be a brief pause while the new expression is written to the production index file and your table's index is re-created with the new expression. You'll return to the Manage Indexes dialog box.

FIGURE 4.9 ▶

Using UPPER() for true alphabetic sorting

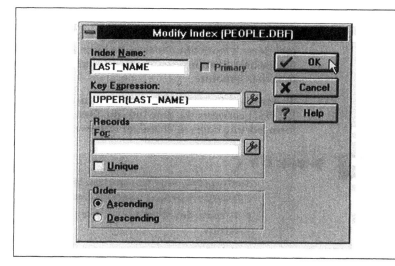

Manipulating Your Data

Adding and Deleting Indexes

From the Manage Indexes dialog box, you can also add and delete indexes. Deleting is a simple matter of selecting an index and clicking on the Delete pushbutton (or pressing Alt-D).

▶▶ WARNING

The Delete option will delete the index without giving you a chance to reconsider. Be sure you want to delete the highlighted index before you click this button or press Alt-D.

To add a new index, simply click on Create .... This launches the Create Index dialog box, which is identical to the Modify Index dialog box, except that it's not filled in. You enter a name and expression, and your index is created.

See Chapter 12 for a full discussion of dBASE for Windows' expressions.

Date Sorting

Unfortunately, choosing to index on a Date field in the Table Structure tool doesn't work like choosing to index on a Character field. The Date field is held in an internal structure, and a default sort on a Date field uses that structure.

To sort dates in date order, you must use the DTOS() function. DTOS() converts the date into the form *YYYYMMDD*. By using this form, sorting dates as character strings puts them into order by date.

 ▶▶ **N O T E**

> Sorting this way ignores the **SET DATE TO** and **SET CENTURY** settings, which is exactly what you want in this case. See Chapter 13 for a discussion of the SET settings.

The following expression correctly sorts records based on the date in the START_DATE field:

    DTOS(Start_date)

Logical Sorting

For many purposes, an index on a logical variable is helpful. This type of index organizes a table into two parts: True and False. For example, your database of attorneys includes a logical field which is True if the attorney is licensed to practice in California. An index on this field would sort those who were licensed in that jurisdiction together, which would be helpful if you needed an attorney for a California legal matter.

You cannot index directly on a logical variable, however. Indexing is only permitted on Character, Numeric, Float, and Date fields. You can use the IIF() expression to convert logical values to character data when you want a logical sort.

This expression will convert the logical field LIC_IN_CA to a single character:

    IIF(lic_in_ca, "Y", "N")

The result is either a Y or an N, depending on the value of the LIC_IN_CA field. (If you want to sort the True values to the top of the table, use descending sequence.)

▶ *Physical Sorting*

The last, and least used, option for putting your records in order is actually sorting the table. In fact, dBASE does not really have an option for sorting a table. It will write a new, sorted table, based on your original (presumably unsorted) table. You can, if you wish, copy this table over the original to get a truly sorted table.

The steps here are not as simple as you might wish. But there's a reason for this. It's to discourage you from doing physical sorts.

 ▶ ▶ **T I P**

You should almost always use indexes or queries to put your data in the order you want. Physical sorting has almost no place in modern data management.

There is one special case where a physically sorted table makes sense, which is why we're going to show you the steps here. Remember that this process is only for this one special case.

The situation that sometimes justifies physical sorting is that static data table. You sometimes meet situations where your data will never change, or change very rarely. In this case, it may be worth the trouble to physically sort your table and dispense with the indexes.

In preparing this book, for example, we built a table of all the object properties available in dBASE 5 for Windows. We don't expect this list to change until dBASE 6.0 for Windows is released. So we waited until we were sure our list was complete, and then we sorted it into name order. We didn't assign IDs until it was sorted.

In the end, we had the table sorted so that the Natural Order, the ID order, and the alphabetic name order were all the same. However, you may find that sorting is enough trouble so that, even in this situation, you go right on using indexes. That's what the dBASE designers had in mind.

Now let's sort the People table. (Sorting is the easy part; the hard part comes next.) We chose the $\underline{S}$ort Records … option from the $\underline{T}$able ➤ $\underline{T}$able Utilities menu.

Selecting $\underline{S}$ort Records … displays the Sort Records dialog box. In Figure 4.10, we've typed the name of the new table into the $\underline{N}$ame entry field for the Target Table. We always use the name TEMP for the file that gets the sorted data.

FIGURE 4.10 ▶

Choosing LAST_NAME to sort to TEMP.DBF

▶▶ **T I P**

If you always sort into the same .DBF file, each sort will overwrite the last one. If you use different names for each sort, you'll have a hard time telling your real .DBFs from the temporary ones.

After you enter a name, select one or more sort fields. The first field is the main sort order. For example, you could sort sales orders by date and then by customer name. The second field would sort records

Manipulating Your Data

where the first field's value matched (all the orders for one date, for example).

Highlight the field on the left, and click on the > pushbutton to shoot it from the Available Fields box into the Key Fields box. After you move a field across, an up arrow icon appears next to it in the Key Fields box.

Click on this arrow and, for a Character field, you will be given four choices: ascending or descending, both with or without case. Choose without case for a true alphabetic sort.

After you've specified your sort and chosen OK, in a very few seconds, the sort will be completed. You'll have a new table, in our case TEMP.DBF, that has the records in the order you specified.

If you had any memo fields, you now have a new copy of the memos in TEMP.DBT. There is no production index for TEMP.

You also have your original .DBF, .DBT (if any), and .MDX files, and probably a .DBK (backup) file as well. Exit from all copies of the Table Records, Table Structure, and Form tools that are manipulating your original file.

In the Navigator, highlight your original .DBF file and right-click to get the Speed menu. From the Speed menu, select Delete. Alternatively you could choose Edit ➤ Delete from the menus, or just press the Del key. You'll see the Delete File dialog box, which will remind you that you will be deleting all the associated files, as well as the .DBF file.

 ▶▶ **T I P**

The Delete File process forgets the .DBK extension. This gives you the opportunity to recover from serious mistakes. On the other hand, it gives you one more cleanup chore to remember.

Once you delete the original file, you can rename the TEMP.??? files to the old name. In the Command window, type

```
rename TEMP.DBF TO oldname.DBF
rename TEMP.DBT TO oldname.DBT
```

With that chore out of the way, you only need to launch the renamed table into the Table Records tool and choose <u>T</u>able ➤ <u>T</u>able Utilities ➤ <u>M</u>anage Indexes. In the Manage Indexes dialog box, you can re-create any indexes you want in your production index.

 ▶▶ T I P

> **If re-creating your indexes is a major job, use the Command window (not the Navigator) to delete your old files one at a time. Don't delete the .MDX file. After you rename your TEMP files to the old name, your old .MDX file has the correct index expressions, but the wrong indexes. Use the <u>T</u>able ➤ <u>T</u>able Utilities ➤ <u>R</u>eindex option to fix the indexes.**

Does this seem like a lot of work? Well, again we remind you that you never need to do it, and that you should do it only in the rare instance of a static file. Even in that instance, you could just use an index and not bother physically sorting.

▶▶ *Fast Updates for Groups of Records*

Sometimes, updating a record is a simple matter of typing a new value over an old one. An acquaintance moves, so you enter a new address in your People table.

Other times, and they are numerous, you want to update a group of records. We just did this when we added ID fields to our People table. In this section, we'll look at some more ways to work with groups of records.

Before we do that, we'll need to have a fair-sized table to work with. For the moment, we'll assume that you have ten records in your People table. If you have a different number, adjust these instructions to fit.

▶▶**WARNING**

If you have a substantial number of live records, copy PEOPLE.* to a backup disk, so that you can restore your files later.

dBASE for Windows will be happy to supply you with data in bulk. This is very helpful for testing. Let's expand our People table to 1000 records. Here's how:

1. From the Navigator, select and launch your People table. (Double-click the table, or select the table and press F2.)

2. If you're not in the Browse Layout view already, select it. (Choose View ➤ Browse Layout, or click on the icon for that view in the speedbar.)

3. Choose Table ➤ Table Utilities ➤ Generate Records ....

4. In the Generate Records dialog box, enter 990 (or as many as you need to get to 1000).

Then click on OK or press Enter.

dBASE for Windows reports its progress in this operation with the color bar at the bottom of the screen in the center of the status bar. When it fills its rectangle, the operation is complete. Bear in mind that dBASE is not just adding records; it is updating its indexes as it goes. This product is fast!

▶▶ W A R N I N G

In version 5.0, there is a harmless but annoying bug. The record number column in the Browse Layout view is not wide enough for four or more digits if you start with fewer than 1000 records. dBASE itself can handle millions of records. This is just a display problem.

Now we have a moderate-size table to work with. Ours is shown in Figure 4.11. As you see, dBASE for Windows has supplied random numbers and text to fill your table. This is the data we will begin to manipulate.

FIGURE 4.11 ▶

dBASE's generated PEOPLE data

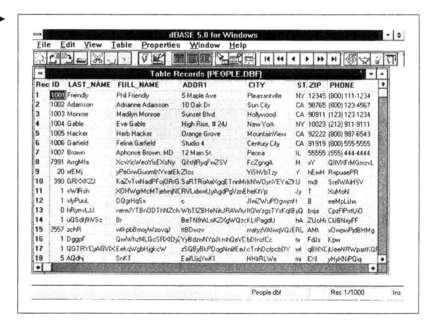

▶ *Locating and Updating Data Groups*

Before we do anything else, the fact that our ID fields are sporting nonunique values bothers us. We hope it bothers you, too. Let's fix that right away. We'll do this from the Command window, because it's the easiest way.

Reestablishing Unique ID Values

First, close any open windows accessing the People table. Then open the Command window. To do so, click on the icon showing Aladdin's lamp on the speedbar (shown in the margin), or choose <u>W</u>indow ➤ <u>2</u> from the menus.

In the Command window, we'll do three things:

- Open the People table and its production index.
- Set unique values in the PEOPLE_ID field and reindex on these values.
- Close our table and index.

Fortunately, none of these is difficult to do. These three commands will do the trick:

```
USE People
REPLACE ALL People_ID WITH RECNO()+1000
USE
```

The first command is USE People. When you USE a table, it's associated production index (if it has one) is automatically opened. As in the Table Records tool, Natural Order (no index) is chosen if there are multiple index tags. (The USE command also opens associated memo, .MDT, files.)

The second command is REPLACE. The ALL keyword specifies the scope, which in this case is every record. The People_ID specifies the field to be replaced. The WITH clause, including the expression, specifies the value to use as a replacement.

Any replacement that affects an indexed field automatically causes the index to be updated, so we don't need to worry about reindexing. This operation would be virtually instantaneous if it were not updating the index every time it replaces the PEOPLE_ID field.

The third command, USE with no table name, closes any open table and its associated files.

Figure 4.12 shows how we entered these commands.

FIGURE 4.12 ►

Reestablishing unique ID fields for the People table

As you can see, we type commands in all lowercase, because it's faster. If we are writing a program (or a book) we use uppercase and lower-case conventions to distinguish dBASE functions and keywords from other elements. dBASE doesn't care either way.

We feel better now that our ID fields are filled with unique values. So much better that we'll allow a little digression right here.

We just did that operation the slow way. If you want to change all, or substantially all, the values in an index, it's better to make the changes with the index turned off, and then reindex when you're finished. For 1000 records, it's faster to forget this and make the change the way shown here. For 100,000 records, do it this way:

```
USE People
SET INDEX TO
REPLACE ALL People_ID WITH RECNO()+1000
USE People EXCLUSIVE
REINDEX
USE
```

The first command, USE People, works as before. The next command, SET INDEX TO, is normally followed by the name of an index file. (You can use this command to have other .MDX files in addition to the production index.) Without a file specification, it turns the indexes off.

The REPLACE command is the same as before. Next, we USE People again, this time specifying EXCLUSIVE use. Then the REINDEX command does just what its name suggests. Finally, the plain USE command closes everything for us.

▶ *Finding Individual Records*

The first choice on the Table menu is for finding records. The Find Records option lets you locate an individual record. The Find tool is also used as part of a find and replace operation to specify a group of records. Let's begin by using Find Records ... to locate a particular record in our People table.

From the Navigator, launch the Table Records tool for your People table. For this example, we'll want the master index to be our UPPER (LAST_NAME) index. Choose Table ➤ Table Utilities ➤ Manage Indexes ....

In the Manage Indexes dialog box, select the LAST_NAME index, and then click on OK or press Enter.

 ▶▶**T I P**

Picking a master index is fastest from the keyboard: press Alt-T for Table, then T and M to get the Manage Indexes dialog box. Press End (assuming your LAST_NAME index is the last index in the list) and Enter. This requires just five keystrokes.

 Press Ctrl-PgUp (or choose Table ➤ Top Record, or click the beginning of file speedbar button) to get to the start of the list.

Now, let's find the first record for a person whose last name starts with the letter *M*. Follow the steps on the following page.

1. Open the Find Records dialog box. There are several ways to get to this dialog box: press Ctrl-F, click on the flashlight icon (shown in the margin) on the speedbar, choose Table ➤ Find Records ..., or right-click to get the Speed menu and choose Find Records ....

2. Type the letter **m** in the Find What entry field.

3. Highlight the LAST_NAME field in the Located in Field box by pressing Tab to reach the box and pressing ↓, or by clicking on that field.

4. Specify that you want the search to start from the top by clicking on the Top Record radio button, or by pressing Alt-T.

5. Begin the search by pressing Enter or by clicking on Find.

You'll now be positioned on the first record where the last name starts with *m* or *M*. If you look at the buttons in the Search Rules box, you'll see that the Standard search is selected. Figure 4.13 shows our search, after execution.

FIGURE 4.13 ▶

Finding the first last name starting with m

If you look in the Start Search From box now, you'll see that the Top Record radio button is no longer selected. Instead, Current Record is chosen. This is done so that if you click on Find again (or press Enter), you'll find the next record that begins with *m*.

Pressing Alt-O or Esc, or clicking on Close, removes the Find Records dialog box.

We recommend using the keyboard for fast searching. Here's a run-down, one keystroke at a time, of the search for the first *m*:

- Ctrl-F opens the Find Records dialog box.
- M places the search target in the Find What entry field.
- Tab switches to the Located in Field box.
- ↓ highlights the LAST_NAME field.
- Enter executes the search.
- Esc removes the Find Records dialog box.

Of course, if you wanted to search for *Masters*, you could type a few more letters into the Find What entry field.

The value you enter in the Find What entry field is the value that dBASE for Windows will look for in the table. It must match the type of field being searched. (Text goes in a Chartacter field, dates for a Date field, Numbers for a numeric field, and so on.)

You may use a dBASE expression in this field, too. Enclose the expression in parentheses, to tell dBASE that it should evaluate the expression before searching. For example, the DATE() built-in function returns today's date. If you wanted to find the first invoice from a week ago, you could type this into the Find What entry field:

```
(DATE()-7)
```

Subtracting 7 from a date backs up exactly one week.

Entering text in the Find What entry field actually is a form of an expression. You're really telling dBASE for Windows to search for a match on the left side of the search field and that the search is not case-sensitive (unless you select otherwise through the Search Rules choices).

In dBASE for Windows, literal strings are enclosed in quotation marks. This is another way you could provide an *m* string:

('m')

You can use either single or double quotation marks, but you must use them in pairs. This is certainly an inconvenient way to do what is simple, but the technique has a very practical use, as you'll see when we come to replace all records operations.

If you look at the buttons in the Search Rules panel, you'll see that you can override these defaults. The search could be for a value that exactly matches the length of your search string. Alternatively, dBASE could search for your string anywhere within the field. It could be a SOUND-EX search (where Smythe and Smith are a match), and it could be case-sensitive.

▶ Finding and Replacing in a Group of Records

The second place where you'll use the Find operation is from the Replace Records dialog box, which appears when you choose Table ▶ Replace Records ... (or press Ctrl-R). Figure 4.14 shows this dialog box.

As you can see, the Find What entry field, the Located in Field box, and the Search Rules choices are identical to those in the Find Records dialog box.

Replacing in Every Record

There is no direct way to specify that you don't want to find particular records; that you just want to do a replace operation in every record in your table. Fortunately, it's simple enough to trick dBASE for Windows into doing exactly what you want.

Recall that the default is to match the length of the string that you type in the Find What entry field. Now if you could type zero characters, then every field would match. If you experiment with typing in this box, you'll see that the very first letter you type enables the grayed Find and Replace All options. If you use the Backspace key to delete the first letter, those options are grayed again.

FIGURE 4.14 ▶

Finding and replacing through the Replace Records dialog box

Similarly, if you type any text, and then use the Del key to delete the last letter, those options are also returned to gray. dBASE for Windows knows that nothing is in the Find What entry field.

This is where we outsmart it. Type in this expression:

    ('')

That's two adjacent single quotation marks, with no space in between. Since the text is in parentheses, dBASE knows that it's an expression. The quotation marks tell dBASE that this is a character string. The fact that there is nothing between the opening and closing quotation marks tells dBASE that we have a zero-length string. If the Exact Length radio button isn't selected, every text field will match this string.

Now that we know how to do a "can't miss" match, let's go on to making some improvements in the test data that dBASE for Windows gave us. While you do this, you'll master this important tool.

A PROPER( ) LAST_NAME

Last names generally begin with a capital letter and are followed by lowercase letters. In dBASE, the PROPER( ) function capitalizes words exactly that way. Let's make all our LAST_NAMEs PROPER( ). Figure 4.15 shows the Replace Records dialog box we used to do this.

FIGURE 4.15 ▶

Making our last names propercase

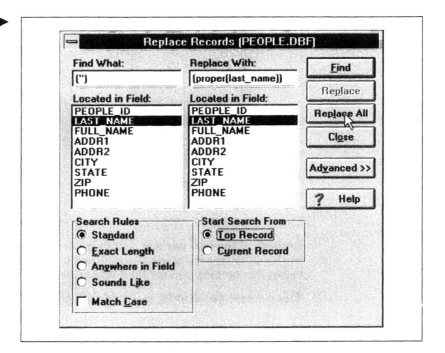

We're searching a text field (it doesn't need to be the LAST_NAME field; any text field will do) for a zero-length string, which will find every record.

Make sure that you put the PROPER( ) function in parentheses:

```
(PROPER(LAST_NAME))
```

This makes dBASE for Windows evaluate the expression. Without the parentheses, it will type the text itself as the replacements. In this case, every field would be replaced with the text *(PROPER(LAST_NAME))*.

When your Replace Records dialog box looks like the one in Figure 4.15, choose Replace All to make the changes.

Fixing the State Codes

We're about to go on to the advanced options for replace operations. Before we do, we'll need to group our data. The states provide a way to do this. First, make the replacement shown in Figure 4.16 to convert all the state codes to capital letters.

FIGURE 4.16 ▶

Capitalizing the two-letter state codes

If you look closely, you'll see that the radio button for Current Record is selected. When you choose Replace All, this setting is ignored.

Make this change, and your state codes will begin to look a little more like U.S. state codes (two-letter codes, always capitalized, identifying the 50 states and a handful of other American territories, such as the U.S. Virgin Islands). The remaining problem, which we'll take as an opportunity, is that dBASE used a mixture of one- and two-character strings. We'll convert all the one-letter strings to CA, to get a generous supply of people living in California.

For this change, the Command window will be handy. Close the Table Records tool and open the Command window. You'll see that the instructions you've been giving are echoed here as if you had typed in equivalent dBASE language commands. These are the commands to type to change the single-letter state codes to CA:

```
USE People
REPLACE ALL State WITH 'CA' FOR 1 = LEN(RTRIM(State))
USE
```

The LEN( ) function returns the length of a character string. The State field is two characters wide, whether it is filled in or not. The RTRIM( ) function trims blank spaces off the right side of a string. Here are some examples of commands given in the Command window and their results:

? state	Reports "X"
? LEN(state)	Reports 2
? RTRIM(state)	Reports "X"
? LEN(RTRIM(state))	Reports 1

If you used an address format appropriate to your country, pick one of your own fields and make a similar change.

Using the For Clause

Now we're ready to explore the advanced options of the Replace Records tool. To get to them, click on the Advanced >> pushbutton in the Replace Records dialog box. This pops out an additional portion of the dialog box. To make a change for all the records where the state is CA, use the For entry field, as shown in Figure 4.17.

The For entry field accepts a logical expression, which is one that evaluates to True or False. The expression

```
state = 'CA'
```

is one example.

Here we've replaced the zip codes with a distinctive value, so we can check the results. Be sure that you've selected the All radio button under Scope.

FIGURE 4.17 ▶

Replacing records with the For clause

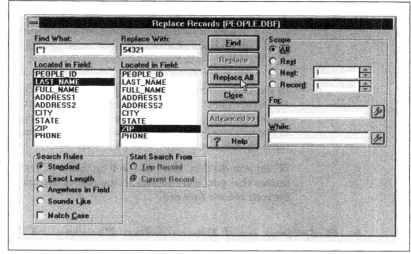

Using the While Clause

Try this change again, but use another replacement value and put the expression into the While entry field. Make sure that your currently selected record is one where the state is CA before you start.

This operation changes only a handful of states. As its name implies, a While selection does its replacements while the condition is true. As soon as it comes to a state that is not CA, it stops.

As you've noticed, running replacements such as these through a 1000-record table is quite quick. However, if you were working with a really large table, it could be important to take advantage of the While clause.

You could create an index on the STATE field and select that index as your master index. Then you could find the first record that has CA in the STATE field. Using

    State = 'CA'

for the While expression will process every record where the state is CA. It will stop on the first record where the state exceeds CA.

Using While expressions with an indexed (or sorted) database can save time if your tables are large.

In the U.S., about one in eight people lives in California. For a representative collection of Americans, indexing by state and replacing While the state is 'CA' will process about one-eighth of your records. Without an index, the For expression will evaluate every record in your table to check to see if the state is CA.

When you do this, click on the Rest radio button for Scope, so dBASE knows that you want to search the rest of the table, starting from the current record forward.

▶ Deleting and Recovering Groups of Records

When you delete a record in dBASE, the record is not physically removed from the file. Its Deleted flag is set and, if you have set Deleted on, your records are not shown in the Table Records tool or in forms.

To see how this works, follow these steps:

1. Launch the People table in the Table Records tool. Choose a Browse Layout view.
2. Choose Properties ➤ Desktop, Table tab. In the Other box, make sure that Deleted is checked.
3. Return to your Browse Layout view.
4. Select a record somewhere in the middle of the window and press Ctrl-U or choose Table ➤ Delete Selected Record. The deleted record disappears.
5. Return to the Properties ➤ Desktop, Table tab. Now remove the check from Deleted and close the dialog box by clicking on OK or pressing Enter.

When you return to your table, you'll see the deleted record. dBASE has added a Del column with a check box to your table to show the deletion status of your records, as you can see in Figure 4.18.

FIGURE 4.18 ▶

People table with Deleted turned off

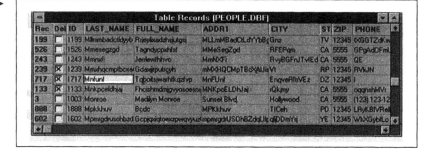

With Deleted turned off, all you need to do to delete a record is check the Del box. To see this, place some checks in the Del boxes, and then use Properties ➤ Desktop to check the Deleted feature. When you return to your Browse Layout view, the deleted records will be gone.

Return to Properties ➤ Desktop and remove the check from Deleted. When you return to your table, the deleted records will reappear.

For the rest of this section, leave the Del column visible so you can see your records' deleted status.

Deleting a Group of Records

Let's delete a handful of records with the Delete Records dialog box. Move to the middle of your People table and select a record somewhere near the middle of your Browse window. From the menus, select Table ➤ Table Utilities ➤ Delete Records ....

As shown in Figure 4.19, in the Delete Records dialog box, choose to delete the Next 4 records. Then choose OK. You'll see that the selected record and the following three are deleted.

Recovering the Deleted Records

Let's retrieve these records, along with any others you may have deleted. From the menus, choose Table ➤ Table Utilities ➤ Recall Records .... This dialog box, shown in Figure 4.20, is similar to the Delete Records dialog box.

FIGURE 4.19 ▶

Delete the selected record and three more

FIGURE 4.19 ▶

Delete the selected record and three more

FIGURE 4.20 ▶

Recalling all deleted records

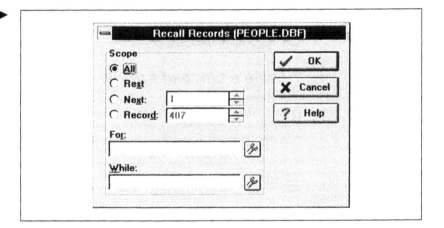

The default for recalling records is A̲ll. Accept the default by choosing OK, and all your deleted records are now returned to nondeleted status.

This is certainly useful for recovering from mistakes, but it can also be used in many other ways.

Using Deletions to Control a Mailing

Suppose you have a mailing which you want to send to all your customers in California. You have used Crystal Reports to prepare a mailing label program. Now it's time to run the labels. One way to make sure you generate just the labels you want is to delete all the customers who are not in California.

Figure 4.21 shows the expression in the For: entry field of the Delete Records dialog box that will delete those customers. The expression uses the dBASE operator <>, which represents "not equal to." Here we are deleting all the records where the STATE field's value is not equal to CA.

FIGURE 4.21 ▶

Temporarily eliminating non-California addresses

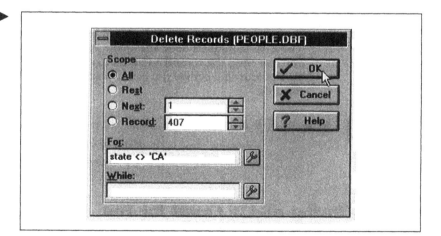

After you print your mailing labels, choose Table ➤ Table Utilities ➤ Recall Records ... and recall all your records.

Making Deletions Permanent

In some cases, you'll want to permanently delete unwanted records. The PACK command performs this function. You can enter the command in the Command window, or with the Table Records tool active, you can choose Table ➤ Table Utilities ➤ Pack Records.

▶▶ W A R N I N G

> **The <u>T</u>able ➤ <u>T</u>able Utilities ➤ <u>P</u>ack Records selection does not give you any warning prompt or other dialog box. It executes immediately.**

Experienced database users develop routine data-maintenance procedures. A common maintenance task is to back up tables first, and then pack them. Backing up your tables outside dBASE guarantees that all records, deleted or not, are backed up. This lets you recover from an eventual Pack mistake.

If you use the PACK command or <u>P</u>ack Records menu option, you'll see that this is a relatively slow, disk-intensive process. It requires physically rewriting the entire table.

You may want to delete every record in a table, to start a fresh table. The ZAP command does this operation in a single, highly efficient step. You can enter the command in the Command window, or with the Table Records tool active, you can choose <u>T</u>able ➤ <u>T</u>able Utilities ➤ <u>Z</u>ap Records.

▶▶ W A R N I N G

> **Zapping your table deletes every record, permanently. Before you use the ZAP command, back up your data!**

▶ *Having dBASE Count for You*

For this section, recall all your records that are marked for deletion (<u>T</u>able ➤ <u>T</u>able Utilities ➤ <u>R</u>ecall Records ...), go anywhere in the People table above the bottom of the table, and delete ten records. Use <u>T</u>able ➤ <u>T</u>able Utilities ➤ <u>D</u>elete Records ..., setting Ne<u>x</u>t: to 10.

We assume that you have 1000 records, of which 10 are now deleted. If you were at or near the bottom of your table when you deleted Ne<u>x</u>t: 10, there might not have been 10 records to delete. Take a good look to be sure.

How many records are in your table? There are two correct answers: there are 1000 records and there are 990 active (not deleted) records.

The answer dBASE gives you depends on the setting of the Deleted flag. Let's go for a count. Here we assume that your Deleted box in Properties ➤ Desktop, Table tab, is not checked, and that the Del column appears in your Browse Layout view.

Counting the Total Records in Table

Choose Table ➤ Table Utilities ➤ Count Records ... to get a count. To select the default All, just press Enter or click on OK. The Counted Records dialog box will report that you have 1000 records:

Counting Active Records

Now return to Properties ➤ Desktop, Table tab and check the Deleted box. Press Enter or click on OK. When you return to Table ➤ Table Utilities ➤ Count Records ..., the count of All records will report that there are 990 records.

TIP

Normal operations are done with the Deleted flag left on. You'll seldom find that counts which include deleted records are useful.

Counting Records that Match a Condition

How many people in this table are in California? Like the Delete Records and Recall Records dialog boxes, the Count Records dialog box provides For: and While: entry fields, which function the same way.

To count your records for people in California, enter this in the For: entry field:

    state = 'CA'

Be sure the scope is A̲ll, and click on OK to count those records.

Counting Contiguous Records

Similarly, the W̲hile: entry field will count only as long as the condition you enter there is True. If your LAST_NAME index is the master index, you can find the first person whose last name starts with *S*, for example. Then you can count W̲hile:

last_name = 'S'

This will tell you how many people you have whose last name starts with the letter *S*.

Counting a Condition in a Range

You can use For and While conditions together. As an example, repeat the previous count, adding this For condition:

state = 'CA'

You'll get a count of all the people whose last name starts with the letter *S* and who are in California. You can use the While condition to specify a range of records, and the For condition to select some of the records in the range.

▶ Letting dBASE Calculate for You

dBASE for Windows can perform any sort of calculations you may require. These half dozen common calculations are defined for you and can be done with only a few mouse clicks (or keypresses):

- Average
- Minimum
- Maximum
- Standard deviation
- Sum
- Variance

Other calculations require programming.

Calculations apply only to Numeric fields. Our People table's only Numeric field is its PEOPLE_ID field, for which these calculations are not meaningful. However, for now, the ID values will be adequate for demonstrating how the calculations are performed.

Let's start by finding the average of our ID values. Choose Table ➤ Table Utilities ➤ Calculate Records .... Figure 4.22 shows the Calculate Records dialog box set to calculate the average of all records in the PEOPLE_ID field.

FIGURE 4.22 ▶

Finding an average value

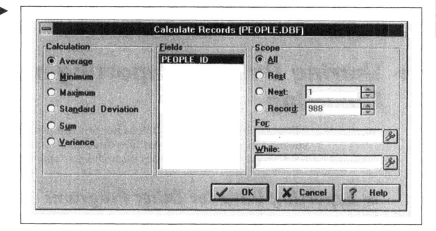

When you click on OK or press Enter, you'll get the Calculation Results dialog box:

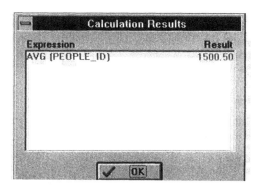

The process is lightning fast.

dBASE for Windows will perform the specified calculation for several fields at once. The Fields box in the Calculate Records dialog box lists all your numeric fields. You select the first field you want by clicking or by using the ↓ and ↑ keys. To select a range, hold down the Shift key and use ↓ or ↑, or click at the end of your range. The Calculations Results dialog box will show all the results at once. Go ahead and experiment with the other calculations.

The Scope box provides the same controls over the scope of the calculation that you can use to control the deletion of records. You can specify a particular number of records as well as For and While conditions.

▶▶ *Sharing Data by Importing and Exporting*

Many modern programs, such as major word processors and spreadsheets, can read .DBF format files directly. For other programs, dBASE for Windows provides capabilities to share its data.

▶ *Exporting Data for Other Programs*

Although many programs can directly read data in .DBF files, you'll find it handy to be able to export your data to other dBASE and Paradox tables, or in standard system formats for programs that don't read .DBF files.

To export data, choose Table ➤ Table Utilities ➤ Export Records .... Figure 4.23 show the Export Records dialog box. In this example, we've chosen the TEMP file, with the SDF (System Data Format) file type. All our fields are selected, and we are exporting the Next 10 records. This will create the file TEMP.TXT in our working directory.

Files and File Types

The file name's default extension is based on the File Type value, which can be one of the following:

- dBASE

FIGURE 4.23 ▶

Exporting ten records to TEMP in System Data Format

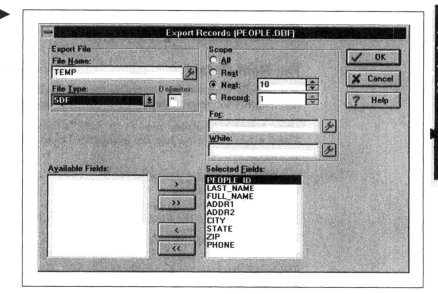

- Paradox
- SDF
- Delimited
- DBMEMO3

Specifying dBASE or DBMEMO3 exports to a .DBF file. The DBMEMO3 type provides compatibility with dBASE III Plus files. Paradox output is directed to a .DB file type. The other two options create .TXT files.

An SDF file is a text file with each field written according to its width. Text fields are left-aligned within their width; numbers are aligned on the right, based on their specified width and decimal places. No extra space is provided between fields.

Delimited data files use delimiters to separate fields in a manner that is compatible with old BASIC program's requirements. Numeric fields are written in whatever width is needed. Character data is enclosed in quotation marks. All fields are separated by commas. (Delimited data is seldom used today.)

The Field Picker

The default selection for exporting records is all fields. You can adjust this to suit your requirements with the field selection pushbuttons.

The >> and << buttons send every field in the direction indicated. The > and < buttons move just the highlighted field in the direction indicated.

In addition to letting you select fields, you can use these buttons to order your fields in whatever way you like. When you use the single-character buttons (> and <), the field that you're moving will be placed immediately below the field that is highlighted in the destination box.

To export a very simple phone list, for example, you could start by clicking on the << button to move all the fields from the Selected Fields box back to the Available Fields box. Then click on the FULL_NAME field to select it and click on the > button to send it to the Selected Fields box. Next, use the same technique to move the PHONE field.

If you wanted to add the CITY field next, you could highlight either of the two fields (FULL_NAME or PHONE) already in the Selected Fields box. Highlighting the first one before you move the CITY field will place the CITY field as the second one in the Selected Fields list. Highlight the last one to put the new field at the bottom of the Selected Fields list.

Setting the Export Scope

The Scope choices in the Export Records dialog box provides the same tools that we've been using throughout this chapter. You can pick All or a limited record range, such as Next: 10.

You can also use For and While clauses to select the records you want. As in the other dialog boxes, you can use these clauses together to select a portion of the records in a range.

▶ *Importing Data*

dBASE for Windows has a limited ability to import data through the Import choice on the File menu. However, it has an almost unlimited ability to import data through the Append Records from File choice on the Table Utilities menu. Any data that you can get in neat columns in a file (such as by printing to file from a word processor or spreadsheet program) can be directly read into a dBASE table.

To import data this way, choose Table ➤ Table Utilities ➤ Append Records from File .... The Append Records from File dialog box supports the same file types as the Export Records dialog box. DBMEMO3 is not listed in the File Type selection list, because dBASE for Windows can read dBASE III Plus files if you simply select dBASE as the file type.

In Figure 4.24, we're using this tool to import the records that we exported in Figure 4.23.

FIGURE 4.24 ▶

Importing System Data Format records

If you choose the Delimited file type, you can also select the delimiter character, which defaults to a double quotation mark.

The For entry field provides a limited means for selecting only a portion of the records in the import file.

►► *Summary*

We've covered a lot of ground in this chapter! We hope you've become comfortable with some of the capabilities dBASE for Windows offers for manipulating your data.

You started by adding a record ID field to your People table and using dBASE's update capabilities to fill in appropriate unique values. Before you dove into the rest of the chapter, you used the record-generation capability to expand your table to 1000 records.

You also used the Properties ► Table Records dialog box to customize your view of your table.

You used indexes to organize your data, and you learned the difference between an ASCII sort and a true alphabetic sort. You also learned how to use indexes instead of physically sorting your table.

You used the Find Records dialog box to quickly locate individual records. Then you used the Replace Records dialog box to do mass updates. You saw how the Find Records capabilities were built into the Replace Records dialog box.

You learned to delete records by groups, for a range of records, for a logical condition, and while a condition was True. You learned that these deletions are not permanent, and you saw that you could use group deletions to temporarily restrict the visible contents of your table. You learned to recall deleted records.

You used dBASE to count records, both all records and just non-deleted records. You used the For and While clauses of dBASE's scope to count records matching particular conditions. You used dBASE's built-in calculation capability to get quick answers to numerical questions.

Finally, you saw how dBASE could export data to other programs and import data from other programs.

As a closing exercise, go back and clean out your People table. First, go back to Natural Order for the index. Then select the first of your generated records. Use the Delete Records dialog box to delete from the selected record through the end of your table. Finally, pack the table (with the Table Records tool active, choose Table ➤ Table Utilities ➤ Pack Records), because you no longer need the test data dBASE generated for you.

Now that you've become adept at manipulating the data in a single table, in the next chapter, you'll use the Query tool to tie together data from multiple tables. This will lead you further into mastering dBASE for Windows.

▶ ▶ CHAPTER **5**

The Two-Way Query Designer

▶ ▶ **I***n* this chapter, we'll explore the Query Designer. The Query Designer is useful for querying tables, as its name suggests. Perhaps more important, the Query Designer is the tool you use to describe your database when you use .DBF or .DB form tables.

With the Query Designer, you tell dBASE for Windows which tables are involved in your database and how these tables are related. This information, called a *view* in earlier dBASE versions, is available to the Table Records tool, to your forms, and to Crystal Reports.

Borland calls the Query Designer a Two-Way-Tool. This means that you can work in a graphical design surface to specify your query. When you save your work, it is written as dBASE program code. If you return to the Query Designer (to add another table, for example), the design surface reads the program to reconstruct its state where you left off.

What this means is that, within limits, you can edit the program generated by the Query Designer, and your changes will be remembered the next time you return to the graphical design surface.

We assume that you have no experience with dBASE program code except, perhaps, for what you've seen pass by in the Command window. You'll find that by letting the Query Designer write your dBASE programs, you can make minor changes quite easily.

As we go through this chapter, we'll explain each dBASE for Windows command that we meet. Don't try to memorize them! Most dBASE commands are quite readable, and they're documented in Chapter 13. The commands that you start using are the ones you'll remember, and they're the only ones you need for now.

Understanding the programs written by the Query Designer won't make you an ace dBASE programmer, but it will extend your control over dBASE for Windows.

▶▶ *You Query a Single Table*

In this section, we'll use the Query Designer with just one table. This will let us do the following:

- Use a table.
- Use selected fields from a table.
- Use indexes to order our table.
- Use logical expressions to find selected records.
- Use calculated fields not actually in the table.

Let's get started with the simplest possible query.

▶ *You Begin at the Beginning*

Let's get started at the beginning. If you have queries from our work in Chapter 2, delete them. In the Navigator, highlight the query and press Del (or right-click and choose Delete from the Speed menu). dBASE for Windows will pop up its Delete File dialog box, asking if you really want to delete the .QBE file from your disk. Tell it Yes. Then dBASE for Windows will ask you if you want to delete the .QBO file. Go ahead and say Yes to that one, too.

With all program files (such as .PRG programs, .WFM Windows' form files, and .QBE query-by-example files), dBASE for Windows must first compile the program into an internal executable form. Whenever it does this, it writes a new file with the last letter of the file extension changed to an *O*. The *O* stands for Object form. Programmers speak of their programs as *source* code, and the 1s and 0s that the compiler writes (which actually drive the computer) is the *object* code. In our case, the .QBE files will be written by dBASE for Windows from our specifications, but they still qualify as source code.

You Build a Plain Query

Now let's build the simplest possible query, using our People data table. From the Navigator, launch the Query Designer for a new query. Select the Untitled query and press Enter, or press Shift-F2, or double-click the mouse. In the Open Table Required dialog box, shown in Figure 5.1, choose the People table.

FIGURE 5.1

Choosing a table for the Query Designer

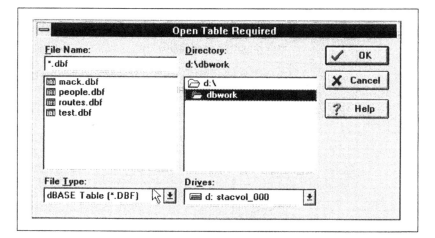

▶▶ **W A R N I N G**

There's a minor bug lurking here. If you press Esc or otherwise don't select a table, you'll still be in the Query Designer. If this happens, right-click and select Add Table ... from the Speed menu.

After you pick the table, you'll be in the Query Designer, shown in Figure 5.2.

Once you're in the Query Designer, press F2 or click the speedbar's lightning icon to run your query. (That's right, do absolutely nothing first—we said we wanted to start plain!)

FIGURE 5.2 ▶

The Query Designer left plain

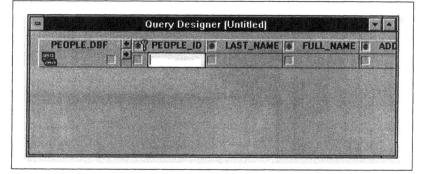

You'll be in a Browse Layout view similar to the first time you browsed your People table. If you're not in a Browse Layout view, choose Properties ➤ Desktop, Files tab. In the Edit Records box, select In Browse Layout. Press Enter or click on OK to commit this change.

After you've taken a look at your data, exit to the Navigator. Let's take a look at the program we just wrote (or, more exactly, that dBASE for Windows wrote for us).

▶▶**N O T E**

We named our query file People. We find it helpful to make the query and table names the same.

The Program Editor is the tool for working with program code. In the Navigator, select the People query and right-click for the Speed menu. Choose Edit as Program to open the file in the Program Editor.

If you are mouseless, open the Command window and enter this command:

MODIFY COMMAND People.qbe

You can set various properties for the Program Editor by choosing Properties ➤ Program Editor. (This choice is only available when the Program Editor is active.) Figure 5.3 shows the Program Editor Properties dialog box, with the PEOPLE.QBE file in the Program Editor in the background.

The Two-Way Query Designer

FIGURE 5.3 ▶

A typical Program Editor setup

Our PEOPLE.QBE file contains this program:

```
* dBASE Windows .QBE file 9
CLOSE DATABASES
SET EXACT ON
SELECT 1
USE PEOPLE.DBF
GO TOP
```

The first line is a comment. The asterisk (*) at the beginning of the line identifies it as a line of commentary, not program code, to both you and the dBASE for Windows system.

The line CLOSE DATABASES closes any databases that you may have open in the current session (you might have several tables open).

We'll learn more about the SET EXACT command when we get to using logical expressions to find selected records.

The SELECT 1 command picks the dBASE for Windows work area for the PEOPLE.DBF file. Available work areas are from 1 to 225.

Since each session has its own set of work areas, we doubt that you'll ever run out.

The USE PEOPLE.DBF command is the one that actually opens the People table. Finally, GO TOP positions the record pointer at the start record. This will be the record selected when your browse begins.

Now exit the Program Editor by pressing Ctrl-Q or by choosing File ➤ Abandon and Close. We'll use the Command window next.

The .QBE file sets the environment for the following command. To simulate the effect of running the query, type these commands in the Command window:

DO People.qbe

BROWSE

After you enter the BROWSE command, control passes to the Table Records tool. Click in the Command window and type the final line:

CLOSE DATABASES

Actually, you can use lowercase, and abbreviate the dBASE for Windows commands to four letters. Here's what that looks like:

Note that you can shorten dBASE commands to four characters, but you can't shorten dBASE function names. They must be spelled out.

Whatever way you type it, you're letting the query you just built set up your environment. Then the BROWSE command launches the Browse Layout view. Finally, you need to clean up after yourself. When you close a form, you end its session, so this cleanup is done for you. The

Command window is the exception; it is its own session, and it's up to you to do proper cleanup.

 ▶▶TIP

> You'll see lots of other commands in the Command window. As you work, each dBASE for Windows surface echoes the dBASE commands that it's executing to the Command window. If you watch this window, it will teach you a lot about dBASE commands.

▶ Selecting Fields for a Query

With that introduction, let's start building more complex queries. First, let's select some fields. Follow these steps:

1. Launch the People query in the Query Designer. If you're still in the Command window, try entering:

MODIFY QUERY People.qbe

2. Tab to the LAST_NAME field and press F5 to select it.

3. Tab to the CITY and PHONE fields and press F5 to select them.

4. Press F2 to run the query. You've now specified a query on just three of the fields, which fit nicely in your Browse Layout view. Figure 5.4 shows the view that this launched for us.

FIGURE 5.4

A restricted Browse Layout view created by a query

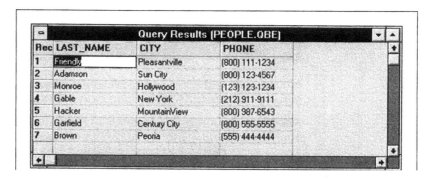

5. Press Ctrl-F4 to exit from the view. The Changes Made - Query Designer dialog box will ask you if you want to save your changes. Tell it Yes.

Now let's launch the Program Editor to examine the code that the Query Designer wrote for you.

6. Choose Edit as Program from the Speed menu in the Navigator, or enter **MODIFY COMMAND People.qbe** from the Command window.

Our program looks like this:

```
* dBASE Windows .QBE file 9
CLOSE DATABASES
SET EXACT ON
SELECT 1
USE PEOPLE.DBF
SET FIELDS TO LAST_NAME, CITY, PHONE
GO TOP
```

There's one new line, which contains the SET FIELDS command. This matches the fields you've selected.

7. While you're in the Program Editor, add the FULL_NAME field to that list of fields. Put the field where you want it to appear when you browse. Ours is shown here:

```
SET FIELDS TO LAST_NAME, full_name, CITY, PHONE
```

▶▶ **N O T E**

> **dBASE for Windows will put the commands in capital letters the next time you run the Query Designer. You don't need to worry about it.**

8. After making this change, press Ctrl-W to write the new version of the file to disk.

9. Reenter the Query Designer, and you'll see the check mark in the FULL_NAME field.

The Two-Way Query Designer

If you're not satisfied with the order of the fields in your query, you can edit the SET FIELDS command in the .QBE file with the Program Editor. Alternatively, you can grab the field with your mouse when you're in the Query Designer. As Figure 5.5 shows, holding the left button down lets you drag your fields into an order you prefer.

FIGURE 5.5 ▶

Dragging a field in the Query Designer

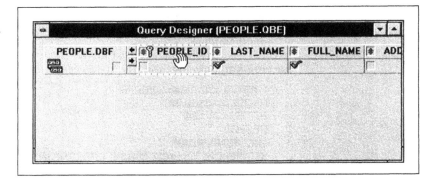

Now let's put an index into use.

▶ Managing Indexes from the Query Designer

It would be nice if our list of names was prepared in alphabetical order, wouldn't it? In the Query Designer, choose Query, and then select Manage Indexes.

In the Manage Indexes dialog box, select the LAST_NAME index and click on OK or press Enter. Then run the query (press F2 or click on the speedbar's lightning icon). Now you can see your table in alphabetical order. There's a problem here, though.

Exit from the Browse Layout view. Then double-click on the People query in the Navigator to return to browsing the query results. You've lost your index selection, as you see.

Selecting a Single Index Tag

What you really want is a permanent selection (or at least one that lasts until you change your mind). Click on the speedbar's design icon or press Shift-F2 to return to the Query Designer. Now press Tab to reach the right end of the table, or click and hold the right-pointing arrow near the file name until you get to the right end. You'll see an unexpected field there, as Figure 5.6 shows.

FIGURE 5.6

An extra field at the end of the table

The "field" is actually our index tag expression: UPPER (LAST_NAME). The key that appears in the upper-left corner of the field tells you that there is a tag for this expression in the production index. Next to the key is a box with a smudge mark.

The smudge mark appears when no index order is selected. (Actually, that smudge is a double-headed vertical arrow.) Here's what happens when we click and hold this box for the STATE field:

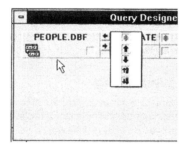

There are five choices here:

- No order (the smudge)
- Ascending, ASCII order (up arrow)
- Descending, ASCII order (down arrow)
- Ascending, alphabetically (double up arrows)
- Descending, alphabetically (double down arrows)

We want to choose the UPPER(LAST_NAME) index. Since this actually is a tag in our production index, when you click on the smudge in this field, there are only two choices: an arrow (the index order) and the smudge (no order). Clicking the box toggles between the smudge and the arrow. Pressing and holding lets you drag to your choice.

Choose the arrow to use the index tag. Now when you run your query (press F2 or click the lightning icon), your records are again in alphabetical order by last name. When you exit from the query, tell dBASE for Windows to save the new design.

If you return to the Program Editor, you'll see that this is what the Query Designer wrote:

```
* dBASE Windows .QBE file 9
CLOSE DATABASES
SET EXACT ON
SELECT 1
```

```
USE PEOPLE.DBF ORDER TAG LAST_NAME OF PEOPLE.MDX
SET FIELDS TO LAST_NAME, FULL_NAME, CITY, PHONE
GO TOP
```

The USE PEOPLE.DBF line has expanded with our new order specification. Actually, this is a more complex form than is needed. This would have been sufficient:

```
USE PEOPLE.DBF ORDER LAST_NAME
```

The OF PEOPLE.MDX clause can be dropped because the production index will be chosen by default. The word TAG only serves to remind us that LAST_NAME is a tag in the production index.

 ►►**N O T E**

> **You need a mouse (or other pointing device) to manipulate the order box (smudge or arrow) in the Query Designer. Without a mouse, you must use the Program Editor to add an ORDER clause to the USE command or to edit this clause to change the order.**

The Two-Way Query Designer

Selecting Multiple Index Tags

Sometimes, you may want a primary order and a suborder. For instance, you might want your People table sorted by state, and sorted by last name within each state.

The documentation suggests that you can select more than one index tag by clicking the appropriate order boxes. They are, it says, used in left-to-right order. Unfortunately, this simply isn't true. Fortunately, you can work around this limitation.

When you choose an index by clicking the order box, the Query Designer sets any other index that was specified back to the no index state. You can have only one index tag at a time active as the master index.

The ORDER clause of the USE command does not accept a list of tags. It takes exactly one tag and reports an error if you try to use more than one.

However, even though you can't use multiple tags, you can get exactly the effect you want by using multiple fields in a single index tag. In dBASE for Windows, the **+** operator concatenates (joins together) strings. (It does addition for numbers, too, of course.)

Test these commands in the Command window:

```
USE People
? LAST_NAME
? STATE
? STATE + LAST_NAME
SKIP
? STATE + LAST_NAME
CLOSE Data
```

The **?** command sends the result of an expression to the results pane of the Command window. (Think of the **?** as "What is …?") You can use it to test any expression, which is exactly what we're doing here.

The SKIP command here is also new. It moves the record pointer. A plain SKIP is equal to SKIP 1. You could SKIP 5 to go ahead 5 records, or SKIP –1 to back up a record, too.

If you examine enough records, you'll see that sorting on the STATE + LAST_NAME combination is the same as sorting on STATE, and then sorting on LAST_NAME within state. This is exactly what we wanted to achieve.

Let's create an index for this combination. To get to the Manage Indexes dialog box from the Query Designer, choose Query ➤ Manage Indexes. If you're running your query (not designing), choose Table ➤ Table Utilities ➤ Manage Indexes.

In the Manage Indexes dialog box, choose Create … to display the Create Index dialog box. You'll probably be presented with the Exclusive Access Required dialog box. This offers to open the table for exclusive access, which you need to adjust the production index, so accept the offer. Figure 5.7 shows the Create Index dialog box we used to add an index combining the STATE and LAST_NAME fields.

After you create that tag, leave it selected when you exit the Manage Indexes dialog box. For the query, check STATE, but deselect CITY. Figure 5.8 shows our Browse Layout view, with people sorted by last names within each state.

FIGURE 5.7 ▶

Making an index combining STATE and LAST_NAME fields

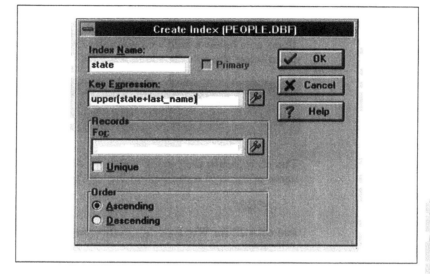

FIGURE 5.8 ▶

The People table sorted on two fields at once

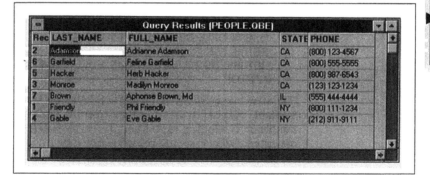

The Two-Way Query Designer

▶ *Selecting Relevant Records*

So far, we've worked with fields, selecting the ones we want and putting them in the order we want. Now we'll go on to selecting sets of records that match our specifications.

A Single Field Selection

The simplest record selection is done by placing a criterion in the condition area below a field's name in the Query Designer. Here's how you could select the records where the STATE field was equal to CA:

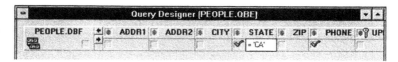

The entry below the record is actually a logical expression, where the name of the field is implied on the left. You enter

='CA'

and dBASE for Windows fills in the complete expression:

STATE = 'CA'

Here's the PEOPLE.QBE program that the Query Designer wrote:

```
* dBASE Windows .QBE file 9
CLOSE DATABASES
SET EXACT ON
SELECT 1
USE PEOPLE.DBF ORDER TAG STATE
SET FILTER TO STATE='CA'
SET FIELDS TO LAST_NAME, FULL_NAME, STATE, PHONE
GO TOP
```

The new line is SET FILTER TO STATE='CA'. A *filter* restricts the available records to the ones that meet the filter condition. The filter condition is a logical expression. If it evaluates to True, the record is accepted. Otherwise, the record is not shown.

> **NOTE**
>
> **Actually, we worked with our first filter in Chapter 4, when we discussed deleting records. The Deleted flag, when set, filters out deleted records. The SET FILTER command adds additional restrictions. Neither one actually deletes any records; they just restrict what you can see when they are in effect.**

Setting Conditions on Multiple Fields

You can use logical conditions on as many fields as you like. The records that appear in your Query Results window will be the ones that meet all the criteria you have established. In Figure 5.9, we show both the Query Designer and the Query Results windows.

The Two-Way Query Designer

FIGURE 5.9 ▶

A query with conditions on two fields

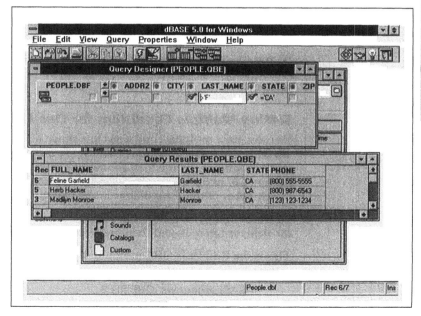

In the Query Designer, we've grabbed the LAST_NAME field and dragged it next to the STATE field, so that you can see both conditions at once. Here, we've selected the records where the state is equal to CA and the LAST_NAME is greater than F.

In an alphabetic sort, *Fa* sorts after (is greater than) *F*, so specifying >'F' includes all the last names beginning with *F* as well as the higher letters. This type of sort has some practical uses. For example, suppose that you're mailing your new price list to your customers. Yesterday afternoon you sent out the mailing for names that begin from *A* through *E*. Today you're finishing the rest.

This is the PEOPLE.QBE program that the Query Designer wrote with conditions on two fields:

```
* dBASE Windows .QBE file 9
CLOSE DATABASES
SET EXACT ON
SELECT 1
USE PEOPLE.DBF ORDER TAG STATE
SET FILTER TO (LAST_NAME>'F' .AND. STATE='CA')
SET FIELDS TO FULL_NAME, LAST_NAME, STATE, PHONE
GO TOP
```

As you can see, the conditions are ANDed together. Note the periods around the AND operator (and the OR operator discussed in the next section).

Setting Multiple Conditions for One Field

You can place multiple conditions in a single field. The records that are available in the Query Results window are the records that meet any of these conditions. Figure 5.10 shows the Query Designer with the conditions ='CA' and ='NY'in the STATE field. You can see the people that match either of these conditions in the Query Results window.

To place multiple conditions in a field, click on the condition area of the field, or tab to it, and then press the ↓ key.

This is the PEOPLE.QBE program that the Query Designer wrote with two conditions on one field:

```
* dBASE Windows .QBE file 9
CLOSE DATABASES
SET EXACT ON
```

FIGURE 5.10 ▶

A query with two conditions on one field

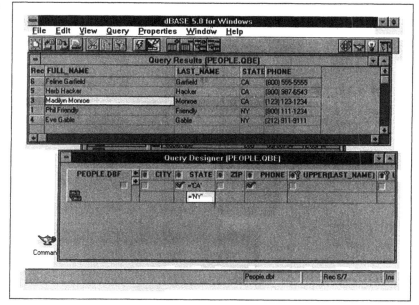

```
SELECT 1
USE PEOPLE.DBF ORDER TAG STATE
SET FILTER TO (STATE='NY' .OR. STATE='CA')
SET FIELDS TO FULL_NAME, LAST_NAME, STATE, PHONE
GO TOP
```

As you see, the conditions are ORed together.

Setting Multiple Conditions for Multiple Fields

You've seen that conditions placed in multiple fields are ANDed together and that multiple conditions in one field are ORed together. The records that pass must meet each condition when you have conditions in multiple fields. When you have multiple conditions for a single field, they pass if they meet any condition.

This was not, in fact, precisely stated. More correctly, the conditions in any row are ANDed together, and the conditions from each row are ORed together.

Figure 5.11 shows conditions accepting any record where the state is NY or the city is Hollywood. Because these conditions are on separate lines, records meeting either one are accepted. If they were on one line, no record would pass (Hollywood is not in New York).

FIGURE 5.11 ▶

Finding records in STATE = 'NY' or CITY = 'Hollywood'

 ▶▶**T I P**

If you look closely at Figure 5.11, you can see that we did not include the equal sign (=) in front of the value. If you don't include a relational operator, dBASE for Windows assumes that you mean "equal to." However, we think it's good practice to include the = to be explicit.

This is the PEOPLE.QBE program that the Query Designer wrote with two conditions on separate lines in their fields:

```
* dBASE Windows .QBE file 9
CLOSE DATABASES
SET EXACT ON
SELECT 1
USE PEOPLE.DBF ORDER TAG STATE
SET FILTER TO (STATE='NY' .OR. CITY='Hollywood')
SET FIELDS TO FULL_NAME, LAST_NAME, STATE, PHONE
GO TOP
```

As before, those conditions are ORed together. You can see how the Query Designer completes your logical expressions for you.

In this example, we specified > 'F' for LAST_NAME on the same line as we specified 'NY' in the STATE field. On a separate line, we specified 'Hollywood' for the CITY field. Here's the PEOPLE.QBE program that was generated:

```
* dBASE Windows .QBE file 9
CLOSE DATABASES
SET EXACT ON
SELECT 1
USE PEOPLE.DBF ORDER TAG STATE
SET FILTER TO (LAST_NAME>'F' .AND. STATE='NY' .OR.
CITY='Hollywood')
SET FIELDS TO FULL_NAME, LAST_NAME, STATE, PHONE
GO TOP
```

The AND operator has a higher precedence than the OR operator. This means that in an expression mixing ANDs and ORs, the AND operators will be applied first. Tied back to our .QBE specification, this means that all conditions on a single line will be evaluated first. If any single line evaluates to True, the record passes.

▶▶**WARNING**

The early documentation stated that AND and OR have equal precedence. This is incorrect. If they had equal precedence, these queries would not have worked whenever there were two or more conditions on any line after the first.

The following are some simple expressions and their results. In these examples, we use values instead of field names, so you can see exactly what this means:

T = .T.	True
F = .F.	False
? T .AND. F	False
? T .OR. F	True
? F .OR. F .AND. T	False
? F .OR. (F .AND. T)	False (same as above)
? (F .OR. T) .AND. T	True

An AND operation is True only if both its parts are True. The OR operation is True if either of its parts are True. The compound expression

    F .OR. F .AND. T

evaluates to False, because the AND operation is done first. If you did ORs first (or just go left to right), the answer would be the opposite.

►► T I P

> **When we write expressions that combine ANDs and ORs, we always use parentheses to group the evaluation precisely as we intend it: (A .AND. B) .OR. (C .AND. D), for example.**

Adding More Conditions

When you place a condition in a field, the field name is implied as the left-hand part of the logical expression. This limits the kinds of expressions you can build.

For unlimited possibilities, you can use the Query Designer's Conditions box. This is added or removed via the Query pull-down menu, which is available when the Query Designer is active. Choose Add Conditions from this menu:

```
Add Table...                        Ctrl+A
Remove Selected Table
Copy Results to New Table...

Manage Indexes...
Set Relation...
Modify Relation...
Remove Relation

Create Calculated Field
Delete Selected Calculated Field

Add Conditions
Remove Conditions
```

Like the conditions for individual fields, the Conditions box originally opens with space for a single line of conditions. You must specify full logical expressions in the Conditions box. For example, 'NY' or ='NY' is not acceptable, because the Conditions box has no idea what is to be equal to NY.

Full dBASE expressions must be used, such as these:

```
STATE = 'NY'
LAST_NAME > 'F'
```

Complex expressions, using AND and OR to connect conditions, may also be used:

```
LAST_NAME > 'F' .AND. LAST_NAME < 'K'
```

Figure 5.12 shows the Conditions box being used to search for records where the state equals NY or the city equals Hollywood.

As with the condition areas under your fields, you can add more conditions by pressing the ↓ key. You can also add multiple conditions on a single line, separating them with commas. These are interpreted the same way as the other field conditions: if they are on one line, all the conditions must be met; if they are on separate lines, records pass if they meet any one of the conditions.

FIGURE 5.12 ▶

Using the Query Designer's Condition box to search for STATE = 'NY' or CITY = 'Hollywood'

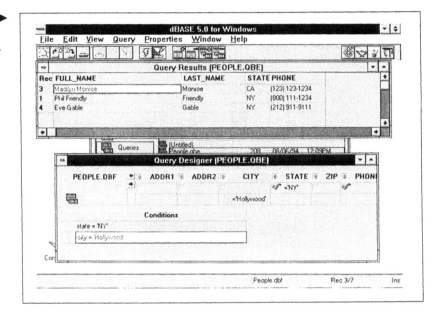

▶ Adding Calculated Fields

Along with the fields in your table, you can use additional fields calculated from the values in your records. Use Query ▶ Create Calculated Field.

When you select this menu choice, a Calculated box, with additional fields, appears. These function in the same way as your original fields in the Query Designer, except that you type in a name and an expression for each field. The width of each field in the Calculated box expands to accommodate the field's name or its expression (whichever is larger).

You can use any valid dBASE expressions, such as numeric and character expressions. In Figure 5.13, we've added three calculated fields and checked two of them for inclusion in the results table. We've used numeric expressions in this example.

Once you have added calculated fields, they function much like your other fields, except that they cannot be used as part of expressions in other calculated fields. Otherwise, you can work with them in the

FIGURE 5.13 ▶

Calculated fields added to the Query Results window

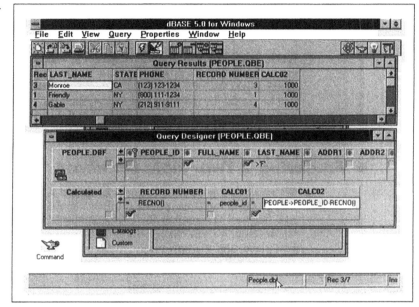

same way as you work with your other fields. Pressing Ctrl-F5 selects (or deselects) all the calculated fields, for example.

Now that you can use the Query Designer on one table, it's time to extend those techniques to building databases with multiple tables.

▶▶ *You Build a Database with Two Tables*

Beginning with dBASE III Plus, a new feature, called the *view*, came into play. This was a powerful concept that never got fully implemented. The basic concept was that a database is built from one or more tables. When there is more than one table, the database needs to know how the tables work together.

Views have now been replaced by queries. The Query Designer lets you describe a database to dBASE for Windows. We'll build a two-table database in this section.

As we work with this powerful capability, bear in mind that you can create as many queries as you like for a single combination of tables. One query might include all the available fields of the related tables, which will be useful for entering and editing data. Another query for the same table might use just the most important fields, which could easily fit into a single Browse Layout view for conveniently examining your data.

▶ Preparing a Two-Table Database

We've already got a People table. If we add a table for employers, we can go on to build the phone number capability that we discussed back in Chapter 1 (remember the BigCo example?). In the two-table system we develop, we can change the phone number for a company in just one place, and the new phone number will appear in the records of all the people in our list who work for that company.

Creating the Orgs Table

We like descriptive file names, but we'll make an exception here. We want a table of organizations, not just companies, since our acquaintances work for companies, schools, hospitals, government agencies, and so on. We don't like any eight-letter abbreviation for *organizations*, so we decided to just use Orgs for our table name.

Figure 5.14 shows the structure of our Orgs table. Build your own using the Table Structure tool (double-click on the Untitled table in the Navigator or select it and press Enter). As with the People table, you can adjust the address fields to suit your national or international needs.

After you set up your table structure, add a handful of organizations to it. Figure 5.15 shows our collection of organizations on a local Main Street.

The importance of the ID field cannot be overstated, as you will see when we relate the People table to the Orgs table. Make sure that you have your own BigCo company (one that several people work for) available for the work that follows. You can change the name to suit yourself, but we recommend that you stick with ID 1001.

FIGURE 5.14

*The structure of the
Orgs table*

FIGURE 5.15

*Some organizations in
Pleasantville*

Updating the People Table

Before we can begin doing two-table work, we'll need to have a linking field, called ORG_ID, in the People table. Figure 5.16 shows the added field, which serves as the foreign key, in the People table.

We make a habit of adding our foreign keys just after the primary key, as you see here. This lets us see our table's parents at a glance. Make sure that the ORG_ID field in the People table matches the one in the

FIGURE 5.16 ▶

*Adding a foreign key
(the ORG_ID field) to
PEOPLE.DBF*

Field	Name	Type	Width	Decimal	Index
1	PEOPLE_ID	Numeric	4	0	Ascend
2	ORG_ID	Numeric	4	0	Ascend
3	LAST_NAME	Character	16	0	None
4	FULL_NAME	Character	32	0	None
5	ADDR1	Character	32	0	None
6	ADDR2	Character	32	0	None
7	CITY	Character	16	0	None
8	STATE	Character	2	0	None
9	ZIP	Character	5	0	None
10	PHONE	Character	14	0	None

Orgs table. Both must be numeric and 4 characters with 0 decimals. You need an ascending index on every foreign key, too.

After you add the foreign key, you need to enter data to tie your people to your organizations. When you enter the Table Records tool for your People table, you won't see the new field you added. This is because we created a Browse Layout view that selects specific fields. Start by updating this layout to include the new field.

Figure 5.17 shows the Table Records Properties dialog box for adding the new foreign key field into our layout. To access this dialog box, choose Properties ➤ Table Records Window ... from the menus.

Remember that the fields you move from the Available Fields box are placed immediately under the highlighted field in the Selected Fields box. Before you select the ORG_ID field and click the > button, highlight the PEOPLE_ID field in the Selected Fields box so the new field will be inserted after it.

FIGURE 5.17

*Adding the new for-
eign key to our layout*

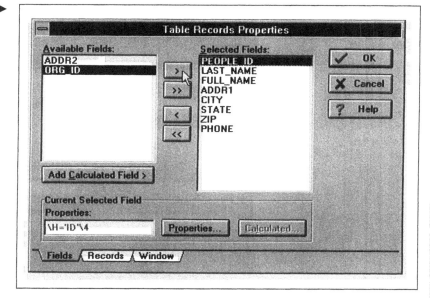

After you add the field, you need to set its properties. Choose the
ORG_ID field in the Selected Fields box and click on the Properties ...
buttton. Figure 5.18 shows the Field Properties dialog box for the field.
We've given it the heading ORG and set the width to 4.

With this setting, we're ready to add data. Figure 5.19 shows the data
we added. When you fill in these fields, make sure that the values here
match the ID values in the Orgs table.

Now we have a table of organizations and a table of people with data
specifying which organization each person works for. (If you look
closely, you'll noticed that our people live all around the country, but
they all work in Pleasantville—they're modern telecommuters.)

What we haven't done is tell dBASE for Windows that these two tables
together form a database. That's our next job.

The Two-Way
Query Designer

FIGURE 5.18 ►

Setting the properties for the new field

FIGURE 5.19 ►

Filling in the ORG_ID fields to specify employers

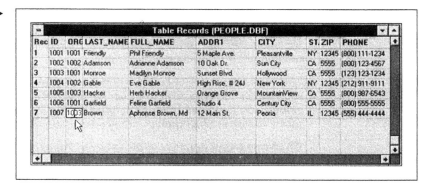

▶ Relating the Tables with a Query

Using the Query Designer to link two tables takes a great deal more explaining than actual work. In practice, you'll find that you can dispense with this chore in a small part of a minute, once you become proficient with multi-table work.

For the first one, however, we'll go very slowly and try not to skip anything.

A Simple Table-Relating Query

To begin, we'll create the simplest possible query that relates our two tables. Begin by launching the Query Designer to build a new query (double click Untitled or select it and press Enter). Now follow these steps:

1. In the Open Table Required dialog box, select the Orgs table.

2. With Orgs in your Query Designer, choose Query ➤ Add Table ... (or press Ctrl-A, or right-click and pick Add Table ... from the Speed menu). Figure 5.20 shows this step.

FIGURE 5.20 ▶

Adding a second table to a query

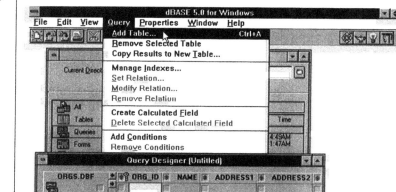

3. Choose the People table from the Open Table Required dialog box.

4. Put your mouse pointer over the relation Set Relation icon in the Orgs table. Press the left button down and drag to the Set Relation icon in the People table, like this:

When you drag this icon, you will see the Relation cursor (as shown above). Be sure to start at the Orgs table (our parent table) and drag to the People table (the People records will be *children* of the organization records).

5. In the Define Relation dialog box, which pops up in response to step 4, click on the ORG_ID field in the Child Table box. dBASE for Windows will automatically select the same named field in the Parent Table box, as shown in Figure 5.21. (If you start by selecting the field in the Parent Table box, you will also need to select it in the Child Table box.)

6. Click on OK or press Enter, and you'll return to the Query Designer, with your relationship in place. It will look like this:

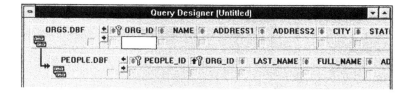

As you can see, the child table, PEOPLE.DBF, is offset to the right, and a double-headed arrow points from the Set Relation icon in the Orgs table

FIGURE 5.21

Selecting the foreign field in the child table

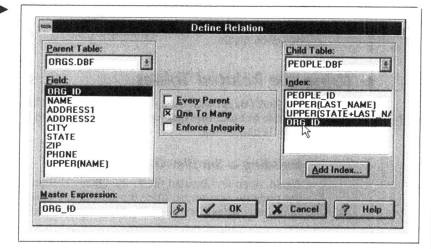

to the People table. This shows that you've properly established the one-to-many relationship.

We're now ready to run the query. But first, save your query. We call ours Orgs1. Before we start running it, take a moment to look at the ORGS1.QBE program that the Query Designer wrote:

```
* dBASE Windows .QBE file 9
CLOSE DATABASES
SET EXACT ON
SELECT 1
USE ORGS.DBF
SELECT 2
USE PEOPLE.DBF ORDER TAG ORG_ID OF PEOPLE.MDX
SELECT 1
SET RELATION TO ORG_ID INTO PEOPLE CONSTRAIN
SET SKIP TO PEOPLE
SET FILTER TO FOUND(2)
GO TOP
```

As you see, it opens the Orgs table in work area 1, with no index. It then opens the People table in work area 2, using the ORG_ID field index. Next, it switches back to work area 1 (the parent table) and sets the relation.

The Two-Way Query Designer

FOUND(2) specifies that the FOUND() function returns True in work area 2. Let's go on to use this query, which will show you what all this code means.

► Using the Related Tables

We won't begin with the query we just built. We'll take a little more trouble to build one that has less data, so we can clearly see exactly what is happening.

Building a Smaller Query

Again, open an Untitled file in the Query Designer. Repeat the steps in the previous section, so that your new query looks just like the old one. (This only takes a few seconds after you get used to the process.)

Now, what we want is a lot less. Check five fields. In the Orgs table, check the ORG_ID and NAME fields. In the People table, check the PEOPLE_ID, ORG_ID, and LAST_NAME fields, like this:

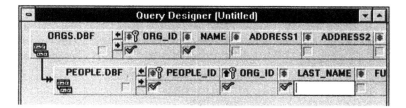

These are the ID fields that the computer will use for identification, and the name fields that we use for identification. Now run the query (click on the lightning icon on the speedbar, choose <u>V</u>iew ► Query <u>R</u>esults, or just press F2).

Our results are shown in Figure 5.22. As you can see, the people are now neatly organized by organization. You'll get from no relation to this point in about 30 seconds. Using the ID fields makes this very fast.

FIGURE 5.22 ▶

People related to employers

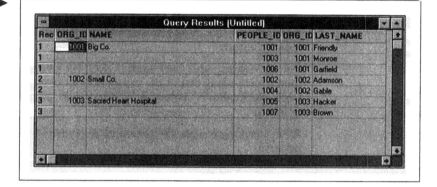

Using the Query

With this query view, you see data from both tables together. Normally, a restricted view such as this one won't be a good choice for data entry. You won't be able to enter data in any of the fields that you didn't include in the query, of course.

However, for our present purposes, let's go ahead and use it anyway. You can learn from it.

First, change your view to either the Form or Columnar Layout (click on the speedbar button, or choose View ➤ Columnar Layout or Form Layout). Go to the beginning of the file and then move down from one record to the next.

In every case, you'll see that each of your fields is filled in. As you go down the Query Results table, you are actually working your way down the child table (in this case, PEOPLE.DBF) of all the children of the first parent. When you finish with the children of the first parent record, dBASE for Windows goes to the parent table (in this case, ORGS.DBF) and advances to the next parent record. It then starts with the first child of the new parent.

If you return to the Browse Layout view, you'll see that the repeated occurrences of the parent data are not filled in (as in Figure 5.22). This is a visual convenience. As far as the database is concerned, the situation is the one you see in the Form or Columnar Layout: each child is matched to its parent's related data. With that in mind, let's edit our data.

The Two-Way Query Designer

First, try editing the ORG_ID field in the Orgs table (change 1001 to 999, for example). You'll see that this change destroys the relationship between the child records and the parent, but dBASE doesn't seem to mind.

Put the correct value back in the ORG_ID field for the parent, and then try changing one of the values in the ORG_ID field of the People table. Again, you're damaging a relationship, but dBASE doesn't seem to mind.

What's lacking is what the relational database scientists call referential integrity.

Enforcing Referential Integrity

Referential integrity means that every ID of an employer in the People table matches one and only one ID in the Orgs table. To achieve referential integrity, you must make sure that you use a proper value when you add the ORG_ID value to the People table, and you must be sure that you change it to another proper value when you edit it.

On the parent table side, you must be sure that each ORG_ID value is unique when you add a new record. You must never edit or delete the value in the parent table if there are child records that match that value.

Fortunately, dBASE for Windows has considerable intelligence. Let's ask it to help.

Switch from Run mode to Design mode (click on the design icon on the speedbar or press Shift-F2). From the Query Designer, we want to get back to the Define Relation dialog box. Select any field in the child table and choose Query ➤ Modify Relation .... (This choice is also available from the Query Designer's Speed menu.)

In the Define Relation dialog box, check the Enforce Integrity box, as shown in Figure 5.23.

With that box checked, click on OK or press Enter and then return to Run mode (click on the lightning icon on the speedbar or press F2). Now try those changes again.

The Two-Way
Query Designer

FIGURE 5.23 ▶

Asking dBASE for Windows to enforce referential integrity

When you try to change the parent key to a new value, dBASE for Windows warns you that records are still attached to that key, and asks you if it should cascade delete these records, with this Alert box:

When you get to the ORG_ID values in the People table records, you'll find that these values have become read-only—you can't change them.

Now try appending new records. If you are in a field from the parent table when you press Ctrl-A, you'll be adding new parent data, in this case, the ID and name. dBASE for Windows will insist that the ID be unique. When you're appending data to the parent, dBASE won't let you add child records.

If you have a child field active when you press Ctrl-A, you'll see the Append to Alias dialog box, shown in Figure 5.24. If you select ORGS here, it will be as if you had pressed Ctrl-A when you were in an Orgs

FIGURE 5.24 ▶

Selecting parent or child tables for appending

table field.

If you select PEOPLE, you'll be adding people automatically related to the currently selected parent record. dBASE for Windows will automatically fill in the ORG_ID value with the correct parent ORG_ID value. This field will still be read-only, so you won't be able to get it wrong.

Showing Every Parent

Select any organization and change its ID value. (In practice, you will *never* change this value.) When the Cascade Delete Alert box pops up, say Yes.

All the children of that record are deleted, and the parent also disappears. Why?

The default setting for the Every Parent question is unchecked. Unless this box is checked, only those parents that have attached children appear in the Query Results window.

To restore your childless parents (Orgs without associated People) return to the Define Relationship dialog box (press Shift-F2 for Design mode, then click on any field in the People table and choose Query ▶ Modify Relation ...). In the dialog box, check the Every Parent box. Select OK and return to Run mode. You'll see that all parents (Orgs) are shown, including the ones that have no related children.

▶ ▶ **T I P**

When we build a relation, we make a habit of checking all three center boxes in the Define Relation dialog box.

When you exit from the Query tools, dBASE for Windows will ask you if you want to save your query. Tell it Yes, and save the query as Orgs2.

This is the program that the Query Designer wrote for our ORGS2.QBE:

```
* dBASE Windows .QBE file 9
CLOSE DATABASES
SET EXACT ON
SELECT 1
USE ORGS.DBF
SELECT 2
USE PEOPLE.DBF ORDER TAG ORG_ID
SELECT 1
SET RELATION TO ORG_ID INTO PEOPLE CONSTRAIN INTEGRITY
SET SKIP TO PEOPLE
SET FIELDS TO ORG_ID, NAME
SELECT 2
SET FIELDS TO People_ID, ORG_ID, LAST_NAME
SELECT 1
GO TOP
```

CLOSE DATABASES closes any data tables or SQL databases (linked through the IDAPI Configuration Utility).

With EXACT off, character strings are considered equal in an expression if the one on the left matches the one on the right to the length of the one on the right. For example, *Mitchell* equals *M*, as do *Morris* and *Mary*. With EXACT ON, strings must match exactly, so *Mary* does not equal *M*.

The next four lines open Orgs and People in work areas 1 and 2. The master index on People is the ORG_ID value.

Returning to work area 1, the parent table's area, the relation is set. CONSTRAIN eliminates any child records whose foreign keys (ORG_ID in the People table) don't match primary keys in the parent table (ORG_ID in the Orgs table). The INTEGRITY clause is added when you check Enforce Integrity. We've seen it in action.

The Two-Way
Query Designer

SET SKIP TO PEOPLE controls the way the records are presented as you move through the table. It specifies that the each child record (in the People table) attached to a parent (in the Orgs table) will be shown before skipping to the next parent record.

Finally, the SET FIELDS commands specify the fields that we checked in the Query Designer.

▶▶ *You Edit the Program*

Normally, using the Query Designer has dBASE for Windows do the programming for us. We work with tools that make visual sense and let dBASE for Windows handle the rather exacting task of creating program statements.

However, the Query Designer is a Two-Way-Tool, so we can also edit the program. This provides a convenient way for us to overcome any limitations that we perceive in the design tool.

One limitation (we actually think it's a bug, but you could argue otherwise) is that the Query Designer always sets EXACT ON. Try this:

1. Launch the Query Designer for your Orgs2 query. (Select the Orgs2 query in the Navigator and right double-click, or press Shift-F2.)

2. In the conditions area of the LAST_NAME field of the People table, type **M**. If EXACT is OFF, this will select all last names starting with *M*. If EXACT is ON, as it always is through the Query Designer, this will only select a person whose last name is the single letter *M*.

3. Launch Run mode. (Press F2 or click the lightning icon in the speedbar.)

Unless one of your people has the a last name *M*, one-letter long, you'll see an Alert box telling you that no records were found. Before the next step, make sure that you use a letter, such as *M* that does, in fact, start at least one last name in your People table.

4. Exit from the Query Designer, saving your query in the ORGS2 file.

Since the Query Designer sets EXACT ON, we need to edit the query as a program and run it from the Command window.

5. In the Navigator, select the Orgs2 query and choose Edit as Program from the Speed menu (right-click on the file).

6. In the Program Editor, change the word ON to **OFF** in the SET EXACT command.

7. Run the .QBE program by pressing Ctrl-D in the Program Editor. This will run all the lines in your Program Editor, and turn control over to the Command window.

8. Give the BROWSE command in the Command window. Figure 5.25 shows our Program Editor and Command window after doing these steps.

FIGURE 5.25 ▶

Launching a query with EXACT OFF

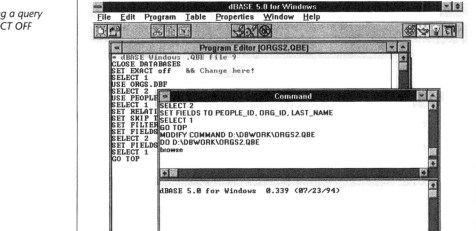

If you look closely in the Program Editor window, you'll see that we have added a comment, starting with two ampersands (&&), in the program. dBASE lets you add notes to yourself in a program. Just be sure to start the comment line with **.

This time, your Browse Layout view will show all the people whose last names start with *M*.

In general, we let the Query Designer handle the programming for us, but there are occasions when we find that we need to take over. As you see, it's not too complex to make your own changes to the code that the Query Designer wrote.

▶▶ *Summary*

In this chapter, you started by doing some cleanup work. You learned that program files, such as the .QBE files written by the Query Designer, are compiled into object files, which have the last letter of their extension replaced with *O*, such as .QBO.

Then you went into the Query Designer to create a simple query. Building from the simplest query, you used the field check marks to control the fields that appeared in your Query Results window.

Then you went on to indexes. You used simple indexes on a single field, and then used index expressions. You used the UPPER( ) function to change ASCII sorting into true alphabetic sorting.

You discovered that it wasn't possible to use more than a single field in an index. But we worked around that limitation by including multiple fields in an index expression.

You then went into selecting records matching your criteria. You used individual field conditions and then you ANDed conditions together across multiple fields. Next, you added multiple conditions on a single field, ORing them with other conditions.

Then you used combinations of AND (across the condition line horizontally) and OR (vertically) conditions for precise control. You also saw that there is a separate Conditions box with similar AND and OR capabilities for the ultimate in selection control.

You then went on to adding calculated fields. You built a separate file skeleton showing calculated fields, and you used it as if it were a normal table-based file skeleton.

After calculated fields, we moved on to relating two tables. You added an Orgs table, and a relating ID field in the People table. With the records related, you built a query that organized your People table by the employing organizations.

Then you created a small (showing only a few fields) query that you used to examine referential integrity. You saw that relational integrity is provided by dBASE for Windows when you check the Enforce Integrity box in the Define Relation dialog box.

Before you left the Define Relation dialog box, you learned to use the Every Parent property to include or exclude Orgs table records that did not have related People table records in your Query Results window.

Finally, you modified the program code to make a change that you could not otherwise get from the Query Designer. You used the Program Editor to edit the code, and launched your own BROWSE command from the Command window.

As you go on in your database work, you'll see that the ability to relate and control multiple tables through the Query Designer is a key to building powerful, flexible databases.

In the next chapter, you'll continue to use your queries when you build your own custom forms.

The Two-Way Query Designer

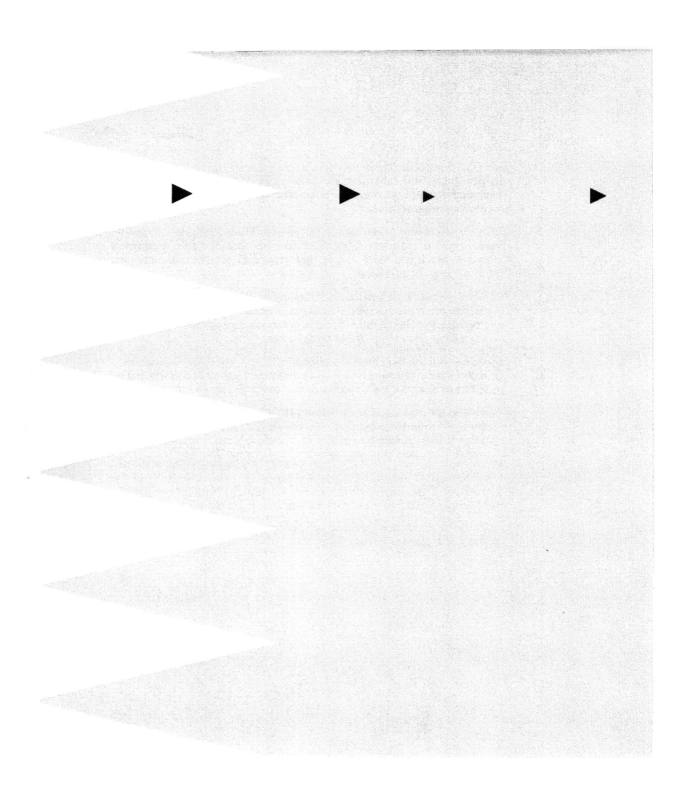

► ► CHAPTER **6**

Building Forms with the Two-Way Form Designer

►► *There's* a secret we want to let you in on, but we don't want it passed along: dBASE for Windows forms are fun. If building Windows forms is part of your job, you'll need to do your best to make it look like a serious, difficult business.

It will help if you talk about all the programming that you need to do in order to really build forms. Let's keep it just between ourselves that these "programs" generally run about one line long.

The Form Designer is a vast tool that addresses all the facets of Microsoft Windows user interface programming. To give it thorough coverage, we've used Part 5 of this book. In this chapter, we'll build MDI (Multiple Document Interface) and non-MDI forms to create a system for our phone lists.

You've already used the Form Expert to build an MDI Windows child form. We'll start by bypassing the Form Expert to create a modal window and then we'll go on to menu building and multi-table forms.

Before we continue, we'll warn you about one of the most annoying bugs in dBASE for Windows. We assume that it will be eradicated in one of the next releases, but it may still show up. You should be prepared for it.

When you build a form, the Form Designer is writing a program for you. When you run the form, dBASE compiles the form (in a .WFM file) into object code (in a .WFO file). It then runs the object code. The problem is that it does not *always* realize that it needs to replace its in-memory copy of the object code when it recompiles. It can go right on running an obsolete copy, even while you're making changes to the form.

The visible effect of this is that you will make changes and your changes won't show up when you run the form. When this happens, you need to exit dBASE for Windows and restart it. (This bug affects only the form design phase; it has no effect when you run the form.)

With that word of warning, let's get started.

▶▶ *You Build a Modal Form*

In Microsoft Windows programs, *modal forms* are those that must be processed by the user before going on to any other part of the system. For example, Alert boxes are modal forms. Frequently, the only processing required is a button click.

One common modal form is the About box, which can be selected from most Help menus. As a simple starter, let's build a modal About box for our phone system.

▶ Creating the Form

To begin, from the Navigator select the Untitled form and launch the Form Designer (press Shift-F2 or double-click the icon). When the Form Expert asks its first question, tell it you want a Blank Form, as you see in Figure 6.1.

This will launch the Form Designer with a blank form. Before we proceed, let's spend a couple minutes organizing the Form Designer so we can work efficiently.

Laying Out the Form Designer Desktop

After many hours in the Form Designer, we've arrived at a layout that is very productive. First select all three of the auxiliary surfaces:

- The Controls palette
- The Object Properties Inspector

Building Forms

FIGURE 6.1 ▶

Using a blank (not Expert-generated) form

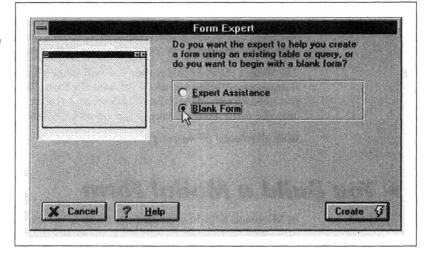

• The Procedure Editor

These tools are available through the View menu pull-down menu or the Speed menu. Figure 6.2 shows them selected through the View menu.

Note the position of the Procedure Editor in Figure 6.2. We'll leave it here, but you won't be able to see its window clearly in the next figures.

The challenge in laying out your Form Designer desktop is to give yourself convenient access to all the tools, all the time. We've solved that problem with the setup shown in Figure 6.3:

• The Controls palette is full height, on the left.

• The Object Properties Inspector is full height, on the right.

• The Procedure Editor is full width, at the bottom.

• The form we're working on is centered, but not so low that it covers the tabs of the Controls palette or the Object Properties Inspector.

FIGURE 6.2 ▶

Turning on the Form Designer tools

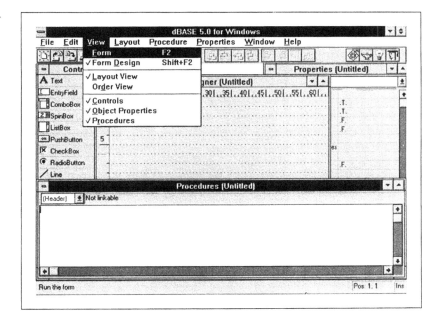

The key points to observe here are that the tabs of the Controls palette and the tabs of the Object Properties Inspector are available with just a click. If you lay out your window this way, the Procedure Editor is also available by clicking in the bottom center, between the Controls palette and the Properties window.

You'll see that the forms we design aren't full height, because that would make working with the three tools extremely difficult.

 ▶▶**T I P**

> **We don't consider the keyboard a viable option for Form Designer work. If you're on a plane without your trackball, use the Form Expert to create its default forms, and then enjoy the in-flight movie.**

Building Forms

Ch 6

FIGURE 6.3 ▶

An efficient Form
Designer layout

Now that we have a plain form and a good working setup, let's build an About form.

Adding Text Objects

First, let's add the form's title. These are the steps:

1. Click on the Standard tab of the Controls palette, to access this tool.

2. Click on the Text object, like this:

3. Press the left button and drag a large Text object on your form. At this point, don't be too fussy about this object's size or placement.

After you drag the Text object, the form becomes the active window. The text you just placed is selected, with resize handles at each of the sides and corners.

4. Use the object's handles, or drag, to make your Text object look like the one you see in Figure 6.4.

FIGURE 6.4

A large Text object for the form's title

Now you have a large Text object with a tiny *text1* up in the corner. That's not what we want to say, and it's not how we want to say it. To fix those problems, we'll work with the Object Properties Inspector.

5. Click on the Properties tab of the Object Properties Inspector.

 ▶▶ N O T E

Objects have data properties, event properties, and method properties. The Properties tab of the Object Properties Inspector refers to just the data properties.

6. Click on the Text property to select it:

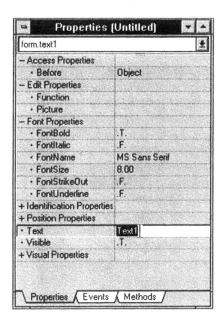

7. Press Backspace to clear the field, and then type **Phone List** (or whatever title you like).

8. If the Position Properties list is not expanded (it shows a + sign), double-click on it to expand it. (It shows a – sign when it's expanded; another double-click reduces it.)

Building Forms

Ch. 6

9. Click on the down arrow next to the Alignment property. Then select 4 - Center from the pop-up menu:

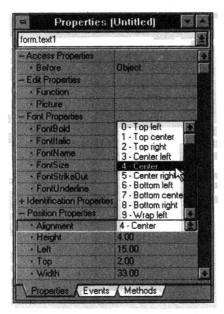

10. If the Font Properties are not expanded, double-click to expand them.

11. Use the spinbutton next to the FontSize property to select a large font.

As you click on higher sizes, you'll see the text (or at least most of the text) grow in your form. You'll also see that some sizes are very readable, and some are not. Multiples of 4 seem to work best.

We now have a big, centered title, as you can see in Figure 6.5.

With that done, add another Text object underneath with your copyright notice. (If you're working for your employer, add your employer's copyright notice, but be sure to sneak in credit for yourself, somewhere.) Figure 6.6 shows our form with the copyright notice added.

FIGURE 6.5

A suitable title on our About form

FIGURE 6.6

A second font for the copyright line adds visual interest.

Building Forms

Ch. 6

> **The copyright line is a good place to be creative with your choice of fonts. We used Times New Roman—an exception to our rule about not choosing serifs for on-screen fonts.**

Making the Form Modal

Now we're ready to turn this form into a modal form. If you haven't done so yet, run the form. Before it runs, you will get the Save Form dialog box. We called our form About. The Save Form dialog box will supply the file extension .WFM.

Note that you can resize the form, minimize or maximize it, and so on. But this is not what we want. We want a form that provides its information and exits when the user tells it to.

Return to the Form Designer (press Shift-F2 or click on the design icon on the speedbar) to change this.

To make the form modal, we need to change the MDI property from True to False. MDI is one of the Window Properties (on the Properties tab), which you will need to expand before you can access the MDI property.

To change MDI to False, click on the MDI property, click on the drop-down arrow, and then click on .F. in the list. Run the form again. It looks the same, but it's very different. Start by minimizing the form.

If your dBASE for Windows is maximized (full screen), your form disappears. It's not a child form anymore. To return to it, press and hold down the Alt key while you press Tab to cycle through all your active Windows applications. You will come to your About form.

When you come to the form, release the Alt key, and your form is selected again. Double-click on the System button or press Alt-F4 to close the form.

►►NOTE

The Alt-F4 combination is for closing non-MDI forms. Ctrl-F4 works for MDI forms.

Our form is still sizable, and can be minimized and maximized, which is what we want.

Return to the Form Designer and set these additional Window properties to False (click on .F):

- Maximize
- Minimize
- Sizeable

Now when you run the form, it's a modal, information-type form.

►►WARNING

A bug in an early version of dBASE for Windows may or may not still be in your version. The Form Designer did not read the settings of Maximize, Minimize, and Sizeable. We needed to reset these to False each time the Form Designer took over in Design mode. If you save the form first, however, you'll avoid this bug.

The EscExit property should get a bit of your thought. If you are used to pressing Esc to exit a form, this is the default behavior of dBASE for Windows forms. Pressing Esc to exit is *not* part of the CUA (Common User Access) specification, however. If you want to follow the CUA conventions, set the EscExit property to False.

Now let's attach an OK pushbutton to our form, so that we can click this familiar button.

Building Forms

►►
Ch.
6

▶ Attaching a Pushbutton

The dBASE Custom Control named OKBUTTON (on the Custom tab of the Controls palette) is precisely what we want. It says OK and it has the distinctive Borland check mark. You could just grab the prebuilt one and use it. However, you'll learn more if you do it yourself. It's not difficult.

Adding a Pushbutton

Start by clicking on the Standard tab of the Controls palette. Then choose the Pushbutton object. On your form, drag a button about 2 lines high and 15 characters wide. Note the shadowed area on the form's rulers (along the top and side of the window). If you adjust your form to a precise width, you can use the rulers for centering objects.

Our button is shown in place in Figure 6.7. Notice that we used the rulers to set the form to 65 characters wide, which makes it easy to position a 15-character pushbutton.

FIGURE 6.7 ▶

A pushbutton centered on our form

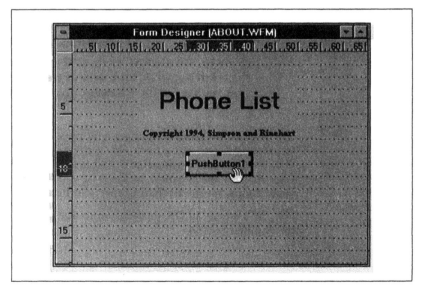

Setting the Text Property

Once again, the Form Designer has chosen the object's class name and added a digit to create a default name (Pushbutton1). As with Text objects, our first order of business is to change the default object to something reasonable.

Click on the Properties tab of the Object Properties Inspector, and then choose the Text property. Replace the text with **OK**. Unlike the Text property of a Text object, there is no Alignment property to set; the pushbutton's alignment works just fine.

Making the Button Work

When you test this form, you'll see that the button is a fine addition, except for one thing: it doesn't do anything.

 ▶▶ **W A R N I N G**

> **Be sure that you close non-MDI windows and return to the Form Designer from the Navigator. If you simply click on the design icon or press Shift-F2, your form will still be in Windows' list of active applications.**

To make a working button, we need to use the Procedure Editor to build an event-handling program that calls the form's Close method. All of this is easier to do than it is to say, fortunately.

So far, we've worked with the Object Properties Inspector's Properties tab. For this task, we'll use the other tabs.

First, select the About form. (Click anywhere in the form outside the objects on the form.) Then click on the Methods tab of the Object Properties Inspector to see these properties:

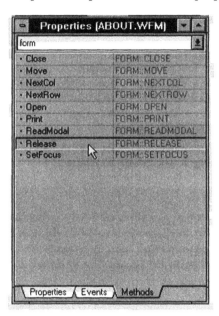

An object's methods are things that it knows how to do. As you can see in the Methods list, a form knows how to open and close itself, how to move and print, and so on.

Let's look at the Event properties of a Pushbutton object. To do this, click the pushbutton, then the Events tab of the Object Properties Inspector.

You'll see the list of events which a pushbutton can respond to. For now, we'll be attaching an event handler to the OnClick event. Click on this event, and then click on the tool icon to the right of the OnClick entry field:

The tool that pops up now is the Procedure Editor. This is another text editor, like the Program Editor, but with a special knowledge of where you called it and how it should organize the programs you enter.

Figure 6.8 shows the Procedure Editor after we entered this program line:

    Form.Close()

FIGURE 6.8 ▶

Calling the Close method from the OnClick event

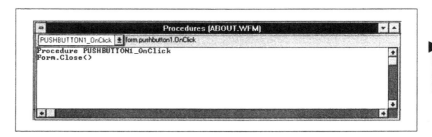

Building Forms

This specifies that we want to invoke the Close method of the Form object.

Enter that line into your own Procedure Editor and then switch to Run mode. This time, when you click on the OK button, your form is closed.

Obviously, this capability would let you write a long, complex program to handle any of the events to which your pushbutton can respond. If you want it to do something special in response to a right double-click, for instance, select the OnRightDblClick event and click on the tool icon. The Procedure Editor will appear and let you enter whatever commands you like.

However, the event handler we just entered is very typical. A simple line of code is often all that is required.

Adding an Icon to the Pushbutton

So far, our form is functional but a bit utilitarian. Let's make a couple improvements.

The Borland buttons all have those decorative images that reinforce the meaning of each button. Let's add one to our pushbutton. Follow these steps:

1. Select (single-click) the pushbutton on the form.
2. Click on the Properties tab of the Object Properties Inspector.
3. Double-click on Bitmap Properties if these properties are not already expanded.

4. Click on the UpBitmap property, and then click on the tool icon (shown in the margin) on its right.

These steps open the Choose Bitmap dialog box you see in Figure 6.9. The Location drop-down list lets you choose between Resource and Filename options. The standard Borland bitmaps are all Resource choices. You can choose the Filename option to use a custom bitmap that you have in a .BMP file.

5. With Resource selected for Location, click on the tool icon at the right of the Bitmap entry field. You'll see the dBASE for Windows Bitmaps dialog box, shown in Figure 6.10.

FIGURE 6.9

Choosing a bitmap for a pushbutton

FIGURE 6.10

The dBASE for Windows Bitmaps dialog box

Of the large collection of available icons, it turns out that the first one is exactly the one we want. Before continuing, you'll probably want to look through the icon collection to see what's available. As you scroll through the icon numbers on the left, the icon is displayed on your right.

6. When you're finished taking a look at the icons, return to ID: 20, the small check mark, and press Enter or click on OK. You will be returned to the Choose Bitmap dialog box, showing #20 in the Bitmap entry field.

7. Again, click on OK or press Enter, and you'll return to the Object Properties Inspector.

Building Forms

RESOURCE #20 now appears in the UpBitmap property's entry field. But you probably overlooked that detail, since your eye is drawn immediately to the check mark on your bitmap! We think these little bits of color add a lot to a form.

 ▶▶ T I P

If you keep your forms mostly monochrome, the colors stand out.

As you've seen, UpBitmap is only one of the possible bitmaps. You could also have selected a bitmap to show when the button was disabled, pushed down, and selected (received focus). In many cases, just assigning an UpBitmap property is adequate.

Customizing the Form's Title

Our form is looking better now, isn't it? Its title in the title bar just says OK, however. We really want that to be something a bit more descriptive.

Again, select the form (click anywhere outside the on-form objects) and click on the Properties tab of the Object Properties Inspector. Click on the Text property. A Form object's Text property refers to the text in the window title bar.

Enter **About My Phone List** (or whatever text you would like to see as the form window's title), and then run your form again. It's looking good, isn't it?

▶ Adding a Memory Report

If you choose Help ➤ About dBASE 5.0 for Windows ..., you'll see the great splash screen with dBASE's transparent globe. To make one of those for your own About message requires a good paint program and considerable skill as an artist. We don't recommend adding those big bitmaps, because they are real resource hogs.

What we do like is the report at the bottom of the About box that shows how much memory is available. Let's add that to our own About form.

Adding More Text Objects

We'll need two Text objects: one to say *Memory:* and the other to actually report the available memory. (Actually, you could do it with just one object, but it wouldn't be as direct a solution.)

With your About form launched in the Form Designer, grab the Text object from the Controls palette and drag a Text object on your form, beneath the pushbutton. Repeat this procedure to place a second Text object. Figure 6.11 shows the two Text objects we added to our form, both selected.

FIGURE 6.11 ▶

Two Text objects just added to our About form

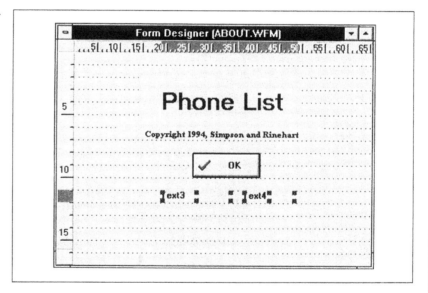

To select multiple objects on your form, click on the first one, then hold a Shift (or Ctrl) key down while you click on the other objects. This is useful, for example, for moving a group of objects. With multiple objects selected, dragging with the left button moves all the selected objects together.

Adjusting the Text Objects

For both Text objects, change the Alignment property to 3, Center left. Do each object separately. Remember, the Alignment property is listed under Position Properties.

Change the first object's Text property to read **Memory:**. Then shrink the Text object so that it is just slightly larger than the text. Position the two Text objects so that they are close enough to make a pleasing display.

For the second Text object's Text property, enter **123456**. You'll see why when we start working with the Picture and Function properties to display the actual memory report.

Using the MEMORY( ) Function

dBASE has a built-in function, MEMORY( ), that returns the available memory in kilobytes. In the Command window, ask

```
? MEMORY( )
```

The MEMORY( ) function gives us the information we want. (Remember, the ? command asks "What is?") You'll see the number of kilobytes available reported in the results pane of your Command window.

But there's a problem with using this function: the value reported by MEMORY( ) is a number, and the Text property of a Text object is a text string. How do we get this information into our second Text object?

Enter these lines in the Command window to see how they work:

```
x = MEMORY( )
? x
? TYPE('x')
? STR(x,6)
? TYPE('str(x,6)')
```

Our results for these commands are shown in Figure 6.12.

In this example, x is a variable that holds the number of kilobytes of available memory, as reported by the MEMORY( ) function. The

FIGURE 6.12

*Assigning MEMORY( )
when the form is
opened*

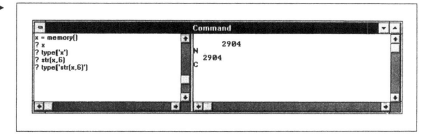

TYPE( ) function reports a variable's type. (See Chapter 12 for a discussion of TYPE( ) and other functions.)

Among other values, TYPE( ) reports 'N' for a numeric value and 'C' for a character string. As you see in Figure 6.12, *x* is a number. The STR( ) function converts a number to a string. In addition to giving the function the number variable that you want to convert, you can give it a second argument that specifies the number of places to include. In our example, the function STR(*x*,6) specifies six places for the result. The actual *x* value converts to a four-place number.

By default, the Command window's results pane will format a number to ten places. This is why the responses to ? *x* and to ? STR(*x*,6) are positioned differently, even through the resulting value is the same.

Now you know how to use the STR( ) function to convert a number to a character string, whose width you control. Next, we need to figure out how to get this string assigned to the Text property at the right time. This isn't something you can precalculate. Your system must query the MEMORY( ) function immediately before displaying the About form. The proper timing will depend on how many other things you have going on.

Using the OnOpen Event Handler

One of the events that almost every object can respond to is the OnOpen event. The code in an OnOpen event handler is called when the form to which the object is attached is opened. So all we need to do is to assign our Text object's Text property when the About form is opened.

Again, all of this is a lot more trouble to explain than it is to program. As you've probably guessed, to assign this at the right time, select your

Building Forms
Ch. 6

second Text object, then click on the Events tab of the Object Properties Inspector. Choose the OnOpen event and click on the tool icon at the right of its entry field.

This launches the Procedure Editor, which has the built-in intelligence to properly attach the program you write to the correct event. a simple, one-line program:

This.Text = STR(MEMORY( ),6)

Figure 6.13 shows the program in the Procedures window.

FIGURE 6.13 ▶

Numbers and character strings in the Command window

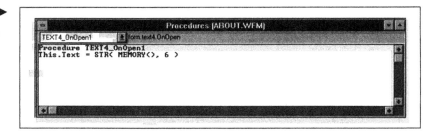

The *This* object in that line refers to the object handling the event. Because we selected the Text object in which we wanted the text, *This* is that Text object. The period (.) operator separates an object from one of its properties. This.Text is the Text property. We assign it the STR( ) function (for character string conversion) of the number that MEMORY( ) reports.

Select your constants, such as using six places for the result of MEMORY( ), very carefully. You want to allow enough room for growth so that you won't run into your own limits during the life of your system.

Using a six-character string will suffice until our desktop computer's memory exceeds a million kilobytes (just under a gigabyte). Our desktop PC's memory is expanding tenfold every seven years or so; six places should carry us at least through the end of the century.

When you run this version, you'll see that your form now reports available memory, in kilobytes.

Formatting the Memory Report

Now we're going to format our memory report with a comma to separate the number into groups of three digits. This is a nice touch with smaller numbers; it becomes increasingly vital as you look at longer numbers. If your national convention isn't a comma, use your own separator.

 ▶▶ **WARNING**

> **In an early version of the Form Designer, there is a bug in the handling of the Function and Picture properties. Because of this bug, the Two-Way feature doesn't quite work. These changes in the program code would get lost if you returned to Design mode.**

We can make this change by using the Program Editor to edit the form as a program. The objects we attached to our program are written into our program file (.WFM for forms) in the order we introduced them as we built our form. This means that our second Text object is the last one in the code, which is very convenient for editing it in the Program Editor.

From the Navigator, right-click on your About form and choose Edit as Program from the Speed menu. Press Ctrl-PgDn to get to the end, and then go up a bit. You'll see the code shown in Figure 6.14.

In a dBASE program, the semicolon at the end of a line means that the line continues. For example, this line:

```
DEFINE Text Text1 PROPERTY Top 1, Left 2, ...
```

is the same as these lines:

```
DEFINE Text Text1;
  PROPERTY;
    Top 1,;
    Left 2,;
    ...
```

FIGURE 6.14 ▶

The bottom part of ABOUT.WFM in the Program Editor

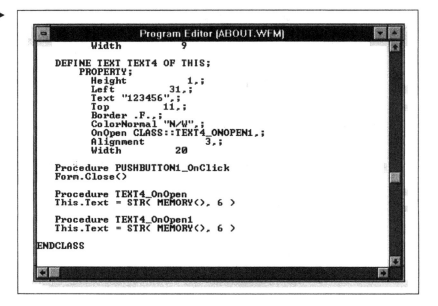

```
                    Program Editor [ABOUT.WFM]
        Width            9
  DEFINE TEXT TEXT4 OF THIS;
     PROPERTY;
        Height              1,;
        Left             31,;
        Text "123456",;
        Top              11,;
        Border .F.,;
        ColorNormal "N/W",;
        OnOpen CLASS::TEXT4_ONOPEN1,;
        Alignment           3,;
        Width            20

  Procedure PUSHBUTTON1_OnClick
  Form.Close()

  Procedure TEXT4_OnOpen
  This.Text = STR( MEMORY(), 6 )

  Procedure TEXT4_OnOpen1
  This.Text = STR( MEMORY(), 6 )

ENDCLASS
```

With that in mind, we want to add two new properties to the Text4 object:

```
Function "R", ;
Picture "999,999k", , ;
```

The "R" function specifies that the text string does not contain the special characters in the Picture property. The "9"s in the Picture property are places where dBASE will substitute digits. The comma and the letter k are special characters that dBASE will just copy.

To test this thoroughly, use the test string "123456" (it should appear as "123,456k"), not the shorter string that your MEMORY( ) function will report. To do this, you "comment out" the OnOpen event handler that gets the real value. To comment out OnOpen, put a semicolon (meaning the line continues) and two ampersands (meaning that what follows is a comment) to the left of the code.

Figure 6.15 shows the two new lines and the commented out change in our Program Editor window. You don't need to add the comments that we used to point out the location of the changes. However, you do

FIGURE 6.15 ▶

*Two lines added, one
line commented out in
ABOUT.WFM*

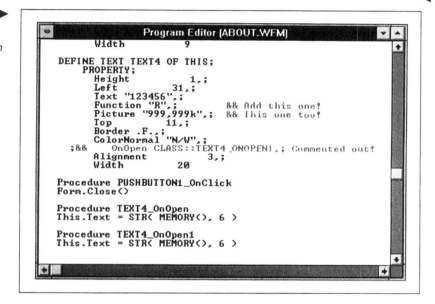

```
                  Program Editor [ABOUT.WFM]
          Width            9
DEFINE TEXT TEXT4 OF THIS;
   PROPERTY;
      Height           1,;
      Left            31,;
      Text "123456",;
      Function "R",;          && Add this one!
      Picture "999,999k",;    && This one too!
      Top             11,;
      Border .F.,;
      ColorNormal "N/W",;
   ;&&    OnOpen CLASS::TEXT4_ONOPEN1,; Commented out!
      Alignment        3,;
      Width           20

Procedure PUSHBUTTON1_OnClick
Form.Close()

Procedure TEXT4_OnOpen
This.Text = STR( MEMORY(), 6 )

Procedure TEXT4_OnOpen1
This.Text = STR( MEMORY(), 6 )
```

need the semicolon and two ampersands (**;&&**) on the line that is commented out.

Now if you press Ctrl-D, your program runs, and your About form looks very good. You should see the Memory value display as 123,456k. Two more changes, and we'll call this complete.

First, "uncomment" (remove the semicolon and asterisks) the line that you commented out, so your program goes ahead and gets the real amount of memory. Second, move the top of the object down a few lines. The default placement is way up there at line 1, which obscures the speed-bar and the menus. Figure 6.16 shows that location changed to 4.

Make sure you make the Top setting change at the correct place in the program. Every object on your form, as well as the form itself, has a Top property. You want to change the form's top. All the other Top settings are relative to the top of the form. Move the form, and everything in it moves along with it.

Press Ctrl-D again, and your About form should have a polished look. What we need now is a form that has a menu with a Help ➤ About choice to launch this form.

FIGURE 6.16 ►

Moving the About form down three lines

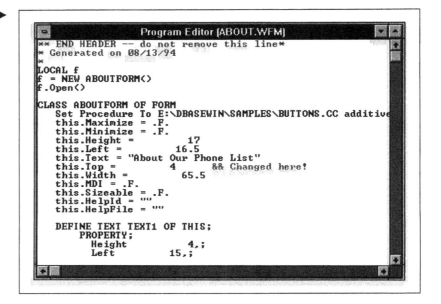

```
Program Editor [ABOUT.WFM]
** END HEADER -- do not remove this line*
* Generated on 08/13/94
*
LOCAL f
f = NEW ABOUTFORM()
f.Open()

CLASS ABOUTFORM OF FORM
    Set Procedure To E:\DBASEWIN\SAMPLES\BUTTONS.CC additive
    this.Maximize = .F.
    this.Minimize = .F.
    this.Height =        17
    this.Left =          16.5
    this.Text = "About Our Phone List"
    this.Top =           4        && Changed here!
    this.Width =         65.5
    this.MDI = .F.
    this.Sizeable = .F.
    this.HelpId = ""
    this.HelpFile = ""

    DEFINE TEXT TEXT1 OF THIS;
        PROPERTY;
          Height           4,;
          Left            15,;
```

►► *You Create a Main Form with a Menu*

We've built an About form. Now it's time to build a form that About can be about.

We'll design a menu with the options File, People, Organizations, Phone List, and Help. The File menu can let us choose a working disk and directory (so you can keep different lists in different directories) and have the expected Exit option. The middle menu choices will launch three forms: one for the People table, one for the Orgs table, and another for a view that shows phone numbers selected from a combination of both files. Help will only have one choice: About.

With older software, all this would have take an experienced programmer a day or more to program. With dBASE for Windows, it will happen in just a few minutes once you master the Menu Designer. Now we'll show you how that tool works.

► *Building a Menu for a Form*

First, we'll need another form for our system. Menus for MDI and non-MDI forms are handled differently. If you have an MDI form, its menu replaces the menu in dBASE for Windows. The dBASE menus return when you close the form. A non-MDI window has its own menu in the standard location. We'll use the non-MDI form for our phone list work.

Creating the Menu

To begin, let's create a blank form and attach a menu. Follow these steps:

1. Launch the Untitled form from the Navigator's list of forms. Tell the Form Expert that you want a Blank Form and click on Create.

2. With the blank form in the Form Designer, set the MDI property to False. To do this, expand the Window Properties if they aren't already expanded, and then click on the MDI property and type **.F.** in the entry field, or click on the tool icon and click on .F. in the list.

3. Select the MenuFile property and Type the word **phone** into its entry field. (You can't create a new file by just clicking on the tool icon.) Then click on the tool icon. The Modify Menu Property dialog box pops up.

4. Choose Design Current Menu, as shown here:

> ▶▶ **N O T E**
>
> **If you forget to enter a menu name for the MenuFile property before you select the Choose Menu option (or click on the tool icon), you'll see the Choose Menu dialog box. This dialog box doesn't include a choice for creating a new menu file.**

You should now be in the Menu Designer, with the insertion point in the upper-left corner, waiting for you to type in your first Menu object.

Entering the Main Menu

The Menu Designer is another of the Two-Way-Tools. It creates an .MNU file of program code, which is a collection of Menu objects. Each Menu object corresponds to one of the prompts on a menu.

Begin by typing **&File**. By preceding the *F* with an ampersand, you tell the Menu Designer to put an underscore under that character. Figure 6.17 shows the first option added in the Menu Designer window.

Note the Object Properties Inspector to the right of the Menu Designer. It is *not* showing the properties of the form from which you launched the Menu Designer. What you see are the properties of the currently selected Menu object (menu option).

What you have, at the point shown in Figure 6.17, is a single Menu object, which would give you a menu system with exactly the one option you've created. Let's continue to add some more.

To switch to the next menu option to the right, press Tab. Then type **&People**. Press Tab again and continue. Use the same procedure to add the other options: **&Organizations, Phone &List**, and **&Help**. (Note that for the Phone List Menu object, you type the ampersand in front of the *L*, not at the start of the first word.) Your menu should look like the one in Figure 6.18.

When you have the focus on the final Help Menu object, check your work. Correct any mistakes (use Shift-Tab to back up; Tab to move forward), and then return to the Help choice. If you Tab past the Help option, simply Shift-Tab to back up without typing anything. When you

FIGURE 6.17

Entering your first menu option

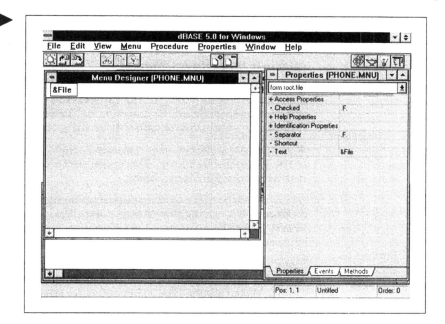

FIGURE 6.18

Finishing the main menu

Building Forms

Ch. **6**

exit a trailing menu choice with no text, the Menu Designer does not create a Menu object.

Making Pull-down Menus

Now we want to make a pull-down menu that will have the About option. To start a pull-down menu, just press the ↓ key. This gives you a new Menu object below the current one. Type **& About Phone List** ... (include the three dots, to show that a dialog box follows).

With the About Menu object entered, press ↑ or Shift-Tab to return to the Help Menu object. Then press Shift-Tab until you have returned to the File Menu object.

Again, press the ↓ key to create a pull-down menu. Enter **Change &Directory** ... in the first Menu object. Press ↓ again and enter **E&xit**. Since these two are logically distinct, you should draw a line between them.

Lines (menu separators) are available from the Menu option of the Menu Designer. Separators are inserted above the currently selected choice. Make sure the Exit Menu object is selected and choose Menu ➤ Insert Separator:

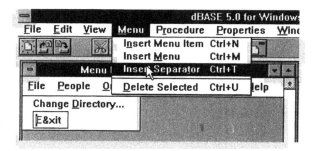

Making a Cascading Menu

Our needs are met without a third-level, cascading menu. But we'll add one anyway, just so you'll know how to make one if you need this type of menu for your own systems. They are as simple to create as the other menus.

Start at the E<u>x</u>it option and press Tab to move to the right. This creates a cascading menu. Type the first item, **&Right Now**, and then press ↓ to add the second: **&Soon**. When you have added the third, **&Whenever**, it should look like this:

Of course, this menu is total nonsense. Now that you know how simple it is to create a cascading menu, let's get rid of it. With one of the cascaded Menu objects selected, choose <u>M</u>enu ➤ <u>D</u>elete Selected. To get rid of the other two, select them and use the shortcut key, Ctrl-U.

Close the Menu Designer. It will save your work as program code in the PHONE.MNU file. Now run the form you are designing. We named ours Fon_Main.

When you run it, you'll get a form with the menu you just designed. It responds appropriately to pressing Alt with the designated letters, or to mouse clicks. Unfortunately, it does absolutely nothing except handle its menus. They haven't been attached anywhere.

That's our next step.

▶ *Attaching Actions to Menu Choices*

Attaching actions to menu selections is similar to adding an event handler for a pushbutton's OnClick event. Let's begin with the <u>F</u>ile ➤ E<u>x</u>it menu option.

Making Exit Work

We want the Exit selection to close and release the form. To make it work, follow these steps:

1. Launch the Form Designer with the Fon_Main form. In the Navigator, right double-click on the Fon_Main file, or select it and press Shift-F2.

2. From the Form Designer, launch the Menu Designer for the PHONE.MNU file. (Click on the Properties tab of the Object Properties Inspector, click on the MenuFile property, click on the tool icon, and choose Design Current Menu from the Modify Menu Property dialog box.)

3. Select the Exit Menu object. Navigate with ↓ and ↑ vertically, Tab and Shift-Tab horizontally, or just click on it with the mouse.

4. Click the Events tab of the Object Properties Inspector. A menu item can only respond to two events, as you see:

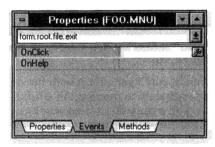

5. Click on the OnClick property, and you'll be in the Procedure Editor. Enter this line:

Form.Release( )

Your Exit Menu object now knows how to respond to a click (or to a selection from the keyboard). This involved traveling a long way from the Navigator to get to the right point at which to add that one line.

A much more efficient way to operate is to add menu event handlers as you build your menu. The method we're using is good practice while you're learning, however.

Let's run the menu and see if it works. Press Ctrl-W to exit the Procedure Editor and the Menu Designer. Then press F2 or click on the lightning icon on the speedbar to run your form. Try pressing Alt-F, then X to close your form.

Now that you've got the Exit choice working, let's get on to launching our About form from the Help ➤ About Phone List... menu choice.

Launching a Form from a Menu Object

First, you need to know how to launch a form by giving a dBASE command. (Obviously, you aren't going to be able to put appropriate mouse movements into the Procedure Editor.)

A form is stored in a .WFM file, which is one type of program file. You execute a program with the DO command. Try typing this in the Command window:

DO About.wfm

This command launches your About form. Since About is a modal form, it will remain on your screen until you click on OK or otherwise close the form, which is what you want for an About form.

Now the only chore that remains is to put that command into the menu. These are the steps:

1. Launch the Fon_Main program in the Form Designer.
2. Using the Object Properties Inspector, MenuFile property, launch the PHONE.MNU file in the Menu Designer.
3. Select the Help ➤ About menu choice in your menu.
4. Click on the Events tab of the Object Properties Inspector and choose the OnClick event. Click the tool icon to get to the Procedure Editor.
5. Enter the line **DO About.wfm** in the Procedure Editor.

Now when you run your Fon_Main file, choosing Help ➤ About Phone List... will launch your About form. Before we leave our menu, lets assign a shortcut key so that we can press Ctrl-D to select a directory.

▶ *Attaching a Shortcut Key*

Attaching a shortcut key (one you can press to go directly to a Menu object's OnClick handler) is straightforward. You simply put the name of the key into the Shortcut property of the Menu object.

Let's try assigning the Ctrl-D keypress to the Change Directory ... choice in our File menu. While we're there, we might as well program this Menu object to actually change directories.

Before you get to the menu's Procedure Editor, try out these commands in the Command window:

x = GETDIRECTORY( )

? x

CD &x

As you can see, the built-in GETDIRECTORY( ) function pops up the appropriate dialog box and lets you choose a directory. The line ? x lets you see your choice in the Command window's results pane.

The CD command in dBASE is similar to the same command in DOS. It changes to the named directory. The ampersand in front of the variable name *x* tells dBASE to substitute the value of the variable, not to use it as the letter *x*.

Now that you know which commands to use, launch the Fon_Main form in the Form Designer, and then open the PHONE menu in the Menu Designer.

Click on the Change Directory ... option to select it and then click on the Events tab of the Object Properties Inspector. Choose the OnClick property, and then click on the tool icon to get to the Procedure Editor.

Add these two lines:

d = GETDIRECTORY( )

CD &d

Your Procedures window should look like this:

Now we have a program that will change directories based on our selection, so it's time to provide convenient access via the Ctrl-D key.

Click on the Properties tab of the Object Properties Inspector. Then click on the Shortcut property. In its entry field, type **Ctrl-D**. When you start typing, the field turns a warning yellow color. When you're finished, press Enter. The field will return to white. If you make a mistake, you'll get an appropriate warning message.

You can use Ctrl, Alt, and function key combinations for your shortcut keys, although function keys higher than F10 are not supported. The following are some valid entries:

- Ctrl-A through Ctrl-Z
- Ctrl-0 through Ctrl-9
- Alt-any letter or number
- F1 through F10
- Ctrl-F1 through Ctrl-F10
- Alt-F1 through Alt-F10
- Shift-F1 through Shift-F10

►►WARNING

The error trapping does *not* detect conflicts with Microsoft Windows special keys, such as Alt-F4 for closing a form. You must be careful not to use these as shortcut keys.

If you haven't done so yet, go ahead and run your modified program. You should be able to choose directories by pressing Alt-F then D, or just by pressing Ctrl-D.

We hope that you don't mind that this program is twice as long as the ones we've used so far!

A final item to fix is the Text property of the Fon_Main form. Change this property's value to **My Phone List** (or something else that's more descriptive than the default *Form*).

Now it's time to go on and use this framework with some real forms that access our tables.

►► *You Build the People Form*

For our phone list system, we'll make a special form that incorporates the best features of a human-assisted form layout and a browse view. Let's begin by letting the Form Expert build a starting form for us, as we did in Chapter 2.

For this form, let's start with a query that has all the People table data, except the employer link, arranged in alphabetical order by last name.

► *Building the Query*

The Query Designer will let us get this result quickly. Follow these steps:

1. Launch the Query Designer on the Untitled query.

2. Choose the People table from the Open Table Required dialog box.

3. Click on the All Fields selection box, like this:

4. Click on the field selection box in the ORG_ID field to remove it from the selected set.

5. Tab to the end of the file skeleton, or hold the right arrow to shift the list toward the end. In the UPPER(LAST_NAME) field, click on the smudge. It will turn into an up arrow, indicating an ascending index on last name, using a true alphabetic sort.

6. Press Ctrl-W to save your work. Give it the name **People_A**.

▶ Building the Base Form

With the query built, it's time to build the basic form. For this, use the Form Expert. Launch the Untitled form and accept the offer of Expert assistance. Choose PEOPLE_A.QBE for your view.

Select all the fields, then send back the two tags (the indexes that are labeled TAG01 and TAG02). Adjust the colors to suit yourself, and then generate the form.

After your form is generated, make some changes. First, stretch it to be about as wide as our sample, which is shown in Figure 6.19.

As you see in Figure 6.19, we've made small adjustments for a better-looking form. For example, we don't use underscores in the Last name and Full name labels.

Make similar improvements in your own form. When you are finished, we'll go on to add a Browse object, which will simplify navigating in the form.

▶ Adding a Browse

We like a form type of layout (really, a Columnar Layout view with some human adjustments—not the built-in Form Layout view) for data entry. We like the Browse Layout view for looking through our data. In this form, we're going to have both!

FIGURE 6.19 ▶

*A base form with
some adjustments*

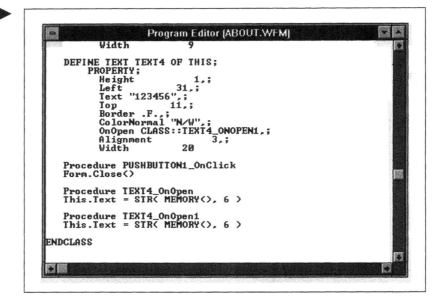

```
┌──────────────────────────────────────────────────┐
│ □       Program Editor [ABOUT.WFM]        ▽ △     │
│         Width         9                           │
│    DEFINE TEXT TEXT4 OF THIS;                      │
│       PROPERTY;                                    │
│          Height        1,;                         │
│          Left         31,;                         │
│          Text "123456",;                           │
│          Top          11,;                         │
│          Border .F.,;                              │
│          ColorNormal "N/W",;                       │
│          OnOpen CLASS::TEXT4_ONOPEN1,;             │
│          Alignment        3,;                      │
│          Width        20                           │
│    Procedure PUSHBUTTON1_OnClick                   │
│    Form.Close()                                    │
│    Procedure TEXT4_OnOpen                          │
│    This.Text = STR( MEMORY(), 6 )                  │
│    Procedure TEXT4_OnOpen1                         │
│    This.Text = STR( MEMORY(), 6 )                  │
│ ENDCLASS                                           │
│ ◄                                                ► │
└──────────────────────────────────────────────────┘
```

From the Form Designer's Controls palette, click on the Browse object. Then drag it onto your form in the empty space you've got on the right. Figure 6.20 shows us adding the Browse object to our form.

Now that the Browse object is on the form, we need to set some properties. Click on the Properties tab of the Object Properties Inspector.

Setting Access Properties

In the Access properties, you can set the TabStop property to .F. for efficient data entry. This means that you will tab from field to field, but not tab into the Browse object. The problem with this is that there will be no access to the Browse object if you don't have a mouse or some other pointing device.

FIGURE 6.20 ▶

Adding a Browse object

  ▶▶**TIP**

Set the TabStop property for your normal situation. If you set it to .F., for instance, you can always change it to .T. when you find yourself without a mouse.

Data-Linkage Properties

You need to select an Alias property. With the People_A query selected, the only choice when you click on the tool icon is People, which is exactly what you want. Choose that, and then click on the tool icon for the Fields property.

We deselected all the fields, then clicked just the LAST_NAME field back into the Browse object. We use this browse to locate the person we want. As we move through the list of last names, every data field about the one we're selecting appears just to the left of the browse, so this arrangement is just right for our purposes.

Building Forms

Ch
6

Edit Properties

If you set the Modify property to False, you'll automatically turn off the Append and Delete properties. This is what we want. Editing will be done in the form layout.

The Toggle property, when True, lets you change between Browse, Form, and Columnar Layout views. You don't want this capability inside this Browse object, so set it to False.

Visual Properties

Set the ShowDeleted property to .F. to turn it off. This eliminates the deleted column, even if the deleted setting in the Desktop Properties dialog box allows showing deleted records.

Also turn off the ShowHeading and ShowRecNo properties. The first eliminates the field names above the data. (It's obvious that w're looking at last names.) The second eliminates the record number column on the left.

▶ Running the Completed Form

After you've finished setting the properties for the Browse object, you can run the completed form. Ours is shown in Figure 6.21.

FIGURE 6.21

*Our completed
People_A form*

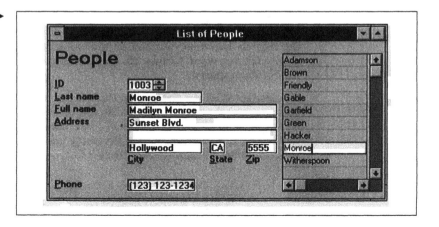

You can navigate in this form with the standard tools (such as the speedbar buttons and PgUp and PgDn keys), as well as with the vertical elevator on the Browse object.

The form layout portion lets you enter and edit the data. We think this type of form gives you the best of both worlds.

▶ Putting Your Form into Your System

Now that we have a completed PEOPLE.WFM, we have something to launch when we choose People from the Fon_Main form. It's time to tie the new form into our system. Follow these steps:

1. Launch the Fon_Main form in the Form Designer.
2. Open the PHONE.MNU menu in the Menu Designer.
3. Launch the Procedure Editor for the OnClick event of the People Menu object.
4. Add a single line that says **DO People.wfm**, and then save your program.

Now you can switch to Run mode from the Form Designer to test our system. When you choose People from your Fon_Main menu, the People_A form we just created will be launched.

Once the People_A form is closed, you may "lose" your Fon_Main window. If this happens, hold the Alt key down and press Tab to cycle through the list of active applications. When you find that window, release the Alt key, and the window will be active again.

If you don't like this behavior, change the Fon_Main form's MDI property back to True. When you do this, the Fon_Main window will still be visible after you open and then close your People form.

Unlike the non-MDI window, an MDI window does not have a menu. Your menu replaces the dBASE for Windows menus. When you close the Fon_Main form, the dBASE for Windows menus return.

►► *You Build the Orgs Form*

To begin building the Orgs form, let's repeat the process we went through in the last section. Build a query, ORGS_A.QBE, that includes all the fields in the Orgs table and indexes in ascending, true alphabetical order.

Have the Form Expert build a form for you. Then change the appearance and text as you like to improve the form.

Next, add a Browse object on the right. Select just the NAME field, and turn off headings and record numbers. Set the Modify property to .F. for this field. Do the same for the TabStop property (unless you'll frequently run this form without a mouse). Our form is shown in Figure 6.22.

FIGURE 6.22 ►

A form for the employers

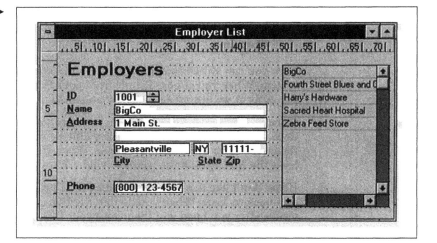

► *Adding Pushbuttons*

If the form has room, we like to include pushbuttons. They provide another option for choosing the most common activities. Let's add a pair of these buttons to our Orgs_A form.

Start by adding more space at the bottom of the form to accommodate the pushbuttons. Then click on Pushbutton in the Controls palette and drag it on your form. In the Object Properties Inspector, change the Pushbutton object's Text property to **Append**.

Repeat the procedure to create a **Close** pushbutton. Figure 6.23 shows our form with these buttons.

FIGURE 6.23 ▶

A form with push-buttons added

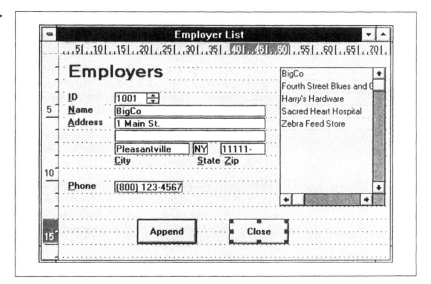

Now let's attach appropriate code to their OnClick events.

For the Append button, enter a one-line program:

    APPEND BLANK

The APPEND BLANK command adds a single, blank record at the end of the table. It also switches the record pointer to this record, which is exactly what you need to add a record.

For the Close button, you want to release the form. Enter this line:

    Form.Release( )

Building Forms

Ch.
6

With those two event handlers attached, we're ready to test our improved form.

▶ Adding Input Templates

When you try your Append button, you'll get a new, blank record, just as we wanted. However, the spinbutton for the ORG_ID field doesn't behave as we wanted.

Spinbuttons default to spinning from 1 to 100 in increments of 1. This is not at all what we want for our ID fields. Let's fix that and make some other improvements.

First, select the spinbutton and click on the Properties tab of the Object Properties Inspector. If it is not expanded, double-click on the Edit Properties category. Set the RangeMin property to 1001 and the RangeMax property to 9999.

Spinbuttons have another bad habit: they may report the number right-justified under the spinbuttons, so you can't see your whole entry. To prevent this, use a Picture property.

The Picture property is a template that controls input. A Picture template is built with special symbols and other characters. The special symbols allow entry of characters where they appear in the template. Regular characters are repeated as they are. The following are some common special characters:

Character	Meaning
A	Alphabetic characters only
9	Numeric digits only
!	Capital letters (no need to press Shift)

The following Picture property will format ten digits in the common North American phone number format:

(999) 999-9999

As you type digits, each one is placed where the 9s occur in the template. The other characters (the parentheses, hyphen, and blank space) do not accept input, so they remain unchanged.

To be sure the spinbutton aligns its digits on the left, use the Picture property **9999**, like this:

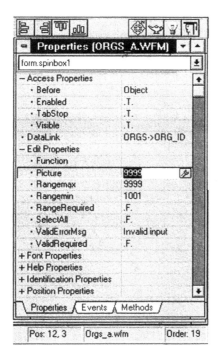

You can also add the Picture format we suggested above—(999) 999-999—for your PHONE field. (Or add a different format if it's appropriate for your national conventions.)

 ▶▶**WARNING**

> **If your list is limited to one country, you can be quite specific about formatting phone numbers, postal codes, and so on. However, if you will be maintaining an international list, you shouldn't use any formatting, because conventions vary from country to country.**

Building Forms

▶ ▶
Ch.
6

▶ *Attaching the Form to the Fon_Main System*

Once you're satisfied with the Orgs_A form, you'll want to attach it to your Fon_Main system. In this section, we'll show you how to sneak into the Menu Designer without going through the Form Designer.

Click the Custom file type in the Navigator. In the Custom Files entry field, enter ***.MNU**, as you see in Figure 6.24.

FIGURE 6.24 ▶

Adding *.MNU files to the Navigator

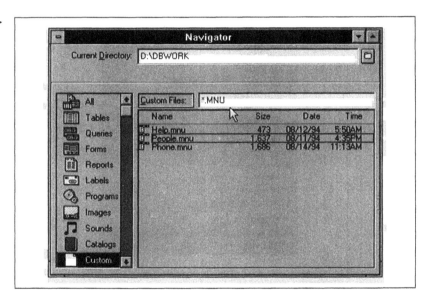

Now you can get to your menus just by choosing Custom and clicking on the files. A right click on the PHONE.MNU file opens its Speed menu, from which you can choose Design Menu. Alternatively, you can right double-click or press Shift-F2 to launch the Menu Designer.

With this trick, enter the Menu Designer and select the Organizations Menu object. On the Object Properties Inspector, click on the Events tab, and then click on the OnClick property. In the Procedure Editor, add this line:

DO Orgs_a.wfm

Save and test your work by running Fon_Main. Your system is now complete, except that it doesn't have the combined people and employer phone list capability.

This is what we will work on in the next section. Before going on, this would be a good time for you to go back to the People_A form and improve it. Add pushbuttons, adjust the ID field, and add Picture properties, as we did in the Orgs_A form.

▶ ▶ *You Build the Combined Form*

You've seen how to build a query that relates people to their employers. However, the query that we built in Chapter 5 won't serve our purposes here. That query related employers to their employees. It showed people in alphabetical order within each employer. For a phone list, you need people in alphabetical order, regardless of their employer. Otherwise, you would have a hard time locating people if you did not already know their employer.

▶ *Building an Inverted Query*

For this query, we'll invert the normal order of parent and child. Normally, you would treat the employer record as the parent, since many employees could be attached to each employer.

But you can do that the other way, too. If you call the People table record the parent, dBASE for Windows will find "every" employer record that matches. Of course, we know that there will only be one, but computers don't have our human knowledge.

One thing we'll lose when we do this is the ability to change an employee's ORG_ID field value, which we would need to do if a person switched employers. But we can still do this through direct access to the People table record in our other forms.

Figure 6.25 shows the query, as we specified it in the Query Designer. Start with the People table, and click on the select all fields check box. Then move to the right and click the smudge mark on the UP-PER(LAST_NAME) index to get people in true alphabetic order.

FIGURE 6.25 ▶

Using an inverted query, keeping people alphabetized

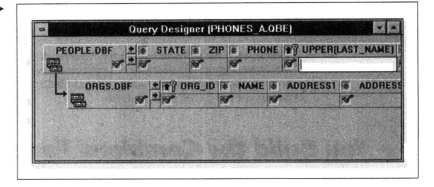

Next add the Orgs table and drag a relation from People to Orgs. Figure 6.26 shows the details of this relationship, in the Define Relation dialog box.

FIGURE 6.26 ▶

The details of the inverted relationship

After you've created the relationship, save the query as Phones_A. Now we can get on to building a form.

▶ Creating the Form

Launch the Untitled form and accept the Form Expert's offer of assistance. Pick the PHONES_A.QBE view, which we just created.

Pick all the fields, and then reject the three tag fields that are associated with indexes. From here, the process is the same as the one we've used for building the individual table forms. Adjust the display of the items until it looks pleasing, and then add a Browse object on the right.

The Alias property of the Browse object is set to PEOPLE. The Fields property is set to just LAST_NAME. The other adjustments are the same ones we made for the Browse objects on the single-table forms.

Our finished form is shown in Figure 6.27.

FIGURE 6.27 ▶

Our completed phone list form

When you run this form for the first time, give it the name Phones_A.

Don't forget to set the title on the form. Also, since you can't change the ORG_ID value in either the People or the Orgs table, you should change these two fields' TabStop properties to False.

Building Forms

When your form satisfies you, give it a test run. Now as you move through the form, your employer data is constantly updated to match the person you've selected.

If you change the BigCo phone number, that change is correctly reflected whenever you look at a person who works for BigCo.

Your system is open for business. The last detail is to bring it in as part of the Fon_Main system.

► Putting the Form in the Fon_Main System

From the Navigator, select Custom tables. Right double-click the PHONE.MNU file to launch it in the Menu Designer.

In the Menu Designer, click on the Phone List menu object and then click on the Events tab of the Object Properties Inspector. Click on the OnClick property, and then the tool icon, to get to the Procedure Editor.

Enter this line in the Procedure Editor:

DO Phones_a.wfm

Now save your work and return to the Navigator. In the Forms file list, double-click on Fon_Main to launch your finished system.

Congratulations! If you've followed this far, you've built some very nice forms and integrated them in a system.

►► *Summary*

You've come a long way in this chapter. First, you learned about modal and MDI forms. You created a modal About form. You added a pushbutton, decorated it with a bitmap from the resource file, and added an appropriate event handler to close the form when the button is clicked.

You used a Text object, supported by the MEMORY( ) function, which you called in the OnOpen event handler, to report memory available. You used Function and Picture properties to format the number appropriately.

Next you went into the Menu Designer. You built a main menu, pull-down menus, and even a cascading menu. You underscored the hot keys and learned to assign shortcut keys. You hooked your Menu objects, through their OnClick events, to the other forms you were building.

For the tables, you learned to start with a query, built in the Query Designer, that you later used as input to each form's design through the Form Expert.

For the People table, you combined the Form Expert and your own work to produce a sophisticated form that combined a Browse object with the basic form layout.

For the Orgs table, you created another combined form. Then you went on to adding pushbuttons. You also used Picture properties to help with entering individual fields on the form.

For the combined table, showing both People and Orgs data, you specified a query that inverted the normal parent-child relationship. This lets you look at each employer attached to the employee's record.

Through this view, you were able to build another form that integrated a Browse object with form layouts from both tables. Changing an employer's phone number in one record effectively changes it for all the employees who work for the same employer.

As you built your forms, you added them to your system through the Menu Designer. You added the .MNU type into your Navigator's Custom table list, to get convenient access to this tool.

In the next chapter, we'll conclude our series of tutorials with a study of the Crystal Reports tool.

Building Forms

Ch.
6

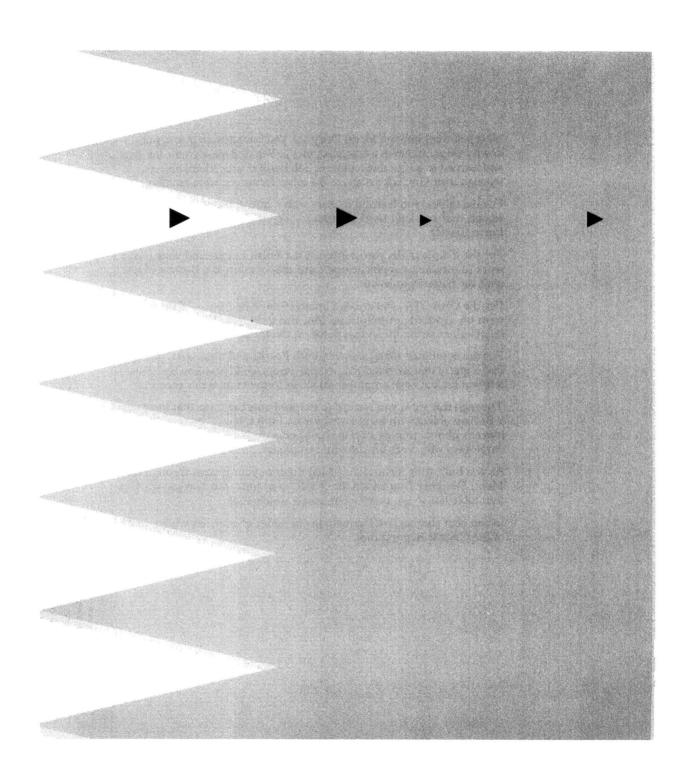

Producing Database Reports

▶ ▶ **I**n this chapter, we'll complete our tutorials with a closer look into the Crystal Reports tool, which we'll call Crystal for short. Crystal is a third-party, add-on report writer that has been bundled by agreement between Seagate (owner of Crystal Computer Services) and Borland.

After Crystal was licensed, Borland acquired the ReportSmith company and software, which was a direct competitor to Crystal. ReportSmith reporting software is now being sold by Borland, and we expect a future version of dBASE for Windows to replace Crystal with ReportSmith.

However, for now, we have Crystal Reports, which is a rich and powerful reporting environment. As you'll see, Crystal makes multi-table reporting simple, and lets you create reports that take advantage of the Microsoft Windows' graphical environment.

▶ ▶ *You Create a Two-Table Report*

To begin, we'll start with a two-table report. We'll list our People table data, grouped by employers. To start, we'll need a query that structures the two tables.

▶ *Building Your Query*

Follow these steps to build the query for the tables:

 1. Launch the Untitled query from the Navigator, and select the Orgs table as your first table.

 2. In the Query Designer, choose Query ➤ Add Table (or press Ctrl-A) and add the People table.

3. For both tables, click on the select all fields check box, and then deselect each of the ID fields. Your query should now look like the one shown in Figure 7.1.

FIGURE 7.1 ▶

Building a query for your report

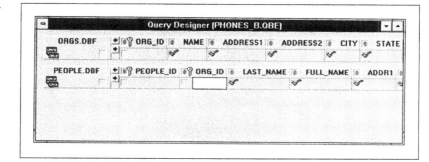

4. With the tables and fields selected, the next step is to establish the relationship between the tables. Drag a line from the set relation icon in the Orgs table skeleton to the set relation icon in the People table skeleton.

5. In the Define Relation dialog box, click on ORG_ID in the child table's Index list, and then click each of the three check boxes in the center. Your relationship should look the same as the one shown in Figure 7.2.

6. With the relationship specified, click on OK or press Enter to return to the Query Designer.

7. Press Ctrl-F4 or Ctrl-W to exit. dBASE for Windows will ask if you want to save your query. Save it as **Phones_B**. (The Phones_ A query is the inverted query we did for our Fon_Main system; our _B series will be for noninverted work.)

▶ *Beginning the Report Definition*

With our query defined, it's time to enter Crystal Reports and define our report. Follow these steps:

1. From the Navigator, click on the Untitled report. This launches the Crystal Reports program.

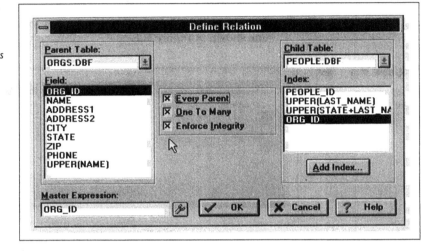

2. Select PHONES_B.QBE in the Open Table Required dialog box. After a moment, Crystal will be loaded, as shown in Figure 7.3. (Crystal is easiest to use if you start by maximizing its window, and then open the report window.)

 ▶▶**WARNING**

If you have any open tables, Crystal will use the open table; it won't prompt you for a table or query selection. If this happens, exit Crystal. Then go to the Command window and type **CLOSE ALL** before returning to the Navigator. With everything closed, you'll be prompted for a table or query name when you launch the Untitled report.

You should see the insertion point flashing in the Details area of the report design screen. (If it isn't there, move the mouse pointer into this area and click the left mouse button.)

FIGURE 7.3

Crystal Reports, ready to accept report fields

3. In the Details area of our report, we want more space than just one line, so press Enter several times. Give yourself about a dozen lines, but don't worry about counting them. You can add or delete detail lines whenever you like.

4. Click on the NAME field in the Insert Database Field window, and then click on the Insert pushbutton in that window. (A shortcut is to just double-click on the field in the Insert Database Field window.)

5. Your cursor will turn into a rectangular shape. Move back to the first line of the Details area, and click to drop your field near the left margin.

After you have placed this field, your report will look like Figure 7.4.

FIGURE 7.4 ▶

The Details area expanded, with its first field

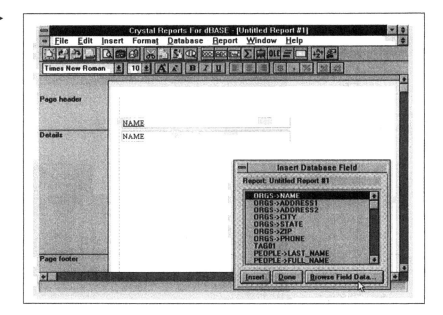

▶ Adding the Other Fields

When you add a field, Crystal helps you out by adding its name above the field in the Page header area. This is fine when your report has multiple fields that run across the page. However, we're building a report of names and addresses, so each column will be a stack of fields.

Unfortunately, when Crystal inserts another field, it stacks the field headings. To see this, add the PHONE field under the NAME field.

▶▶ W A R N I N G

When you have more than one table, you can have duplicate field names. Be sure you pick the Orgs table PHONE field when it's appropriate, and the People table PHONE field when it's the right one.

As you can see, you now have two column headings disagreeing about who has the right to occupy the heading space. Click on the argument and press Del. A heading will be deleted. Press Del again, and the argument is settled. They're both gone.

Fortunately, the Crystal Reports authors anticipated work such as we are doing. Choose File ➤ Options.... In the Options dialog box, shown in Figure 7.5, you'll see these four categories:

- General
- Database
- Format
- Fonts

FIGURE 7.5

Setting Crystal Reports options

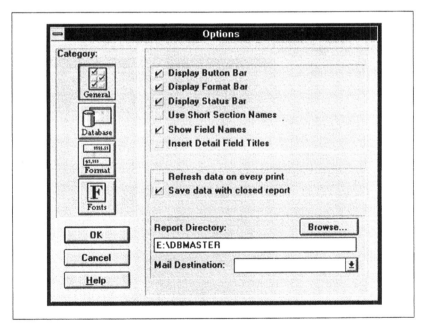

The General option is the default. The last check box in the upper-right section of the dialog box is Insert Detail Field Titles. Click on it to remove the check mark, and then press Enter or click on OK. From now on, Crystal will *not* put those column headings up for you.

►►**TIP**

Sometimes computer programs put labels on everything. Human beings are smarter than computers—we don't need a label that says "Address" if we're looking at an address. Skip unnecessary labels.

Now shift the report design window a bit to the right and add the address information from the Orgs table. Place the fields to the right of the name and phone number. Figure 7.6 shows our report at this stage. As you can see, we moved the Insert Database Field window to a location that was more convenient.

FIGURE 7.6 ►

The Orgs table details in place

When you're finished adding data from the Orgs table, add the data from the People table in a similar fashion, but offset it to the right by an inch or so (about 3 centimeters). We put the LAST_NAME field above the PHONE field. To the right of these, we put the full address, starting with the FULL_NAME field.

If you don't have enough space in the Details band, put the insertion point into this band and press Enter. Pressing Backspace on a blank Details line deletes the line.

▶ Previewing Your Work

After you have these fields in place, click on the looking glass icon (shown in the margin) on the speedbar, which is the fifth from the left, to preview your report. This button launches the Preview window, where you can look at your report.

Actually, the Preview window could also have been correctly called the Report to Screen window, because it lets you look at your whole report.

The default preview is full size. If you click on the looking glass (shown in the margin) on the Preview window's speedbar (at the bottom of the window) you can zoom out to two smaller sizes. Two clicks put the whole page on the screen, as shown in Figure 7.7.

If you click on the looking glass again, you return to the full-size view. In this view, you'll see that you have repeated the name of the employer with every employee record. It would be better to have the employer data just once, and have each employee listed below the employer's listing.

We'll make that improvement soon. For now, let's add a page header and footer to our report.

▶ Adding Headers and Footers

When we started Crystal, we were in the Details band of a three-band design surface. The other two bands are for a page header and footer. What we put in these bands will be part of each page of our report.

Let's add a title and a page number.

FIGURE 7.7 ►

The full-page view in the Preview window

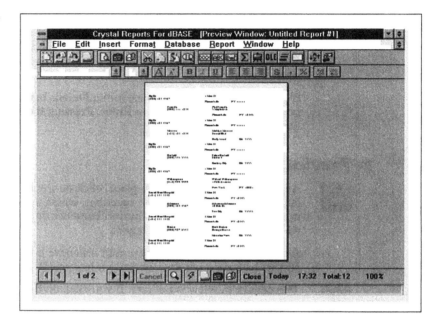

Putting a Title in the Page Header Area

Move the mouse pointer into the Page header area and click. The insertion point will be located to the far left of this area, where you could begin typing the header text directly into that band. Actually, you can type text directly in any area of the report. However, we recommend that you always use text fields for fixed text.

To insert a text field, choose Insert ➤ Text Field ... from the menus. The Edit Text Field window pops up.

Enter your text in this box. Obviously, you could write an extended essay here, but we used a simple, two-word title:

When you click on the Accept pushbutton (pressing Enter is interpreted as part of the text you're entering, not an Accept action), your
cursor again becomes the field-placement rectangle. Put the rectangle
in the center of your report's Page header section and click to drop it.

Now we have a rather unimposing title, to say the least. When you
dropped your title, it was selected; it was outlined in yellow and had
resize handles at the left and right sides.

If the title is not still selected, click on it. Now go to the fonts bar and
click on the down arrow next to the point size box. This will drop down
a menu of font sizes:

Use the elevator to scroll to something a bit larger than the default size.
We use 24 points for a title.

To the right of the point size box are big and small *A*s, which tighten
and loosen the kerning. To the right of these are three icons that specify
font style information:

These are for boldface, italics, and underlining.

For our title, we chose all three: bold, italic, and underlined. Our selections look like this:

Numbering the Pages in the Page Footer

Numbering your report pages is simple. Choose Insert ► Special Field to see a menu of special items. Each of these is a field that you can insert, just as you would add a database or text field. For our work, click on Page Number. Your cursor again turns into the rectangular field-insertion cursor.

Position it in the Page footer area and click in the center. This gives the report a page number centered at the bottom of every page. If you like, you can leave it selected and adjust the font size and style to suit your tastes.

►► You Produce a Two-Table Grouped Report

Most multi-table reports benefit from grouping the data, and our list is no exception. What we want are detail records for employees grouped by employer. We don't really want to repeat the employer data once for each employee.

► Creating a Group

To create a group, choose Insert ► Group Section ... from the menus. This will pop up the Insert Group Section dialog box, shown in Figure 7.8. The default setting is for the employer name, in ascending sequence. This

FIGURE 7.8

Accepting the default grouping suggestion

dialog box will let you pick a field and sequence to suit your needs. But in this instance, the defaults are precisely right. Just click on OK or press Enter.

Groups have a Group header and Group footer area. In this case, since we're grouping on the NAME field, the report design screen labels these areas NAME. They appear above and below the Details section.

But we want to put the employer data into the Group header area, so that it precedes the details about each employee. (The Group footer area prints after all the details about the group.)

▶ Putting the Employer Data into the Group Header

Begin by clicking in the Group header area to position the insertion point there. Press Enter twice to expand this area to three lines, so that it will accommodate all the employer data.

You can move fields in Crystal Reports by selecting them and dragging them, just as you move objects in the Form Designer. (The cursor doesn't change into the little hand, but the operation is the same.)

 However, for moving a group of fields, the lasso is the best tool. The lasso (shown in the margin) is available on the speedbar. It's the one that looks a little like a squashed baseball, under the *base* part of the Database menu selection.

Click on the lasso on the speedbar. Your cursor changes to cross-hairs. Position the cross-hairs at the top and to the left of the first Orgs table field. Then click and hold the mouse button down while you drag to the lower-right corner of the area that holds all the Orgs table fields.

When you release the mouse button, all the fields within the rectangle you just sketched are selected. Again as in the Form Designer, with multiple fields selected, you can move the fields by dragging with the mouse.

Put the mouse pointer over any one of the selected fields, and press and hold the mouse button while you drag the fields into the Group header area. When they are in position, release the mouse button.

Now return to the Details section of your report and click to position the insertion point in the blank space above the People table data. Use

the Del and Backspace keys to delete the blank lines. These keys remove characters in the same way that they do in any text editor.

The result we want is shown in Figure 7.9.

FIGURE 7.9

*The employer group
with employee details*

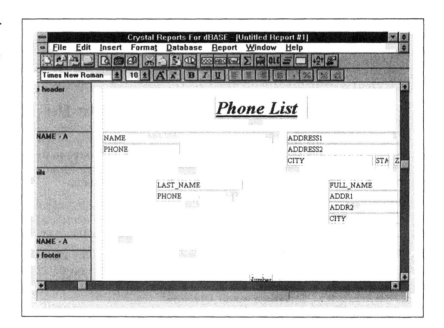

▶ Previewing the Improved Report

With the employer data in the Group header area and the space adjusted in the Details area, click on the Preview window button (the
looking glass icon) to preview your report again.

Crystal makes its own copy of your reports data. The second and subsequent times that you preview your report, Crystal asks if you want to use the saved data:

This dialog box tells you the time and date when it last saved the data. Unless you change the default setting, when you save a report, you also save a copy of the data. Using the copy is faster and avoids the problems possible in a multi-user environment, where one person could be updating data as another is running a report.

Make a choice. Normally, you'll accept the default choice to reuse the saved data. Click on the button reflecting your choice, or press Enter to accept the default. In the Preview window, click on the glass at the bottom to zoom out to a full-page view of your report.

You may or may not see a problem, depending on your data. Crystal may have come to the bottom of the page in the middle of printing data about an employee or employer, and split the address between two pages. Use the navigation buttons on the bottom speedbar to page through your report to see if this happens in your report.

▶ *Preventing Section Splitting*

To make sure the address lines appear on the same page, you need to tell Crystal that you don't want it to start a detail group or a section header if it can't finish it on the current page. To do this, choose Format ▶ Section ... from the menus. In the Format Section dialog box, choose Details, as shown in Figure 7.10.

After you choose a section, Crystal launches another dialog box, also titled Format Section, where you can provide formatting details about the section you have chosen. In Figure 7.11, we're choosing the Keep

FIGURE 7.10

*Choosing to format
the Details section*

FIGURE 7.11

*Choosing to print only
complete Details
sections*

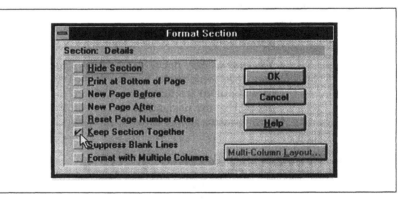

Section Together option for the Details section. This choice tells Crystal that we don't want it to start the section if it can't fit the whole section on the current page.

After choosing this option for the Details section, go back and repeat the process for the Group header section. Note that although this keeps the Group header section together, it doesn't keep all the details together with the header. Keeping the entire group together is not an option in Crystal Reports.

▶▶ *You Add Embellishments to Your Report*

One of the best features of Crystal is that it lets you work in the Preview window, where you see the results of your work on live data. When you get to the position we are now in—you have the right data in the right order—you begin to address the appearance of the report. Being able to do this in the Preview window is invaluable.

  ▶▶ T I P

> **Make regular use of the zoom icon spy glass at the bottom of the page as you make improvements.**

You will need to be in the full-size view to select fields. Your selections remain in the other views, but you can't select different fields unless the window is full size.

▶ *Manipulating Font Sizes and Styles*

The simplest, and one of the most effective, ways to dress up a report is to vary your font sizes and styles. To begin, let's make the employers' names stand out.

Click on an employer's name to select this field. You'll see that every occurrence of the field in the Preview window is selected. With the name selected, set the font size to 16 points and choose boldface. To change the font size, click on the font size box and use the elevator to select a size. To boldface the text, click on the B button for boldface.

► ►**T I P**

> **Varying font sizes and styles adds emphasis. Using multiple fonts makes reports look garish. Stick with one font for most of your work. Used with discretion, using two fonts sometimes works. Using three or more fonts almost always looks foolish.**

We've used a 16-point, boldface font for the employers' names, and a 16-point, regular font for their phone numbers. Now try a 12-point, boldface font for the employees' names and a 12-point, regular font for their phone numbers.

► *Drawing on Your Report*

You can use lines and boxes to dress up your report. Before we go on, however, let's save what we've got. If you haven't saved your work yet, you'll see that your report is untitled (look in the Crystal Reports main window's title).

Choose File ➤ Save or File ➤ Save As ... to save your work. (Crystal will ask for a name if your report is untitled.) We saved our report as Phones_B.

Now let's put a box around the employer's data. Choose Insert ➤ Box from the menus. Your mouse pointer will turn into a pencil (as shown in the margin). From the upper-left area, above the employer's name, drag to the lower-right, area, just below the end of the employer's address. Your box should surround all the employer data.

When you release your mouse button, you might get the mixed-up result shown in Figure 7.12.

What's going on here? The answer is simple. The box you just drew is covering some of the Details section, as well as the Group header section. The portion in the Details section is repeated for every detail.

Close the Preview window (click on the Close button at the bottom) to go back to the report design window. Click on the box you just added to select it, and drag any convenient handle back into the Group header section.

FIGURE 7.12 ▶

*A box causing
problems*

Phone List

BigCo (800) 123-4567	1 Main St. Pleasantville		NY	11111
Friendly (800) 111-1234	Phil Friendly 5 Maple Ave. Pleasantville		NY	12345
Monroe (123) 123-1234	Madilyn Monroe Sunset Blvd. Hollywood		CA	5555
Garfield (800) 555-5555	Felina Garfield Studio 4 Century City		CA	5555
Witherspoon	Wilfred Witherspoon			

▶▶ **N O T E**

**You may find that trying to grab a box handle selects a
field instead. Drag the field out of the way before you
adjust the box.**

With the box located in the Group header section, you can return to
the Preview window. Your box is now well-behaved, neatly enclosing the
employer data, as shown in Figure 7.13.

▶ Formatting the Box

With the box in place, we can add decorative effects. Click on your
box, then choose Format ▶ Box ... from the menus. (You can't access
the Box option of the Format menu unless you've selected a box first.)
You'll see the Box Format dialog box. Figure 7.14 shows this dialog
box with our settings.

We chose a gray fill color (which Crystal calls Silver). For our border, we
used a 3-point, solid-black line. Choose whatever combinations you like.

A well-behaved box

Phone List

BigCo (800) 123-4567	1 Main St.		
	Pleasantville	NY	11111

Friendly
(800) 111-1234

Phil Friendly
5 Maple Ave.

Pleasantville   NY   12345

Monroe
(123) 123-1234

Madilyn Monroe
Sunset Blvd.

FIGURE 7.14 ▶

*Choosing box format-
ting options*

◎ ▶▶ W A R N I N G

**Adding gray areas can increase the print time
dramatically. An eight-page-per-minute printer can
be slowed to one or two pages per minute.**

As you add decorative effects, remember that individual characters are
transmitted to your printer 8 bits per character. Bitmaps and gray areas
are transmitted at 300 dots per inch (dpi). (Both lower and higher den-
sities are available, but 300 dpi is the most common.)

A square inch of gray area takes 90,000 bits. For pure character information, 90,000 bits would handle 11,250 characters (about four pages of single-spaced text). You might consider two versions of your reports: one with embellishments and one that prints quickly.

▶ *Emphasizing Names*

With our employers standing out so clearly, we need to do something to add emphasis to the employees' names. The work we are about to do should be done with discretion. If you use too much emphasis, nothing will stand out.

The potential to abuse, rather than use, the field-emphasis features may have led the designers of Crystal to place these capabilities in an obscure portion of the product.

To add emphasis, select a field (we chose the last name field), and then choose Format ▶ Borders and Colors .... Figure 7.15 shows our choices in the Format Borders and Colors dialog box.

In this dialog box, we've chosen to place a border line on all four sides of the field. We've also asked for a Drop Shadow, to really pop the field up off the page.

FIGURE 7.15 ▶

*Boxing and shadow-
ing last names*

With these improvements made, it's time to preview the report again. Our Preview window now shows the report as it appears in Figure 7.16.

FIGURE 7.16 ▶

Previewing a hand-some report

If your report looks something like ours, you'll probably be pleased with the results. This is just one example of the results you can achieve with Crystal Reports, with very little effort.

Now you can exit from Crystal Reports. You'll return to dBASE for Windows.

 ▶▶ **W A R N I N G**

Don't close dBASE for Windows while you're in Crystal Reports. Crystal Reports runs partly under Windows independent of dBASE for Windows, and partly as a child of dBASE for Windows.

▶ *Running the Report from the Navigator*

You now can choose your new PHONES_B.RPT file in the Navigator's Reports area and launch it with a double-click or by pressing F2. This will *not* return you to Crystal Reports. That tool is only for designing reports, not running them.

The Report window, shown in Figure 7.17, is the tool for running your reports. As you can see, it's a child window in dBASE for Windows.

The navigation buttons on the speedbar let you browse through your report. Clicking on the print button (or pressing Ctrl-P) sends your report to the printer. When you choose to print, the Printing Reports dialog box appears. It reports on the progress of your print job and gives you a chance to cancel it.

FIGURE 7.17 ▶

Running your report inside dBASE for Windows

▶ *Running the Report from Fon_Main*

Now that we have a report that can be run from the Navigator, we also have a report that should be added to the Fon_Main File menu, as the Print ... option.

Choose the Custom file type in the Navigator and launch the Menu Designer on the PHONE.MNU file. (Right double-click or press Shift-F2 after selecting it.)

Press the ↓ key from the File choice to get to the Exit menu item. Choose Menu ➤ Insert Menu Item, or press Ctrl-N, to put a new Menu object above the Exit choice. Its text should read **Print** ....

Now add the OnClick property for this option. Choose the Events tab of the Object Properties Inspector, click on the OnClick property, and then click on the tool icon to get to the Procedure Editor. Add this two-line program:

> **SET VIEW TO Phones_b**
>
> **REPORT FORM Phones_b**

The first line uses the view we've created, and the second line runs the report we've created.

As a final touch, add another menu separator between the Print ... and Exit options. Then save your work.

From the Navigator, choose Forms and launch Fon_Main. You should be able to choose File ➤ Print ... and have dBASE for Windows launch your new report.

► Handling Inverted Relationships

With the 5.0 release, there is a bug in Crystal Reports that won't let it correctly run a report with an inverted relationship. However, this doesn't mean that you can't use an inverted list, such as our PHONES_A.QBE file. It just means that you must work around the problem.

One way to get your inverted relationship to Crystal is by preparing a single table. Then with the data correctly drawn together into a single table, you can design a single-table report in Crystal.

Preparing a Single Table

To build a consolidated results table from your query, first launch the inverted query by double-clicking on it or selecting it and pressing F2. Choose Table ➤ Table Utilities ... ➤ Export Records .... You'll see the Export Records dialog box, shown in Figure 7.18.

Type a name for your new table and click on OK or press Enter. The export defaults are all exactly what you want. You will get all records and all fields in the exported file. It will be another dBASE data table.

After you have exported your data to a new, single table, select the Untitled report in the Navigator and open it. In Crystal, you can just go ahead and create an attractive report for your single table.

FIGURE 7.18 ▶

*Exporting the
PHONES_A file into
a single table*

There is one problem in this procedure that has been solved for you. In Phones_A, our People and our Orgs tables have fields with the same names; for example, they both have a field named PHONE.

As you scroll through the field list in Crystal, you'll see that the second PHONE field (in the Phones_A query, the fields in the Orgs table are second) has been named PHONE_1. This gives you all the fields, without name conflicts.

▶▶ *You Create Mailing Labels*

Crystal Reports makes the mailing label generation process as simple as it can possibly be. However, there are some tricks of the trade that you may want to use.

For these instructions, we assume that you'll be doing relatively low-volume work, using peel-and-stick labels. For high-volume runs, you would use continuous-form labels suited to automated mailing equipment. The techniques here are still applicable.

To begin with, mailing label work depends on a precise knowledge of the placement of the labels on the label sheet. Specifically, your printer needs to know exactly how far from the paper edge the first label should be placed.

Crystal makes this easy by including a database of the most common label types. If you have Avery (or compatible) labels, you just need to look at your label number, and Crystal will take it from there.

Unfortunately, Crystal cannot look at your hardware, which is a key variable. Your paper-feed path determines the actual placement of text on your label stock. Your labels may be feeding a bit more to the right or left than our labels. You'll need to print test labels to be sure.

The last time we bought labels, each sheet (three across, ten down) cost about 40 cents. That's just over a penny a label, which is not a lot. However, it may take you five or ten test runs to get your labels positioned exactly.

We take a single sheet of labels and make photocopies. If you use a dark setting, you'll be able to see the label borders on your copies. These copies will substitute for the real labels when you do your test printing.

With photocopies loaded in your printer to test your labels, let's get started.

▶ *Generating a Single-Table Label Set*

If you've been running other reports and forms, begin by giving a CLOSE ALL command in the Command window. If any of your data tables are open, Crystal Reports will use those tables, rather than asking you to choose a table or query.

Without any tables open, choose the Untitled option in the Labels file type in the Navigator. Double-click on it or press F2 to launch it in Crystal Reports.

On your way to Crystal, dBASE for Windows will prompt you with an Open Table Required dialog box. Choose your basic People query, PEOPLE_A.QBE.

> In the U.S., you can get a reduced postage rate by presorting your mail on the postal codes. For high-volume work, check with your postal authorities and prepare a modified .QBE file to take advantage of any savings.

Choosing a Label Type

When you enter Crystal Reports from the Labels section of the Navigator, you begin with the Mailing Labels dialog box. The default type is User Defined Label, which lets you describe a nonstandard type of label. The Choose Mailing Label Type drop-down list gives you a selection of the most common Avery labels. If you're using Avery or compatible labels, pick your type from this list, and the rest of the data will be filled in for you. We choose the Avery 5260 type, as shown in Figure 7.19.

Before you leave this dialog box, take a good look at the options you have. Even though Crystal's label database has the correct setting for the left margin, for example, you may need to change it because your printer is feeding paper a little to the right or left of center.

When you click on OK or press Enter, you'll proceed to the Crystal label design screen.

Designing Your Labels

On the design screen, pick your fields from the Insert Database Field dialog box (double-click for quick picking) and position them in the Details band.

FIGURE 7.19 ▶

Choosing Avery 5260 labels

 ▶▶**TIP**

> **Stay to the right of the left margin by two or three characters, to avoid paper-path alignment problems.**

Crystal will repeat each Details section across the page according to the number of labels specified in the Mailing Labels dialog box. For example, the 5260 type is three labels across and ten down. You don't need to worry about this; just position your fields to print correctly on a single label.

Here's the Details section for our Avery 5260 labels:

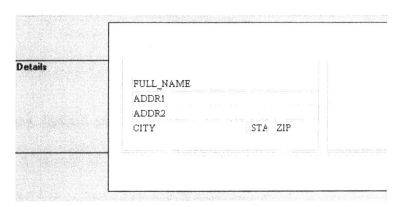

You can see that we've avoided the left margin and stayed away from the very top and bottom of the label. Our fields have been moved in on the right to stay within the boundary of the label.

Checking Your Labels

For a quick check of what Crystal intends to do with your specifications, look at your label design in the Preview window. If it looks reasonable, print a test sheet. (Just one sheet—there's no need to run your whole table.)

You may find that your data is slightly off to the left or right, or slightly too high or low on your label. If necessary, return to the Mailing Labels dialog box and adjust the top and left margins appropriately. You can get to this dialog box by choosing File ➤ Set Label Layout ....

Running Your Labels

Once you are satisfied with the label layout, you can begin to print the real labels from Crystal Reports. Alternatively, you can return to dBASE for Windows and run the labels from there.

When you exit, you'll be given a chance to save your layout. We chose to save it under the file name PEOPLE_A.RPL (the .RPL extension is added automatically), to correspond to the query we use with the labels.

From dBASE for Windows, launch the People_A label file in Run mode. Your labels will appear in the Labels window, just as reports run in the Reports window. From here, you can print them (from the File menu or by clicking on the speedbar icon).

Remember that you can modify the People_A query before you run your labels in dBASE for Windows. For example, you may need to select only the first half of your table.

▶ Generating a Multiple-Table Label Set

Generating labels from a multi-table query is generally no more difficult that generating labels from a one-table query. However, there are some special considerations.

To illustrate these, let's prepare a mailing label job that will send mail to all the people in our People table at the business addresses in our Orgs table.

Selecting the Query and Label Type

If you simply return to Crystal Reports at this point, it will continue to use the last tables you had open. You need to issue a CLOSE ALL command in the Command window before you launch the Untitled file in the Navigator's Labels file type.

When you get the Open Table Required dialog box, choose the PHONES_B.QBE query that we prepared earlier for our multi-table report. This has all the data we need.

Again, you could modify this query to suit your mailing. For example, if you were doing a high-volume mailing, you could sort the table by zip code to take advantage of discounted postal rates.

Launch Crystal Reports and make your selections in the Mailing Labels dialog box (pick the type of label you will be using, or enter custom coordinates for a User-Defined label).

Designing for More Fields

Next, lay out your fields on the label design screen. The only special consideration here is that you'll certainly have more data when you combine employee names with employer names and addresses.

Here's our design for these labels:

```
Details

        FULL_NAME
        NAME
        ADDRESS1
        ADDRESS2
        CITY                    STA  ZIP
```

It includes the full name from the People table, along with the name and three lines of address data from the Orgs table.

In our single-table label design, we avoided problems with the data printing too high or low on the label sheet by not using the first or last label line. With five lines, we recommend using half-line spacing.

The setting for the top margin depends on the size of the font you're using. With a 10-point font size, you're printing six lines per inch. Each line is one-sixth inch—about 0.1666 inch tall. To get a half line vacant at the top of the label, set the top margin at 0.0833 inch.

If your printer's top margin is 0.50 inch, change it to 0.58. That will start the first label line down a half line. The sixth label line (the one we don't use in a five-line label) would be half on the current label and half on the top of the next label.

In some cases, you may find that you need to use a full, six-line label. The simplest way to accommodate this is to switch to a larger label size. If you must put six lines on a ten-deep set of labels, you'll need to experiment with your equipment.

It may work, if your paper feed is extraordinarily accurate, to just use all six lines. More likely, you'll need to bump the top margin up a bit and print with a smaller type size.

Testing and Printing Your Labels

The testing and printing processes for mutiple-table labels are the same as with single-table labels, except that you should be aware of a possible subtle problem with your test sheets. When you photocopied from the labels to test sheets, the copying process could have introduced slight errors. You might, for example, have not adjusted the labels in the precise center of your copying area.

If you've designed a full, or nearly full, label, there is no substitute for doing your final testing on actual label stock.

Once you are satisfied that your labels print correctly, exit Crystal Reports. On the way out, save your new label job as Phones_B (the extension .RPL is automatically applied) to match the query it runs on.

▶▶ Summary

You began your work with Crystal Reports by preparing a new query tying the People table to the Orgs table. With the results of this query, you built a simple report, showing employer and employee data. You used the Preview window and its zoom feature to check your results.

Moving out of the Details area of the Crystal Reports design window, you added a text field in the Page header area for a report title. You adjusted the font size and style to make the title stand out.

In the Page footer area, you used the Insert menu to insert a special field. You chose the Page Number option as a Page footer field.

Your first report repeated the employer data with each employee's data. You improved this by creating a group, grouping on the employer's name field in ascending order. You moved the employer data from the Details section into the Group header section, to have it print before any employee data. This report showed the employer data once, preceding as many employees as needed.

Again, you used the Preview window to check and to edit the results. You used the Format ➤ Section ... menu choice to tell Crystal Reports that your data in each section should be printed together, not split across pages.

With the content of your report set, you went on to improve its appearance. You started with varying the font sizes and styles, highlighting the most important fields.

You added a box around the employer data. You used the Insert ➤ Box choice to add the box and then the Format ➤ Box ... choice to select fill and border characteristics.

You added emphasis to the employee's last name field with the Format ➤ Borders and Colors ... choice. In the Borders and Colors dialog box, you specified a single line around all four sides of the field and added a drop shadow beneath it.

After creating an attractive report, you saved your work and returned to dBASE for Windows, where you ran your finished report in the Reports window, launched from the Navigator. You set up this report as a Print ... choice, which you added to your Fon_Main system.

You learned that a problem in Crystal Reports prevents the current version from handling inverted queries directly. For these queries, you learned to use the Table Utilities tools to export your data into a single table, and then report from that table.

Finally, you went on to create mailing labels. You learned to use the Mailing Label dialog box to select an appropriate label type, and then use the design surface to paint labels in the Details area.

You tested your labels on photocopies of the real label stock. You learned to adjust the margins to compensate for the characteristics of your printer.

Finally, you used the label capability to generate labels drawing data from two tables. You learned to adjust the margins to center five lines of text in a six-line label.

Congratulations! You have finished the tutorial section of this book. Now we'll go on to more advanced topics. At this point, you can pick and choose the topics that are most relevant to your own work with dBASE for Windows.

PART THREE

In this part, we'll examine all the tools and surfaces of dBASE for Windows in depth. Our goal in Part 2 was to be good teachers. We selected the features that we thought were most important and showed you how to use them.

Our goal in this part is to be totally exhaustive, even if we risk being exhausting in the process. We'll cover every menu choice, every mouse-click possibility, and every combination in dBASE for Windows.

Obviously, not all of this information is relevant. In fact, a great deal of it may be irrelevant to your daily use of dBASE for Windows. On the other hand, we think that every bit of it will be relevant to at least someone, doing something. The designers of dBASE for Windows went to the trouble of adding all these features so that they could meet real, working database needs.

In Chapter 8, Mastering the Menus, Navigator, and Command Window, we'll look at the control surfaces for dBASE for Windows. You can drive almost every feature in dBASE for Windows from all three control surfaces, and we explore them all in depth. The menus are particularly fascinating to track down. The menus of dBASE for Windows are constantly changing to reflect the capabilities of the active design or run surface.

In Chapter 9, Mastering Table Tools, we'll cover the Table Structure tool, the Table Records tool, and the Table Utilities in depth. When you get tired of grabbing the bars separating your fields and want dBASE for Windows to remember how wide you like each column, this is the place to turn for help. If you must export selected records and fields to your spreadsheet or word processor, here's where you'll find out how.

In Chapter 10, Mastering Crystal Reports, we'll continue our exploration of the report writer, covering all of its menus, dialog boxes, and speedbars.

In Chapter 11, we complete the Master classes with a thorough treatment of the remaining Crystal Reports topics. We'll look at the cross-tab and mailing label topics that we passed by in Chapter 10, and also study the use of Crystal Reports for generating form letters.

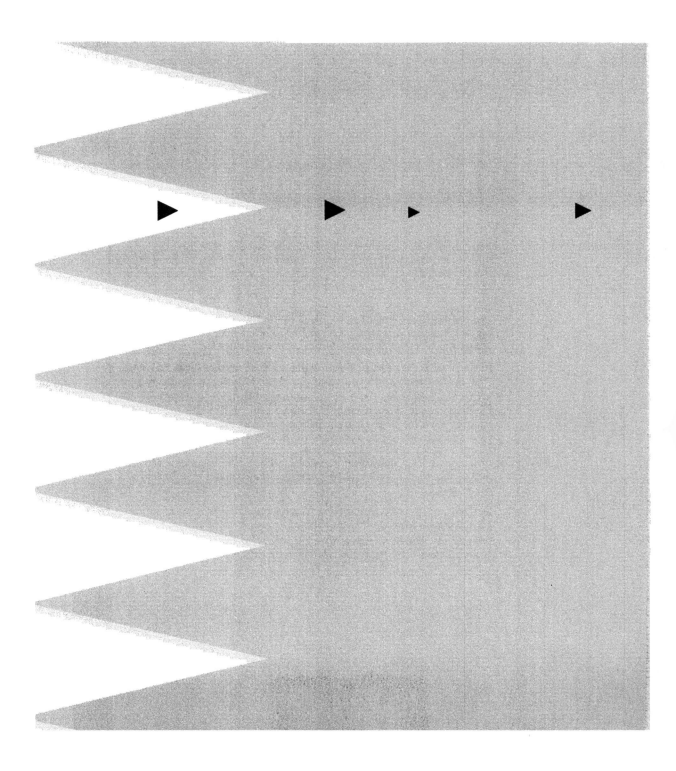

Mastering the Menus, Navigator, and Command Window

▶▶ **I**n Parts 1 and 2 of this book, we've covered the basics of using dBASE for Windows to design tables, manage and manipulate your data, and create reports. Now we'll begin to go into detail about the great variety of features offered by dBASE. This chapter covers the main menus, the Navigator, catalogs, the Command window, and the Expression Builder. Yes, we know you've already worked with some of these features. But here we'll discuss every nook and cranny of these elements, so you'll know where to find whatever options and settings you need.

We'll start with the dBASE for Windows main menus. As you've seen, the menu choices vary depending on the active child window. Here we'll cover the parts that are common to all child types.

▶▶ *Using the File Menu*

The File menu choices vary depending on the type of object that is active. However, the following options are always available when an object of some type is active:

- New (Ctrl-N)
- Open … (Ctrl-O)
- Save (Ctrl-S)
- Close (Ctrl-F4)
- Print … (Ctrl-P)
- Printer Setup …
- Exit
- 1, 2, 3, 4 and 5

Choosing File ➤ New displays this submenu of dBASE file types:

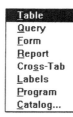

These options work as follows:

- Table launches the Table Structure tool.
- Query invokes the Query Designer.
- Form starts the Form Expert.
- Choosing Report, Cross-Tab or Labels enters Crystal Reports.
- Program starts the Program Editor.
- Catalog starts the Create Catalog process.

Choosing File ➤ Open displays the Open File dialog box. This is a common dialog box that you've seen in one form or another during your work with dBASE for Windows. Appendix B provides a complete discussion of its options.

Items 1 through 5, at the bottom of the menu, are the Most Recently Used (MRU) files: the five files you've used most recently. So, for example, you could choose File ➤ 1, and get to the appropriate file immediately. You can choose to have more or less than five files in the MRU list, via the Application tab in the Properties ➤ Desktop window.

When you use one of the MRU options, the file automatically opens in Run mode, not Design mode. If you choose File ➤ Open, radio buttons give you a choice between modes for most file types.

 ➤➤ **T I P**

For Design mode, open a file through the Navigator. Use the Speed menu or press Shift-F2.

The other options, including Close, Print, Printer Setup, and Exit, do precisely what they say.

▶▶ Using the Edit Menu

The Edit menu always includes the following options:

- Undo (Ctrl-Z)
- Cut (Ctrl-X)
- Copy (Ctrl-C)
- Paste (Ctrl-V)
- Delete (Del)

For most operations from the Navigator, all of the Edit menu choices are dimmed (unavailable). Other times, this menu will contain different options, depending on the active object. For example, when the Command window is active, Edit menu options include copying to and from files and using the Expression Builder.

▶▶ Using the Properties Menu

The Properties menu always includes the Desktop ... choice. Its other options depend on where you are in dBASE for Windows.

Selecting Properties ➤ Desktop brings up a form with six tabs:

- Country
- Table
- Data Entry
- Files
- Application
- Programming

▶ *Setting Country Properties*

The Country tab (Properties ➤ Desktop ➤ Country), shown in Figure 8.1, offers Numeric, Currency, and Date settings. Each group of choices also includes an Example display, which shows how the current selection appears.

FIGURE 8.1 ▶

Properties ➤ *Desktop, Country tab*

Numeric
Separator: |
Point: .
Example: 1,000,000.00

Currency
Position: ⦿ Left ○ Right
Symbol: $
Example: $129.99

Date
Date Format: MDY
Mark: /
☐ Century
Example: 07/27/94

✓ OK
✗ Cancel
? Help

Country / Table / Data Entry / Files / Application / Programming /

Menus, Navigator, and Command

The two Numeric choices are Separator and Point. The Separator is the character that separates whole numbers into groups of three digits (as in one million: 1,000,000). Point refers to the character that separates the whole part from the fractional part (as in 1.23).

The Currency choices include the location of the currency symbol (radio buttons for Left or Right) and an entry field to select a Symbol.

The Date selections give you a choice of Date Format (GERMAN, JAPAN, USA, YMD, MDY, and DMY) and the Mark to separate the components or the date (such as a /, as in 1/1/96). You can also check the Century check box if you wish the full four-digit version of the century to be displayed (1996 if checked; 96 if unchecked).

▶▶ **N O T E**

In all the Desktop Properties tabs, the OK, Cancel, and Help pushbuttons perform their standard functions.

▶ Setting Table Properties

The Table tab (Properties ➤ Desktop ➤ Table), shown in Figure 8.2, offers Multiuser, Default Table Type, Block Sizes, and Other settings.

FIGURE 8.2 ▶

The Properties ➤ Desktop, Table tab

Multiuser Choices

The Table tab's Multiuser selections include check boxes for Lock and Exclusive. With Lock (the default) selected, your table records are locked when you add or update them. When Exclusive is checked, you have exclusive access, which means that no one else can use the table when you are using it.

The Refresh counter lets you set the number of seconds that elapse before any change one user makes in a database is reflected on all other users' screens (when dBASE for Windows is running on a server). The default setting, 0, does no refreshing.

The Reprocess button sets the number of times dBASE for Windows will retry access to a record or table before reporting an error. It defaults to 0, for no retries.

Default Table Type Options

You can choose either dBASE or Paradox as the default table type for dBASE for Windows. With dBASE (the default) selected, if you ask for access to your People table, for example, dBASE for Windows will get data from the PEOPLE.DBF file. If Paradox was selected as the default type, data would be read from the PEOPLE.DB file.

Choosing Block Sizes

The Block Sizes choices let you adjust the size of blocks for indexes (Index Block) and memo files (Memo Block). These adjustments allow you to make performance tradeoffs. Larger block sizes can improve performance, at the cost of wasting disk space.

Your Other Table Choices

The Other section of the Table tab includes the following check boxes:

- Autosave, which saves additions, changes, and deletions to disk after each record is processed. This helps to ensure against data loss (in case of a power outage or computer crash), but it can slow down processing.

- Exact, which determines when one character string is equal to another. If the language driver is French, for example, the letter *e* may or may not have an accent. If Exact is not checked, all the *e*'s are considered equal, regardless of accent. If Exact is checked, the letter and the accent must match.

- Language Driver Check, which warns you if your table was created with a language driver that is incompatible with the ones you have available.

- Deleted, which determines how deleted records are handled. If Deleted is checked, deleted records are not shown in your tables. If it is not checked, deleted records remain visible, with their deletion status shown in a Del column.

- Near, which controls where dBASE for Windows stops after it can't find something you've asked it to look for (with a SEEK or FIND command, for example). When Near is checked, the operation will stop at the first index entry after the target if the target cannot be found. For example, you could SEEK for "Simp" and the SEEK might stop at "Simpson." When Near is not checked, the operation will stop at the end of the file.

▶ Setting Data Entry Properties

The Data Entry tab (Properties ➤ Desktop ➤ Data Entry), shown in Figure 8.3, offers Keyboard, Delimiters, and Bell settings.

FIGURE 8.3 ▶

The Properties ➤ Desktop, Data Entry tab

Keyboard Options

The Keyboard options include the following selections:

- Confirm, which controls whether or not the user must press a key to leave an entry field. If Confirm is checked, the user must press a key, such as Tab, after typing the last character in an entry field. If it is not checked, typing the last character immediately moves the entry point to the next entry field or next control.

- CUA Enter, which controls the effect of pressing the Enter key. Checking CUA Enter enforces the CUA default meaning for Enter, which is the same as clicking an OK pushbutton. When it is not checked, the Enter key is used to complete a field and move to the next field, which is consistent with older dBASE applications.

Menus, Navigator, and Command

Ch.
8

►►N O T E

Checking CUA Enter maintains consistency with other Microsoft Windows applications at some cost in convenience and in breaking with dBASE's older behavior. Leaving this box unchecked is consistent with older dBASE applications and very convenient, but not consistent with other Windows applications.

- Escape, which controls the effect of pressing the Esc key. If Escape is checked, pressing the Esc key exits from the current dialog box. This is consistent with dBASE's former behavior, but is not defined to work in Windows. If this box is not checked, one of the Windows exits (such as Ctrl-F4) must be selected.

- The Typeahead spinbutton, which sets the size of the keyboard typeahead buffer.

Your Choice of Delimiters

The Delimiters choices include a check box for Delimiters and an entry field where you can specify the delimiter Characters. In dBASE IV and earlier, setting Delimiters on made dBASE put the specified characters before and after an entry field. Checking the Delimiters box here does not have this effect in dBASE for Windows forms.

Bell Selections

The selections in the Bell area set the bell's characteristics. If the Bell check box is unchecked, the bell is turned off. The Frequency spinbutton lets you choose a higher or lower note. (Middle C on a piano is about 256.) The Duration spinbutton lets you select the length of time that the bell sounds, in DOS clock ticks. A DOS clock tick happens about 18.2 times every second.

►►T I P

We like the bell—it rings when you come to the end of an entry field, among other places. But a short, high bell (1 tick at 1000 Hz) is all it takes.

The Play Bell pushbutton lets you test the choices you have made.

► Setting File Properties

The Files tab (Properties ➤ Desktop ➤ Files), shown in Figure 8.4, offers Location, Editors, Edit Records, Add Records, and Other settings.

FIGURE 8.4 ►

*The Properties ➤
Desktop, Files tab*

Choosing Locations

The Location section has two entry fields: Search Path and Current Directory. Each entry field has a pushbutton with the tool icon to its right.
You can click on this button if you want to go into the Choose Directory dialog box. Alternatively, you can simply type the directory (with
optional drive specification) in the entry field.

dBASE for Windows will look for files that are not qualified with a directory specification in the current directory first. If it does not find
them, it will continue looking through any directories in the search
path, in the order you specify them.

Choosing Editors

The Editors area has two entry fields: Program Editor and Memo Editor. As with the Location selections, each field has the tool icon pushbutton to its right. Clicking on the icon takes you to a Choose File

dialog box. Alternatively, you can type the name of the editor in the entry field.

Edit Records Choices

The Edit Records section lets you select the default way to look at a table in Run mode. The three radio buttons show your choices:

- In Browse Layout
- In Form Layout
- In Columnar Layout

Add Records Choices

The Add Records section lets you choose the default view for adding new records. The two radio buttons show your choices:

- In Form Layout
- In Columnar Layout

> **The Form Layout choice is generally better, unless you normally have more fields than will fit on a screen.**

Other Selections

The Other selections include four check boxes:

- Older File Types, which controls the file types that appear in file lists.
- Full Path, which is useful to dBASE programmers. If checked, it tells functions that return a file name to return the full path along with the name.
- Sessions, which can be turned off if you need to emulate a dBASE III or older dBASE version. With Sessions on, each table you launch runs in a separate session, as if you were multiple users.
- Title, which turns on prompting for item descriptions when you use a catalog.

If Older File Types is checked, the list of dBASE file types includes the following:

- View (*.VUE)
- Filter (*.QRY)
- Format (*.FMT)
- dBASE/DOS Report (*.FRM)
- dBASE/DOS Label (*.LBG)
- dBASE/DOS Label (*.LBL)
- dBASE/DOS Report (*.FRG)

These types are included to support dBASE IV and earlier systems. They are not used in Microsoft Windows programs. If this box is not checked, these file types are not shown in the file lists.

▶ Setting Application Properties

The Application tab (Properties ➤ Desktop ➤ Application), shown in Figure 8.5, offers Speedbar Position, Status Bar, and Other settings.

FIGURE 8.5 ▶

The Properties ➤ Desktop, Application tab

Speedbar Position Choices

For Speedbar Position, you have six choices for positioning the speedbar:

- Horizontal, Top
- Horizontal, Bottom
- Vertical, Right
- Vertical, Left
- Horizontal, Floating
- Vertical, Floating

Vertical speedbars lose the end icons: Tutor, Expert, Command, and Navigator. (You can use Window ➤ 1 for the Navigator and Window ➤ 2 for the Command window.) The floating speedbars can be dragged with the mouse.

We prefer a horizontal speedbar for most use. The one exception is when we are programming. Then we use a vertical speedbar, because it gives us a few more lines of code in the Program Editor.

Menus, Navigator, and Command

Ch. 8

Status Bar Choices

The Status Bar check box controls whether not the status bar appears. You can uncheck it if you want to turn the status bar off. The entry field, Status Bar Message Font, shows the currently selected font. You can select another font for the status bar. Clicking on the tool pushbutton to the right of this field opens the Font dialog box.

Other Selections

The Object Properties Outline check box in the Other section controls the appearance of the Object Properties Inspectors. Unchecking it turns the outlining feature off in the Object Properties Inspector. All the object's properties (and events and methods) are shown in a single, long list.

▶▶**T I P**

Turning off the outlining feature might be useful if you're teaching a class and want to simplify the Object Properties Inspector tool for beginners.

The MRU Size spinbutton controls the number of MRU files that you can access as 1, 2, and so on in the File menu.

▶ Setting Programming Properties

The Programming tab (Properties ➤ Desktop ➤ Programming), shown in Figure 8.6, offers Command Output, Program Development, and Other settings.

FIGURE 8.6 ▶

The Properties ➤ Desktop, Programming tab

Command Output Choices

The Command Output area has the following spinbutton choices:

- Decimals, which specifies the number of decimals to display when showing numbers. The default is 2, and the range is 0 to 18. Internally, dBASE for Windows stores floating-point numbers accurate to 15 decimal places, regardless of the setting of Decimals.

- Precision, which sets the number of decimal places dBASE for Windows stores for Numeric data (not for Float data). This defaults to 16 and ranges from 10 to 20.

- Margin, which establishes a default left margin for printed output. It defaults to 0 and ranges from 0 to 254. Crystal Reports handles margins when you use that tool. This setting affects your dBASE for Windows File ➤ Print printouts.

The Command Output section also includes three check boxes:

- Space, which determines whether the output of ? and ?? commands inserts a space between items in the command's parameter list (for example, between names when you give the command ? First_name, Last_name). This setting is retained for compatibility with dBASE IV and earlier programs.

- Talk, which controls whether or not results are shown in the Command window's results pane. It is on by default. If it is checked, it directs the results of assignment statements in programs and in the Command window to the results pane of the Command window. For example, if you entered x=2+2 in the Command window, the number 4 would show in the results pane if this option is checked.

- Headings, which controls the use of field names over columns displayed with commands such as LIST and SUM. By default, it is on, and field names are used as column headings.

Program Development Choices

The Program Development section has two check boxes. Coverage turns on the program coverage feature, which programmers use to get a detailed analysis of which parts of their programs are most heavily used.

The Ensure Compilation setting is also used by programmers. With this box checked, dBASE for Windows will always check to see if a program source file (such as a .PRG or .WFM file) has been modified since the corresponding object file (.PRO or .WFO file) was created. If the program source has been changed, dBASE for Windows will recompile the source, creating a new object version.

If you are not developing programs by directly editing .PRG files, leaving Ensure Compilation checked only slows down dBASE for Windows. The tools that create programs for you, such as the Form Designer, handle compilation.

Other Choices

The Other section has Design and Safety check boxes, which are both checked by default. If Design is not checked, the Design abilities of dBASE for Windows are turned off (presumably, for users who only run a system created by others). With Safety checked, operations that could destroy existing data (creating a new file which has the same name as an existing file, for instance) trigger a warning dialog box.

►► **WARNING**

Always leave Safety checked, for safety's sake! Sometimes programs will turn safety off temporarily (for example, to create a TEMP.DBF for some temporary data, deliberately overwriting the previous TEMP.DBF) but Safety will save you from a lot of mistakes.

►► *Using the Window Menu*

The Window menu has these options:

- Cascade (Shift-F5)
- Tile Horizontally
- Tile Vertically (Shift-F4)
- Arrange Icons
- Close All Windows
- 1 Navigator
- 2 Command
- 3 (and higher) your windows

▶ *Arranging Your Windows*

The Cascade, Tile Horizontally, and Tile Vertically options make neat (if not always helpful) arrangements of your windows. If you have not used this feature in other Microsoft Windows programs, open several windows and try it. Figure 8.7 shows cascaded windows. Figures 8.8 and 8.9 show tiled arrangements.

FIGURE 8.7

Cascaded windows

The Arrange Icons option makes a neat arrangement of your icons. Figures 8.10 and 8.11 show a before-and-after example of using this option.

▶ *Closing and Opening Windows*

The Close All Windows option does just what it says. You don't need to worry about saving your work. If any window contains new or changed

FIGURE 8.8 ►

Horizontally tiled windows

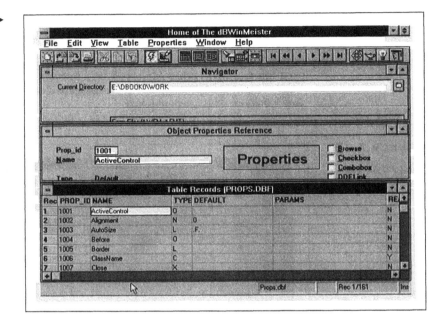

data, dBASE for Windows will ask you if you want to save the file before closing. This is the same close procedure that takes place when you exit from dBASE for Windows.

Window 1 is always the Navigator window. Choosing Window ➤ 1 brings the Navigator into focus on top of any other open windows. Similarly, window 2 is the Command window, which can be given focus by choosing Window ➤ 2.

The remaining numbers are for your open child windows. If you have more than seven child windows (nine, including Navigator and Command), an additional menu option appears: More Windows. Selecting

FIGURE 8.9 ▶

*Vertically tiled
windows*

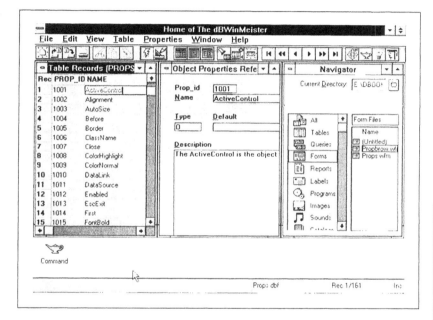

this option opens the Select Window dialog box, which will look something like this:

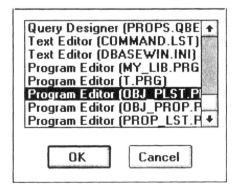

FIGURE 8.10 ▶

Before Arrange Icons

▶▶ Using the Help Menu

The Help menu has these options:

- Contents (Shift-F1)
- Search ...
- Views and Tools
- Language
- Keyboard
- Experts
- Interactive Tutors ...
- How to Use Help
- About dBASE 5.0 for Windows ...

You can go immediately to the Table of Contents by choosing the Con-tents option (or by pressing Shift-F1). The Search ... option brings up Windows' Search dialog box.

The Views and Tools, Language, and Keyboard options name three of the most commonly accessed sections in the Table of Contents. Choos-ing Keyboard, for example, is the same as choosing the Keyboard topic from the Table of Contents.

The Experts option brings up the Experts submenu. From this menu you can choose the Form Expert.

The Interactive Tutors ... choice takes you to the main menu of the Tu-tors. This is the same as clicking on the tutor button on the speedbar (the one on far right).

The How to Use Help choice takes you into this topic in Windows' Help system.

The About dBASE 5.0 for Windows ... brings up an information win-dow, such as the one shown in Figure 8.12.

FIGURE 8.12 ▶

About dBASE for Windows

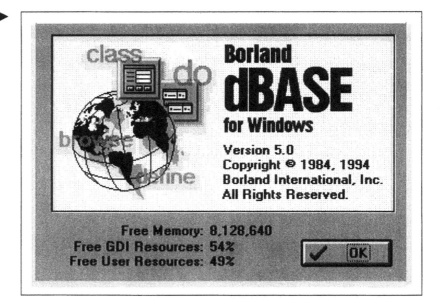

▶▶ *Working with the Navigator*

The Navigator, an MDI child window, is a simple, powerful tool for directing all your work in dBASE for Windows. You can operate it fully with only a mouse, and you can operate it fully with only a keyboard. (In fact, there are two different ways to drive it from the keyboard!) Of course, you can combine the two.

There are three main areas in the Navigator window:

- Directory area
- File Types menu
- Files list

Changes in Navigator settings can substantially impact the appearance of your Navigator. Compare the Navigators shown in Figures 8.13 and 8.14 to see just how different these can be. You can control the appearance of

FIGURE 8.13 ▶

One Navigator

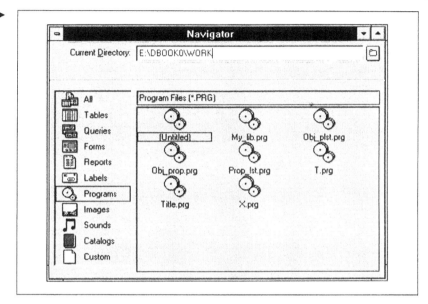

FIGURE 8.14 ▶

A different Navigator

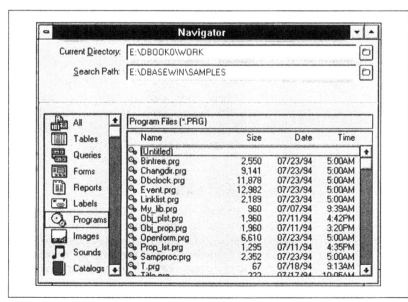

the Navigator window through the Properties ➤ Navigator choice, as discussed later in this chapter.

▶ The Directory Area

The directory area, the top part of the Navigator, has one or two entry fields, Current Directory and Search Path. The pushbuttons to the right of each entry field access the Choose Directory dialog box, which lets you choose a different directory than the current one. Its icon is a file folder (we think; we're not sure that miniscule icons are terribly helpful).

The Current Directory

The current directory is the directory in which you're storing your work for a particular project. If you're working on multiple projects, you simply switch from one current directory to another, to switch projects. The Navigator will change all its files accordingly. (See Appendix C for information about using multiple DBWIN.INI files for different projects.)

You can type the directory into the entry field, or choose the pushbutton to access the directory list. You can click the pushbutton, or tab to it and press the spacebar (or Enter).

 ▶▶ T I P

In the directory list, the spacebar functions like a mouse click, and the Enter key functions like a double-click. For example, pressing the spacebar will expand a directory or, if the directory is expanded, hide the subdirectories.

The Search Path

The Search Path entry field and pushbutton are shown if the Use Supplemental Search Path check box is selected in the Navigator's Properties dialog box. dBASE for Windows will look at all files in the current directory, and in the Search Path directory. One common use for a supplemental path is to use local programs to access data on a network drive.

You can have more than one supplemental directory. Type them into the entry field, separated by commas. (Don't use the Choose Directory dialog box, because that overwrites anything in the entry field with a single choice.)

▶ The File Types Menu

The file types list on the left side of the Navigator window is a custom menu (a slick, Borland-designed menu, not standard Windows) that lists the different types of files you can manipulate:

- All
- Tables
- Queries
- Forms
- Reports
- Labels
- Programs
- Images
- Sounds
- Catalogs
- Custom

Since each type of file corresponds to a major functional area of dBASE for Windows, this lets you control your dBASE for Windows work by picking files.

You can select a file type by clicking on it in this menu. With the keyboard, you can press Tab to reach this menu, then use the ↑ and ↓ keys to select a particular type, or type the first letter in the file type to move to that type.

▶ The Files List

The files list is in the area to the right of the file type menu. This has two parts: a title line and the list itself.

The title line reflects the choice you made in the file type menu. The file name extensions that appear depend on whether or not the Older File Types check box in the Desktop Properties Files tab is checked, as follows:

File Types	With Older File Types On	With Older File Types Off
dBASE files	All	All
Table files	*.DBF, *.DB	*.DBF, *.DB
Query files	*.QBE, *.VUE, *.QRY	*.QBE
Form files	*.WFM, *.FMT	*.WFM
Report files	*.RPT, *.RPC, *.FRM, *.FRG	*.RPT, *.RPC
Label files	*.RPL, *.LBL, *.LBG	*.RPL
Program files	*.PRG	*.PRG
Image files	*.BMP, *.PCX	*.BMP, *.PCX
Sound files	*.WAV	*.WAV
Catalog files	*.CAT	*.CAT

If you have selected Custom files, an entry field follows the text *Custom Files:*. You can enter any other file type(s) you wish here. Enter them as DOS file masks (for example, in the format *.*XXX*). You can enter multiple types, separated by commas.

The list itself includes your files, of whatever type you chose. The appearance of this listing is determined by your selection in the View menu. Here's the list with large icons:

Here's the same list with small icons:

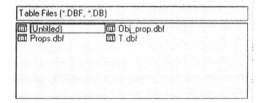

And here's what it looks like when Details is selected:

As you can see, each option shows an icon and file name. The details version adds file size, and the date and time of last update, as well.

In this list, you can choose a file by clicking on it or by moving to it using the arrow keys. Alternatively, you can type the first letter of the file name to move to it. (Tab and Shift-Tab move from the file types menu to the files list.)

Double-clicking on a file launches it in Run mode. For example, double-clicking on a form (.WFM file) runs the form. Double right-clicking brings up a file in Design mode. Right-clicking brings up a Speed menu. You can press F2 to run the selected file. Pressing Shift-F2 launches the file in Design mode.

▶ Using the Navigator Main Menu

The File, Window, and Help menus are not changed in the Navigator. Two new menu choices are added, and the Edit and Properties choices are changed. The new menu options are View and Navigator.

The Edit menu has one additional choice in the Navigator: Delete, with Del as the shortcut key. When an Untitled file is selected in the files list, this choice is grayed (not available). When a named file is selected, choosing this option will delete the selected file.

 ▶▶ **T I P**

> **Files can also be deleted from the Speed menu. Right-click on the file, then click on Delete.**

Using the View Menu

The Navigator's View menu looks like this:

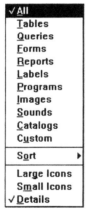

The choice corresponding to the currently selected file type is checked. A second check indicates which of the display options (Large Icons, Small Icons, or Details) is currently selected.

 ▶▶ **T I P**

> **View gives you a keyboard shortcut for selecting a file type. For Queries, for example, press Alt-V, then Q.**

The last three choices control the files list display, selecting the displays shown earlier, in the section about the files list.

The Sort choice displays this submenu:

> √ by **N**ame
> by **T**ype and Extension
> by **S**ize
> by **D**ate and Time

These options control the order in which your files are displayed in the files list.

Using the Navigator Menu

The Navigator menu generally has a New option, and it always has a Refresh Items option. The Refresh Items option forces the Navigator to reexamine the current and search path directories for files that may have appeared since the last time the Navigator looked. For example, you might use this option after you run a form that creates or deletes other files.

The New choice depends on the type of file selected in the files list, and whether it is a named file or Untitled. For untitled files, the new choice is the type of file, such as New Table when the Table type is selected, or New Query when the Query type is selected. The shortcut key is Shift-F2 for all the new file types. When the type is Reports, an additional choice is New Cross-Tab. The New Catalog choice leads to the Create Catalog dialog box. The default type is *.CAT. For the Custom type, the choices are Design Menu (Shift-F2) and Edit As Program.

For named files, the Navigator menu choices are as follows:

- **Tables:** Edit Records (F2), Add Records, and Design Table Structure (Shift-F2)

- **Queries:** Run Query (F2), Design Query (Shift-F2), and Edit as Program

- **Forms:** Run Form (F2), Design Form (Shift-F2), and Edit as Program

- **Reports:** Run Report (F2) and Design Report (Shift-F2)

- **Labels:** Run Labels (F2) and Design Labels (Shift-F2)
- **Programs:** Do (F2), Debug, and Design Program (Shift-F2)
- **Images:** Display Image (F2) and Design Image (Shift-F2)
- **Sounds:** Play Sound (F2) and Design Sound (Shift-F2)
- **Catalogs:** Open Catalog (F2)
- **Custom:** The choices vary depending on the file extension.

▶ Using the Navigator's Properties Menu

In the Navigator, the Properties menu has the standard Desktop choice (discussed earlier in the chapter) plus the Navigator ... and Selected File Item ... (Alt-Enter) choices.

Setting Navigator Properties

Choosing Properties ▶ Navigator displays the Navigator Properties dialog box. This is a single tab with three sections: Large Icons, Small Icons, and Details.

The Large Icons choices include two spinbuttons. One lets you adjust the X Spacing (horizontal), and the other is for adjusting the Y Spacing (vertical). These spacings are in pixels. The X default is 100; the Y default is 47.

The Small Icons choices are similar. Its two spinbuttons are X Spacing and Y Spacing. These default to 117 and 13, respectively. The small icons are wider, but very short, because the file name appears to the right of the small icon.

The Details section has just one spinbutton, for Y Spacing, which defaults to 13. If you have lots of files to list, it can be reduced to its minimum: 12.

The Navigator Properties dialog box also has a Use Supplemental Search Path check box. As discussed earlier, checking this box enables the supplemental path and adds the Search Path entry field to the Navigator window.

In addition to the three normal pushbuttons (OK, Cancel, and Help), a fourth pushbutton, Reset, is added. This lets you reset the spacings to their original default values.

Selected File Items

When you choose Properties ➤ Selected File Item, you see a dialog box giving details about the file. A sample is shown in Figure 8.15. This dialog box is also available from the Speed menu and by selecting a file and pressing Alt-Enter.

FIGURE 8.15 ▶

*File Item Properties
dialog box*

▶ The Navigator Speed Menus

The Navigator has a Speed menu that you can access by right-clicking in the Navigator window, anywhere outside the files list rectangle. This Speed menu has the following choices:

- Navigator Properties …
- Cut (Ctrl-X)
- Copy (Ctrl-C)
- Paste (Ctrl-V)

Choosing Navigator Properties is just like choosing Properties ➤ Navigator from the main menu. It accesses the Navigator Properties dialog box.

The Clipboard-related choices apply to text in the three entry fields (Current Directory, Search Path, and Custom Files).

Navigator Files List Speed Menus

If you right-click on any file in the Navigator's files list, you'll see a Speed menu for the type of file you have selected. There are separate Speed menus for the Untitled and for the named files in the files list.

With an Untitled choice, the only option on its Speed menu is to create one. For example, when the file type is Tables, the Speed menu will have the choice New Table (Shift-F2).

The Speed menus for named files have the following choices:

- **Tables Speed menu:** Table Properties ... (Alt-Enter), Delete (Del), Edit Records (F2), Add Records, and Design Table Structure (Shift-F2)

- **Queries Speed menu:** Query Properties ... (Alt-Enter), Delete (Del), Run Query (F2), Design Query (Shift-F2), and Edit as Program

- **Forms Speed menu:** Form Properties ... ((Alt-Enter)), Delete (Del), Run Form (F2), Design Form (Shift-F2), and Edit as Program

- **Reports Speed menu:** Report Properties ... (Alt-Enter), Delete (Del), Run Report (F2), and Design Report (Shift-F2)

- **Labels Speed menu:** Label Properties ... (Alt-Enter), Delete (Del), Run Labels (F2), and Design Labels (Shift-F2)

- **Programs Speed menu:** Program Properties ... (Alt-Enter), Delete (Del), Do (F2), Debug, and Design Program (Shift-F2)

- **Images Speed menu:** Image Properties ... (Alt-Enter), Delete (Del), Display Image (F2), and Design Image (Shift-F2)

- **Sounds Speed menu:** Sound Properties ... (Alt-Enter), Delete (Del), Play Sound (F2), and Design Sound (Shift-F2)

- **Catalogs Speed menu:** Catalog Properties ... (Alt-Enter), Delete (Del), and Open Catalog (F2)

- **Custom Speed menu:** Depends on the type of file selected

▶▶ *The Other Navigators: Catalogs*

Some work can be organized conveniently in disk directories. We've used our \DBWORK directory to organize our phone list system by keeping it all in one place. There are times when this works well, and there are times when it doesn't work. Here are a few examples of situations in which you wouldn't be able to keep all your system's files in the same directory:

- You may have tables that are critical to several systems. If the systems each have several forms and reports, keeping them all together in a single directory leads to a situation that is, at best, difficult to manage. (Take a look at your \WINDOWS directory to see what happens when you have far too many files in one place.)

- You may develop or acquire libraries of useful routines and functions that you want to use in several systems. Again, you'll need to draw work from multiple directories into a single system.

- If you're working on a network, your forms may be local while your tables are remote.

In each of these situations, the catalog is your answer.

You can think of a catalog as a Navigator that is not built from the files in a directory (or a directory plus a search path). A catalog is assembled from whatever components you choose. With a catalog, you can have forms in one location, library routines in another place, and data spread over one or more local and remote drives. Whatever organization makes sense for your work makes a fine catalog.

▶ *The Catalog Window*

Figure 8.16 shows a catalog that we constructed for our phone list system, active over the Navigator.

Our Navigator is using a default working directory on the E: drive. As you can see, the catalog does not depend on the current directory or supplemental search path setting.

FIGURE 8.16 ▶

The catalog is a type of Navigator

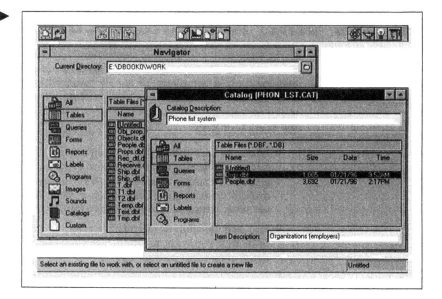

The catalog itself shows a system description where the Navigator shows a directory. On the lower right, it shows a description of the individual catalog item.

You can see that the Navigator includes more file types than the catalog does. The following types are not available in a catalog:

- Images
- Sounds
- Catalogs
- Custom

When you include images and sounds in your forms or reports, they are linked with the item to which you attach them, so they can be part of your system, even though they are not listed in the catalog.

▶ ▶ **N O T E**

> **You obviously don't need a Catalog file type inside a catalog, but we do miss the Custom file type. We like including *.MNU or whatever else is needed in the Custom section, a capability that you lose with a catalog.**

▶ *Building a Catalog*

Creating a catalog is no different than creating any other item from the Navigator. Pick the Catalog type, select the Untitled entry, and press F2 or double-click.

This launches the Create Catalog dialog box. You enter a name (optionally changing the drive and directory), and press Enter or click on OK.

Next, you go to the Catalog Item Description dialog box, shown in Figure 8.17. This dialog box appears, appropriately labeled, for the catalog and for every item that you enter in the catalog. Type in a description and select OK.

FIGURE 8.17 ▶

Entering a description for the catalog

Catalog Item Description

Catalog Name: CATALOG.CAT
Catalog Item Name: TMP.CAT
Catalog Description:

✓ OK   ✗ Cancel   ? Help

Menus, Navigator, and Command

▶ ▶
Ch.
8

Don't labor over the descriptions. The catalog fields that display the catalog and item descriptions are entry fields, so you can add to or change the descriptions whenever you see them.

▶ Adding Items to the Catalog

There are several ways to add items to the catalog. The simplest way is to open the catalog and leave it open as you continue your work. You can minimize it to an icon so that it doesn't get in your way.

As you open tables, queries, and so on, each one is added to your catalog. If the item is not part of the catalog, the Catalog Item Description dialog box is launched so you can add a description.

You can click the Cancel pushbutton if you do not want to add a description, but the selected item will still be added to your catalog. We're not sure if this is a bug or a feature. If you don't want an item in your catalog, select it and choose Delete from the Speed menu.

After you choose Delete from a catalog, you'll see two dialog boxes in succession. The first one asks you if you want to delete the item from the catalog. If you say yes, the next dialog asks you if you want to delete it from your disk. Obviously, you can say no in the second dialog box if you want to save the item but remove it from the current catalog.

With your catalog active, these are the other ways you can add an item to that catalog:

- Click on the add a file speedbar button (shown in the margin).
- Choose Catalog ➤ Add Item ....
- Press Ctrl-A.
- With the mouse, drag the file from the Navigator to the catalog.

Each of these actions launches the Add Catalog Item dialog box. Select a file from this dialog box, and dBASE for Windows will open the Catalog Item Description dialog box so you can add a description.

► *Using a Catalog*

Using a catalog is essentially the same as using the Navigator. There are some minor differences, however. First, the Navigator menu choice is replaced by the Catalog menu choice. The choices in the Catalog menu are the ones that are appropriate to the item selected in the catalog. For example, here are the choices that are available when the Tables file type is selected:

Edit Records	**F2**
Add Records	
Design Table Structure	Shift+F2
Add Item...	Ctrl+A

When a catalog is active, the Properties menu has the Catalog Window... choice. If you select this choice, it launches the Catalog Properties dialog box, which is identical, except for the title and the absence of the Use Supplemental Search Path check box, to the Navigator Properties dialog box.

Another difference is that the add a file speedbar button is located just to the left of the delete file button. With the Navigator active, you add files by creating them. With a catalog, you add existing files (or create new ones).

► *The Catalog Is a Table*

The catalog that is created is stored as a table on your disk, like any other dBASE for Windows table, except that the extension is .CAT, not .DBF. To launch a catalog as a table, in the Command window, give these commands:

```
USE catalogname.cat
BROWSE
```

You must provide the .CAT extension to the USE command, because it defaults to a .DBF of .DB table.

When you give these two commands, the Table Records tool is launched with your catalog data. Ours is shown in Figure 8.18.

FIGURE 8.18 ▶

Browsing a catalog

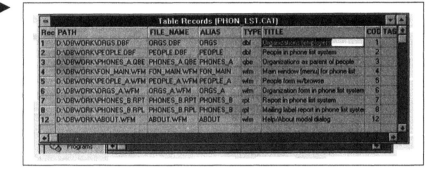

▶▶ *Working in the Command Window*

The Command window is always available from the speedbar, via the Aladdin's lamp button, or from the keyboard as <u>W</u>indow ➤ <u>2</u>. A sample Command window is shown in Figure 8.19.

FIGURE 8.19 ▶

One Command window setup

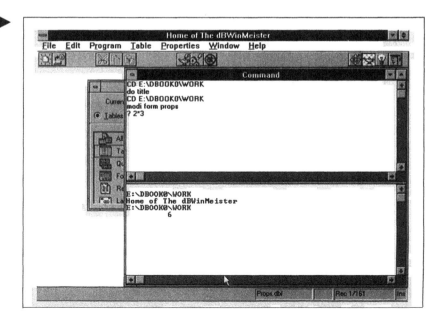

The Command window provides an alternative to the Navigator for driving dBASE for Windows. Most dBASE for Windows users will operate from the Navigator for most operations, because it's a much friendlier tool. On the other hand, while the Navigator provides ease of use, the Command window provides *total* power for the true dBASE for Windows master.

The end result of most dBASE for Windows operations is a command given to the dBASE engine. These commands are echoed, as native dBASE commands, to the Command window, as you may have noticed while you worked in the Navigator.

The Command window has two panes, which default to the arrangement shown in Figure 8.19. The top pane is for input, and the bottom pane shows the results of commands given in the input pane.

You can drag the bar between the panes to divide the window into proportions that suit your requirements. The window can be mostly commands, with a tiny results pane, or vice versa. When a dBASE for Windows program (.PRG file) is running, the input pane disappears, and the results pane shows all non-Windows output.

 ▶▶ **N O T E**

> **dBASE IV and older systems run in the results pane of the Command window.**

▶ *Entering Commands in the Input Pane*

The input pane is a memory-only text editor. You type a command, and it executes immediately. As you accumulate commands, you add text. This text can be cut or copied into the Clipboard, and commands can be pasted in from the Clipboard. Through the Command window menus, you can bypass the Clipboard, reading and writing directly from .PRG files or other files.

When the Command window is active, the input pane is active by default. If you switch focus to the results pane (for example, by selecting results to copy into the Clipboard), you can just click in the input pane to position the insertion point (I-beam) wherever you want.

The ? Command

One of the simplest dBASE for Windows commands is the ? command, which you've met in earlier chapters. The ? command writes the results of any valid dBASE for Windows expression into the results pane. Here are some expressions you can try typing in the input pane:

```
? 2+2
? 'John ' + 'Smith'
? DATE()
? DATE()+1
? LEFT('abcdefg',3)
? 'Mary' + 1
```

The last one gives you an error.

►►NOTE

You can build expressions in the Expression Builder, which is covered later in this chapter, or just type them in directly.

Most of today's dBASE programmers got started programming by typing simple commands in the dBASE dot prompt environment, which was the predecessor to the Command window. Most of tomorrow's dBASE programmers will get their start typing commands in the Command window. It's a wonderful place to try things out. The ? command is used constantly by experienced dBASE users and programmers to try expressions out.

The MODIFY Command

Another command commonly used in the input pane is MODIFY. The full command is:

```
MODIFY <file type> <file name>
```

For example, you could give any of the following commands (assuming you have file with these names):

```
MODIFY FORM people.wfm
MODIFY QUERY people.qbe
MODIFY REPORT people.rpt
MODIFY LABEL people.rpl
```

```
MODIFY COMMAND people.prg
MODIFY FILE any.txt
```

dBASE for Windows commands are not case-sensitive. They can all be abbreviated to just their first four letters. Additionally, most of the file extensions above are implied by the object type. These are the commands as a dBASE master would really enter them:

```
modi form people
modi quer people
modi repo people
modi labe people
modi comm people
modi file any.txt
```

The USE Command

To use a data table in the Command window, you give a USE command. Your subsequent table commands apply to that table. These are some typical examples:

```
USE e:\dbmaster\people.dbf
MODIFY STRUCTURE
BROWSE
DO people.wfm
```

The DO command runs a program, form, or report.

If your current directory includes the file, you don't need the drive and directory specification. Additionally, the USE command implies the .DBF file type, so you can omit the extension. Again, you can abbreviate to four letters and use lowercase letters. Here are the more likely versions of those commands:

```
use people
modi stru
brow
do people.wfm
```

Note that you cannot abbreviate the file name. The default file type for the DO command is .PRG, so the .WFM is needed here.

Running Commands from the Input Pane

If you've tried any of these examples, you've seen that you type a command and then press Enter. The command then runs. But that's not the only option.

If you select any set of one or more commands (drag the mouse to select text), pressing Enter causes the currently selected set to execute. If there is no selected text, the command that has the insertion point, before you press Enter, is executed. This latter is the case when you type a command and press Enter.

But there's more to that last option. If you want to repeat a command that is anywhere in the input pane, simply use the ↑ or ↓ key to move the insertion point to the line that has the command, and press Enter. Alternatively, click anywhere on the command and press Enter.

This means that sometimes its easier to repeat operations from the Command window than it would be in the Navigator.

For more on commands, refer to Chapter 13.

 ▶▶ **W A R N I N G**

With the exception of the ? command, all the commands that direct output to the results pane are supported only so that dBASE for Windows can still run dBASE IV and earlier applications. dBASE for Windows uses objects and properties on forms outside this window. Don't use commands that write to or read from the results pane, except for the ? command.

▶ *Checking the Output in the Results Pane*

You don't do any operations in the results pane, except for copying results to the Clipboard and the input operations for legacy (dBASE IV and earlier) applications. dBASE 5.0 and later programs all use windows outside the results pane.

We think the results pane, combined with the input pane, is invaluable for testing commands and expressions, so we expect this use of the results pane to have a very long future.

▶ *The Command Window Speedbar*

When the Command window is active, its speedbar looks like this:

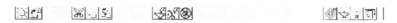

Table 8.1 shows the functions of the speedbar buttons in the Command window.

▶ **TABLE 8.1:** *Command Window Speedbar Buttons*

BUTTON	FUNCTION
	Create one of the primary types of files
	Open one of the primary types of files
	Cut selected text to the Clipboard
	Copy selected text to the Clipboard
	Paste the contents of the Clipboard at the insertion point
	Run the currently selected commands
	Run a program
	Launch the dBASE for Windows Debugger
	Launch the Navigator
	Launch Command window (current selection)
	Run an Expert
	Run a Tutorial

Menus, Navigator, and Command

Ch.
8

▶ *The Command Window's Main Menu*

The File, Window, and Help menus are not changed in the Command window. Two new menus are added, and the Edit and Properties menus are changed. The new menus options are Program and Table.

▶ *Using the Edit Menu*

The Edit Menu always includes the following standard options:

- Undo (Ctrl-Z)
- Cut (Ctrl-X)
- Copy (Ctrl-C
- Paste (Ctrl-V)
- Delete (Del)

It also includes these options:

- Select All
- Clear Results
- Insert from File ...
- Copy to File ...
- Search ➤
- Build Expression ... (Ctrl-E)
- Execute Selection

These new options are discussed in the following sections.

Edit ➤ *Select All*

The Select All option selects (highlights) all the text in the input pane. (You can also do this by dragging with the mouse.) This is useful to either reexecute the commands or to cut or copy the commands to the Clipboard or another file.

Edit ➤ *Clear Results*

The Clear Results option clears the results pane. This choice is the same as issuing a CLEAR command in the input pane.

Edit ➤ *Insert from File* ...

The Insert from File option is used to copy in the contents of a file (normally a .PRG or .WFM file). It brings up an Insert from File dialog box, in which you specify the file you want to insert. The default file type is Text (*.TXT).

Edit ➤ *Copy to File* ...

The Copy to File option is used to copy the contents of the input pane to a program file (normally a .PRG or .WFM file). It displays a Copy to File dialog box, in which you specify the file you want to write. The default file type is Text (*.TXT).

Edit ➤ *Search* ➤

Choosing Edit ➤ Search choice displays this text search submenu:

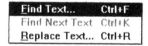

Edit ➤ *Build Expression* ...

The Build Expression choice launches the Expression Builder. You can build your expressions using this tool and then paste them into the Command window input pane. The Expression Builder is discussed later in this chapter.

Using the Expression Builder is much slower, but much more reliable, than typing expressions directly into the input pane. You'll want to try both methods to find which one gets your results most quickly.

►►**T I P**

> **Don't use the Expression Builder just to avoid mistakes. The Command window will trap mistakes and you can try again, editing the erroneous line. Your data is not at risk from a syntax error.**

Edit ➤ Execute Selection

The Execute Selection option gives mouse users a convenient substitute for pressing the Enter key. Is this worthwhile? We think so. How else can you sip your coffee without stopping your work?

► Using the Program Menu

The Command window's Program menu has four options:

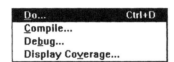

These options are discussed in the following sections.

Program ➤ Do

The Do option opens an Execute Program dialog box, which is like the other Open File dialog boxes. The available file types are *.PRG, *.PRO, and *.WFM. The program you select is run when you choose OK in this dialog box.

 ►►**N O T E**

> **There are no radio buttons, so you cannot choose Design mode here.**

Program ➤ *Compile*

The Compile option opens the Compile Program dialog box, which is similar to the Execute Program dialog box. The only difference between this dialog box and the one displayed by Edit ➤ Do is that is that the compiled file type *.PRO is not available here.

Unlike the Do option, this choice compiles the source program into an executable form, but does not run it. This choice is used during programming to check that your syntax is all correct, without actually starting your program.

Program ➤ *Debug*

The Debug choice opens the same Execute Program dialog box as the Do option. However, once you have chosen the program, it then starts the dBASE for Windows Debugger.

This is a tool primarily useful to advanced programmers. It lets you examine and tinker with the inner workings of a dBASE for Windows program while it is running.

Program ➤ *Display Coverage*

The Display Coverage option opens a Display Coverage dialog box. This lets programmers choose a coverage file (the only extension is .COV).

Coverage files are an option available to programmers. They show how often each section of a program is used. This information lets the programmer focus on the most frequently used portions of the code in tuning for optimum perfomance.

▶ *Using the Table Menu*

The Table choice on the Command window's main menu displays this menu:

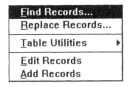

```
Find Records...
Replace Records...

Table Utilities      ▶

Edit Records
Add Records
```

Menus, Navigator, and Command

Ch. 8

These choices are all documented in Chapter 9, which covers the Table tools.

▶ Using the Properties Menu

The Properties menu choice adds one new choice to the universal Desktop choice: Command Window .... This option displays the Command window Properties dialog box, which is shown in Figure 8.20.

This dialog box lets you adjust the look of the Command window to suit your tastes and work habits. It has two sections: Input Pane Position and Fonts.

FIGURE 8.20 ▶

Command Window Properties dialog box

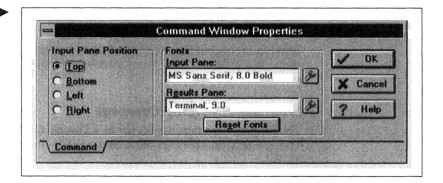

Input Pane Position Choices

The Input Pane Position section has four radio buttons:

- Top
- Bottom
- Left
- Right

Top is the default choice. (We fiddle with this occasionally, just to keep from getting bored.)

Font Choices

The Font section has two pseudo entry fields, Input Pane and Results Pane, with associated tool pushbuttons. These name the font used for the respective panes. Clicking on the tool pushbutton (or tabbing to it and pressing the spacebar) brings up the Windows Font dialog box, where you can select your fonts.

These are pseudo entry fields. You cannot type in them, though they look like you can. Their information is taken from the Font dialog box. They report the font name, size, and style.

▶ The Command Window's Speed Menu

If you right-click in the input pane, you bring up the Command window Speed menu. It offers six options:

- Command Window Properties ...
- Cut (Ctrl-X)
- Copy (Ctrl-C)
- Paste (Ctrl-V)
- Build Expression ... (Ctrl-E)
- Execute Selection

The Command Window Properties choice opens the Command Window Properties dialog box—the same one that you see when you choose Properties ▶ Command Window.

The Cut, Copy, and Paste options provide access to and from the Clipboard for text selected in the input pane.

The Build Expression option starts the Expression Builder.

Menus, Navigator, and Command

Ch. 8

The Execute Selection option provides another way for you to work without touching the keyboard. (This is Enter on the keyboard.)

▶ The Results Pane Speed Menu

If you right-click in the results pane, you bring up another Speed menu. Its three options are:

- Command Window Properties...
- Copy (Ctrl-C)
- Clear Results

The first choice launches the Command Window Properties dialog box.

The Copy choice lets you copy to the Clipboard after you have selected a rectangle by dragging.

The Clear Results choice clears the results pane. It is the same as giving the CLEAR command in the input pane.

▶▶ Using the Expression Builder

The Expression Builder lets you build dBASE expressions that you can use throughout dBASE for Windows. Whenever you see the tool icon next to a field that accepts expressions, the Expression Builder is just a click away. If the Command window is active, the Expression Builder is also available from the Edit menu.

In the Command window and in the editors, the Expression Builder is launched when you press Ctrl-E. From the Program Editor, you can click on the Einstein button (shown in the margin) to launch it. You'll see the Build Expression dialog box.

After you create an expression in the Build Expression dialog box and choose OK, dBASE for Windows pastes your expression into the tool you were using when you launched the Expression Builder.

▶ *Building Simple Expressions*

Let's start by entering a simple expression. Launch the Expression Builder from the Command window (choose Edit ➤ Expression Builder...). Notice the Safety Net check box at the top of the Build Expression dialog box. When Safety Net is checked, you can't type in the expression itself. For now, let's begin with Safety Net off. Make sure that the Safety Net check box is *not* checked, and type this expression: **2 + 2**. Figure 8.21 shows this expression entered in the dialog box.

FIGURE 8.21 ▶

Adding two and two in the Expression Builder

With this trivial expression entered, click on the Evaluate pushbutton at the top of the dialog box. Below your expression, the Expression Builder will report Result: 4.

Now let's go for a small increase in complexity. Delete the 2+2 expression and add this one: **2 + 3 * 4**. (You can use spaces freely within your expressions; they can be a big help when you get to more complex expressions.)

▶▶**N O T E**

If you're like us, you'll press Enter when you didn't mean to in the Expression Builder. Simply select the expression and press Ctrl-E to return to the Expression Builder with the expression exactly where you left it.

Can you predict the result of this expression? Give it a guess, and then click on E̲valuate. The result is 14, because multiplication is done before addition, unless you specify otherwise. If you added 2 and 3, then multiplied by 4, the answer would be 20. Let's get this done next.

Click on the Safety Net check box to turn this feature on. Then drag to select 2 + 3 and click on the G̲roup button at the top of the dialog box. It should look like this:

After you click on the G̲roup button, the Expression Builder inserts parentheses around the sum, turning the expression into:

(2 + 3) * 4

Now click on E̲valuate. The Expression Builder will report 20 as your result.

▶ Using the Category, Type, and Paste Options

The three lists near the bottom of the dialog box are labeled C̲ategory, T̲ype, and P̲aste, unless the Field choice is highlighted in the Category list. In this case, the middle list is labeled T̲able. We'll call it the Type list, since this is the most common name.

So far, you've discovered that the Expression Builder can be used as a clumsy calculator. Let's go beyond this for our next example.

We're approaching the turn of the century. At midnight at the end of December 31, 1999, we'll usher in a new century. (Some will say that the twentieth century actually ends on 12/31/2000, but this detail won't stop us from having a big party on 12/31/1999.) Let's start getting ready to celebrate by finding out what day of the week 12/31/99 is.

dBASE for Windows has a function that returns the day of the week, given any date. We presume that you don't know the name of that function (do your best to forget, for the moment, if you do know). Begin by deleting any expression (drag to select the current expression and press Del) and turning Safety Net on.

Often, a rough idea of what you want is enough to find the exact expression that will do the job. Start in the Category list and click on Function, since you know you want a function. Now the Type list will show the various types of functions. One of the choices is Date/Time data, which seems promising.

Click on Date/Time data and look in the Paste list. This list shows the actual functions from which you can choose. Underneath the Category, Type, and Paste lists, the highlighted function is explained, very briefly.

As luck would have it, the first of the Date/Time data functions is CDOW. As you see at the bottom of the dialog box, this function returns the day of the week for the given date expression, which is exactly what we want to know. Figure 8.22 shows our selections in the lists.

FIGURE 8.22 ▶

Finding a day of the week function

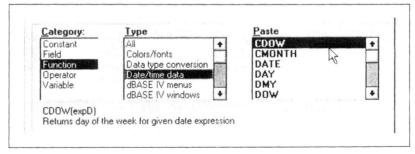

The last list is called Paste because this is what you do when you find what you're looking for: you paste the result into the expression. Paste the CDOW( ) function into the expression by double-clicking on the function, or by dragging it into the Expression area, like this:

When you put a function into the Expression area, it is shown in black, but its arguments (the values you supply for its operation) are shown in yellow. In this case, its argument is *expD*, which means that it needs a date expression.

We want to know what the day of the week will be on 12/31/99. This is a date constant, so return to the Category list and click on Constant. One of your Type choices is now Date, which is the one that we want.

Click on Date in the Type list. Now your choices in the Paste list are LastWeek, NextWeek, Today, Tomorrow, and Yesterday. If you don't happen to be reading this book in late December 1999, these choices aren't what you want.

Don't worry; you'll be able to get the correct constant in there. For now, drag any one of these date constants from the Paste list to the expression and drop it right on top of the *expD* value. Don't double-click, because that would made it a separate expression. (If you had selected a numeric constant, your only choice would be zero; it's just a place to start.)

Your expression is now all black, and you can click on Evaluate. We dragged LastWeek to the *expD*. Since today is Wednesday, the Expression Builder reported Wednesday when we clicked on Evaluate.

▶ Editing Constants in the Expression

The important result you have is that you are now looking at a correctly formed expression that will evaluate a date constant and return the day of the week. The last item to be done is to type 12/31/99 where it is reporting the date constant. Just click on the date and start typing.

An entry field will open underneath the date constant, like this:

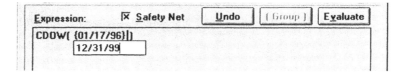

Don't enter the { } delimiters around a date constant (and don't enter the quotation marks that surround a character string constant, either).

Once you have 12/31/99 entered in the CDOW( ) function, click on the E<u>v</u>aluate button. You'll find that this important New Year's Eve is on Friday. That means that we'll have the whole weekend to clean up and recover from our big party.

▶ *Adding a Date Operator Expression*

Of course, Friday might not be the best choice for the widest number of people. If this will put a damper on your celebration, perhaps you want to think about having your big celebration on 12/31/2000, which will be, after all, the last day of the century.

If you recall, the argument to the CDOW function was *expD*, a date expression. Let's try to add 366 days to 12/31/99 to get the day of the week a year later. (Sure, you could just change the 1999 to 2000, but that wouldn't teach you about using the Expression Builder, which is our real point.)

Start by clicking near the right side of the date constant in the CDOW expression. Your insertion point (vertical bar) will appear to the right of the date, just to the left of the closing parenthesis. Here you want to add 366 to get the date one year later (2000 a leap year).

Return to the Category list and click on Operator. The Type list now shows the types of operators you can choose. Select Numeric, and the Paste list will show a menu of numeric operators. Select the plus sign to add the value. Figure 8.23 shows these selections in the Category, Type, and Paste lists.

FIGURE 8.23 ►

Choosing the add operator

When you choose an operator, the Expression Builder also adds any needed operands. In this example, an operand called *Value* has been added, waiting for our action:

This *Value* could be replaced by anything that will create a numeric value. We want the numeric constant 366. Return to the Category list and select Constant, and then choose Numeric in the Type list. The Paste list will show the constant zero. Drag the zero over the value operand and drop it. *Value* will be replaced by the 0.

Just as we did with the date, click on the 0 and start typing. An entry field will open beneath the constant. Type in **366, as shown here:**

Now the value 366 replaces the 0.

With that value inserted, we can now ask for an evaluation of the expression:

    CDOW({12/31/99} + 366)

This is the day of the week that New Year's Eve falls on in the year 2000: a Sunday.

▶ *Pasting to and from the Command Window*

If you launched the Expression Builder from the Command window, you can press Enter (or click on OK) to paste your expression back into the Command window. When you send an expression to the Command window, it is automatically written at the location of the insertion point in the Command window. The expression is not a complete command, but you can use the ? command to see the value of an expression.

To reverse the process—paste an expression from the Command window into the Expression Builder—select an expression (drag from the first character to the last) in the Command window and press Ctrl-E. This launches the Expression Builder with the expression already in place.

▶▶ *Summary*

In this chapter, you examined the dBASE for Windows menus, the Navigator, and the Command window. You also learned about catalogs and the Expression Builder.

You started with the menu options that are available for most file types, including the File, Edit, Properties, Window, and Help menus. You reviewed the Properties ▶ Desktop option, which is available from anywhere in dBASE for Windows.

Then you moved onto the Navigator. You learned about the features for selecting directories, file types, and files. You also explored the Navigator menus, including the Navigator menu and the Properties ▶ Navigator choices, as well as the Speed menu.

Next, you became acquainted with catalogs, which work like the Navigator, but for files that aren't in the same directory. You learned that you can build a catalog simply by picking the Catalog type from the Navigator and then opening the files that you want the catalog to contain.

Then you learned how to work in the Command window. You saw that the Command window has an input pane, in which you enter commands, and a results pane, which shows the results of your commands.

Menus, Navigator, and Command

▶ ▶

Ch.
8

You tried out a few of the more commonly used commands. You also explored its menus, including the Speed menus for the results and input panes.

Finally, you took a look at the Expression Builder, which helps you create expressions. The Expression Builder provides one way to put expressions in your commands.

In the next chapter, you'll get thorough coverage of the Table tools, including Table Structure, Table Records, and Table Utilities.

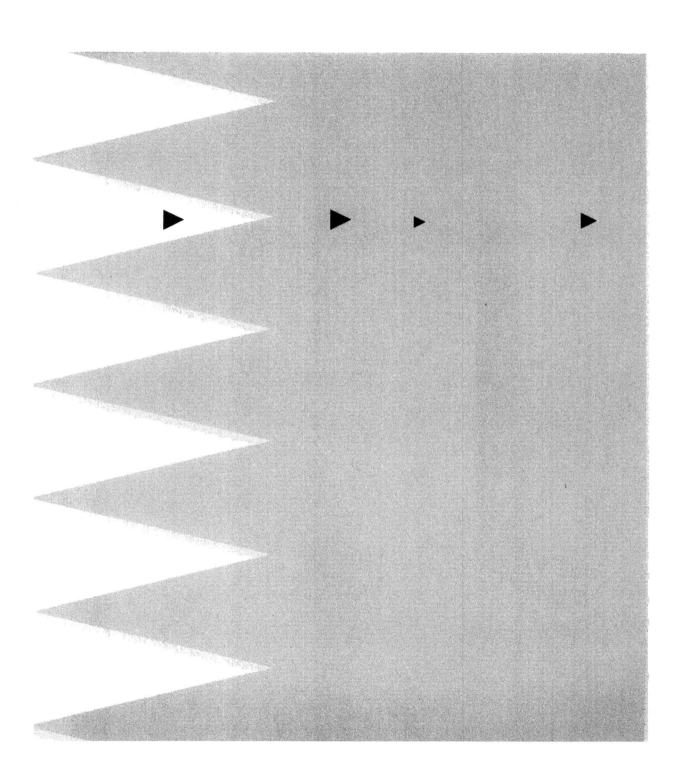

▶ ▶ CHAPTER **9**

Mastering Table Tools

▶▶   **I**n this chapter, we'll dissect the table-related tools. Table Records tools let you examine, edit, add, and delete data in one of the Browse, Form, or Columnar Layout views. A tool with a lower profile is Table Properties, which is a design tool that lets you customize your Table Records tools.

Finally, we'll examine the other Table tools. These are accessed through the Table Utilities menu, which presents a collection of data-manipulation tools.

▶▶ *Using the Table Structure Tool*

As you've seen in your earlier work, the Table Structure tool lets you design tables and modify the design of tables. Here, we'll examine every feature of the tool. We'll also consider the key problems and solutions when it comes time to use this tool to modify a table with live data.

▶ *A Browse for Your Table Structure*

The main part of the Table Structure tool is a specialized Browse window. A sample is shown in Figure 9.1.

The columns are the same columns that you find in a structure-extended file:

- Name, for the field's name
- Type, for the field's type

FIGURE 9.1 ▶

Browsing in a Table Structure window

• Width, for the field's width, in characters

• Decimal, for Numeric or Float fields, the number of places to the right of the decimal point

• Index, for the type of index (if any)

▶ Adding the Fields

The data-entry characteristics of this Browse window are tailored to the requirements of designing a table structure. The requirements discussed in the following sections may give you some ideas for your own work.

Field Name

The Name field restricts entry to valid field names. The first character must be alphabetic (you get a beep when you try anything else). The remaining characters must be alphabetic, numeric, or underscore characters. Invalid keystrokes are simply ignored.

Ch.
9

Field Type

The Type field choices are given in a drop-down list box:

With the mouse, click on the down arrow next to the field, and then click on your choice. From the keyboard, the first letter of your choice is adequate. Pressing the down arrow cycles through the choices.

dBASE for Windows supports the following field types:

- Character fields hold text (for names, addresses, and so on).
- Numeric fields store numbers, usually for business data.
- Memo fields are used for memoranda, notes, and other long blocks of text.
- Logical fields contain True/False or Yes/No data.
- Date fields store dates.
- Float fields store numbers, usually for scientific and engineering data.
- OLE fields are used to link to OLE (Microsft's Object Linking and Embedding protocol) objects, such as spreadsheets or word processing documents. (OLE lets you access one application when you are working in another one.)
- Binary fields hold data that cannot be entered from the keyboard, such as sounds and pictures.

Field Width

The Width field is a spinbutton. It is available for Character, Numeric, and Float data types. Memo, OLE, and Binary fields are 10 characters wide, which is the width needed to link to those data types. Date fields are 8 characters wide. Logical fields are 1 character wide.

Field Decimals

The Decimal field is a spinbutton available for Numeric and Float fields. For both those types, its range is 0 through 8.

Field Index

The Index field is a drop-down list box:

The default choice, None, does not index the field. The other two choices, Ascend and Descend, create an index from low to high, or high to low, respectively.

  ►►T I P

> **Almost never index a character field. The default index is based on the ASCII collating sequence, in which A–Z come before a–z. This will sort *Zebra* before *aardvark*, which is seldom what you want. Use the Manage Indexes dialog box (choose $\underline{S}$tructure ➤ $\underline{M}$anage Indexes) and index on UPPER (or LOWER) of the character field, for an alphabetic sort.**

With the mouse, click on the down arrow, and then click on your choice. From the keyboard, press A or D to override the default None selection.

If you choose indexing on a single field, that index will be the main index, by default. If you choose indexing on more than one field, the dBASE does not pick one for you. Instead it defaults to the physical order. You must use the Manage Indexes dialog box (choose Structure ➤ Manage Indexes) to select the primary index.

▶ Working in the Browse Area

As in the Table Records tool's Browse Layout view, placing the mouse pointer at the top (title) of a column turns the mouse pointer into the hand (grabber) icon. By pressing down and holding, you can drag the columns into a different order.

As is also true in the Table Records tool's Browse Layout view, placing the mouse pointer on the line between columns gives you the double-headed arrow that lets you drag the column separator left or right. In the standard setup, you can see all of each column, so this is seldom used.

Unlike the behavior of the Browse Layout view in the Table Records tool, moving the mouse pointer to the field number column turns it into the grabber hand. You can grab your records here and move them up and down. This will change the order of the columns in your table.

In a Table Records Browse window, clicking on the record number selects the field, letting you copy or cut it to the Clipboard. Pasting it elsewhere gives you a similar capability. The Table Records Browse window is more useful in large tables. The grabbing capability in the Table Structure tool is convenient for smaller tables, which table structures generally are.

A vertical elevator appears when you have more rows of data than fit in the window.

▶▶ NOTE

Perhaps it was an oversight, but no horizontal elevator appears if you reduce the width of the Table Structure window to the point that not all columns fit. Data on the right is just not accessible.

▶ Looking Above the Browse Area

The combobox above the Browse area shows the file name. The default type (also shown) is dBASE. The other types available depend on the choices made in your IDAPI configuration installation. (If your organization is not using Paradox tables or remote relational database management systems, this will not be relevant to you.)

A continuous display shows you four items: the date the table was last updated, the number of records in the table, the bytes used, and the bytes available. The bytes available are 32,767 minus the amount of bytes you have used. (This is the space for your table structure; data space is limited by your disk space.) Since each record takes 10 to 14 bytes, this gives you space for a table with 2500 to 3000 columns—more than anyone should ever need.

▶ Using the Table Structure Menus

The File and Edit menus in the Table Structure tool are standard, as described in Chapter 1.

The View menu includes two options:

- Table Records (F2)
- Table Structure (Shift-F2)

The Structure menu has five choices:

- Add Field (Ctrl-A)
- Insert Field (Ctrl-N)
- Delete Selected Field (Ctrl-U)
- Go to Field Number ... (Ctrl-G)
- Manage Indexes ...

The first three choices let you add a new field, insert a field, and delete the selected field.

The Go to Field Number ... choice opens the Go to Field dialog box. This dialog box contains a spinbutton that ranges from 1 to the number of fields you have, plus OK and Cancel buttons.

The Manage Indexes choice launches the Manage Indexes dialog box. If you've made changes to the table structure, it begins with the Changes Made dialog box, which gives you a choice of saving or discarding those changes. Whether you save your changes or not, the next step is the Manage Indexes dialog box. This dialog box is discussed later in this chapter, in the section about Table Utilities.

The Table Structure tool's Properties menu has two choices:

- Desktop
- Table Structure Window ...

The Desktop choice offers the standard multi-tab form, which you've learned about in earlier chapters. Choosing Properties ➤ Table Structure Window ... opens the Table Structure Properties form. This form has a single tab, Table Structure, with only two choices: Horizontal Grid Lines and Vertical Grid Lines. These check boxes turn the specified grid lines on or off.

 ►►**N O T E**

In all the dialog boxes, the OK, Cancel, and Help pushbuttons perform their normal duties.

► Right-Clicking for the Table Structure Speed Menu

Right-clicking with your mouse in the Table Structure window brings up a Speed menu, with the following choices:

- Table Structure Window Properties ...
- Cut (Ctrl-X)
- Copy (Ctrl-C)
- Paste (Ctrl-V)
- Add Field (Ctrl-A)

- Insert Field (Ctrl-N)
- Delete Selected Field (Ctrl-U)

The Table Structure Window Properties choice launches the Table Structure window (the same result as choosing Properties ➤ Table Structure).

The three editing choices—Cut, Copy, and Paste—work on the contents of the Name field or the numbers in the Width and Decimal fields. (If you're wondering if this might be less than overwhelmingly useful, we agree.)

The Add, Insert, and Delete options are the same as the Structure pull-down menu's Add Field, Insert Field, and Delete Selected Field choices.

▶ Using the Table Structure Speedbar Buttons

The speedbar for the Table Structure tool looks like this:

Three special buttons appear on the speedbar when the Table Structure tool is active:

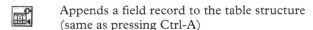

Appends a field record to the table structure (same as pressing Ctrl-A)

Inserts a field record above the selected record (same as pressing Ctrl-N)

Deletes the selected field record (same as pressing Ctrl-U)

These choices are also available on the Speed menu and from the Structure pull-down menu.

Mastering Table Tools

▶ ▶
Ch.
9

▶ *Avoiding Data Loss from Restructuring*

This warning box might appear when you're using the Table Structure tool to modify the structure of an existing table:

The two pushbuttons in the Data Loss Potential warning box let you choose a Yes or No response. Often, you can simply ignore this dialog box—just click on Yes and proceed. But not always. The following sections give the rules for making successful changes.

Make a Backup Copy

Before editing a table structure, make a backup copy of the table. With a backup copy, you can proceed to make any changes you want. If you've made a mistake, there's no harm done.

Sometimes, you'll find yourself working with a very large table—too large to back up on disk. (We presume that you have backed up on tape or some other backup medium.) When this happens, copy the first few dozen records to a temporary table. Make your changes on the temporary table and test the result. If there's a problem, try again with another copy of a dozen records. When you have a set of changes that work, apply them to the full table.

Make Multiple Passes

Changing field names and reordering fields never triggers the Data Loss Potential dialog box. Do these changes first.

Increasing field widths is also never a problem. Make these changes second.

Increasing a Numeric or Float field's decimal places might leave too little space to the left of a decimal point. If you know that all your data will continue to fit, or if you have increased the field's width so that this will not be a problem, go ahead with this change. You *will* trigger the Data Loss Potential dialog box, but you'll know that you can safely continue.

Similarly, decreasing a field's width will trigger the Data Loss Potential dialog box, but if you know that you've allowed enough space, you can select Yes and continue.

Check Maximum Widths

To be sure that you allow enough space for the largest number in a Numeric or Float field, choose Table ➤ Table Utilities ➤ Calculate. Use the Calculate Records dialog box to find the highest value. (The Calculate Records dialog box is discussed later in this chapter.)

▶▶ **W A R N I N G**

> If you have mixed positive and negative values, you must check both the maximum (largest positive number) and minimum (largest negative number) to be sure you allow for the widest number in your table.

To find the width of the widest character field, use the CALCULATE MAX( ) command in the Command window. For the expression, you want the LEN( ) of the TRIM( ) of the field. (Without the TRIM( ), the LEN( ) of the field is its width as defined in the table's current structure.) This will work in the Command window for a character field named LAST_NAME:

```
CALCULATE MAX( LEN(TRIM(Last_name)) )
```

▶▶ **T I P**

> The extra blank spaces inside the parentheses are discarded by dBASE for Windows, but we like them since they help make nested function calls, like this one, more readable.

Ch.
9

That command will show its answer in the Calculation Results dialog box.

Read the Dialog Box Message

The message explicitly states the conditions that trigger the Data Loss Potential dialog box:

- Changing a field's type
- Changing a field's decimal value
- Decreasing a field's width
- Deleting a field

Changes to the field's type may or may not cause problems. dBASE does its best to preserve your data. It works extra hard when you change a field's type. These are the changes:

- **Numeric to Float:** The internal representation of the number is changed. This may make a difference in round-off error, but is probably negligible.

- **Float to Numeric:** With any difference in precision between the Float field's decimal places and the Numeric field's decimal places, dBASE for Windows rounds the number to the nearest value that fits (for example, 0.04 rounds to 0.0 at one decimal place; 0.05 rounds to 0.1). This will cause significant loss of precision, which may or may not be important, depending on your application.

 ▶▶ N O T E

As an example of changing a Float field to a Numeric field, suppose that your Float field contained the fraction ⅓, stored to eight decimal places (the default for Float field data). Converting to a numeric with two decimal places will truncate 0.00333333 (to .00). Then again, this truncation may actually improve the accuracy of your calculation if, for example, you are dealing with currency amounts that should be rounded.

- **Character to Memo:** The character data will be moved into the Memo field. Ignore the Data Loss Potential dialog box. There is no data loss.

- **Memo to Character:** As much of the Memo field text that will fit is moved into the Character field. Any memo longer than the field is truncated.

- **Numeric or Float to Character:** The number is written as a character string into the Character field. It is left-justified. Precision or data may be lost if the number does not fit in the Character field.

- **Character to Numeric or Float:** The VAL( ) of the Character field is moved into the Numeric field if, and only if, the entire character string can be converted to a number. For example, "123" is converted to the number 123; "123a" is not entirely numeric, so the Numeric field is blanked. (A blank field is treated as a zero in most dBASE for Windows operations.)

- **Date to Character:** The DTOC( ) of the date is written into the Character field. There is no data loss as long as the Character field is wide enough to fit the date as a string.

- **Character to Date:** The Character field data is interpreted as a date constant and placed in the Date field. If the character string is not a valid date, the Date field is blanked.

- **Logical to Character:** .T. values are converted to Y, and .F. values are converted to N.

- **Character to Logical:** If the Character field data is an acceptable input to a Logical field, the appropriate value is entered into the Logical field. Y, y, T, and t are .T.; N, n, F and f are .F. The character string ".T." is *not* recognized as True. All other character strings are converted to .F. values.

- **Numeric or Float to Logical:** Zeros are converted to .F. values. Nonzeros (positive or negative) are converted to .T. values. Blank Numeric fields are converted to .F.

- **Logical to Numeric or Float:** .T. values are converted to 1. .F. values are converted to 0.

No other conversions are attempted. The existing data is discarded and the new fields are blanked.

We've already considered the impacts of changing the data decimal value or decreasing a field's width. If you delete a field, the data in it will be lost, of course. If this is what you have in mind, you can proceed.

Remember that your computer is not as smart as you are. You may have just looked at the data and know that you have plenty of room to increase the decimals from 2 to 4, for instance. dBASE for Windows doesn't check; it just displays the Data Loss Potential dialog box and lets you decide.

►► *Using the Table Records Tools*

The Table Records tools are the primary tools for entering and editing data (unless you build custom forms).

► *Using the Table Records Menus*

In the Table Records views, the only standard menus are Window and Help. The other menus have custom options or are entirely new.

File Menu

The File menu has two changes from the standard File menu: the Save section has modified options, and there is a new section for importing spreadsheet data.

The Save section has the following options:

- Save Record (Ctrl-S)
- Save Record and Close (Ctrl-W)
- Abandon Record
- Abandon Record and Close (Ctrl-Q)
- Close (Ctrl-F4)

The two Abandon options eliminate any changes made to an existing record or they discard a record that you were appending.

The new option for importing a spreadsheet is Import .... This option opens the Import dialog box, shown in Figure 9.2.

FIGURE 9.2 ▶

Importing data with
File ➤ Import

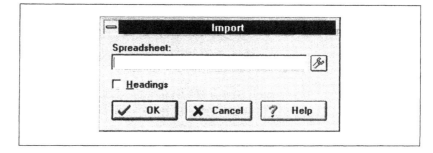

The tool button next to the entry field launches an Open File dialog box titled Choose Spreadsheet. Its available file extensions are .WB1 for Quattro Pro spreadsheets and .WK1 for Lotus 1-2-3 spreadsheets. (See Appendix B for more information about Open File dialog boxes.)

Importing a spreadsheet creates a new table with each field in the table corresponding to a column in the spreadsheet.

If the Headings box is checked, the data in the first row of the spreadsheet is used for field names. The data is adjusted as needed. For example, blanks are converted to underscores, and text is truncated to 10 characters.

The import process is *not* intelligent. Except for row 1 (when Headings is checked), all data in each column is read into your table, so you must have exactly zero or one row of header in the spreadsheet.

Only Lotus 1-2-3 and Quattro Pro spreadsheets are supported.

Edit Menu

You can use the Clipboard to copy field contents (including Memo fields). You can select text by either dragging with the mouse or holding down the Shift key while using the ← or → key.

In the Browse Layout view, you can also click on the record number to select the entire record. Doing this lets you copy the whole record to the Clipboard.

Mastering Table Tools

▶▶
Ch.
9

▶▶ **N O T E**

The Cut option is not available; you can only Copy a record to the Clipboard.

You can't Shift-click to select multiple records. However, dragging with the left button over the record numbers lets you select a range of records in the Browse Layout view.

When you paste from the Clipboard, the current field is overwritten with the Clipboard's contents. If you have copied a record, the entire current record is overwritten. (Picture all paste operations as if you were using an editor in overstrike mode.)

If you've copied multiple records to the Clipboard, each record from the Clipboard overwrites one record in the table, beginning with the currently selected record.

Pasting from the Clipboard will *not*, however, add records to the table. The paste operation stops when it reaches the end of the file.

The only non-overwrite option is the new choice added to the Edit menu: Paste Add Records. This option appends enough blank records to fit the Clipboard's contents, and then pastes the Clipboard's record(s) into the new record(s).

View Menu

The View menu is divided into three sections. In the first, you choose one of the following:

- Table Records (F2)
- Table Structure (Shift-F2)

The current choice is checked.

The second section has three options:

- Browse Layout (F2)
- Form Layout (F2)
- Columnar Layout (F2)

Again, your current choice is checked. You can press F2 to switch between these layouts.

A Browse object may disable toggling between the different layouts, in which case these options are grayed. (This is the Toggle property of the Browse object, discussed in Chapter 18, which can also be set for a Browse in the Table Properties dialog box, discussed later in this chapter.)

The last section has a single choice: Field Contents (F9). This choice is available when you have selected a Memo, Binary, or OLE field. It activates the text editor for a Memo field, or the appropriate editor for Binary and OLE fields.

Table Menu

The Table menu has four sections. The first one has two choices:

- Find Records ... (Ctrl-F)
- Replace Records ... (Ctrl-R)

These are covered in Chapter 4 of this book.

The next section also has two choices:

- Create Query
- Table Utilities

The Create Query choice launches the Query Designer, which is covered in Chapter 5. The Table Utilities choice is one of the routes to the Table Utilities menu, discussed later in this chapter.

The next section has four choices:

- Add Records (Ctrl-A)
- Delete Selected Record (Ctrl-U)
- Lock Selected Record (Ctrl-L)
- Blank Selected Record

You've probably been using the Ctrl-A and Ctrl-U shortcut keys in your Table Records work. We don't recommend using the Ctrl-L method for coordinating multiple, simultaneous table users. If you're

Ch.
9

updating the table while others are also updating it, pressing Ctrl-L is *not* a reliable way of coordinating multiple users. This should be done under control of a program designed for this purpose.

If you have the Deleted flag off (the view shows deleted records) and the current record is deleted, the Delete Selected Record choice is replaced by its opposite: Recall Selected Record (Ctrl-U).

The last section of the menu provides record-navigation options:

- Goto Record Number ... (Ctrl-G)
- Previous Record (Up Arrow)
- Next Record (Down Arrow)
- Previous Page (PgUp)
- Next Page (PgDn)
- Top Record (Ctrl-PgUp)
- Bottom Record (Ctrl-PgDn)

Properties Menu

The Properties menu adds one choice: Table Record Properties .... The Table Records Properties dialog box is accessed from this menu choice (as well as from the Speed menu). This dialog box is a form with three tabs:

- Fields
- Records
- Window

These tabs are discussed in the section about setting Table Record properties, later in this chapter.

▶ *Using the Table Records Speedbar Buttons*

The speedbar for the Table Records tool looks like this:

Up to 12 special buttons appear when you run the Table Structure tool. Table 9.1 shows the functions of this speedbar.

▶ **TABLE 9.1:** *Speedbar Buttons for the Table Records Tool*

BUTTON	FUNCTION
	Changes to the multicolumn Browse Layout view (same as choosing View ➤ Browse Layout or pressing F2 to cycle through the available layouts).
	Changes to the single-record Form Layout view (same as choosing View ➤ Form Layout or pressing F2 to cycle through the available layouts).
	Changes to the single-column Columnar Layout view (same as choosing View ➤ Columnar Layout or pressing F2 to cycle through the available layouts).
	Opens the Find Record dialog box (same as choosing Table ➤ Find Records ... or pressing Ctrl-F).
	Appends a new record (same as pressing Ctrl-A or attempting to navigate to the record past the end of the table).
	Launches the Query Designer for this table.
	Goes to the first record in the table (same as pressing Ctrl-PgUp).
	In Browse Layout view, goes to the previous page of records (same as pressing PgUp).
	Goes to the previous record (same as pressing ↑ in Browse Layout view; PgUp in Form and Columnar Layout views)
	Goes to the next record (same as pressing ↓ in Browse Layout view; PgDn in Form and Columnar Layout views)

▶ **TABLE 9.1:** *Speedbar Buttons for the Table Records Tool (continued)*

BUTTON	FUNCTION
▶▶	In Browse Layout view, goes to the next page of records (same as pressing PgDn).
▶|	Goes to the last record in the table (same as pressing Ctrl-PgDn).

▶▶**N O T E**

In Form or Columnar Layout view, there are four record-navigation buttons on the Table Records speedbar. Since there's more to move through in the Browse Layout view, that window has six record-navigation buttons on its speedbar.

▶ Setting Table Records Properties

You can adjust the properties of field, records, and the Table Records window as a whole through the Table Records Properties dialog box. This dialog box can be accessed by selecting Properties ➤ Table Records Properties ... from the pull-down menu, or by choosing Table Records Window Properties from the Speed menu.

Fields Tab Properties

The Fields tab of the Table Records Properties dialog box is shown in Figure 9.3.

The main part of the upper-left portion of this dialog box is a field selector. Using the field selector, you can choose the fields to include, as well as the order of those fields. (See Appendix B for more information about using the field selector.)

FIGURE 9.3 ▶

Table Record Properties, Fields tab

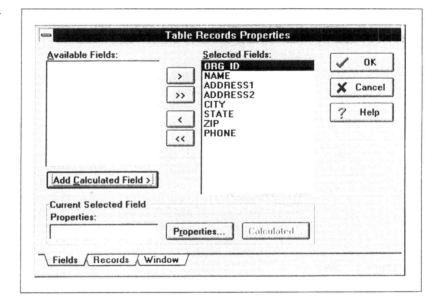

Calculated Fields Beneath the field selector on the left is the Calculated Field pushbutton. Pushing this button launches the Calculated Field dialog box, shown in Figure 9.4.

FIGURE 9.4 ▶

Calculated Field dialog box

To add a calculated field, enter a name and then an expression. If you fill in these two fields and click on OK or press Enter, your new calculated field is added to the Selected Fields list in the Table Records Properties dialog box.

Clicking on the tool icon next to the Expression: entry field launches the Expression Builder, which lets you build a dBASE expression. (See Chapter 8 for information about using the Expression Builder.)

To edit the characteristics of a calculated field, select it in the Selected Fields list to make the Calculated ... pushbutton at the bottom of the Fields tab available. Clicking on this button returns you to the Calculated Field dialog box for the selected field.

Field Properties   To set field properties, click on the Properties ... pushbutton, just to the left of the Calculated Field ... pushbutton. You'll see the Field Properties dialog box, shown in Figure 9.5.

FIGURE 9.5 ▶

The Field Properties dialog box

The Heading entry field accepts a column or field heading that replaces the default field name heading. The Width spinbutton sets the visual width. If the field width is wider than the visual width, the field will scroll as you enter data.

The Template entry field lets you enter formatting information, just as you can with the Picture property. Clicking on the tool icon launches the Choose Template dialog box.

The Read Only check box can make the field read-only (so that it cannot be modified). This can be very useful for ID fields.

The When entry field is a more sophisticated version of the Read Only check box. It allows editing the field when the contents of the When expression evaluate to True. Clicking on the tool icon launches the Expression Builder.

The Valid and Range settings have a similar function: to allow entry of only allowable values into the field. You can enter a logical expression into the Valid Expression entry field. You can enter numbers or dates, depending on your field's type, in the Limit (Lower Limit and Upper Limit) entry fields. A number or date must be within the specified range, or the entry will be rejected. For any field type, the Valid expression must evaluate to True, or the entry won't be accepted. For each of these fields, clicking on the tool icon launches the Expression Builder.

Normally, the Valid Expression and Range entries are evaluated when you enter data. If you select the Required check box for either field, every field that you navigate over is checked for these conditions. If you get to a field that doesn't meet the conditions, you will not be able to go past it without entering an acceptable value.

After you use the Field Properties dialog box to set values for each field, the Properties reporting field (it looks like an entry field, but you can't type in it) in the Table Records Properties dialog box is updated with a compressed version of the data you entered.

Ch.
9

▶▶**N O T E**

> **All your work in the Field Properties dialog box will be entered into your DBASEWIN.INI file, for use in later dBASE for Windows sessions. See Appendix C, which is about the DBASEWIN.INI initialization file, if you want to try your hand at entering this data as a compressed text string.**

Records Tab Properties

The Records tab of the Table Records Properties dialog box is shown in Figure 9.6. It includes three sets of choices:

- Editing Options
- Scope
- Index Range

FIGURE 9.6 ▶

Table Record Properties, Records tab

In the Editing Options choices, if Append is checked, you can add new records to the table. If the Edit option is checked, you can modify the values in your fields, in accordance with any other specifications you've made for particular fields. If it isn't checked, every field is read-only, overriding any other field settings you've made.

The Delete option, if checked, lets you delete records. For some tables, such as a table of U.S. two-letter postal codes, you would not normally want to allow deletion of records, so you would not check this option.

The Follow Index option selects one of two behaviors, either of which can be confusing at times. Assume that your master index is on the Name field and you're correcting the invalid entry Zenith, changing it to Azimuth. The question is, what should dBASE for Windows do when you make this change?

If you choose Follow Index, when you change the master index value, dBASE for Windows will relocate its position in the table. In the example above, it would change from the *Z*'s to the *A*'s. If Follow Index were not checked, when you changed the master index value to Azimuth, your record would disappear from the page full of *Z*'s that you could see. Your position in the table wouldn't change. For most applications, you'll want Follow Index checked.

The Index Range selections are available whenever a master index is selected. You enter expressions in these fields that evaluate to the same data type as your master index. If the current record is between the Low Key and High Key values, it is shown. If it is not in range, it disappears.

This is a method for limiting the table to a portion of the available data. For instance, on Monday, you might be updating data from *A* through *E*, so you use this range to make the rest of your table disappear (it is masked out until you change the range).

The Exclude check box specifies whether the end points of the range are considered in range. If your range is dates between 12/1/95 and 12/31/95, checking Exclude would eliminate the start and end dates. Only records from 12/2/95 through 12/30/95 would be accepted. If it isn't checked, records exactly matching the end values are considered part of the range.

Ch.
9

Window Tab Properties

The Window tab of the Table Records Properties dialog box controls settings that affect the whole window. It is shown in Figure 9.7.

FIGURE 9.7 ▶

Table Record Properties, Window tab

The Title entry field lets you replace the default window title (Table Records, followed by your table name in parentheses) with one of your own choosing.

The Toggle Layout check box, if checked, lets you toggle between Browse, Form, and Columnar Layout views. The Horizontal Grid and Vertical Grid check boxes let you turn these grid lines on or off.

The Field Options choices let you set the number of fields that will be frozen on the left (Lock), the maximum display width of fields (Width), and a single field to take all data entry (Freeze).

The Lock spinbutton locks the specified number of fields into the left side of a Browse Layout view. It's handy when, for example, you have a name on the left and want it to stay in place while you scroll through the other fields.

The Width setting is the second place dBASE for Windows looks when deciding on the display width for your fields. It starts with width settings specified for individual fields, which take top priority. Without a setting for the individual field, the setting here applies, if it is smaller than the actual field width. Finally, the field's width is used if this Width setting is equal to 0 or the field is smaller than the width set here. This is a convenient way to make a large number of wide columns temporarily shrink.

The Freeze drop-down list lets you pick a single field that will be the only one available for data entry. It will remain in your Browse window regardless of your horizontal scrolling, and all your other fields will be read-only.

▶ ▶ *Using Table Utilities*

To get to the Table Utilities, you must go through the Table pull-down menu, which is available in the Command window or when the Table View tool is active. In both cases, choose Table ▶ Table Utilities Alt-T, then T) to access the Table Utilities.

 ▶ ▶ N O T E

One of the design changes we would make if dBASE for Windows were our product is to not hide the Table Utilities. As you'll see, this is a powerful set of data-manipulation tools. We think it deserves a place on the main menu and on the speedbar. Maybe in a later version...

This selection displays the Table Utilities menu:

Manage Indexes...
Reinde**x**
Close Table
Close All **T**ables
Delete Records...
Recall Records...
Pack Records
Zap Records
Append Records from File...
Export Records...
Sort Records...
Generate Records...
Cou**n**t Records...
Ca**l**culate Records...

As you can see, the utilities themselves are divided into five groups:

- Index Management
- Table Closing
- Record Deleting and Recalling
- Record Import and Export, Sorting and Generating
- Counting and Calculation

The five sections that follow discuss each of these capabilities in detail.

► Working with Indexes

The two index-related utilities are represented by the **M**anage Indexes and Reinde**x** choices in the Table Utilities menu.

Managing Indexes

The **M**anage Indexes choice lets you control the indexes in the production index (the .MDX file with the same name as the table). You can create, modify, and delete indexes, and you can select the current master index (the one which controls the apparent order of the records). Figure 9.8 shows the Manage Indexes dialog box being used to select a master index.

 ▶▶**NOTE**

The Manage Indexes dialog box is also available from the Structure menu of the Table Structure tool and the Query menu of the Query Designer tool.

The dialog box presents three choices:

- Create …
- Modify …
- Delete

If the (Natural Order) index is highlighted, the Modify and Delete choices are grayed (not available). When an index is highlighted, those choices become available.

Choosing Create … allows you to specify a new index (see Chapter 4). To remove an index, highlight it and choose Delete. Selecting an existing index and clicking on the Modify … button takes you to the Modify Index dialog box, as shown in Figure 9.9. This looks just like the Create Index dialog box, except that it shows the current settings for the index you chose. You can change the settings for this index, and then choose OK to put those changes into effect.

FIGURE 9.9 ►

The Modify Index dialog box

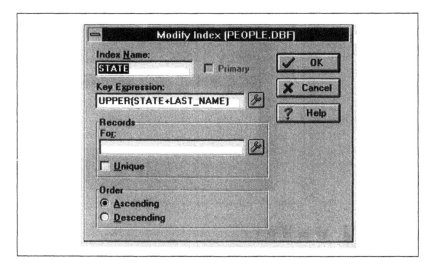

Reindexing

Choosing Reindex rebuilds the production index. The production index is maintained automatically as you add, edit, and modify your data, so this choice is only necessary if you need to recover from a hardware or software failure.

However, rebuilding the indexes periodically can lead to faster operation. The internal index structure, called a B-tree, depends on spreading the index data evenly over the index pages (called *balancing* the index) for maximum efficiency.

dBASE for Windows balances indexes as it builds them. However, the index can become unbalanced over time as data is added, changed, and deleted. So reindexing is a sensible maintenance procedure.

The reindex process should be run on the machine that holds the data, as it involves reading every record in the table multiple times. You should plan to reindex when you have exclusive use of the table and don't object to a time-consuming process.

▶ Closing Tables

There are two table closing choices: C̲lose Table and Close All T̲ables. Selecting C̲lose Table is equivalent to choosing C̲lose from the Table Records tool's System menu or pressing Ctrl-F4. It closes the current table. If you have multiple related tables open, it closes all of them. It also closes any related .MDX and .DBT files.

The Close All T̲ables choice closes all open tables and related .MDX and .DBT files. If sessions are on, it closes all the tables in the current session, which also ends the session. If sessions are off, all open tables are closed.

▶ Minimizing Waste and Recovering from Mistakes

The next section of the Table Utilities menu deals with deleting and re-calling records. It includes four choices:

- D̲elete Records ...
- R̲ecall Records ...
- P̲ack Records
- Z̲ap Records

Deleting Records

The D̲elete Records dialog box is shown in Figure 9.10. As you can see in that example, the Delete Records dialog box is simply a Scope panel plus the three standard pushbuttons. The default scope is Next 1. Next starts counting at the current record. (The Scope panel is the same as the one that appears in the Find and other dialog boxes; see Appendix B for more information.)

The default settings in this dialog box delete a record in the same way that selecting T̲able ➤ D̲elete Selected Record (or pressing Ctrl-U) deletes a record.

▶ ▶
Ch.
9

FIGURE 9.10 ▶

Removing California records from the table

 ►►**W A R N I N G**

> The Delete Records dialog box does *not* recall records. Unlike when you use Ctrl-U on a record that has been deleted (its Delete flag is on), the record does not become "undeleted." Any record in the scope of the deletion that is already deleted simply stays deleted.

Recalling Records

dBASE for Windows tables use a single byte to indicate a record's deletion status. This Deleted flag is set when the record is deleted (or, more correctly, marked for deletion). Deleting the record sets this flag. If the Deleted setting is on, the record disappears from view. If the Deleted setting is off, the record stays in view but the Deleted flag is set.

◉ ►►**W A R N I N G**

> Deletion status does not apply to Paradox .DB or SQL records, which are physically deleted when you delete them. They cannot be recalled.

Figure 9.11 shows the operation performed in Figure 9.10 being reversed. All the records where the state is California are being recalled.

FIGURE 9.11 ▶

Recalling deleted records

Recall Records (ORGS.DBF)

Scope
- ⦿ **A**ll
- ○ Re**s**t
- ○ Ne**x**t: |
- ○ **R**ecord: |

For:
state = 'CA'

While:

✓ OK

✗ Cancel

? Help

Packing Records

The **P**ack Records choice physically deletes records from a .DBF file. After packing, the .DBF file contains only records that do not have the Deleted flag set. (Paradox .DB tables and SQL tables are continuously packed.)

If you're responsible for maintaining your tables, we recommend the following routine maintenance procedure:

- Make backups of your tables.
- Pack your tables.
- Reindex your tables.

Note that the backup must come before the pack operation. If your data is auditable, your auditors will require that you do it this way. If you are your own auditor, you should require it of yourself.

Ch.
9

There is no way to recover data that has been packed out of existence. The nondeleted records overwrite the locations of the deleted records. Except for deleted records at the very end of the table, other deleted records cannot be recovered records after a pack operation, unless you have a backup copy.

Zapping Records

Zapping a file kills every record in the file—quickly! Zap resets the internal record count in the table to 0, and it tells DOS that the end of the file is the end of the header area. The portion of the file that holds the records is returned to DOS's free space pool.

This process is virtually instantaneous. The equivalent process is deleting all records, then packing the table. To delete all the records, every record's Deleted flag must be written. Since the pack operation does not know what you have been doing before you tell it to start, it will read every record to check the Deleted status. This means that the process must first write every record, and then read every record. Obviously, with a large table, this can be a long process.

If the safety setting is on, the Zap Records dialog box will prompt you to confirm that you want to empty your file.

If you have not opened the table for exclusive use, dBASE for Windows will ask you if you want to open the table for exclusive use. (Obviously, you cannot zap a file if others are accessing it.)

▶ Sharing Your Data with Other Applications

There are four data-sharing and file-manipulating choices on the Table Utilities menu:

- Append Records from File ...
- Export Records ...
- Sort Records ...
- Generate Records ...

Appending Records from a File

The Append Records from File ... selection opens the Append Records from File dialog box, shown in Figure 9.12.

FIGURE 9.12 ▶

Appending records from a temporary table

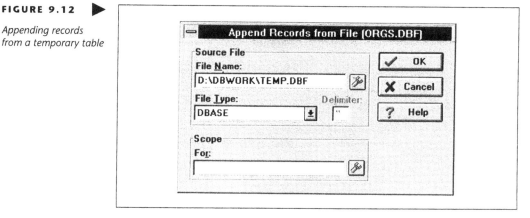

The File Type selection in the Source File section lists the type choices on a drop-down list:

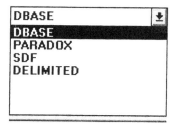

Clicking on the tool icon next to the File Name entry field launches an Open File dialog box titled Import File. For dBASE files, the default file type is .DBF. For Paradox files, the default is .DB. For SDF (System Data Format) and delimited files, the default type is .TXT.

Mastering Table Tools

Ch.
9

SDF files are text files with the columns lined up (also known as fixed field lengths):

```
Friendly   Phil Friendly      Pleasantville   NY12345(800) 111-1234
Adamson    Adrianne Adamson   Sun City        CA55555(800) 123-4567
Monroe     Madilyn Monroe     Hollywood       CA55555(123) 123-1234
Gable      Eve Gable          New York        NY12345(212) 911-9111
Hacker     Herb Hacker        Mountain View   CA55555(800) 987-6543
```

Delimited files use delimiters:

```
"Friendly","Phil Friendly","Pleasantville","NY","12345","(800) 111-1234"
"Adamson","Adrianne Adamson","Sun City","CA","55555","(800) 123-4567"
"Monroe","Madilyn Monroe","Hollywood","CA","55555","(123) 123-1234"
"Gable","Eve Gable","New York","NY","12345","(212) 911-9111"
"Hacker","Herb Hacker","Mountain View","CA","55555","(800) 987-6543"
```

The Delimiter entry field lets you choose your own delimiter if the default is not suitable. It is only available when the File Type is DELIMITED.

The Scope choices let you establish a logical condition that limits the records appended. The For condition only applies when you are importing from dBASE tables.

When you import from dBASE tables, the Deleted setting controls the import of records marked for deletion. If Deleted is checked, only non-deleted records are imported. If Deleted is not checked, all records are imported.

Exporting Records

The Export Records ... choice opens the Export Records dialog box, shown in Figure 9.13.

The Export File section is similar to the Source File section in the Append Records dialog box. The only difference is that a fifth file type is available: DBMEMO3.

The default file extension for DBMEMO3 data is .DBF. This type is a dBASE III+ compatible .DBF format.

The dialog box offers the full range of Scope choices. You can select and order fields through the field selector at the bottom of the dialog box. (The Scope options and field selector are described in Appendix B.)

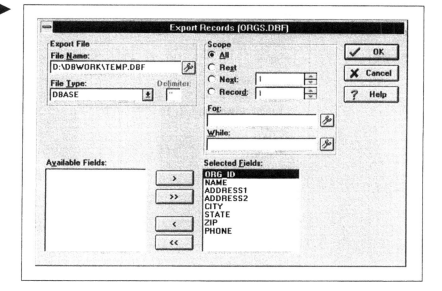

Sorting Records

The Sort Records ... choice opens the Sort Records dialog box, shown in Figure 9.14.

The sorting process does not sort a table's records. Rather, it sorts from the active table into another table.

The Name field is used to enter the .DBF or .DB file into which you will sort the records of the current table. Clicking on the tool icon launches an Open File dialog box titled Save File.

The Target Table Type box lets you choose between dBASE (.DBF) and Paradox (.DB) tables. Your choice determines the default extension in the Open File dialog box.

The Field Selection box is a modified field selector. There is no **>>** button in this selector, because moving every available field into the Key Fields list would not normally be a sensible operation.

Mastering Table Tools

Ch. 9

The field or fields that you select are the ones on which the result table
will be sorted. Using multiple fields sorts on each, in order. For example, if you sort on State and Name, the data will be ordered by State
and, within each state, by Name.

When you select a field for sorting, an up arrow appears next to its
name. If you click on this arrow, you get a drop-down list of sort
choices:

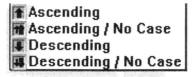

The arrows indicate your choice (just as they do in the Query Designer). The Scope choices are the standard ones.

Generating Records

The Generate Records ... choice launches the Generate Records dialog
box, which allows you to enter the number of records you want to generate (as we did in Chapter 6 to get some test data).

Generating records is very useful when you are designing a system and need to check possible response times. Test files of a few records give you no idea of what your performance will be with tens of thousands of records. The dBASE for Windows record-generation feature lets you test your system on a filled file.

This dialog box is simple. Just spin the button or, for larger values, type the number of new records you want generated, then click on OK or press Enter.

dBASE for Windows' progress is reported in the center of the status bar by a colored area that moves from left to right, showing the proportion of the new records that have been generated. A percentage figure is also displayed in this area.

To generate a lot of records (10,000 or more), eliminate all tags from your production index, then generate. Add the indexes after your table is filled.

▶▶ **W A R N I N G**

Before you use the Generate Records dialog box for a substantial number of records, check that you have disk space available. Multiply the record length by the number of records that will be generated. The record length is given in the Table Structure tool.

▶ *Analyzing Your Data*

There are two Table Utilities menu choices for data analysis: Count Records ... and Calculate Records ....

Counting Records

The Count Records ... choice launches the Count Records dialog box, shown in Figure 9.15.

One of the most frequently asked questions of any database is, "How many ...?" In Figure 9.15, we are asking how many of our records are for California.

FIGURE 9.15 ▶

Counting the records in California

The Count Records dialog box answers these questions. It reports its results in the Counted Records dialog box, which shows your answer and waits for an OK click or Enter press.

You can use the Scope panel to set your criteria and proceed to click on OK or press Enter. If you're counting in a small table, your answer will be virtually instantaneous. If your count is For or While a condition that matches an index expression, the answer will be pulled from the index, and will also be virtually instantaneous, even on very large tables.

Counting for a nonindexed condition on a large file requires reading every record, which may take some time.

If you give the command

```
? RECCOUNT( )
```

in the Command window, you get an immediate response in the results pane, showing the total records in the file. If the Deleted setting is off, this will match the Count Records results (when your Scope is All).

If the Deleted flag is on, the Count Records dialog box will exclude deleted records from its count, so it may be lower than RECCOUNT( ).

Calculating on Records

The Calculate Records ... choice launches the Calculate Records dialog box shown in Figure 9.16. The following calculations are available:

- Average
- Minimum
- Maximum
- Standard Deviation
- Sum
- Variance

FIGURE 9.16

Performing calculations

For those of you who are not statisticians, the standard deviation of a set of data points measures the amount by which they vary from the arithmetic average (mean). It is the square root of the average of the square of the deviations from the mean. Variance is the square of the standard deviation.

In the Fields box, you'll see a list of all the Numeric and Float fields in your active table. You can select one by clicking on it. You can select a range of fields by clicking on the first field and Shift-clicking at the other end of the range. If you want to select multiple fields, but not a range, use Ctrl-click.

▶▶ T I P

All the calculations require far more time spent reading records than actually calculating, so you might as well get your answer for all Numeric fields.

On our test machine, a generic 33 MHz 80486, we calculate the standard deviation of a single Float field in a 1000-record database in a little under two seconds. We calculate the standard deviation of all six Float fields in the same table in a little under two seconds, too. (The time difference is not measurable with a stopwatch.)

The dialog box has a Scope panel, so you can limit your calculations to a subset of your available records.

▶▶ Summary

In this chapter, you've reviewed the features of the Table Structure and Table Reports tools.

You started with the Table Structure tool, which is a special Browse window for table structures.

You looked into every part of what you could do in the fields, between and outside the fields, with the menus, and with speedbar buttons.

You studied the Data Loss Potential dialog box. Some changes to table structures can lose data, and dBASE warns you. However, it warns you about the *potential*. You learned about what type of loss you might expect, and what could be done to prevent it.

Next you went on to the Table Records tool. You examined every new choice menu choice. You spent a lot of time on the Properties menu's Table Records Window … choice, which launches a three-tab form.

You learned to use the Table Properties dialog box to customize your Table Records tool for your forms, and you learned that these customized settings were saved for you in the DBASEWIN.INI file.

After going into every aspect of the Table Records tool, you went on to the Table Utilities menu choices. This menu lets you control your indexes, close tables, delete and recall records (in .DBF files), share data with other applications, and perform data analysis.

In the next chapter, you'll begin taking an equally comprehensive look at Crystal Reports.

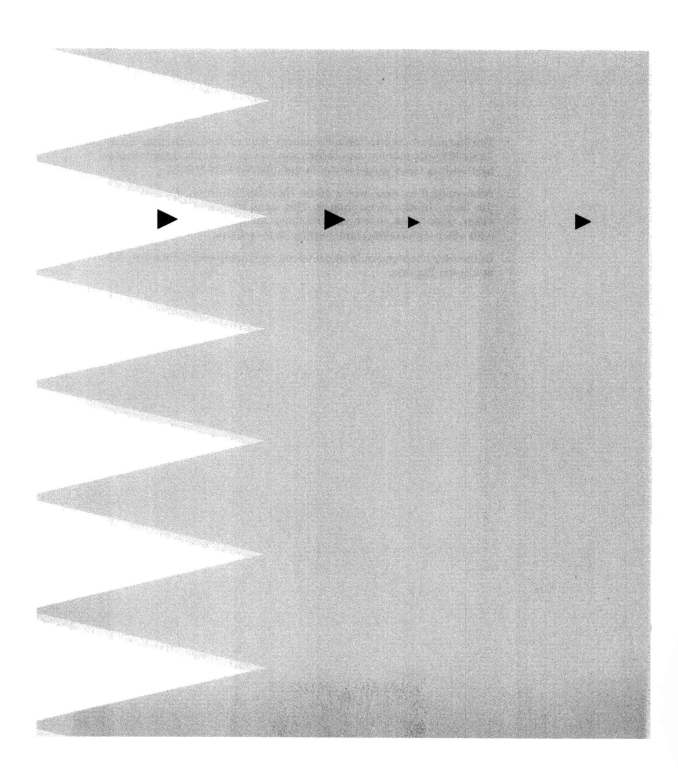

10

Mastering Crystal Reports

___

►► ***This*** chapter and the next cover the Crystal Reports tool. In this chapter, we'll go through every menu choice, dialog box, and speedbar button in detail. We'll attempt to treat Crystal Reports (Crystal, for short) exhaustively, at the risk of getting exhausting.

Here, we'll cover every tool at your disposal, so you'll know just how much you can do with Crystal. This will prepare you for getting creative, as we'll do in the next chapter.

Unlike dBASE for Windows, which changes menu options for the different tools, Crystal has a single main menu. Each pull-down menu has a single list of options, which are grayed or active, as appropriate to your work. The main menu for Crystal has eight choices:

File	Edit	Insert	Format	Database	Report	Window	Help

We'll go through each of these pull-down menus and the options they offer. Then we'll cover the speedbar, the format bar, and the Preview window's speedbar. We'll complete the chapter with a discussion of Crystal's Speed menus.

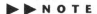 ▶▶ **N O T E**

In Chapter 11, we'll treat some special types of reports that you can create using what you'll learn here. Frankly, Chapter 11 is more fun, and we won't mind if you turn right past this chapter to get to it. If you're stuck on a particular report you want to create, go right ahead and try to find something similar in Chapter 11. But you'll still need the information in this chapter. As you go through Chapter 11, you can flip back to this chapter to pick up on all that you've missed.

▶▶ *Using the File Menu*

The File pull-down menu includes choices for opening, saving, printing, and closing files, as well as setting file options.

We'll cover the New choice in the next chapter, when we discuss cross-tabs and labels. The Open ..., Save, Save As ..., and Close menu choices work as you would expect.

► *Printing Files*

The File ➤ Print menu let's you print to a printer, to the Preview window, or to a file:

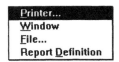

You can also print the report's definition—a text file that documents your report.

The Saved Data Dialog Box

Once your data has been saved, any of the first three File menu choices launch the Saved Data dialog box, shown in Figure 10.1.

FIGURE 10.1 ►

The Saved Data dialog box saves your time

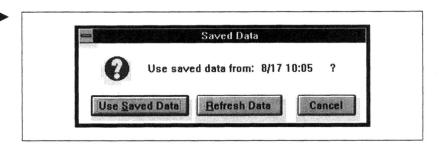

When Crystal is launched with a view or .DBF file selected, it will make a copy of the data that it will use in a temporary .DBF file. This can be a time-consuming process, especially if your tables are large and your view is complex. Once the temporary data table is created, its use is almost instantaneous.

Most of the time, you will use your saved data. For a final report, you may refresh your data to make sure that you have the latest information. If you are not on a network with multiple users, your saved data will be identical to the result from refreshing your data (unless you are running dBASE for Windows in another session and editing your data while your work in Crystal).

Printing and Previewing Files

The File ➤ Print ➤ Printer ... choice launches the Windows Print dialog box. From this dialog box, you can choose to print your entire report or a range of pages.

The File ➤ Print ➤ Window choice launches your report in the Preview window (see Chapter 7).

Exporting by Printing to a File

The File ➤ Print ➤ File choice launches the Export dialog box, shown in Figure 10.2. This is an important dialog box, because it provides a backdoor export facility that is much more robust than the export facilities built into dBASE for Windows.

FIGURE 10.2 ▶

The Export dialog box

 ▶▶ **N O T E**

As any major software company does, Borland competes with Microsoft and Lotus, among others. It is not overly enthusiastic about providing links from its programs to competing programs. In contrast to Borland, Crystal sells add-ons, not major software. An add-on vendor's existence depends on good support for the software of major vendors, so it is not surprising that its list of supported products is much more extensive than Borland's.

The direct export support available from the pull-down menu on the left side of the Export dialog box includes the following:

- Character-separated values
- Comma-separated values (CSV)
- Crystal Reports (RPT)
- Data Interchange Format (DIF)
- Excel 2.1 (XLS)
- Excel 3.0 (XLS)
- Excel 4.0 (XLS)
- Lotus 1-2-3 (WK1)
- Lotus 1-2-3 (WK3)
- Lotus 1-2-3 (WKS)
- Quattro Pro 5.0 (WB1)
- Record style (columns of values)
- Rich Text Format
- Tab-separated text
- Tab-separated values
- Text

When you choose the Character-separated values option, you move to the Character-Separated Values dialog box, shown in Figure 10.3. In this dialog box, you can choose the character that will separate fields and the character to use to surround character fields (by default, the double-quotation mark).

FIGURE 10.3 ▶

The Character-Separated Values dialog box

After you choose these characters, the Number and Date Format dialog box is launched, as shown in Figure 10.4.

FIGURE 10.4 ▶

*The Number and Date
Format dialog box*

Next, the Choose Export File dialog box is launched. This is a standard Open File dialog box (see Appendix B). If you are attached to a network mail system, the destination may be a disk file or a network mail system. If you are not on a network, the destination is a disk file.

Getting a Report on Your Report Design

The File ➤ Print ➤ Report Definition choice prints documentation about the design of your report. This is a five-section report. The easiest way to get a feel for this report is to choose this option and examine its output.

The output is directed immediately to your default printer, without any prompts. Be ready to print a report before you choose this option.

▶ Setting Up the Printer and Page Margins

There are two additional choices in the printer section of the File pull-down menu: Printer Setup ... and Page Margins ....

The Printer Setup ... option launches the Print Setup dialog box, common to Windows applications. This lets you choose a default printer, portrait or landscape orientation, upper or lower paper trays, and the other options that your printer supports.

The Page Margins ... choice launches the Printer Margins dialog box, shown in Figure 10.5.

FIGURE 10.5 ►

*The Printer Margins
dialog box*

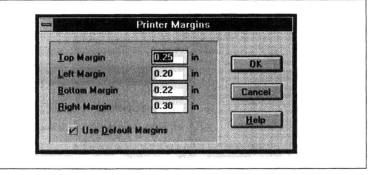

This dialog box lets you set margins for your printed pages (hence the
difference in the names of the menu choice and the dialog box).

 ►►T I P

> **Leave the default choices unless you know that your
> printer needs special choices. Click on the Use Default
> Margins check box to return to the standard setting if
> you are having problems.**

► Setting File Options

The File ► Options ... choice launches Crystal's Options dialog box. The
Options dialog box is functionally similar to the multi-tab dialog boxes in
dBASE for Windows. As you click on the four choices in the Category section, the rest of the dialog box changes to reflect your choice. Figure 10.6
shows the Options dialog box for the General choice.

The Options Dialog Box General Options

The first three general options let you control the work surface for
Crystal Reports. You can turn the button bar (speedbar) on or off, and
do the same for the format bar and the status bar.

FIGURE 10.6 ▶

The Options dialog box, General category

Ch.
10

The Use Short Section Names choice abbreviates the section names to the left of the report to something that barely suggests the section. The Page header becomes PH, the Details band becomes D, the first Group header is GH1, and so on.

 ▶▶ **T I P**

> **Don't choose Use Short Section Names until you are comfortable with Crystal Reports. Once you know the sections well, you may appreciate having more of your work surface available for the report you are working on.**

The Show Field Names choice toggles between showing the field names in the report's fields or showing characters which suggest field contents. For example, without field names a character field will show *X*'s.

By default, as you add fields to the Details band, the field names are added over the Details band as field titles. If you don't want these default titles, remove the check from the Insert Detail Field Titles box.

The next panel lets you control the use of saved data. If you check Refresh data on every print, the Saved Data dialog box will not appear. Each time you print, your data will be retrieved from its tables. This option is a time-waster if you are not running on a network with multiple simultaneous users.

The Save data with closed report option, if checked, saves a copy of the temporary data when Crystal saves your report's definition. If your data is not time-consuming to pull together from multiple tables, of if your data takes lots of disk space, don't choose this option.

Clicking on the Browse ... pushbutton launches the Set Directory dialog box, shown in Figure 10.7.

FIGURE 10.7 ►

The Set Directory dialog box

The Mail Destination choice in the Options dialog box has a drop-down list of the mail choices supported on your network.

The Options Dialog Box Database Options

The Options dialog box with the Database category selected is shown in Figure 10.8.

FIGURE 10.8 ▶

The Option dialog box, database category

The first choice in this dialog box is Data Directory. This defaults to the same location as the Report Directory in the General category. Clicking on the Browse ... button launches the Set Directory dialog box (Figure 10.7).

The Database Selector shows the choices from which your table or query will be chosen. The Index Selector shows the extensions used for finding indexes. When you call Crystal from dBASE for Windows, the exact names of your tables and their indexes are supplied by dBASE, so these choices are not relevant.

The Use Indexes For Speed choice should be left checked except in extraordinary circumstances. (You might not want an index used if you had inadvertently used an index that Crystal Reports needed to do a partial index, when you wanted a full report.)

The Translate DOS Strings and Translate DOS Memos check boxes let you use the characters you supplied in DOS applications in Character and Memo fields, respectively. This applies to the *hi-bit* characters (from 128 and up). In Windows, the hi-bit characters are different from those in DOS. Checking either of these boxes directs Crystal to translate the DOS characters to their Windows equivalents.

The Options Dialog Box Format Options

Figure 10.9 shows the Options dialog box for the Format category. The settings here are your general settings, which you can override for any or all fields in your report. Choosing one of the options in the Options dialog box's Field Format panel launches another dialog box for the type you selected.

FIGURE 10.9 ►

The Options dialog box, Format category

The Format String Dialog Box Choosing File ► Options ... Format category and pressing the String ... pushbutton launches the Format String dialog box, shown in Figure 10.10.

This dialog box controls the default formatting for character-based fields. In dBASE tables, for example, these are called *character strings*. In other databases, they are called by other names, such as *text* or *string fields*.

FIGURE 10.10

The Format String dialog box

The Suppress if Duplicated option prevents a field's value from being repeated on successive lines of a report. The individual value will be printed only on the first line on which it occurs.

The Hide when Printing option is not available when you select Options ... from the File menu, since this would not be a sensible general option. However, the Format String dialog box is also available when you format an individual field. For individual field formatting, the Hide when Printing Option is active. This lets you exclude the field from the printed report. For example, you might use this option for a column that does a calculation for the report, but does not need to appear in the printed version.

The Alignment choices are Default, Left, Centered, and Right. The Default alignment is right-justified for numeric data (columns of numbers line up) and left-justified for all other types (names line up on the left). You can override this here. For example, you could choose to center all dates.

The second section in the Format String dialog box lets you specify the treatment of text fields that are too long to fit on one line. The default is *not* to print long strings on multiple lines. If you check the Print on multiple lines box, the Maximum number of lines box applies. You can specify a maximum number, or leave it at zero, which will let Text fields take as many lines as needed.

►►**N O T E**

Word wrapping is used to print text fields over multiple lines. If the text doesn't fit in the number of lines allowed (1 by default, or the number specified in the Maximum box), the text is truncated to fit.

The Format Number and Format Currency Dialog Boxes Choosing File ➤ Options ... Format category and selecting the Number ... pushbutton launches the Format Number dialog box, shown in Figure 10.11.

FIGURE 10.11 ►

The Format Number dialog box

Format Number

Number Default Options

☑ Use Windows Default Format

☐ Suppress if Duplicated   ☐ Currency Symbol: [$]
☐ Suppress if Zero   ☐ One Symbol Per Page
☐ Hide when Printing   ◇ Fixed   ◇ Floating
Alignment: [Default ▼]   Position: [-$123 ▼]

Decimals: [1.00 ▼]   Decimal Separator: [.]
Rounding: [0.01 ▼]   ☑ Thousands Separator: [,]
Negatives: [-123 ▼]   ☑ Leading Zero

Sample:
        -5,555,555.56

[OK] [Cancel] [Help]

The Currency ... pushbutton brings up the Format Currency dialog box, which looks just like the Format Number dialog box. The Format Number dialog box applies to dBASE Numeric and Float fields. The Format Currency settings apply to money type fields, such as those in Paradox.

The Use <u>W</u>indows Default Format check box has the formatting default to the specifications provided in the Windows Control Panel.

 ►►**N O T E**

> **Using the Windows defaults may limit your other choices in a way you don't want, or it may quickly adjust your formatting to your national standards. You can try it to see if it is helpful or limiting.**

The <u>S</u>uppress if Duplicated option prevents a field's value from being repeated on successive lines of a report. The individual value will be printed only on the first line on which it occurs. Suppress if <u>Z</u>ero prevents a field's value from being printed if it is zero. Hide when <u>P</u>rinting is unavailable when you get to this dialog box from the File menu. When you are formatting an individual field, you can choose this option to prevent the field from appearing in the printed report. The <u>A</u>lignment choices are Default (right-justified for numbers and left-justified for other data), Left, Centered, and Right.

The currency-related choices let you choose a symbol (such as $) for currency. The rest of the options, such as printing the symbol just once on each page, apply when you are formatting currency fields, not when you access this dialog box through the Format Number choice.

Your choices in the Format Currency dialog box are to print the symbol only once, at the top of a column; to print the symbol in a fixed position (to the left or right of the number portion of the field, inside or outside optional parentheses for negative numbers); or to let it float, printing adjacent to the nearest digit.

To specify the number of decimals, you choose from a drop-down list that shows the alternatives. You can have from none through ten places to the right of the decimal point. Similarly, you choose rounding by picking a value between 0.01 and 1,000,000.

For negative values, you can have the number in parentheses or with the minus sign on the left or right. The decimal separator and thousands separators can be selected to meet your requirements. The thousands separator and leading zeros can be printed or suppressed.

The value in the Sample section shows what a number or currency field will look like based on the settings you've selected.

The Format Date Dialog Box Choosing File ➤ Options ... Format category and clicking on the Date ... pushbutton launches the Format Date dialog box, shown in Figure 10.12.

FIGURE 10.12 ►

The Format Date dialog box

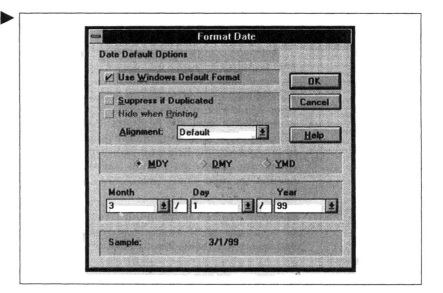

As in the dialog boxes for formatting numbers and currency, your first option in the Format Date dialog box is Use Windows Default Format. As with numbers, checking this box will conform your selection to the default set in the Windows' Control Panel.

The Suppress if Duplicated, Hide when Printing, and Alignment options work the same as they do in the other Format dialog boxes.

The next section lets you choose from MDY, DMY, and YMD orders for the month, day, and year in your date. The choice you make here is *not* reflected in the next section, where you choose specific options for Month, Day, and Year. However, it does control the output of your dates, as you can see in the Sample section.

The Month, Day, and Year options let you choose specific options for each component of your date. The month can be a single digit (if appropriate), a two-digit number, a three-letter abbreviation, or the month fully spelled-out. The day can be a one- or two-digit number. The year can be two or four digits long.

The separators between the three components specify the separation. The separation will be between the components you chose when you specified MDY, DMY or YMD—which may *not* be the order in which the three components are labeled in this section.

For a display such as 12/31/95, you can use the default / character or choose a different one. For a spelled-out date, such as December 31, 1995, you would type a single blank space for the first separator, and a comma followed by a blank space for the second separator.

The Sample section at the bottom shows the results of your choices (for the date March 1, 1999).

FIGURE 10.13 ▶

The Format Boolean dialog box

Format Boolean
Boolean Default Options

Suppress if Duplicated

Hide when Printing

Alignment: Default

Boolean Text: True or False

OK

Cancel

Help

The Format Boolean Dialog Box Choosing File ➤ Options ... Format category and choosing the Boolean ... pushbutton launches the Format Boolean dialog box, shown in Figure 10.13.

In dBASE tables, Boolean fields are called Logical fields. Other databases could use other names, such as Bit fields. Whatever the name, these are the fields used for True/False or Yes/No answers.

All the options here are discussed above in the Format String dialog box section, except for the Boolean Text option, which provides the following choices:

• True or False

• T or F

• Yes or No

• Y or N

• 1 or 0

By convention, 1 is synonymous with True or Yes; 0 is synonymous with False or No.

The Options Dialog Box's Fonts Options

Figure 10.14 shows the array of choices that you are faced with when you select the Fonts category from the File ➤ Options ... menu.

Here you can choose from each of the main bands, from headers through details to totals and footers. In each band, you can choose a font for the fields, or for the text you have typed in the band outside your fields.

Each of these pushbuttons launches the Windows Font dialog box (see Appendix B). This dialog box lets you choose a font name, a size, and a style (bold, italic, and so on).

FIGURE 10.14

The Options dialog box, Fonts category

 ▶▶ **T I P**

Critics of the overuse of fonts suggest that this many choices will lead to *ransom-note* typography. That name suggests what you would get by cutting individual letters from a newspaper or magazine and pasting them together. To avoid ransom-note typography, tread lightly here, if you tread at all.

Probably the best use of this set of choices would be either to ignore it or to replace every one of the choices with another font family. The default is Times New Roman, which is an excellent proportional font with serifs. The only reason that you might want to replace it is that it is very common. However, it has earned its popularity, since it is a well-designed, highly readable font. Don't change it unless you are sure that your alternative is better.

►► *Using the Edit Menu*

The Edit menu provides the standard Clipboard-related options and an OLE-related choice:

Cut	Ctrl+X
Copy	Ctrl+C
Paste	Ctrl+V
Paste Special...	
Clear	Del
Select Fields	
Formula...	
Text Field...	
Summary Operation...	
Show/Hide Sections...	
Group Section...	
Delete Section...	
Browse Field Data...	
Show Field Names	
Object	
Links...	

The Cut, Copy, and Paste options allow standard interaction with the Windows Clipboard. The fourth menu item, Paste Special ..., allows interaction with OLE applications.

► *Object Linking and Embedding through Paste Special*

If you activate an OLE-enabled application and copy to the Clipboard, the Edit ➤ Paste Special ... menu choice becomes available. Choosing it launches the Paste Special dialog box, shown in Figure 10.15.

Through this dialog box, you can embed any of the following in your report:

- A graphic (or other OLE result)
- A graphic with a link to the program that created it

FIGURE 10.15 ▶

The Paste Special dialog box for OLE links

- A link accessed by an icon in your report

If you choose the Paste radio button, you can then choose to paste the object, or just an image of the object. If you choose an image, you will have pasted an image into your report. If you choose the object, you will include an OLE connection to the program that created the object along with the object itself. Then you can use the program that created the image to edit the image from within your report.

If you choose the Paste Link radio button, you will have created an active link between the object's creating program and your report. If you change the object in the creating program, the change will be shown in your report.

When you choose Paste or Paste Link, the Display As Icon check box is activated. If you choose this option, your report will show an icon of the creating application.

If you have an icon for the creating application, an additional pushbutton, labeled Change Icon ..., appears in the lower-right corner of the Paste Special dialog box. Clicking this button launches the dialog box shown in Figure 10.16.

This dialog box lets you choose from among the icons available in an executable file. By default, this file is the creating object's executable file. If you choose the From File option in this dialog box, you can select icons from any Windows executable file on your system, such as Windows .EXE and .DLL files.

FIGURE 10.16 ►

The Change Icon dialog box

The icons available in the selected file are shown in the unlabeled rectangle below the From File choice. Clicking on the Browse ... pushbutton launches the Browse dialog box, which lets you specify a file from which to choose icons.

► Deleting and Selecting Fields

The next two choices in the Edit menu allow additional keyboard access to two common functions: deleting and selecting.

The Clear choice has the same effect as pressing the Del key. If you select any report component, you can choose this option in lieu of pressing the Del key.

 ►►TIP

While menu choices are often used as keyboard alternatives for mouse actions, the Clear choice also provides mouse access to a keyboard function. After you select your report element, clicking the Edit choice followed by clicking Clear is an alternative to pressing the Del key.

The Select Fields choice is an alternative way of selecting the lasso from the speedbar. After choosing this, you select report elements by dragging a rectangle on the report.

Note that the lasso in Crystal is *not* the same as the lasso in the Form Designer. First, you can start the lasso in the Form Designer simply by beginning a drag action anywhere that is not on top of a Form object. In Crystal, you must choose the lasso from the speedbar or by the Edit ➤ Select Fields menu choice.

Second, the lasso in the Form Designer selects only those fields that are entirely inside the lasso. The lasso in Crystal also selects all fields that are touched by the lasso. To put it another way, fields that are touched by the lasso are *not* selected in the Form Designer but *are* selected in Crystal Reports.

▶ Editing Formulas

The Edit ➤ Formula ... choice launches the Expression Builder (see Chapter 8) to edit the formula in a formula field. This choice is only available when you have a formula field selected. If you have more than one formula field selected, Formula launches the last selected formula field in the Expression Builder.

▶ Editing Text Fields

The Edit ➤ Text Field ... choice launches the Edit Text Field dialog box, shown in Figure 10.17.

This dialog box lets you enter extensive text in a field, which is not a practice we recommend. See Chapter 11 for information about form letters, which are one area where you will want extended text in a report.

Note that you can't exit the Edit Text Field dialog box with an Enter keypress, because this keystroke is interpreted as part of the text you are entering or editing.

▶ Editing Summary Fields

The Edit ➤ Summary Operation choice is available when you have selected a summary field, such as a subtotal or total. It launches the Summary Field dialog box, shown in Figure 10.18.

FIGURE 10.17 ▶

The Edit Text Field dialog box

FIGURE 10.18 ▶

Selecting a summary field operation

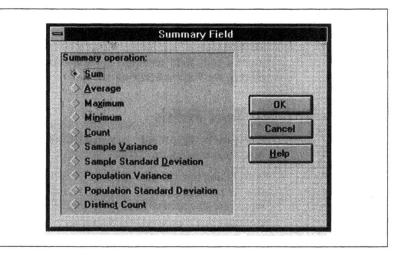

The Summary Field options are standard mathematical operations you can perform, such as calculating a sum or average. (See the Table Utilities section in Chapter 9 for definitions of the variance and standard deviation calculations.) For this dialog box, a *sample* is a portion of the total series, similar to a group subtotal. The *population* is the entire set of data, similar to a grand total.

► *Hiding Report Sections*

The Edit ➤ Show/Hide Sections ... choice lets you temporarily suppress individual report sections. It launches the Show/Hide Sections dialog box, which lists all the available sections in your report.

In Figure 10.19, we chose to hide the Grand total section of a report. This section will not appear on the report layout surface, nor will it appear in the report itself.

FIGURE 10.19 ►

Temporarily eliminating a report section

▶▶ TIP

If you're designing a report with lots of items, hiding sections is a good way to make room for your work. That way you can focus on only the sections of a report that need attention.

The radio buttons at the bottom of the dialog box, Show section and Hide section, reflect the current status of each section.

▶ Editing Report Groups

The Edit ➤ Group Section ... option launches two successive dialog boxes, both titled Edit Group Section. The first dialog box lets you choose from a list of your report's group sections. You must select a group section before you can click on OK or press Enter to proceed to the second Edit Group Section dialog box.

The second Edit Group Section dialog box is shown in Figure 10.20.

FIGURE 10.20 ▶

The second Edit Group Section dialog box

The first of the two drop-down lists lets you choose from any available data field. The second lets you choose between ascending and descending order.

The Browse Field Data ... pushbutton lets you examine the contents of the selected field.

▶ Deleting Report Sections

The Edit ➤ Delete Section ... option launches the Delete Section dialog box, shown in Figure 10.21.

This dialog box is another instance of the first Edit Group Section dialog box. It provides a list of your report's group sections so that you can choose a group section or total section for deletion.

Deleting all the fields from a section does not delete the section itself. Deleting the section gets rid of all the fields in the section.

FIGURE 10.21

Choosing a section to delete

WARNING

There is no warning in Crystal Reports when you choose to delete a section that contains fields. All your fields will be deleted. Look carefully before you delete a section.

▶ *Browsing the Selected Field's Data*

When you choose Edit ➤ Browse Field Data ..., you see a dialog box, titled by the field you have selected, which shows the data in that field. You cannot choose this option until you have selected a field. If you have selected more than one field, the last field in the selection is used.

▶ *Showing Field Names*

The Edit ➤ Show Field Names choice is documented to toggle between the display of letters and the display of field names in the fields in your report layout surface. It is not operable in the current release of dBASE for Windows. Choose File ➤ Options ..., General category and check the Show Fields Name box to change this setting.

► Editing Objects

The next to last choice on the Edit menu is dimmed and labeled Object if you have not selected an object on your report. If you have selected an object, this choice is labeled according to the object you have selected. For example, here's the command when a Microsoft drawing object is selected:

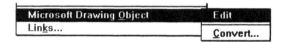

When you've selected an OLE object in your report, you can edit it (launch Microsoft Draw, in this case) or convert it (from an object link to just a graphic, for example). For more information, see the discussion of the Edit ► Paste Special choice.

► Managing Links

The Edit ► Links choice is available when you have established a link to an OLE object (see the discussion of Edit ► Paste Special). If you have selected a linked object, this choice launches the Links dialog box, shown in Figure 10.22.

FIGURE 10.22 ►

Editing OLE links

![Links dialog box showing: Links list with "E:\...\ARCADE.BMP|2 2 32 32   Paintbrush Picture   Automatic" highlighted. Buttons on right: Cancel, Update Now, Open Source, Change Source, Break Link. Below: Source: E:\WINDOWS\ARCADE.BMP|2 2 32 32, Type: Paintbrush Picture, Update: ● Automatic ○ Manual]

The Links dialog box shows the link and provides options to update, open, or change the link's source. You can also break the link.

▶▶ *Using the Insert Menu*

The Insert pull-down menu is used to add items to your reports after you have finished your basic layout:

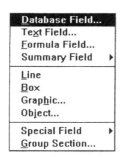

▶ *Inserting a Database Field*

Choosing Insert ➤ Database Field ... launches the Insert Database Field dialog box, shown in Figure 10.23. From this dialog box, you can add as many fields as you like to your report. This dialog box is in a modeless child window, so you can leave it open as you do other work on your report.

From this dialog box, you can select a field to place in your report in three ways:

- Select it and click on the Insert pushbutton.
- Double-click on the field.
- Drag the field from the dialog box to the report.

In addition to the Insert choice, the Browse Field Data ... pushbutton lets you look at the data in the field you have selected. When you're finished with this dialog box, choose the Done pushbutton.

FIGURE 10.23 ►

The Insert Database Field dialog box

► *Inserting a Text Field*

The Insert ► Text Field ... choice launches the Edit Text Field dialog box, shown earlier (Figure 10.17). You can create your text field in this dialog box.

When you're finished entering text, click on Accept. Your cursor will turn into the field-insertion rectangle. Position the field in the report and click to drop it.

► *Inserting a Formula Field*

Choosing Insert ► Formula Field ... launches the Insert Formula dialog box, shown in Figure 10.24.

This dialog box lets you manage your list of formula fields. You can enter a new name in the top entry field, or click on one of the existing fields listed in the middle section to enter its name in the entry field automatically.

If you enter a new name in the entry field, clicking on OK or pressing Enter launches the Expression Builder (see Chapter 8). After you've created a new expression or selected an existing formula, your cursor turns to the field-insertion rectangle. Position the field and click to drop it into your report.

FIGURE 10.24

Managing your list of formula fields

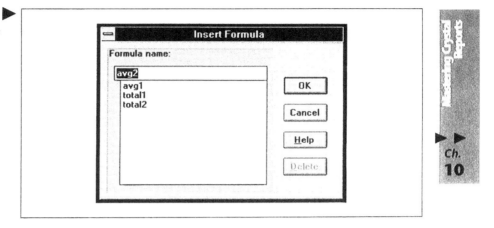

▶ *Inserting a Summary Field*

To insert a summary field, you begin by selecting a Numeric or Date field to summarize. After you have selected one, choosing Insert ➤ Summary Field brings up this cascading menu:

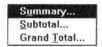

Adding a Summary Calculation

If you choose Insert ➤ Summary Field ➤ Summary ..., the Insert Summary dialog box, shown in Figure 10.25, is launched.

The summary choices are the same as those in the Summary Field dialog box (see the discussion of Edit ➤ Summary Operation ...). You can also choose the group if you've inserted multiple groups. The Browse Field Data ... choice launches a dialog box that shows you the data in your field.

FIGURE 10.25 ▶

Inserting a summary field

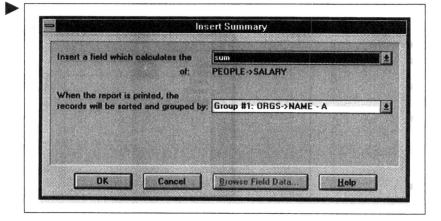

Inserting a Subtotal for a Data Field

If you've selected a data field (not a summary field), you can choose to insert a subtotal. The Insert ➤ Summary Field ➤ Subtotal ... choice launches the Insert Subtotal dialog box, shown in Figure 10.26.

FIGURE 10.26 ▶

The Insert Subtotal dialog box

If you access the first drop-down list, the dialog box allows you to pick from all your data and calculated fields. If you drop down this list, you can choose a different grouping variable. The second drop-down list lets you choose ascending or descending sequence.

If you do not drop down the first list, you will be given an existing grouping as the default.

FIGURE 10.27

Inserting a grand total

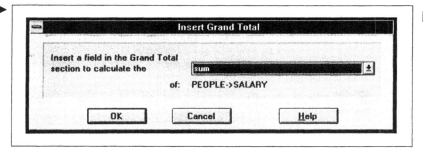

Adding a Grand Total

Choosing Insert ➤ Summary Field ➤ Grand Total ... launches the Insert Grand Total dialog box, shown in Figure 10.27.

Inserting a grand total is simpler than inserting a subtotal, because it does not respect groups—it computes a grand total across all groups. Inserting a grand total adds an additional band to your report, titled Grand total. (If you are using short section names, it's GT.) The grand total field is automatically placed in this band.

 ►►**TIP**

> It's almost always a good idea to add a text field to label the grand total field.

▶ Inserting Lines and Boxes

When you choose Insert ➤ Line or Box, the cursor changes to the pencil shape. To draw a line, you drag from one end of the line to the other end. You draw a box by dragging from any corner of a rectangle to the opposite corner.

For those who find the mouse a somewhat imprecise drawing instrument, you'll be happy to know that the designers of Crystal assumed that you would only use vertical and horizontal lines.

If your end is more or less to one side or the other of your starting point, you will get a perfectly horizontal line. Similarly, if you move more or less up and down, you get a perfectly vertical line.

 ▶▶ **T I P**

You can insert a graphic to add lines other than horizontal and vertical ones.

You can use Format ➤ Line ... to add color to lines, to change line width, and to select line styles. Use Format ➤ Box ... to change box widths and border styles, add colors to your box, and choose other features.

▶ Inserting Graphics and Objects

The Insert ➤ Graphic ... choice launches the Choose Graphic File dialog box. In this dialog box, you can choose from .BMP, .GIF, .PCX, .TIF, and .TGA graphics files.

Choosing Insert ➤ Object ... launches the Insert Object dialog box, shown in Figure 10.28. This dialog box lets you pick any OLE-enabled application to supply an object to place on your report.

You can create a new object of any of the specified types, or use one from a file. To display this object as an icon, check the Display As Icon check box (see the discussion of Edit ➤ Paste Special ...).

FIGURE 10.28 ▶

Choosing to insert an OLE application

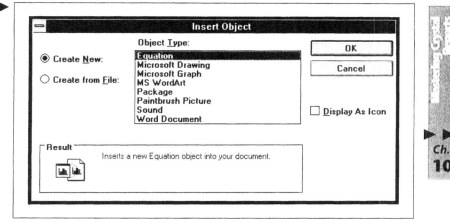

▶ *Inserting a Special Field*

The Insert ➤ Special Field choice displays this cascading menu:

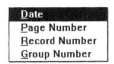

The Date choice is today's date (actually, the system date in your computer, which is probably today's date). This is frequently used in the Page header area.

The Page Number choice is used to number pages, as it is in any publication. This is commonly used in the Page footer or Page header area.

You can also choose to use record numbers and number your groups, with the Record Number and Group Number choices, respectively.

When you make any of these choices, your cursor turns into the field-insertion rectangle, which you position wherever you like and then click to drop the field.

To format these fields, choose Format ➤ Field ... after selecting the special field. The Date special field is formatted as a date; the others are formatted as numbers.

▶ Inserting a Group Section

Choosing Insert ➤ Group Section ... launches the Insert Group Section dialog box, shown in Figure 10.29.

FIGURE 10.29 ▶

Inserting a group section

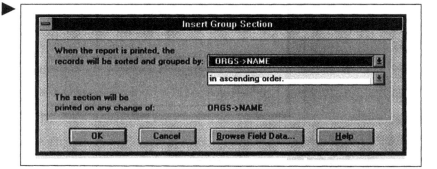

The default grouping field is the first field in the Details band. If you have a typical one-to-many relationship (one employer with many employees, for example), this is frequently the correct choice. You can access the other fields in your report and the other fields in your table or query through the drop-down list.

The default order is ascending. You can change this to descending through the second drop-down list. The section is printed every time the selecting grouping item changes.

Through the Browse Field Data ... pushbutton, you can take a look at the data in the field that you selected for grouping.

▶▶ Using the Format Menu

Each element you add to your report is given a default format, which you can set with the File ➤ Options ... choice. The Format menu lets you give specific format characteristics to each field and other object on your report.

Font...
Field...
Border and Colors...

Graphic...
Line...
Box...

Section...
Report Title...

Send Behind Others

  T I P

A very light hand with the format features will yield more effective reports. Before you add any formatting, ask yourself if it will help the report communicate its message. When you add features, keep your final output device(s) in mind. The most effective use of color is useless if you are going to reproduce the report on a black-and-white photocopier.

Some of the Format menu choices, such as Section ... and Report Title ..., are always available. Other choices, such as Graphic ..., Line ..., and Box ..., are only available when you have selected an object of the appropriate type.

The Format ➤ Font ... choice lets you select a font, size, and font style for the text in the object you have selected. It launches the Windows Font dialog box (see Appendix B).

➤ *Formatting Fields*

The Format ➤ Field ... choice launches one of the following dialog boxes, depending on the field's type:

- Format String

- Format Number
- Format Currency
- Format Date
- Format Boolean

These are the same dialog boxes you can get to through File ➤ Options, Format category (Figures 10.10 through 10.14).

▶ Formatting Borders and Colors

Choosing Format ➤ Border and Colors ... launches the Format Borders and Colors dialog box, shown in Figure 10.30.

FIGURE 10.30 ▶

Setting field border and color characteristics

By default, your fields have black text and no fill color, which normally will mean printing with black ink on white paper. You can change the color of the text (the foreground color) and the fill color (the background color). The check box next to the Fill choice must be checked to choose a fill color other than None.

A border is not normally used. If you check the box next to the Border choice, it will trigger checks in the boxes for all four of the field's sides.

If you use a border, it will be drawn on the sides specified by these checks. Figure 10.31 shows some sample uses of the border.

FIGURE 10.31

Various border characteristics

plain border	double line
top and bottom	left and right
drop shadow	border and shadow
width of field	width of data
height of line	height of font

▶ *Formatting Graphics*

The Forma**t** ➤ **G**raphic ... choice launches the Graphic Format dialog box, shown in Figure 10.32.

FIGURE 10.32

Cropping and scaling a graphic

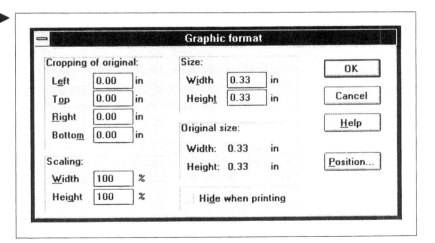

Graphic format

Cropping of original:
- L**e**ft   0.00   in
- T**o**p   0.00   in
- **R**ight   0.00   in
- Botto**m** 0.00   in

Scaling:
- **W**idth   100   %
- Hei**g**ht   100   %

Size:
- W**i**dth   0.33   in
- Heigh**t** 0.33   in

Original size:
- Width: 0.33   in
- Height: 0.33   in

Hi**d**e when printing

OK

Cancel

Help

Position...

The Graphic Format dialog box provides options for cropping, scaling, and sizing graphics:

- Crop a graphic on any of its four sides.
- Set scaling in both the horizontal and vertical dimensions.
- Adjust the size of a graphic.

▶▶ **T I P**

> **If you adjust the scaling differently for width and height, you will change the aspect ratio. This lets you be creative about how you stretch an image.**

The Hide when printing check box lets you show a graphic on the screen but not print it. (Printing graphics ranges from time-consuming to impossible, depending on its size and your printer's capabilities.)

Clicking on the Position ... pushbutton launches the Graphic Position dialog box, shown in Figure 10.33.

FIGURE 10.33 ▶

Positioning the graphic

The values in this dialog box default to the position at which you drew the graphic. You can change the position by dragging the graphic or by adjusting the coordinates in this dialog box.

▶ Formatting Lines

Choosing Format ➤ Line ... launches the Line Format dialog box, shown in Figure 10.34. This dialog box lets you adjust the color, width, and style of your line.

FIGURE 10.34 ▶

The Line Format dialog box

Here are some examples of lines in different widths, ranging from one pixel to the thickest available (3.50 points), and the dashed and dotted line styles:

Dashed and dotted line styles are not available if you have selected a thick line.

▶ Formatting Boxes

Choosing Format ➤ Box ... launches the Box Format dialog box, shown in Figure 10.35. This is similar to the Line Format dialog box, but it adds a check box for closing the box at the top and bottom of pages. This applies when the printing would otherwise start a box on one page and finish it on another.

FIGURE 10.35 ►

The Box Format dialog box

Here are examples of a standard-width box, a thicker box, and boxes drawn with dashed lines and dotted lines:

► *Formatting Sections*

The Forma**t** ➤ **S**ection … choice launches two dialog boxes, both named Format Section. The first one lets you choose one of your report's sections. The second dialog box lets you choose formatting characteristics for the section you selected. Figure 10.36 shows the Format Section dialog box after the Details section was selected.

The **H**ide Section option hides the section you have selected (it doesn't show on the screen or in the printed version). For example, you might hide a section that includes calculated fields that you use in other sections but don't want to show in detail.

The **P**rint at Bottom of Page option is used for group values, such as a subtotal section, which you want to appear at the bottom of a page. Invoices are a typical use for this feature.

The New Page B**e**fore option forces a new page to be started before starting the selected group. New Page A**f**ter forces the page to be completed

FIGURE 10.36

*Formatting a report's
Details section*

when this section is printed. (Pages still start and end with the normal
Page header and Page footer sections.)

The Reset Page Number After option sets the page number back to 1 after printing the section. You would use this feature if you were printing
long groups where you wanted each group numbered starting with 1.

The Keep Section Together option prevents the section from being
split at the end of a page. Note that this does not support keeping a
group together; only the selected section (such as a Group header section) is kept together.

Suppress Blank Lines suppresses those lines that have fields that are
suppressed (for example, by using blanks for zero values). It does not suppress blank lines that you have included for spacing in your layout.

The Format with Multiple Columns option enables the Multi-Column
Layout ... pushbutton, which launches the Multi-Column Layout dialog box, shown in Figure 10.37.

This dialog box lets you specify formatting for a multiple-column (telephone book) style layout. This is the layout used for most mailing labels.

▶ *Formatting Report Titles*

The Format ▶ Report Title ... choice launches the Edit Report Title
dialog box, shown in Figure 10.38.

FIGURE 10.37 ►

Setting a multiple-column layout

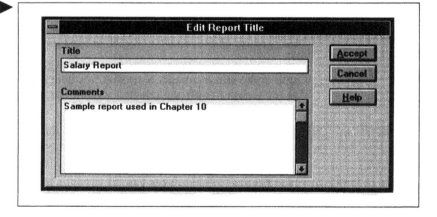

FIGURE 10.38 ►

Entering a report title and description

The title you enter here (as well as the comments) is for your use in identifying the report. It does not appear in the Report window when you run the report in dBASE for Windows, nor does it appear on the printed report. (Use a text field with the same text to put a title on the printed report.)

The title, but not your comments, is printed as part of the report definition when you choose File ➤ Print ➤ Report Definition.

▶ Restacking Items

If you have multiple items stacked on top of each other, they are in what the Form Designer calls the z-order. In Crystal, you can use Format ➤ Send Behind Others to push the top item in the stack to the bottom.

▶▶ Using the Database Menu

The Database pull-down menu lets you specify the location of your data and verify that the report is consistent with the latest version of your tables.

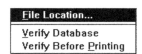

▶ Changing the Database File Location

If you want your report to use data from a different location than the one you specified when you created it, use the Database ➤ File Location … option. This choice launches the Set Location dialog box, shown in Figure 10.39.

The Set Location dialog box does *not* let you move your data. It lets you specify the location of your data. For each database (SQL database, query, or table), you can choose the Set Location … pushbutton. This takes you to the Choose New Location dialog box, in which you can specify another location.

The Same as Report pushbutton sets the location of the data to the same location as the report. This button is available only after you have saved your report.

▶ Verifying Your Databases

The Database ➤ Verify Database choice checks that your database tables exist in the location you specified. If the tables exist, it continues to check that they have the fields used to create your report.

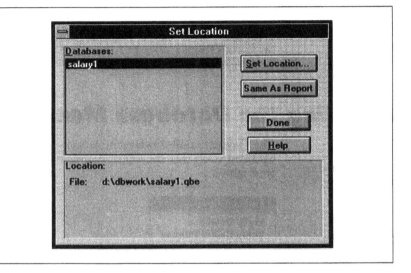
FIGURE 10.39 ▶

Choosing a database location

You are given appropriate messages if your tables are not found, or if they do not have all the fields used in your report.

Crystal will try to run a report with different fields. If you have added fields to the table since you built the report, Crystal will ignore them. If you have deleted fields used in the report, Crystal will also delete the field(s) from your report and run just the remaining portions. Alert boxes advise you if this is the situation.

The Database ➤ Verify Before Printing menu option is a toggle, which defaults to not checked. If you turn it on, each time you choose to print the report, Crystal will check that your database tables exist in the location you specified and that they have the fields used to create the report (like Database ➤ Verify Database).

▶▶ *Using the Report Menu*

The Report pull-down menu's choices let you filter and sort records, as well as specify how report data is handled.

```
Record Selection Formula...
Record Sort Order...

Group Selection Formula...
Group Sort Order...

Refresh Report Data
Save Data with Closed Report

Set Print Date...
```

Ch.
10

▶ Specifying Record or Group Selection Formulas

The Record Selection Formula ... and Group Selection Formula ... choices both launch the Expression Builder. They require a logical expression. If you select Record Selection Formula ... and enter an expression, only those records that evaluate to True are selected. This is the same as using a filter in dBASE for Windows. If you choose Group Selection Formula ... and enter an expression, only the groups for which the formula is True are selected.

▶ Specifying Record or Group Sort Order

The Record Sort Order ... option displays the Record Sort Order dialog box, shown in Figure 10.40.

FIGURE 10.40 ▶

Choosing a record sort order

The default sorting is done by groups, as you specified when you added groups to your report. The Record Sort Order dialog box lets you sort the records within your groups. If you add fields from the list (the fields in your Detail band), the Sort Direction choices become available. These give you a choice between ascending or descending sort order.

If you choose the Group Sort Order ... option, the Group Sort Order dialog box is launched. This dialog box is almost identical to the Record Sort Order dialog box. The difference is that the fields are those that are in your Group summary bands. Choosing one or more of these groups will sort your groups into the order you specify. Again, the Sort Direction choices are available after you choose a sort field.

► Refreshing and Saving Report Data

The Refresh Report Data option reads the report's data from the databases or tables you have specified, so that your report will reflect the latest changes to the data.

The Save Data with Closed Report is a toggle. When checked, this option saves a copy of the report's data with the report. This is a particularly useful option when you are building a report.

► Specifying a Print Date

The Set Print Date ... choice launches the Print Date dialog box, shown in Figure 10.41.

The default choice is to use today's date (actually, the system date stored in your computer). If you check the Other box, you can add a date in the fields shown.

FIGURE 10.41 ▶

Setting the print date

▶▶ *Using the Window Menu*

The Window menu is a standard Microsoft Windows Window menu, with the same features as the dBASE for Windows Window menu.

Tile Vertically
Tile Horizontally
Cascade
Arrange Icons
Close All
1 Salary Report
√2 Preview Window: Salary Report

▶▶ *Using the Help Menu*

The Help menu has the choices that are common to most Windows Help menus:

Contents	**F1**
Search...	
Using Help	
Personal Trainer	
Register / Change Address...	
Technical Support Request...	
Crystal Library...	
About Crystal Reports For dBASE...	

There is a notable extra capability here. Through Crystal's Help menu, you can register and change your registration information with Crystal Computer Services, the company that built Crystal Reports.

After you enter or update your name and address information, the registration options include registering via modem. If you have a modem, you select your modem's speed and COM port (Com1, Com2, and so on) and the registration software takes over. This Help option will dial Crystal's computer and transfer your registration information. It will inform you of its progress (it takes a minute or so), and it is totally automatic—a very nice feature.

If you want to change your registration information (you move, for instance), you can do so by choosing the appropriate choices on the Help menu and using your modem to automatically update your data in Crystal's database.

►► *Using the Crystal Speedbar*

The speedbar in Crystal Reports looks like this:

The functions of the buttons are listed in Table 10.1.

► **TABLE 10.1**: *Crystal Reports Speedbar Buttons*

BUTTON	FUNCTION
	Creates a new report (same as File ➤ New ➤ Report...)
	Opens an existing report (same as File ➤ Open...)
	Saves the report (same as File ➤ Save)

▶ **TABLE 10.1:** *Crystal Reports Speedbar Buttons (continued)*

BUTTON	FUNCTION
	Prints the report (same as File ➤ Print ➤ Printer…)
	Previews the report (same as File ➤ Print ➤ Window)
	Exports the report (same as File ➤ Print ➤ File…)
	Mails the report (like File ➤ Print ➤ File … but the destination default is a network mail system, not a disk file)
	Cuts selected text to the Clipboard (same as Edit ➤ Cut, or Ctrl-X)
	Copies selected text to the Clipboard (same as Edit ➤ Copy, or Ctrl-C)
	Pastes text from the Clipboard (same as Edit ➤ Paste, or Ctrl-V)
	Selects (lasso) fields (same as Edit ➤ Select Fields)
	Inserts a database field (same as Insert ➤ Database Field…)
	Inserts a text field (same as Insert ➤ Text Field…)
	Inserts a formula field (same as Insert ➤ Formula Field…)

Ch.
10

► ► *Formatting with the Format Bar*

► **TABLE 10.1:** *Crystal Reports Speedbar Buttons (continued)*

BUTTON	FUNCTION
Σ	Inserts a summary field (same as Insert ➤ Summary Field ➤ Summary...)
	Inserts a graphic (same as Insert ➤ Graphic...)
OLE	Inserts an OLE object (same as Insert ➤ Object...)
	Inserts a line (same as Insert ➤ Line)
	Inserts a box (same as Insert ➤ Box)
	Selects the record sort order (same as Report ➤ Record Sort Order...)
	Allows you to enter or edit the record selection formula (same as Report ➤ Record Selection Formula...)

Crystal's format bar includes buttons for formatting your report. You can use these buttons instead of the Format menu choices.

▶ *Formatting Fonts*

The font name and size drop-down lists let you choose their respective properties (like Format ➤ Font...):

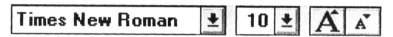

The two buttons to the right or this group let you increase and decrease the font size by one unit. Click on the large A to increase the size; click on the small A to decrease the size.

The font style buttons can be used in any combination you like:

The **B** button toggles the boldface style. The *I* button toggles the italic style. The U button toggles underlining. (The menu choice is Format ➤ Font....)

▶ *Aligning Fields*

The alignment buttons let you pick an alignment for your fields:

These buttons select left, center, or right alignment, respectively. (The menu choice is Format ➤ Field....)

▶ Formatting Numbers

The number formatting buttons are toggles:

Their current setting reflects the state of the highlighted number or currency field. (The menu option is Format ➤ Field ....)

Clicking on the $ button turns on (or off) the use of the currency sign. The default setting is to show the $ to the left of the number, but you can change the symbol and position through the File ➤ Options ... menu's Format choice.

The comma button toggles the display of commas (or the separator character you specified in the File ➤ Options ..., Format category) in the selected Numeric field.

The % button toggles the display of a percent sign to the right of the selected field. Note that the number 1 will display as 1%, not 100%—the assumption is that your number is already a percentage.

The decimal selection buttons control the decimal places shown:

The button on the left increases the number of decimal places displayed in the selected field. The button on the right decreases the number of decimal places. (The menu choice is Format ➤ Field ....)

▶▶ *Using the Preview Window's Speedbar*

The speedbar at the bottom of the report Preview window looks like this:

Table 10.2 lists the functions of these buttons.

▶ **TABLE 10.2:** *Preview Window Speedbar Buttons*

BUTTON	FUNCTION
⏮	Moves to the first page
◀	Moves one page at a time toward the first page
▶	Moves one page at a time toward the last page
⏭	Moves to the last page
Cancel	Cancels activity, during processes such as refreshing report data.

▶ **TABLE 10.2:** *Preview Window Speedbar Buttons (continued)*

BUTTON	FUNCTION
🔍	Toggles among three zoom levels
⚡	Refreshes your report's data (same as Report ➤ Refresh Report Data)
🖨	Prints the report (same as File ➤ Print ➤ Printer ...)
📷	Exports the report's data (same as File ➤ Print ➤ File ...)
✉	Mails the report (like File ➤ Print ➤ File ... but the destination default is a network mail system, not a disk file)
Close	Closes the report Preview window (same as Close from the Preview window's System menu)

►► *Using the Speed Menus*

Clicking the right mouse button launches a Speed menu from almost every point in Crystal Reports. The following sections describe the Speed menus, grouped as follows:

- Speed menus in report bands
- Field-related Speed menus
- Special-item Speed menus

▶ *Speed Menus for the Report Bands*

You access the Speed menus for report bands by right-clicking in the area to the left of the report, in either the report layout window or in the Preview window.

The following choices are available in the Speed menus for report bands:

- Hide Section
- Show ➤ Hide Sections …
- Format Section …
- Add Line
- Delete Last Line
- Cancel Menu

The Group header and Group footer Speed menus have two addtional options:

- Change Group …
- Delete Section

The Grand Total Speed Menu

The following choices are available in the Grand Total Speed menu:

- Hide Section
- Show ➤ Hide Sections …
- Format Section …
- Add Line
- Delete Last Line
- Delete Section
- Cancel Menu

The Page Footer Speed Menu

The Page Footer Speed menu offers the following options:

- Hide Section
- Show/Hide Sections ...
- Format Section ...
- Add Line
- Delete Last Line
- Cancel Menu

▶ The Field-Related Speed Menus

There are two similar Speed menus for fields. One is for database or table fields, and the other is for report fields, such as subtotals and grand totals. These Speed menus appear when you right-click over the related field type.

Database and Table Field Speed Menu

The Speed menu choices available for database and table fields are as follows:

- Change Font ...
- Change Format ...
- Change Border and Colors ...
- Browse Field Data ...
- Insert Subtotal ...
- Insert Grand Total ...
- Insert Summary ...
- Send Behind Others
- Delete Field
- Cancel Menu

Text Field Speed Menu

The following choices are available for text fields:

- Change Font ...
- Change Format ...
- Change Border and Colors ...
- Edit Text Field ...
- Send Behind Others
- Delete Field
- Cancel Menu

Summary Field Speed Menu

The following choices are available for summary fields:

- Change Font ...
- Change Format ...
- Change Border and Colors ...
- Change Summary Operation ...
- Send Behind Others
- Delete Field
- Cancel Menu

▶ The Special-Item Speed Menus

Speed menus are also associated with the following:

- Text areas
- Special fields
- Lines
- Boxes
- Graphics
- Objects

The Speed Menu for Text Areas

Text areas are the areas of your report that are outside fields or other items but within the report itself.

The following Speed menu options are given for a text area:

- Change Font ...
- Paste ...
- Cancel Menu

The Speed Menu for Special Fields

Special fields are the fields added by the Insert ➤ Special Field choice: date, page number, record number, and group number. The Speed menu choices for these fields are as follows:

- Change Font ...
- Change Format ...
- Change Border and Colors ...
- Send Behind Others
- Delete Field
- Cancel Menu

The Speed Menus for Lines and Boxes

The following choices are on the Speed menus for lines and boxes:

- Change Format ...
- Send Behind Others
- Delete Line (or Box)
- Cancel Menu

The Speed Menus for Graphics and Objects

The following Speed Menu choices are available for graphics and objects:

- Change Format ...
- Change Position ...
- Send Behind Others
- Delete Graphic
- Cancel Menu

When you've selected an OLE object, the first choice of the Speed menu is the name of the object. Choosing this option displays a cascading menu that lets you edit or convert the object.

▶▶ *Summary*

In this chapter, we explored almost every part of the Crystal Reports program. (We've saved a couple of the best parts, including cross-tab reports, for the next chapter.)

We started with the File menu, which has more choices than you might expect. The Print options in particular offer a wider range of choices. Exporting provides a richer set of export file types than the export option within dBASE for Windows.

The File ➤ Options dialog box provides a comprehensive set of default settings. It is roughly comparable to the dBASE for Windows Desktop Properties dialog box (although Crystal doesn't uses the multi-tab format).

Along wilth the standard Clipboard operations, the Edit menu covers many other operations, including controlling which sections of the form are visible and manipulating OLE links to other Windows programs.

The Insert menu lets you add items to your report. You can insert lines, boxes, graphics, and special fields, as well as summary fields such as subtotals and grand totals.

The Format menu lets you apply all kinds of formatting to the items on your report. You can change colors, draw lines around some or all of your items' sides, add drop shadows, and more.

The Report, Window, and Help menus provide typical Windows' program services.

After the menus, we discussed the speedbars, the format bar, and the Speed menus in Crystal Reports.

In the next chapter, we'll conclude Part 3 with a closer look at some specialized reporting, including building cross-tab reports.

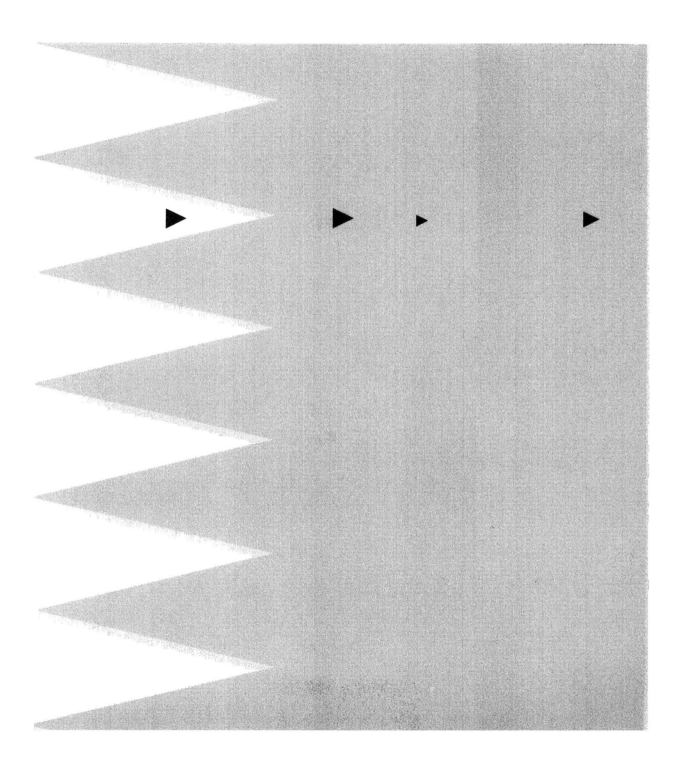

► ► CHAPTER **11**

Mastering Cross-Tab Reports, Labels, and Form Letters

———

▶ ▶ **I**n this chapter, we'll conclude Part 3 with an in depth look at three types of specialized reports: cross-tabs, mailing labels, and form letters.

Cross-tab reports are used when you want to look at your data in two or more dimensions simultaneously. This is a common requirement with, for example, sales data.

Mailing labels let you prepare mailing labels from your data, as we did in Chapter 7. In this chapter, we'll explore your choices and the label settings in detail. You'll find that you can use the mailing label feature for a lot more than simple mailing labels.

Form letters are the final type of report that we'll examine in depth. The way Crystal Reports lets you handle your text makes it an ideal tool for preparing form letters.

We'll begin with cross-tab reports, which are designed using another one of Crystal Report's design surfaces.

▶ ▶ *Generating Cross-Tab Reports*

Cross-tab reports let you group your data on two criteria simultaneously, presenting a spreadsheet-style view. For example, with a cross-tab report, you could view your company's sales by product line within geographic regions.

In Crystal Reports, creating a cross-tab report is a simple matter of dragging your fields into the appropriate box.

▶ *Sample Data for Cross-Tab Reporting*

For our example of cross-tab reporting, let's suppose that we've built a database system for a seed company that does business in three states in the center of the U.S.: Indiana, Illinois, and Iowa (IN, IL and IA, respectively, in U.S. postal codes). Figure 11.1 shows the structure of the portion of an Orders table that we'll use. Create a similar ORDERS.DBF file for your own use.

FIGURE 11.1 ▶

A table structure for cross-tab reporting

Table Structure (ORDERS.DBF)

Name: ORDERS.DBF   **Type:** DBASE

Updated: 02/09/96   **Bytes Used:**   35
Records: 12   **Bytes Left:**   32,732

Field	Name	Type	Width	Decimal	Index
1	ORDER_ID	Numeric	8	0	None
2	ORDER_DATE	Date	8	0	None
3	ITEM	Character	8	0	None
4	QUANTITY	Numeric	8	0	None
5	STATE	Character	2	0	None

Figure 11.2 shows our Orders table filled in with some sample information. Fill in your own Orders table with data similar to that in Figure 11.2.

Note that we have taken some liberties here. In practice, we would have at least three tables. Through the Query Designer, we would link an Orders table to a Customer table. Assume that we've done this in the example, using the STATE field from the Customer table. Similarly, we would link the Orders table to a Product table. Again, assume that we've created this link, using the ITEM field from the Product table.

FIGURE 11.2 ▶

*Sample Orders
table data*

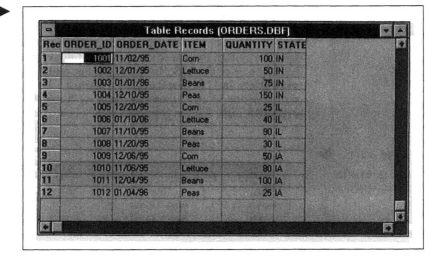

▶ *Building Your First Cross-Tab Report*

You can create a cross-tab report from the Navigator, but it is much simpler if you use these commands in the Command window:

```
USE orders
CREATE REPORT CROSSTAB
```

This command sequence—USE orders and then CREATE REPORT CROSSTAB—selects the table and launches the Cross-Tab window in Crystal Reports, as shown in Figure 11.3.

The alternative method for getting to the Cross-Tab window is to select the Untitled report from the Navigator, which takes you into Crystal Reports. In Crystal, you'll be creating a standard banded report. Cancel that process and choose File ➤ New ➤ Cross-Tab.

In the Cross-Tab window, your first task is to pick the field that will contain your summary data. From our Orders table, we want to summarize the QUANTITY field by STATE and by ITEM.

With the mouse pointer, drag the QUANTITY field into the Summarized Field rectangle of the Cross-Tab window, as shown in Figure 11.4. As you drag the field, you'll see that your cursor turns from a "stop" shape circle

FIGURE 11.3

*The Cross-Tab window
in Crystal Reports*

FIGURE 11.4

*Dragging the QUAN-
TITY field into position*

into a document marked with a cross (as in cross-tab report, we presume) when it is in a position where it can be dropped.

Now that the QUANTITY field is in the Summarized Field position, let's put the states across the top of our report and the items down the side. Start by dragging the STATE field to the rectangle marked Columns. Here we are beginning to drag that field out of the Fields rectangle:

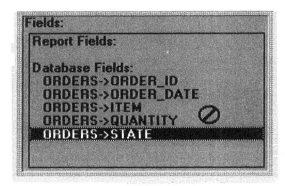

Notice the cursor is still in its "stop" shape, which tells us that the field can't be dropped yet.

Next, drag the ITEM field to the Rows rectangle. When you have dragged the three fields into position, the top of the window should look like this:

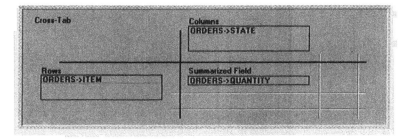

We've now completed the specification of a basic cross-tab report.

▶ *Viewing Your Report*

With your three fields in place, click on OK or press Enter. Your new cross-tab report is complete. Figure 11.5 shows our report in Crystal. For this figure, we maximized Crystal Reports itself and also maximized the child window labeled Untitled Report.

FIGURE 11.5 ▶

Our cross-tab report in Crystal Reports

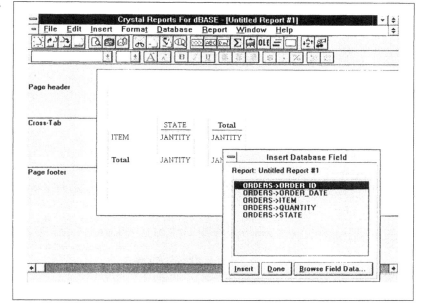

As you see in Figure 11.5, there are three bands in a cross-tab report:

- Page header
- Cross-Tab
- Page footer

► Adding Page Headers and Footers

The Page header and Page footer bands have their usual uses, and you can treat them as you would for any other report. For now, try adding a title in the Page header band and a page number in the Page footer band.

We've called our report Seed Sales. To add a title, choose Insert ➤ Text Field .... In the Edit Text Field dialog box, type the report title.

When you click on Accept, the text field is attached to your cursor. Position it in the Page header band and click to drop it. While the text field is still selected, set the point size to 24 (or something similarly emphatic).

To add the page number in the Page footer band, choose Insert ➤ Special Field ➤ Page Number. Again, the field is attached to your cursor. Drop it in the Page footer area.

► Previewing the Report

With these preliminaries completed, click on the spyglass icon to look at your report in the Preview window. Figure 11.6 shows our first version.

At this point, if we were preparing a banded report, we would start selecting individual fields to make the formatting improvements that transform a plain report into an elegant report. Unfortunately, you can't edit fields in the Cross-Tab band from the report's Preview window. You must close the Preview window and return to the Crystal design surface to make changes.

► Formatting a Cross-Tab Report

For this example, we'll make a few simple improvements. The column titles would look better if they were right-justified, and the totals would stand out if they were in boldface.

Formatting the Column Titles

To begin, click on the Close button in the Preview window's speedbar to return to the report design surface. Then click on the lasso icon or choose Edit ➤ Select Fields to get the cross-hair cursor that allows you to draw a rectangle around a group of fields.

►►**N O T E**

The Crystal Reports lasso is different from the Form Designer lasso. In Crystal Reports, every field that is touched by the lasso is selected. In the Form Designer, only fields that are fully enclosed are selected.

FIGURE 11.6 ►

Previewing our cross-tab report

```
Preview Window: Untitled Report #1
```

Seed Sales

	IA	IL	IN	Total
Beans	100	90	75	265
Corn	50	25	100	175
Lettuce	80	40	50	170
Peas	25	30	150	205
Total	255	185	375	815

```
  |◄  ◄   1 of 1   ►  ►|  Cancel  🔍 ⚡ __ 📷 📲  Close    12 of 12   Total
```

With the cross-hair cursor, drag from the upper left of the column-title fields to a point far enough down and to the right to touch both the STATE and Total column-title fields. Then choose Forma**t** ➤ F**i**eld ... to launch the Format String dialog box.

In the Format String dialog box, set the **A**lignment to Right, and then click on OK or press Enter. Your two column-title fields will now be right-justified.

If both column-title fields are selected, click any field to deselect them and return to single-field selecting. With one field selected, we can consider the differences between the two column-title fields shown here.

Remember that there is a key difference between the STATE column-title field and the Total column-title field. To see this, click on the Total field and choose Edit ➤ Text Field .... This choice will let you edit the text.

Now try the same thing with the STATE field. When you choose Edit ➤ Text Field ..., you'll find that the selection is grayed; it's not available. Why?

The STATE field isn't really a column heading at all. It's a proxy for data that will come from the database. You will have one STATE field for each different state value in your table. In our report, we have IN, IL, and IA.

Formatting Row Labels

As you've seen, the column titles are actually made up of data from your tables, plus a Total column at the end. The rows are also built this way.

The ITEM field in your Cross-Tab band is the same as the STATE column title; you can't use Edit ➤ Text Field ... to change it. The values will be supplied from your database.

You can, however, use Edit ➤ Text Field ... on the Total row. You can also use Format ➤ Field on either the ITEM or Total row label.

Formatting the Bottom Totals

To format the totals at the bottom, use the lasso to select both of the QUANTITY fields at the bottom of the Cross-Tab band. As shown in Figure 11.7, our fields are right-justified (the default for numbers), and they don't quite fit. The Q in QUANTITY is chopped off.

FIGURE 11.7 ▶

Lassoing the QUAN-TITY fields

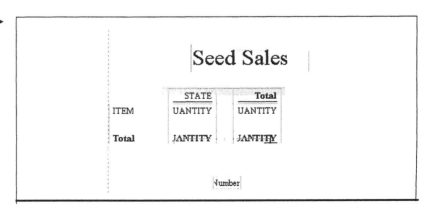

When these fields are selected, click on the **B** icon to convert them both to boldface. If you return to your Preview window, you'll see a more attractive report.

▶ *Adding Another Dimension*

As you may have noticed when we built the cross-tab report, you could put more than one field in the columns or rows of your cross-tab report. Putting additional fields here is similar to selecting multiple group levels in a banded report. We'll work through an example, breaking down our sales by month within item types.

Changing the Cross-Tab Layout

The Cross-Tab window lets you define and change the selection of your cross-tab report's fields. To return to the Cross-Tab window to make changes, choose Format ➤ Section .... In the first Format Section dialog box, you'll see the list of each band in your report, as shown in Figure 11.8.

FIGURE 11.8 ▶

The first Format Section dialog box for a cross-tab report

Choose the Cross-Tab section from the Format Section dialog box, and then click on OK or press Enter. This will launch the Format Section dialog box for the Cross-Tab section. From this second Format

Section dialog box, choose the Cross-Tab Layout ... pushbutton, as you see us doing in Figure 11.9. This will return you to the Cross-Tab window, where you can modify your layout.

FIGURE 11.9 ▶

The Format Section dialog box for the Cross-Tab section

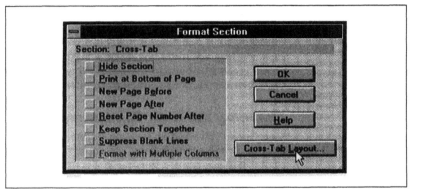

▶▶**NOTE**

The Cross-Tab Layout ... pushbutton does not appear unless you have already built a cross-tab report.

In the Cross-Tab window, we could add the ORDER_DATE field as an additional row, but this would not give us what we want. Each field in either the rows or the columns is another grouping item. If we added the ORDER_DATE field, we would group our orders by individual days. This might be interesting for some purposes, but for our data, grouping the orders by month would be much more useful.

Adding a Formula to Group by Month

To group by month, we'll need to use a formula field, and enter a dBASE for Windows expression that will give us the month from the date data we have available. We'll cover dBASE for Windows expressions and functions in detail in Chapter 12. For now, we'll go over the ones we need for our sample cross-tab report.

dBASE for Windows has a built-in function, MON( ), which returns a month number, given a date. For example, MON({1/1/96}) returns 1, meaning January. We could use MON( ) as the base for our formula field's expression:

MON(Order_Date)

This function will return 11 for November orders, 12 for December orders, 1 for January orders, and so on. This will do a good job of sorting our orders by month, except for one problem: computers are stupid.

When you give Crystal an expression that returns a number, you and I may think about farmers ordering seeds during the winter, but Crystal only knows that it has some numbers used to group data. So it will do what it always does: put them in order.

The order of your data will come out like this:

January (1)
November (11)
December (12)

But we want a numbering scheme that will make the months come out like this:

November
December
January

We'll need to devise a trick that returns the months of late fall and early winter in a numeric sequence that will put January after December. As is frequently the case, the method is a lot more complicated to explain than it is to implement.

Another dBASE built-in function is INT( ), which stands for INTeger part. The INT( ) of any number is the whole part, with any fractional part chopped off. INT( ) doesn't do rounding.

If we asked for INT(1/30), we would get 0 (zero). If we asked for INT(29/30), we would still get 0. Similarly INT(30/30) would give the result 1 (one), and INT(59/30) also returns 1.

In dBASE for Windows, if you subtract one date from another, you get the number of days between the two dates. Here are two examples that evaluate to 30:

{11/1/95} – {10/2/95}
{12/1/95} – {11/1/95}

As you can see, dBASE does real date arithmetic. It knows that there are 31 days in October and that there are only 30 days in November.

Now that you know all this, here's what we can do. We'll subtract {10/2/95} from the order date. It will give us the following results:

- A number from 1 to 29 for any order in October
- A number from 30 through 59 for any order in November
- A number from 60 through 90 for any order in December
- A number from 91 through 121 for any order in January

If we divide these numbers by 30 and take the INT( ) of the result, we'll have 0 for October, 1 for November, 2 for December, and 3 for January.

You might have realized that December 31 will give us a 3, as if it were in January. Similarly, January 30 and 31 will give us a 4, as if they were in February. This is an approximation that gets sloppier as more months pass. But if you look at the data we have, it gets every order in our table right, so we can go with it.

Adding a Formula Field

To add a formula field to our report, click on the pushbutton labeled New Formula ..., under the Report Fields list in the Cross-Tab window. You'll see the New Formula dialog box. We called our formula field ord_month, as shown in Figure 11.10.

FIGURE 11.10 ▶

Entering a formula field's name

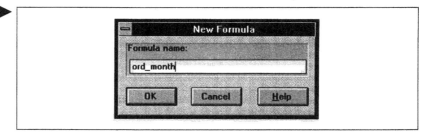

After you enter the name and press Enter or click on OK, the Expression Builder is launched. We entered this expression:

```
INT( (Order_date-{10/2/95})/30 ) + 10
```

Adding 10 at the end converts November dates from a 1 to an 11, December dates from a 2 to a 12, and so on.

When you're finished entering your formula field's expression in the Expression Builder, click on OK or press Enter to return to the Cross-Tab window. (See Chapter 8 for details on using the Expression Builder.)

In the Cross-Tab window, your new formula field will be highlighted. You can drag it to the Rows rectangle and drop it underneath the ITEM field, but there is another way.

Specifying a Cross-Tab without Dragging

You may have noticed that the pushbuttons in the Cross-Tab window are enabled and disabled as you work with your layout. If you have a field selected in the Fields rectangle, the first three buttons are available:

- Add Row to Cross-Tab
- Add Column to Cross-Tab
- Set Summarized Field

Note that the first two choices are to *add* a field, but the third is to *set* the field. You can have multiple row or column fields, but only a single summarized field.

If you have any of the fields in the Cross-Tab section, the Remove Field from Cross-Tab pushbutton is available. This button lets you clear the selected field from the report.

With your formula field (Crystal labels it @Ord_month) selected in the Fields rectangle, click on the Add Row to Cross-Tab pushbutton. The formula field is added underneath the ITEM field.

Running the Revised Cross-Tab Report

With your date formula field added to the Rows section, click on OK or press Enter. You'll return to the Format Section dialog box. Again, click on OK or press Enter. Now you'll see your report layout, which should look like the one shown in Figure 11.11.

FIGURE 11.11 ▶

A date dimension added to the layout

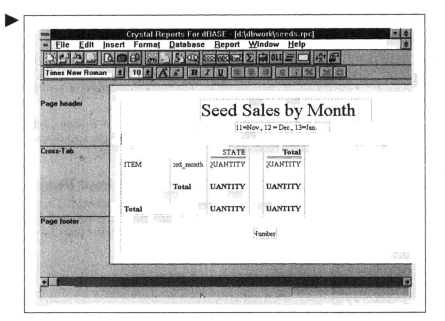

If you look carefully, you'll see that we changed our title text field and added another, explanatory field underneath the title. When you preview the report, your Preview window should look like the one in Figure 11.12.

As you can see, adding the months has added another dimension to the report. You can examine sales by month for individual items, for individual states, or for both. While our sample data is not going to help anyone who is in the seed business, it's enough for you to see that this type of report will go a long way toward helping you examine your own data for trends.

As you can also imagine from studying our sample report, adding more dimensions by adding more row or column fields will let you continue to break down your analysis to whatever degree is required.

FIGURE 11.12

Previewing the cross-tab report with months added

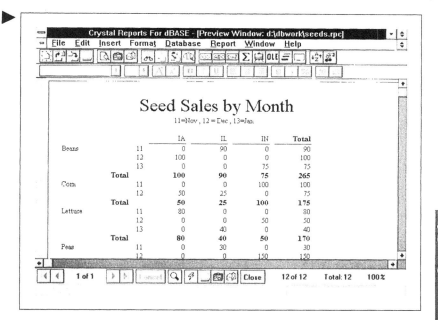

Crystal Reports For dBASE - [Preview Window: d:\dbwork\seeds.rpc]

File Edit Insert Format Database Report Window Help

Seed Sales by Month
11=Nov , 12 = Dec , 13=Jan

		IA	IL	IN	Total
Beans	11	0	90	0	90
	12	100	0	0	100
	13	0	0	75	75
	Total	**100**	**90**	**75**	**265**
Corn	11	0	0	100	100
	12	50	25	0	75
	Total	**50**	**25**	**100**	**175**
Lettuce	11	80	0	0	80
	12	0	0	50	50
	13	0	40	0	40
	Total	**80**	**40**	**50**	**170**
Peas	11	0	30	0	30
	12	0	0	150	150

1 of 1   Cancel   Close   12 of 12   Total: 12   100%

▶▶ **TIP**

If your cross-tab report runs to several pages, see if you can create a summary on a single page that shows the data aggregated in the most informative way possible.

A single-page cross-tab report is often worth more in providing information than the most detailed banded report. Use cross-tab reports whenever you can.

▶▶ *Creating Labels*

In Chapter 7, we generated our first mailing labels. Crystal makes this simple, but the vagaries of our hardware make it a job that still takes a little human intelligence. Here, we'll consider the mailing label design

Cross-Tab Reports, Labels

Ch. 11

tools in depth. You'll see that a wide variety of labels—ranging from standard Avery mailing labels to name tags to VCR labels—come under the heading mailing labels.

To specify a label layout, choose File ➤ New ➤ Mailing Label .... Crystal displays the Database File dialog box so that you can select a table or query. After you choose a file, the Mailing Labels dialog box appears, as shown in Figure 11.13.

FIGURE 11.13 ►

Specifying mailing label layout

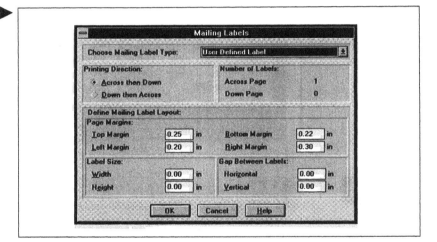

► Choosing a Label Type

The first option in the Mailing Labels dialog box is Choose Mailing Label Type. The following list gives the available types and counts (columns per page by rows per page). The counts give you a rough idea of the size of each label. For the exact size, select the label type and look at the Label Size section of the Mailing Labels dialog box, which will show the exact specifications of the selected type.

These standard labels are white, with other colors noted:

- Address (3×10, 3×6, 3×5, 2×10, 2×7, 2×3)
- Address/Shipping (2×5, 2×3, 2×2)

- Address, $5\frac{1}{4}$ diskette (2×6)
- Address, $3\frac{1}{2}$ diskette (3×3)
- Audio Cassette (2×6)
- Clear Address (3×10, 2×7, 2×6, 2×5, 2×3)
- Diskette, $3\frac{1}{2}$-inch (3×3) (also in red and blue)
- Diskette, $5\frac{1}{4}$-inch (2×6) (also in red and blue)
- Diskette, $3\frac{1}{2}$-inch (2×3)
- Diskette, $5\frac{1}{4}$-inch (1×7)
- File Folder (2×15)
- Full Sheet (1×1)
- Index Card (1×3)
- Index/Post Card (1×2)
- Mini Address (5×12) (also clear)
- Name Badge (2×4) (also in blue)
- Name Tag (2×4) (also in blue)
- Name Tag (2×2)
- Return Address (4×20)
- Rotary Index Card (2×4, 1×3)
- Round (3×4)
- Video Cassette Face (2×5)
- Video Cassette Spine (1×15)

Cross-Tab
Reports, Labels

Ch.
11

As you can see, the range of labels is substantial, covering far more than just mailing labels.

One good use of mailing labels is for return addresses for yourself. Enter your name and address into a table and then copy your record to another record. Then copy the two records to two more. Then copy the four records, and so on. In short order, you'll have a table full of copies of your name and address.

Generate a few pages of labels for yourself and keep them handy. Even if you send most of your correspondence in preprinted envelopes, you'll find an amazing number of times when you can stick on a return address. They work on large envelopes, packages, and postcards. They are especially handy when you pay your bills, using the envelopes your creditors supply for this purpose.

You can test your creativity by trying to come up with the best use yet for the round labels. We think using a fancy graphic to make awards to give your kids for bringing home good test scores is one good idea. Have you got a better one?

Crystal has provided thorough coverage for the Avery label series; however, one important category it omits is Cheshire labels. In the mailing trade, Avery labels are known as *peel-and-stick* labels, since that is exactly what you do to apply one.

Cheshire labels are named after the brand of equipment that applies these labels (which don't peel) to envelopes. If you're doing large-volume mailings, your mail house will supply the exact specifications for its range of Cheshire labels. You can enter those specifications in the Mailing Labels dialog box. Either choose User Defined Label as the label type, or pick the closest type and edit the specifications.

► *Specifying the Printing Direction*

In the Printing Direction section, you can choose to print labels Across then Down, or Down then Across. In many applications, your choice here doesn't matter. However, in some cases, the printing order can be an important consideration.

If you're printing personalized letters and using mailing labels, you'll start with sheets of labels and a stack of letters, both in alphabetical (or some other) order. You'll want to be absolutely certain that the labels are applied in the same order as the envelopes are stuffed.

Decide beforehand which way makes it easiest to peel your labels from their backing and stick them onto the envelopes. You may find, for example, that 2-up labels (labels in 2 columns per page) are easiest to peel across and then down, but 3-up labels may be easier to peel down the columns. Whatever you decide, make your printing conform to your manual procedures.

► *How Crystal Determines the Number of Labels*

The Number of Labels section tells you how many labels you will get across the page and down the page. It does *not* let you enter these values. They are calculated from two sources:

- The values entered in the Mailing Labels dialog box
- The paper size Windows lists for your printer

The values in the Mailing Labels dialog box determine how many labels fit across and down on a page. The values that Crystal chooses are the maximum number of full labels that can be printed on a page. If, for example, your label specification would give you room for 3.9 labels across, Crystal would print only 3 across.

The page size is determined by the settings in the Windows Control Panel's Printer Setup dialog box (or Crystal's Printer Setup dialog box if you've filled that in).

  T I P

> In some cases, you may want to use paper smaller than the maximum size that your printer can support. For example, you could be running 8½-inch-wide labels in a printer that supports up to 15-inch-wide paper. You can always reduce the available paper size by setting a large right or bottom margin value in the Mailing Labels dialog box.

► *Defining the Mailing Label Layout*

The Define Mailing Label Layout section is divided into three panels:

- Page Margins
- Label Size
- Gap Between Labels

Setting Page Margins

In the Page Margins panel, you enter the margins that are the greater of either of these:

- The area your printer cannot reach
- The margins on your label stock

For example, many laser printers that use $8^{1}/_{2}$-by-11-inch paper cannot print on the leftmost or rightmost $^{1}/_{2}$ inch, nor on $^{1}/_{6}$ inch at the top and bottom. (Your page dimensions may be given in centimeters, not inches, depending on your Windows setup's international settings.)

Your labels will also have margins. For example, the Avery 7664 labels for $3^{1}/_{2}$-inch diskettes have 0.71 inch (about 2 centimeters) left and right margins. These are the controlling margins for these labels.

If you're using paper that is smaller than the size listed for your printer, increase the bottom and/or right margins accordingly. For instance, a $4^{1}/_{2}$-inch right margin would let you run $8^{1}/_{2}$-inch-wide paper through a printer that can support 13-inch-wide paper.

Specifying the Label Size

In the Label Size section, you can enter the maximum width and height of your labels. For round or other odd shapes, measure the maximum width and height and enter those dimensions here.

Setting the Gap between Labels

In the Gap Between Labels section, enter the amount of space between your labels that is not available for printing. Bear in mind that the width of the first label plus the gap between labels must be the exact location of the left edge of the second column of labels.

Always compute the location of the left edge of the last column of labels from the dimensions you specify and compare that to an actual label measurement.

▶ *Leaving and Returning to the Mailing Labels Dialog Box*

After you select your label specifications from the Mailing Labels dialog box and click on OK or press Enter, you'll return to the report layout window.

In your label layout, the Details band is sized correctly, according to the settings in the Mailing Labels dialog box. The layout shows as many rectangles across the page as you have columns of labels. You only need to put your fields into the first label; the rest are filled in automatically.

If you need to make changes, or just want to review the settings, you can return to the Mailing Labels dialog box for your labels. From the layout window, choose Forma<u>t</u> ➤ <u>S</u>ection ..., and then choose the Details section. In the second Format Section dialog box, click on the <u>La</u>bel Layout ... pushbutton to launch the Mailing Label dialog box again.

▶ *Tips on Printing Labels*

Making your selections in the Mailing Labels dialog box and setting up the Details band in the layout window may be all that you need to do to print your labels. However, as we've mentioned, your printer may not print the labels correctly for one reason or another. Be sure to make some dummy labels with your photocopier and to run these samples before using your real label stock. If your printer doesn't print the labels properly, you can try some of the adjustments noted in the following sections.

Cross-Tab Reports, Labels

Ch. 11

Margin Variation

Some printers have an inherently imprecise margin mechanism. For example, feeding single sheets into a laser printer can provide quite a bit of error to the left or right.

To compensate for margin variation, specify a left margin that is slightly large, a gap between labels that is similarly oversized, and a label width that is undersized. For example, if your variability is 0.1 inch, you could specify a left margin that is 0.1 inch too large, a label width that is 0.2 inch too small, and a gap that is 0.1 inch too large.

Again, remember to calculate the location of the rightmost column of labels from your specifications, and compare it to an actual label measurement.

Labels and Field Sizes

Remember that your selection of labels has no effect on your table's field width. If you have chosen 60 character-wide names and addresses, you won't be able to fit them on 3-up labels on $8^1/_2$-by-11-inch paper. You can, however, accommodate a reasonable variation in field widths by varying the point size of the field's font.

Lines per Label

If at all possible, leave at least one line unprinted to provide a margin between the printing and the edge of the label. Again, the number of lines that fit are a function of the size of the font you choose.

If you can leave, for example, 0.16 inch free between labels, set your label layout to begin at the top of the Details band in Crystal. Leave the blank space at the bottom of the label. Then, before you print, add 0.08 inch to the top margin of your paper in the Mailing Label dialog box. This will divide the free space evenly between labels.

▶▶ Producing Form Letters

Crystal Reports lets you put large amounts of text in any text field, and in any band of your report. Its limit is 32,000 characters per field (just a little shorter than this chapter, for example). While Crystal isn't going to replace your favorite word processor for text entry and manipulation, it is more than capable of handling your most demanding form letter requirements.

▶▶ **N O T E**

> **To generate form letters, you can use Crystal or you can use the mail-merge capabilities of your word processor. If you're familiar with Crystal, it will be the simpler tool. If you've already been using the mail-merge features of your word processor, there's no reason to switch.**

▶ *Database Design for Form Letters*

Before you do any work on form letters, you need to design your database to support this application.

The first principle of database design for form letters is to assume nothing. Don't try to extend your letters past the edge of your actual knowledge.

Alan likes being known as Alan. If you wanted him to respond to your letter, you wouldn't begin with "Dear Al,"—he would know that you're a stranger, and he may be offended at your presumption. On the other hand, none of Marty's friends would ever send him a letter that began, "Dear Martin,"—he would know that it was a half-baked form letter and probably toss it without a second thought.

The second principle to observe is to never assume that anything about addressing a letter is simple.

Here in the U.S., we are a relatively egalitarian people. You correctly address both Joe Jones, the maintenance man at BigCo, and Sam Jones, the Chief Executive Officer of BigCo, as Mr. Jones.

However, a simple Mr. or Ms. will not work for Dr. Brown, Professor Green, or Senator Smith. Judges and clerics have their own forms of address. Some lawyers prefer an Esq. after their names. These are just a few of the many exceptions to Mr. or Ms.

Beginners generally start with a database design with fields like these:

- SALUTATION (for Mr., Ms., and so on)
- FIRST_NAME

- MID_INIT
- LAST_NAME

Then they build the address by combining the salutation, first name, middle initial, and last name on one line. For the salutation that comes after "Dear" in the letter, they often try the first name.

We suggest that you don't make these beginners' mistakes. The only method that is guaranteed to give sound results is to have one field for the individual's full name and a second field for the name you will use after "Dear" in your letters.

With those two fields, you could address a letter to "Ms. Mary Smith," and open it "Dear Mary," or you could address it to "The Hon. Mary Smith, M.S., J.D." and open it with "Dear Judge Smith."

For our example, we copied PEOPLE.DBF to MAILLIST.DBF and modified it for form letter application. Figure 11.14 shows our new structure.

FIGURE 11.14 ▶

A mailing list table's structure

Table Structure [MAILLIST.DBF]

Name: MAILLIST.DBF   Type: DBASE

Updated: 02/10/96   Bytes Used: 156
Records: 11   Bytes Left: 32,611

Field	Name	Type	Width	Decimal	Index
1	MAILLISTID	Numeric	4	0	Ascend
2	LAST_NAME	Character	16	0	Ascend
3	DEAR	Character	16	0	None
4	FULL_NAME	Character	32	0	None
5	ADDR1	Character	32	0	None
6	ADDR2	Character	32	0	None
7	CITY	Character	16	0	None
8	STATE	Character	2	0	None
9	ZIP	Character	5	0	None

The field we've called DEAR is for the name that will come after the "Dear" in a letter. You could fill in Bill for "Dear Bill," or you could fill in Mr. President, for "Dear Mr. President."

After modifying the structure, we went through our PEOPLE.DBF data and modified it so that we can use it for form letters. As you see in Figure 11.15, we filled in our close personal friends' nicknames, but we've been safe and formal with our more remote acquaintances.

FIGURE 11.15 ▶

Data for mailing list applications

Rec	MAILLISTID	LAST_NAME	DEAR	FULL_NAME	ADDR1
1	1001	Friendly	Phil	Mr. Philip Friendly	5 Maple Ave
2	1002	Adamson	Ms. Adamson	Ms. Adrianne Adamson	10 Oak Dr.
3	1003	Monroe	Mandy	Miss Madilyn Monroe	Sunset Blvd
4	1004	Gable	Winnie	Ms. Eve Gable	High Rise, # 24J
5	1005	Hacker	Herb	Mr. Herb Hacker	Orange Grove
6	1006	Garfield	Fatso	Meow Feline Garfield	Studio 4
7	1007	Brown	Dr. Brown	Alphonse Brown, Md	12 Main St.
8	1008	Witherspoon	Wil	Mr. Wilfred Witherspoon	1 Fifth Avenue
9	1010	Smith	John	Mr. John Smith	747 Plane St.
10	1015	Joplin	Ms. Joplin	Ms. Jane Joplin	Pop Festival
11	1019	Fitzgerald	Frank	Mr. Franklin S. Fitzgerald	Gatsby Plaza

Table Records (MAILLIST.DBF)

Cross-Tab Reports, Labels

Ch. **11**

▶▶ WARNING

When you fill in your data for a form letter application, be sure that you don't make any guesses. The great actor Leslie Howard would probably *not* respond to your appeal if you sent him a letter addressed to "Dear Ms. Howard."

▶ Creating Your Form Letter

With your database designed and filled in for a mailing application, your next concern is the creation of the letter itself. Any text editor can be used with good results. One of your authors (we won't say who, but one of us is a bit old-fashioned) likes to use a DOS text editor. Even that works.

You can use the built-in dBASE editor, if you like. From the Command window, launch the text editor with:

MODIFY FILE t.let

Choose Properties ➤ Text Editor ... to launch the Text Editor Properties dialog box, where you can set word wrap and an appropriate margin.

For more extensive writing, use the text editor or word processor you like best. You can even type your letter directly into Crystal (but editing text in a report writer is not our idea of fun).

Whatever editor you choose, prepare the fixed part of your letter and revise it as necessary. Finish all the changes before you go to Crystal Reports, where text editing is much less convenient. When you're finished, select all your text and copy it to the Clipboard.

From a Windows program, copying to the Clipboard is generally a one-button choice, or available by pressing Ctrl-C. If you're running a DOS editor under Windows, press Alt-Enter if you are running full-screen. With your letter in a DOS window under Windows, click on the System button or press Alt-spacebar to get the System menu. Choose Edit from this menu. From the cascading menu, choose Mark and use your mouse to select text as if you were in a Windows program. When you have selected your whole letter, press Enter to copy the text to the Clipboard.

When you have your letter in the Windows Clipboard, it's time to launch Crystal Reports. From the Navigator, select the Untitled report and press F2 or double-click. Or, from the Command window, type

CREATE REPORT

Pick your mailing list database and let Crystal start up. Once Crystal is launched, maximize it and the design window. Click in the Details band if your insertion point is not already there. Then choose Edit ➤ Paste or press Ctrl-V to paste your letter into the Details band. Figure 11.16 shows our form letter in Crystal.

We clicked on Done in the Insert Database Field dialog box, so it would get out of the way. You can leave yours in place, or do likewise.

FIGURE 11.16 ▶

*A form letter in the De-
tails band*

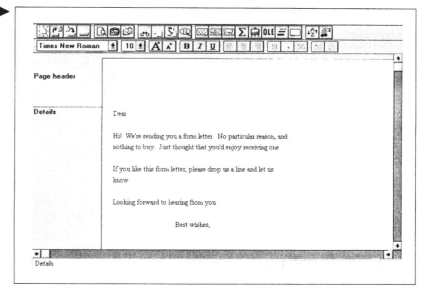

Page header

Details

Dear

Hi! We're sending you a form letter. No particular reason, and
nothing to buy. Just thought that you'd enjoy receiving one

If you like this form letter, please drop us a line and let us
know

Looking forward to hearing from you

Best wishes,

Details

At this point, we recommend using the File ➤ Save As command to
save your work.

▶ *Adding the Name and Address Fields*

With your letter safely saved in Crystal, put your insertion point in
front of the *Dear* and press Enter several times to make enough space
for the address. If you closed the Insert Database Field dialog box,
choose Insert ➤ Database Field … to bring it back.

Drag the full name field and the address fields into the space you
made. Also copy the Dear field after the word *Dear*. When you have
done this much, your result should look similar to the Details band
shown in Figure 11.17.

Now we're ready to run our report in the Preview window. Click on the
spyglass icon and look at a few of your letters. Do you see what the biggest problem is?

FIGURE 11.17 ►

The name, address, and Dear fields in place

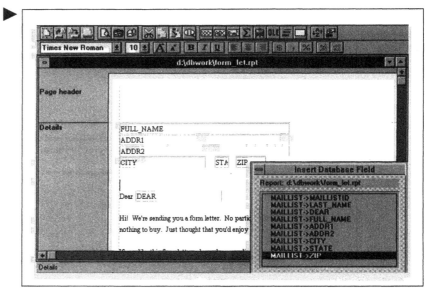

Crystal Reports has no idea that we are sending form letters. It repeats the Details band as many times as it can, including fractional times, on a page.

To get a new letter on each page, choose Format ► Section ... and choose the Details band. In the second Format Section dialog box, check the New Page After option.

Now return to the Preview window. This time, you'll see that you have a separate letter on each page.

► Using Formula Fields to Improve Your Letters

Our first letter begins:

Dear Phil

There's no comma or colon after Phil's name.

If you were to simply add a colon (or comma) after the Dear field, you would have a letter that starts like this:

    Dear Phil   :

The colon will come after the end of the Dear field. Of course, you allowed enough space in this field to hold the longest name you might include, so there is a lot of blank space after almost every name in your table.

Cleaning Up the Salutation Field

To print a comma or colon after the salutation, we need to replace the DEAR field from our data table with a formula field. We need an expression that will trim the trailing blanks from the DEAR field and append a colon. The RTRIM( ) function trims blanks from the right of a character field. The plus operator (+) puts two strings together. This is the expression that we want to use:

    RTRIM(Dear)+":"

To add a formula field, click on the Einstein icon on the speedbar or choose Insert ➤ Formula Field .... Either one will launch the Insert Formula dialog box, where you enter the name of your formula field.

After you enter a name and click on OK or press Enter, the Expression Builder is launched. In the Build Expression dialog box, enter the expression above. If you like, you can double-click on the DEAR field instead of typing it in. (For our table, this entered MAILLIST->DEAR, which would help us get the correct DEAR field if we had a multiple-table view open.)

After you enter your expression, ask the Expression Builder to Evaluate it, just to check. Then click on OK or press Enter to return to Crystal's design window. Your field is now attached to your cursor.

Position it anyplace near the existing DEAR field and drop it. Then select the DEAR field and press Del to delete it. (If Del doesn't work, which is sometimes the case with our copy, choose Edit ➤ Clear.) With the old field gone, you can position the new one after the *Dear* in the letter, and get the result shown in Figure 11.18.

Cross-Tab
Reports, Labels

Ch.
11

FIGURE 11.18 ►

Dear handled correctly

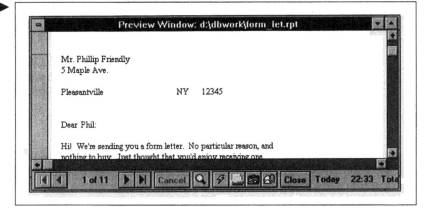

Handling the Address Fields

Figure 11.18 shows fine style in handling the *Dear* line, but take a look at the city, state, and zip code line in the address. You'll see a rather clumsy line with lots of extra space (it probably reminds you of every poorly programmed computer form letter you've ever seen). Let's fix this up next.

We want is to print the city, followed immediately by a comma and a single space, followed by the two-letter state code and another space, and then the zip code. (We assume that you'll adapt the methods we describe here as necessary to suit the address format appropriate to your country.)

Again, we need to replace the database fields with a formula field. Just as with the DEAR field, the RTRIM( ) function and + operator will work here. This is the expresson we need:

    RTRIM(City)+", "+State+" "+Zip

This is going to become part of a more extensive formula when we address the next problem, so copy this one carefully.

Begin by adding a new formula field (choose Insert ➤ Formula Field ... or click on the Einstein button). Name this formula **line4** (the reason will become apparent shortly). In the Build Expression dialog box, type the expression above, and then ask the Expression Builder to Evaluate your results. If you had our data, your result would be:

Pleasantville, NY 12345

Test our line4 expression by running your report in the Preview window. You should see that the city, state, and zip code line looks just fine. However, we still have a problem with the address.

Three- or Four-Line Addressing

The problem we face is that we have allowed for two address lines before the city, state, and zip code line. In many cases, the ADDR2 field will be blank, so we will be addressing the letter with something like this:

Mr. Phil Friendly
5 Maple Ave.

Pleasantville, NY 12345

If this letter were typed, we certainly wouldn't leave a blank line in Phil's address just because we might want another line in someone else's address. For the sake of this discussion, let's call the city, state, and zip code line the CSZ line. We want to print the CSZ line at line 3 if the ADDR2 field is blank. If the ADDR2 file is not blank, then the CSZ line should be the fourth line printed. Here's the algorithm we should follow:

Print the full name

Print the Addr1 value

IF the person has an Addr2 field value
    Print Addr2
  ELSE
    Print the CSZ line
ENDIF

IF the person had an Addr2 field value
    Print the CSZ line
  ELSE
    (do nothing -- the address is done)
ENDIF

As you see, we need a more complex expression for the third and fourth lines. As you've probably guessed, we'll call the third one **line3**.

We can use the IIF( ) function to make a choice. Here's an example of IIF( ) that returns "genius" or "normal" depending on whether or not the value of Person is "Einstein":

    IIF(person="Einstein", "genius", "normal")

The IIF( ) function takes a logical expression and returns one of two values following that expression. If the logical expression is True, it returns the first value. In our example, if the person is Einstein, it returns "genius." If the expression is False, it returns the second value.

Using IIF( ) functions, here is our address algorithm:

    Print the full name

    Print the Addr1 value

    IIF(.NOT. EMPTY(Addr2), Addr2, CSZ)

    IIF(.NOT. EMPTY(Addr2), CSZ, "")

In the last line, we use quotation marks with nothing in between for an empty string—it will print nothing.

Now our final point is that the CSZ expression must be spelled-out in full (Crystal Reports hasn't been reading this chapter). So here is the full expression for line 3:

    IIF(.NOT. EMPTY(Addr2), Addr2, RTRIM(City)+", "+State+" "+Zip)

In Crystal, delete the third line field (ADDR2) and then create a new formula field named line3 with this expression. Use the Preview window to check your work.

When you have line 3 complete, edit the formula in line 4. Choose Edit ▶ Formula Field ... after you select the line 4 formula field. This will launch the Expression Builder with the line available for editing. This is the formula we want to use:

    IIF(.NOT. EMPTY(Addr2), RTRIM(City)+", "+State+" "+Zip, "")

Now you have an address that will print without blank lines, as shown in Figure 11.19.

FIGURE 11.19 ▶

The correct address for Phil's letter

These same expressions can be used for other applications that require mailing addresses, such as for printing the envelopes or mailing labels for our form letters.

▶▶ *Summary*

In this chapter, we examined cross-tab reports, labels, and form letters. We started by developing a simple approximation of a sales data system for building sample cross-tab reports.

Launching Crystal from the Command window with a CREATE RE-PORT CROSSTAB command is a simple way to begin building a new cross-tab report. Alternatively, you can select the Untitled report in the Navigator, and then choose File ➤ New ➤ Cross-Tab in Crystal Reports. In the Cross-Tab window, we used our items as rows, our states as columns, and summarized our quantity field.

Crystal prepared a cross-tab report for us, after we added a title and page number in the Page header and Page footer bands.

We edited our report in the Crystal report design window, because you can't edit the Cross-Tab band in the Preview window.

After this, we added a formula to subgroup our data by the month of the sale. We used an approximation to get January to sort after December. This additional grouping added another dimension to our cross-tab report.

Next, we went on to discuss mailing labels. The first thing you saw was that a wide variety of label types are available. You can use the mailing label feature to produce far more than just standard mailing labels. We examined the Mailing Label dialog box settings in detail. You can make adjustments here to compensate for the variability in your equipment and to force Crystal Reports to use smaller paper than the maximum supported by your printer.

Finally, we went on to form letters. You saw that a simple database design, using one field for the recipient's full name and another for the data that comes after the word *Dear* in the letter is the best design to correctly address the people on your list.

You used your favorite word processor to create and edit your letter, and then used the Windows Clipboard to paste it into the Details band of Crystal's standard banded report. Setting the New Page After option for the Details band produces one letter per page.

You used your table to add name and address fields. You then used formula fields to place the punctuation after the *Dear* line; to correctly format the city, state, and zip line; and to correctly format the address, accommodating varying numbers of lines.

This concludes Part 3. The next part deals with programming basics. In Chapter 12, you'll learn more about using expressions and functions to get the results you want.

PART FOUR

In this part, we'll go through some of the basics that you'll need to know to write simple dBASE for Windows programs. Actually, it would almost be correct to call this part Procedural Programming Basics, since most of it (though not all) is about the tools and techniques needed to write programs that run one step at a time, directly under your control.

In the next part, Working with Forms, you'll be working with dBASE for Windows' objects and object properties, including events. That is all about object-oriented programming, but we hesitate to use the word *programming*. You do most of that "programming" by clicking on tools from the Controls palette and by entering properties in the Object Properties Inspector.

As you learned in Chapter 6, event handlers that you attach to your objects are, indeed, programs. Many of them are only a line or two long, as all the examples in Chapter 6 were. Sometimes, however, you'll want to establish longer chains of commands. Other times, you'll find that something you're doing in the Table Records tool was interesting the first time, but has become boring by the sixth time, and you want to automate the task. For both these reasons, knowing a little bit about dBASE programming helps.

In Chapter 12, Working with Expressions and Functions, we'll dive into dBASE expressions in detail. Then we'll divide the functions into categories. We'll also provide an alphabetic reference to all the functions, which you can browse through to find ones that meet your needs.

In Chapter 13, Using Command Window Commands, we'll cover the commands that you can give in the Command window. The chapter doesn't include the commands that control the operation of dBASE programs or those that are in dBASE for Windows just to support dBASE IV and earlier applications (those are listed in Appendix D). Even so, there are still more than 200 commands here!

Our goal is to present the commands in a form that you can read through, getting an idea of the types of commands that are available. Then while you're working, you should recognize that what you want to do can be achieved by the right command. Turn to the listing by topic, and you should be able to find the right command. Then turn to the alphabetical listing, and you'll see it explained and, frequently, you'll see examples and tips or warnings about the command.

In Chapter 14, Basics of Programming Statements, we explain the commands, which we call *statements*, that control the operations of dBASE for Windows programs. These are the core of the dBASE language. You'll see that unlike the huge sets of functions and commands, the core statements comprise a small, easily mastered group.

With one reading of Chapter 14, you should be able to understand the way that the Form Designer structures its dBASE for Windows programs. And you'll be prepared when it comes time to create more elaborate event handlers as you work with the object-oriented tools presented in Part 5.

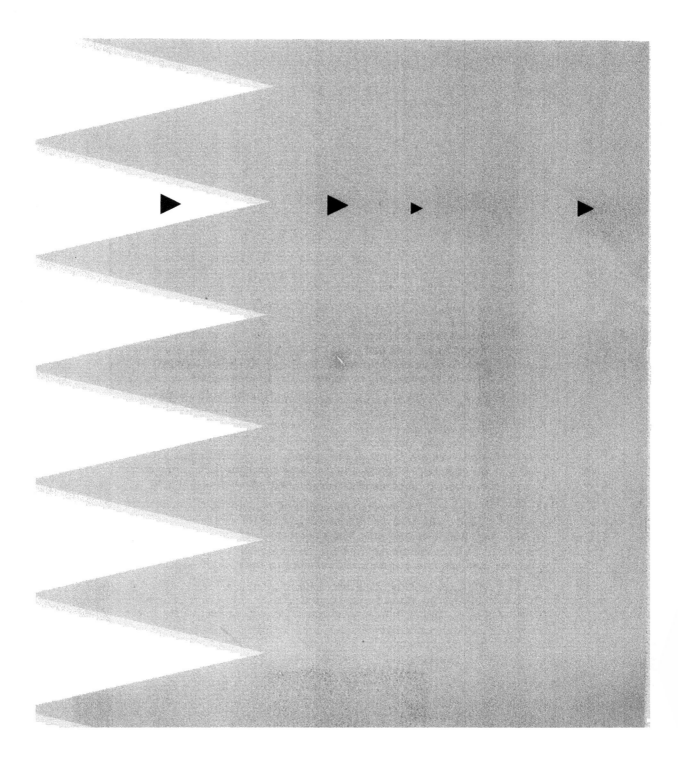

► ► **CHAPTER 12**

Working with Expressions and Functions

d*BASE* for Windows supports a wide variety of expressions and an even wider set of functions to use as part of those expressions. They are used everywhere. In an index expression, you might specify UPPER(Last_name) to get a true alphabetic sort. In a calculated field you specify Price*Quantity to compute a currency amount.

The list of rules for properly forming expressions is very long, and every one of those rules is given in this chapter. But don't be intimidated. If an expression seems reasonable to you, it's probably acceptable to dBASE, too.

dBASE's language designers have always had typical users, not programmers, in mind as their target audience. You may wonder, "Can I add 7 to a date to get the date a week later, or subtract 7 to get to last week?" The answer is yes.

If you subtract 7 from the 3rd of January, you'll get the 27th of December in the prior year (not the -4th of January). dBASE does its best to take good care of you.

We'll begin with expressions. Functions are a component of expressions, but they get their own section in the second part of this chapter.

 ►►T I P

Read this chapter quickly to get an idea of the things you can do. Then use it for reference as you develop requirements for expressions in your database work.

▶ *Forming Expressions*

dBASE expressions are built from operators and operands. Any dBASE expression can be evaluated in the Command window by using the ? command (to pose the question "What is …?"). In this example, the ? command outputs the value of the expression 2+2 to the results pane of the Command window:

        ? 2+2

This command contains two *2* operands and a + operator. Figure 12.1 shows several sample expressions in the Command window's input pane, along with their values in the results pane.

FIGURE 12.1

Some expressions and their results in the Command window

 ▶▶ **T I P**

> **The left-to-right orientation of the input and results panes is our preference for evaluating expressions. Select Properties ➤ Command Window from the menus to change the window layout.**

In the following sections, we'll discuss operands and operators in depth, beginning with operands.

▶ *Using Operands*

The following are the seven different types of operands, from the simplest to the most complex:

- Constants
- Memory variables
- Fields
- Object properties
- Object references
- Function calls
- Subroutine references
- Expressions

We'll cover each in turn.

Types of Constants

The five types of constants are numeric, character string, date, logical, and other.

Numeric Constants

Numeric constants begin with integers, which can be signed, such as the following numbers:

```
0
1
123456789
-5
```

Your numeric input cannot include grouping separators, such as commas. For example, 1,234,567 is not a valid numeric constant.

Numeric constants can include decimal fractions, as in these examples:

```
0.5
14.3456
-28.43210
```

dBASE for Windows defaults to carrying decimal numbers to 16 significant digits, so you don't need to worry about numeric accuracy except in extreme cases.

Leading zeros are not significant, and may be omitted. These are pairs of identical values:

```
0.5
.5

-0.456
-.456
```

You can also use integral exponents in scientific notation, as in these examples:

```
1E6
-1.4E-8
```

The scientists and engineers who understand scientific notation will comprehend that immediately. For you nonscientists, we offer the following tip.

▶▶ **TIP**

Large numbers are sometimes better written in scientific notation. 1E6 is a million (1, followed by six zeros). 1E9 is a billion. 1000000000 is impossible to read without stopping to tick off the zeros in groups of three.

Character String Constants

Character string constants are any string of characters that you can type, delimited by single or double quotation marks or by square brackets. For example, these are all the same:

```
"Smith"
'Smith'
[Smith]
```

dBASE reads a string constant from the opening delimiter to the matching closing delimiter. This means that you need to decide if your string should include one or more of the delimiters before forming your expression. These examples are correctly specified:

```
"Single 's inside doubles"
'Double "s inside singles'
"Brackets [inside] either"
'Brackets [inside] either'
[Brackets surrounding both: "Don't go," she said.]
```

Date Constants Date constants are written according to the settings of Desktop Properties Country tab (choose Properties ➤ Desktop, Country tab to check). They are enclosed in braces. The following examples assume the *M/D/Y* format:

```
{6/28/94}
{12/31/95}
{1/1/96}
{12/31/1999}
{1/1/2000}
```

(The first date above was the date that dBASE for Windows was officially launched.)

Logical Constants Logical constants are one of two values:

```
.T.
.F.
```

These mean True and False, respectively.

▶▶ **W A R N I N G**

Although you can also use Y and N (or y and n) in logical entry fields, and you never include the surrounding dots, these forms are not permitted in expressions.

Other Types Other constant data types include binary types, such as sounds and images. These constants can be supplied to commands, but cannot be used in expressions.

Memory Variables

A memory variable is created, most simply, by assigning an expression to a variable name. A constant is the simplest form of expression. These are all statements that create memory variables:

```
days_per_week = 7
tax_rate = .0675
last_name = "Smith"
full_name = 'Ms. Jillian Smith, PhD.'
launch_date = {6/28/94}
is_project_complete = .F.
```

Memory variable names begin with an alphabetic character and continue with any combination of letters, digits, and underscore characters. Valid memory variable names include the following:

```
x
x_ray
product_1
P17_A40
```

dBASE does *not* consider differences in case to be significant. The following names are all identical:

```
on_hand
On_hand
On_Hand
ON_HAND
```

By convention, memory variable names are typed in lowercase.

The name x-ray is not valid because the – operator is not allowed in names. The names 01P47 and _target are not valid either, because variable names must start with a letter.

 ▶▶NOTE

> **An exception to the rule for naming memory variables is the dBASE internal global variable names, which all start with an underscore character.**

There are no formal restrictions on the sorts of names you can make up. However, it is good policy to make your name reflect the variable's contents. The following are perfectly acceptable to dBASE, but will make your job much harder than it should be:

```
days_per_week = "Smith"
tax_rate = 'Ms. Jillian Smith, PhD.'
last_name = .0675
full_name = {6/28/94}
launch_date = .F.
is_project_complete = 7
```

In dBASE IV and earlier, you could use only 10 characters in a variable name. (Actually, you could use 11 but only the first 10 were significant.) dBASE for Windows lifts this restriction. There is no limit to the length of variable names. Use names that are just long enough to describe the value they will hold, but are not unnecessarily verbose.

Field Names

A field name is an alphabetic character, followed by up to nine letters, digits, or underscore characters. For example, these are all valid field names:

```
Address1
Last_name
Ship_date
Qty_on_hnd
```

The field name width is limited to 10 characters. This is because the field name is written into a strictly formatted header in the .DBF file.

A field name may include an optional data table alias specification. The table's alias is the table's name, unless an alternative is specified with the USE command (see Chapter 13). We always use these table alias specifications to be sure we're getting the data we want. For instance, you could have tables for Company, Product, and Customer, each with a NAME field. The following field names would keep the name data *Amalgamated Widgets, Inc.*, *Large Widgets*, and *Fred Smith* sorted out:

```
Company->name
Product->name
Customer->name
```

If a field name matches a memory variable name, the field takes precedence. Choosing a different (longer always works) memory variable name can eliminate this conflict. You can also prefix a memory variable with M-> as a pseudo table alias. For example if name is a field, M->name can be used as a memory variable.

Object Properties

Object properties can be referred to in expressions. Using the Properties tool in the Form Designer, you have assigned many properties. Properties can also be assigned with statements such as these:

```
my_form.Top = 2
pushbutton1.Left = my_form.Width - 12
my_form.Maximize = .F.
```

As you see in the second example, the property my_form.Width can be used as part of an expression. Since it is a number, it can be used like any other number.

You can create your own properties, just as you create your own memory variables. Property names follow the same rules as memory variable names, except that there is no M-> pseudo-table prefix. These are some examples using property names:

```
my_form.is_complete = .F.
my_form.start_date  = {12/31/95}
```

  ► ► N O T E

> **dBASE for Windows uses mixed uppercase and lowercase names for properties, such as Left, OnClick, and ColorNormal. To keep our custom properties separate, we use the lower_with underscores style you've seen above. Keep in mind that this is a convention; dBASE doesn't care about uppercase and lowercase.**

Object References

If you examine your .WFM file output from the Form Designer, you'll see that it is dBASE program code, and that the vast majority of the lines of code define and assign properties to your form's objects. By default, the object that the Form Designer creates is named *f*.

This is known as an *object reference variable*. It can be used in expressions, although its usage is specialized. Examples are given later in this chapter, in the section about structure operators.

An object reference is at least one of the properties of most of the dBASE built-in objects. For example, all the objects that you attach to forms have a Parent property. That is an object reference to the parent form.

The parent form's First property is the first on-form object in the form's tabbing order. All the on-form objects that are tab stops (including buttons and entry fields, but excluding lines and rectangles) have a Before property, which is the on-form object that they precede in the tabbing order. (The Before property of the last object in the tabbing order is an object reference to the First object, so tabbing goes in a circle.)

 ▶▶ **N O T E**

> **Subroutine references can also be used to refer to procedures, functions, or code blocks. However, these references are seldom used outside advanced programs.**

Function Calls

A function is a subroutine that returns a value. A function call is the function's name followed by parentheses enclosing the function's arguments, if any. All function calls require the parentheses. Arguments may or may not be needed, depending on the function.

A function call may be used as an operand anywhere that the appropriate result can appear in an expression. Here are some valid numeric function calls in ? commands that you can test in the Command window:

`? LEN("Smith")`	Returns 5
`? RECNO()`	Returns number of current record (or error if no table is in use)
`? PAYMENT(100000, .07/12, 30*12)`	Returns 665.3025
`? YEAR({12/31/95})`	Returns 1995

These are valid character string function calls:

? CHR(65)	Returns "A"
? STR(1/3, 5, 3)	Returns "0.333"

These function calls return dates:

? DATE()	Returns today's date
? CTOD('12/31/99')	Returns date of big New Year's Eve

These function calls return logical results:

? EOF()	Returns .T. at end of table; .F. otherwise (or error if no table is open)
? ISALPHA('9')	Returns .F.
? ISUPPER('A')	Returns .T.

In these examples, some of the functions have no argument at all, such as DATE( ), EOF( ), and RECNO( ), and some have as many as three arguments, such as the PAYMENT( ) and STR( ) functions. Other functions can be called with varying numbers of arguments.

In each function that accepts one or more arguments, the arguments can always be expressions. Here we've shown constant values. These are some valid expressions called with expressions more complex than simple constants:

? DTOS(DATE( ))	Returns a string for today, such as "December 31, 1995"
? CHR(10*6 + 5)	Returns "A"
? ISUPPER(CHR(65))	Returns .T.

These examples all use dBASE for Windows built-in functions. By convention, these are typed in all uppercase letters; however, as with other names, dBASE is not case-sensitive.

You can also create your own functions. These participate in expressions exactly as the built-in ones do. See Chapter 14 for information about writing your own functions.

 ▶▶ **N O T E**

> **By convention, your own functions, called UDFs (user-defined functions) are typed in lowercase (but again, dBASE doesn't care). Following the conventions makes it easy for you to distinguish calls to UDFs from calls to the dBASE built-in functions.**

Expressions as Operands

You can build expressions using other expressions as operands. This is a simple example:

    ? 4 + 1/3

which returns 4.33. In this case, the value of the expression 1/3 (0.33) was used as the operand of the addition operator.

Expressions can be enclosed in parentheses. An expression in parentheses is evaluated fully before it is used as an operand. Consider these two expressions:

`? 4 + (1/3)`	Returns 4.33
`? (4+1)/3`	Returns 1.67 (that's 5/3)

In our first example, without parentheses, dBASE decided to do the division before the addition, because its internal rule is that division has higher precedence than addition. The precedence follows this order:

- Exponentiate first
- Multiply and divide second
- Add and subtract third

The rules of precedence also extend to all other types of operators. We're not going to present those rules here, and we recommend that you ignore them if you stumble across them. However, the one rule to remember is that expressions in parentheses are fully evaluated before being used as an operand. By using parentheses, you control the order of execution. In fact, your expressions will be more readable and less prone to errors if you always use parentheses.

 ►► T I P

> **Here's one way to remember the order of precedence: "Please Excuse My Dear Aunt Sally," for Parentheses, Exponentials, Multiplication, Division, Addition, Subtraction.**

► Using Operators in Expressions

You can use half a dozen different kinds of operators in your expressions:

- Arithmetic
- Date
- String
- Logical
- Structure
- Relational

The following sections discuss each one in turn.

Arithmetic Operators

Arithmetic operators include the big four: +, −, *, /. We'll start with these, then round out the set with the others.

The big four numeric operations do just what you would expect:

? 2+3	Returns 5
? 2-3	Returns -1
? 2*3	Returns 6
? 2/3	Returns 0.67

As you will see below, the + and – operators are also string and date operators. They examine their operands to pick an appropriate type of operation. The arithmetic operations are performed if both their operands are one of the numeric types.

You may have noticed that dBASE for Windows keeps two types of numbers: N and F. The N type is used for integers—numbers that have no decimal fraction part. The F type is used for numbers that do have a fractional part. dBASE picks the appropriate types and handles the conversion from one to the other automatically.

For instance, dBASE for Windows will add the integers 2 and 2 and produce an integer 4. It will divide integer 4 by integer 3 and produce a floating-point number: 1.33. The number of digits you display is set in the Desktop Properties Programming tab. The number of places kept internally is also set there. In most cases, you'll want to display only a small portion of the available digits.

The other arithmetic operators are –, for unary negation, and ^, for exponentiation.

The operators we have looked at so far have all been binary, meaning they take two operands—one on either side. The – operator can also be used in a *unary* fashion, meaning with a only a single operand (on its right).

The – sign can precede an expression, meaning to reverse its sign. Here are some examples:

```
x = 2
? -x          Returns -2
? -(2+3)      Returns -5
? -(2-3)      Returns 1
```

The ^ operator means "raise the operand on the left to the power on the right." Here are some examples:

```
? 3^2         Returns 9
? 3^3         Returns 27
? 3^4         Returns 81
```

Neither operand need be integral, as in these examples:

? 1.2^2   Returns 1.44

? 3^2.5   Returns 15.5885

The ** operator is a synonym for the ^ operator.

The arithmetic operators are used only with arithmetic operands and produce arithmetic results.

Date Operators

Unlike numeric operators, the date operations use mostly mixed operands and do not always produce date results.

 ▶▶ **N O T E**

> **Other authors classify operators by the type of result they return. For example, subtracting two dates yields a number, so it is categorized as a numeric operator. We call them date operators if one (or both) operands is a date.**

The date operators are +, for date/number addition, and –, for date subtraction. The date/number addition operation adds a number to a date (or a date to a number) and produces a date result, as in these examples:

? DATE( )+7   Returns the date a
               week from today

? 30 +   Returns {12/31/99}
{12/1/99}

Date subtraction has more rules. But if you ignore the rules and think about the operation, it all makes sense, as in these examples:

? DATE( )-7   Returns the date one week past

? {12/31/99}-DATE( ) Returns the number of days
                      until the big New Year's Eve

Expressions and Functions

? 7-DATE( )	Returns error (because it's meaningless)

Date operators are supplemented by a wide range of date functions.

String Operators

There are three string operations, two involving a form of string concatenation and the third performing a string search:

- +, for simple concatenation
- –, for concatenation, trimming blanks
- $, for search (member of)

Concatenation is the operation of putting two strings together to form a single, longer string. The simple concatenation operator (+) abuts two strings. The result is precisely the combined length of both strings.

The trimming operation (–) removes trailing blanks from the left argument string. Here are some examples:

? 'John'+'Smith'?	Returns 'JohnSmith'
? 'John '+'Smith'?	Returns 'John Smith'
? 'John '-'Smith'?	Returns 'JohnSmith'
? 'John'-' Smith'?	Returns 'John Smith'
? 'John?'-' Smith'	Returns 'John Smith'

 ▶▶ **T I P**

The result of the – concatenation is the same as using the RTRIM( ) (right side trim) function on the right argument, then using the + operator for a simple concatenation. You may prefer that form, since it's more explicit.

The *member of* operator returns a logical result. It looks for the first string in the second, returning .T. if it is found. These examples show the operator in operation:

```
? 'a'$'abc'      Returns .T.
? 'at'$'abc'     Returns .F.
? 'at'$'Hat'     Returns .T.
```

The $ operator is case-sensitive. For example, this expression:

```
? 'A'$'abc'
```

returns the result .F.

For a case-insensitive search, use UPPER( ) or LOWER( ) on the operands, as in:

```
? UPPER('A')$UPPER('abc')
```

This expression returns .T.

Logical Operators

The following logical operators let you manipulate True and False results:

- .AND. returns True if both operands are True.
- .OR. returns True if either or both operands are True.
- .NOT. is a unary operator, which returns the reverse of the operand.

These are the operators that you will use constantly in expressions that test for two or more conditions. Here are some examples:

```
credit_limit = 500
balance = 450
frequent_buyer = .T.
buying_power =            Returns 50
credit_limit-balance
hi_buy_power = buing_     Returns .F.
power > 100

? frequent_buyer         Returns .T.
```

? frequent_buyer .AND. hi_buy_power	Returns .F.
? frequent_buyer .OR. hi_buy_power	Returns .T.
? .NOT. hi_buy_power	Returns .T.
? .NOT. (frequent_buyer .OR. hi_buy_power)	Returns .F.
? .NOT. (frequent_buyer .AND. hi_buy_power)	Returns .T.

►►**WARNING**

Parentheses are vital when working with logical operators. You need to use them to force dBASE for Windows to evaluate the expression as you want it evaluated.

Structure Operators

There are three complex structures in dBASE for Windows: tables, arrays, and objects. The structure operators are **[ ]** (brackets), which is the subscript operator) and **.** (period), which is the "property of" operator.

►►**NOTE**

The field value operator (->) is technically an operator, but it was covered earlier as part of a field name operand. We think of it as part of the name, despite its technical status.

The subscript operator can be applied to either an array or an object, as in these examples:

? arr[10]	Returns the tenth value in arr, or error if arr is less than 10 long

`? arr[2,3]`	Returns the value in second row, third column of arr; returns error if arr does not have two dimensions or if either subscript is too large
`? obj[10]`	Returns property number 10 of obj, or error if property 10 is not assigned

Arrays must be DECLARED before they can be used. See Chapter 14 for information about array declarations.

Objects come into existence by the NEW operator or by the DEFINE command. Numbered properties are created when you assign them a value. They cannot subsequently be unassigned. You can assign a value to obj[10], for example, without assigning any preceding property number. (obj[1] through obj[9] do not need to exist to have obj[10].)

  T I P

> **You can use an object's .Parent dimensions to make resizable forms. For example, assign Line1.Parent.Width to Line1.Right. That way, the line will grow or shrink as the parent form is resized.**

The . and [ ] operators may be used repeatedly in a single structure expression, as long as the value reached from left to right is appropriate to the operation. The following are examples:

`? Line1`	Returns object
`? Line1.Parent`	Returns object (form holding line1)
`? Line1.Parent.Width`	Returns width of parent form
`? Line1.Width`	Returns number (width of line, in pixels)

`arr[1] = Line1`

`? arr[1]`	Returns object (Line1)
`? arr[1].Width`	Returns width of Line1
`? arr[1].Parent.Width`	Returns width of parent form

▶▶ W A R N I N G

The Two-Way Form Designer is not totally two-way. It will replace any expressions you assign in properties with numeric constants. Get your form design right, then abandon the Two-Way tools to make final changes in the Program Editor.

Relational Operators

The following relational operators allow you to compare two values:

- <, for less than
- <=, for less than or equal to
- =, for equal to
- <> or #, for not equal to
- >=, for greater than or equal to
- >, for greater than

The operands must be matching types: numeric, character, date, or logical. Here are some examples:

`? 5.5 < 5.5`	Returns .F.
`? 5.5 <= 5.5`	Returns .T.
`? 'Smith' <= 'Smythe'`	Returns .T.
`? DATE( ) < {12/31/99}`	Returns .T. (as this is written)
`? .T. > .F.`	Returns .T.

All relational operators return results when applied to logical operators. .F. equals .F. and .T. equals .T.; .T. is greater than .F. (or .F. is less than .T.). A beginners mistake is writing:

```
buy_power = credit_limit - balance
hi_buy_power = buy_power > 100

? hi_buy_power = .T.      && silly!
? hi_buy_power      && same thing, good style
```

 T I P

> **We've never seen a good reason to use relational operators solely with logical operands.**

That finishes covering the operators.

▶ *Calling Functions*

Technically speaking, the parentheses that follow a function name are also an operator: the function call operator. However, unlike any other operator, function calls may not contain any operand at all, or they may have one or more operands (up to a limit imposed by your equipment's available memory).

All syntax (ours, the on-line help, printed documentation, and other books) documents the arguments to functions as expressions of specified types. For example, the ABS( ) (absolute value) function takes a single numeric argument. Its syntax is

```
ABS(<expN>)
```

It takes one argument, which is any expression evaluating to a number. This is why we say that a constant is the simplest form of expression. This syntax then covers all of these possibilites:

```
ABS(-2.5)
ABS(total_due)
ABS(invoic->total_due)
ABS(arr[1])
```

```
ABS(Form.First.Top)
ABS(ASC(LEFT(UPPER(last_name),1))-100)
```

You "unpeel" deeply nested function calls, like the last one, from the inside out. Here's an example:

`last_name = "Smith"`	
`? UPPER(last_name)`	Returns "SMITH"
`? LEFT(UP-` `PER(last_name),1)`	Returns "S"
`? ASC(LEFT(UP-` `PER(last_name),1))`	Returns 83
`? ABS(ASC(LEFT(UP-` `PER(last_name),1))-100)`	Returns 17 = ABS(83-100)

In a program, such as an event handler, it is better to provide named variables for the portions of the expression and build it in stages. (This is slightly less efficient, but massively less prone to error.) Here's an example:

```
last_name = "Smith"
uname = UPPER(last_name)
first_char = LEFT(uname,1)
...
```

Unfortunately, in many uses, such as in index expressions, you do not have this choice—you must provide a single expression. If you find yourself using more and more complex expressions, consider writing a user-defined function to hold the expression. See Chapter 14 for information about writing your own functions.

► *Using Functions in Expressions*

The rest of this chapter is devoted to the dBASE for Windows functions that are commonly used in expressions. It excludes those that are solely used to support obsolete dBASE IV syntax, functions used only in programming, and other functions that are not commonly used. (These other functions are listed in Appendix E.)

▶ *Function Categories*

Functions can be grouped into the following categories:

- Database-related
- Date manipulation
- Financial
- Low-level file I/O
- Miscellaneous

▶ **TABLE 12.1:** *Database-Related Functions*

FUNCTION	RESULT
ALIAS([*<alias>*])	Name of table in work area
BINTYPE([*<field name>*])	Type of Binary field
BOF([*<alias>*])	True if attempted to move before first record
BOOKMARK( )	Alternative to RECNO( ) for SQL tables
CATALOG( )	Name of current catalog
DATABASE( )	Name of open SQL database
DBF([*<alias>*])	Name of current of specified table
DELETED([*<alias>*])	Is record deleted?
DESCENDING(...	Is index descending?
EOF([*<alias>*])	True if moved past last record
FDECIMAL(*<field number expN>* ...	Number of decimals in field
FIELD(*<field number expN>* [...	Name of field, given number
FLDCOUNT([*<alias>*])	Number of fields in table
FLDLIST([*<field number expN>*])	Fields in SET FIELDS TO ...
FOR([[*<.mdx filename>*,] ...	FOR expression used to create tag
FOUND([*<alias>*])	Was last search successful?

▶ **TABLE 12.1:** *Database-Related Functions (continued)*

FUNCTION	RESULT
ISTABLE(<*table name*> ...	Is table in database?
KEY([<*.mdx filename*>,] ...	Key expression of an index
KEYMATCH (<*exp*> ...	Is there an index on the expression?
LUPDATE([<*alias*>])	Date of last update
MDX(<*index tag expN*> ...	Name of .MDX file containing a tag
ORDER([<*alias*>])	Order # of master index tag
RECCOUNT([<*alias*>])	Number of records in database
RECNO([<*alias*>])	Number of current record
RECSIZE([<*alias*>])	Size of record
RELATION(<*expN*> ...	Relation expression of specified relation
SEEK(<*expC*> ...	Search index for expression
SELECT([<*alias expC or expN*>])	Select a [new] work area
SQLEXEC(<*SQL statement*> ...	Execute an SQL statement
TAG([<*.mdx filename expC*> ...	Return selected tag
TAGCOUNT([<*.mdx filename*> ...	Number of tags in MDX file
TAGNO([<*tag name expC*> ...	Index tag number
TARGET(<*expN*>[, <*alias*>])	Table that is target of relation
UNIQUE([[<*.mdx filename*> ...	Is index UNIQUE?

▶ **TABLE 12.2:** *Date-Manipulation Functions*

FUNCTION	RESULT
CDOW(<*expD*>)	Character day ("Sunday" ...)
CMONTH(<*expD*>)	Character month ("January" ...)
DATE( )	Today's date

▶ **TABLE 12.2:** *Date-Manipulation Functions (continued)*

FUNCTION	RESULT
DAY(<*expD*>)	Day number (1 through 31)
DOW(<*expD*>)	Day of week (Sun.=1, ... Sat. = 7)
MONTH(<*expD*>)	Month number (1 through 12)
YEAR(<*expD*>)	Year number, two to four digits

▶ **TABLE 12.3:** *Financial Functions*

FUNCTION	RESULT
FV(<*payment expN*> ...	Future value of constant stream
PAYMENT(<*principal expN*> ...	Mortgage-type payment
PV(<*payment expN*> ...	Present value of constant stream

▶ **TABLE 12.4:** *Miscellaneous Functions*

FUNCTION	RESULT
FLENGTH(<*field number expN*> ...	File length from DOS (categorized as a low-level I/O function)
IIF(<*expL*>, <*exp1*>, <*exp2*>)	In-line IF test
INSPECT(<*object reference*>)	Inspect object properties
LOOKUP(<*return field 1*> ...	Look up value in table
SET(<*expC*>)	Set commands (on/off)
SETTO(<*expC*>)	Set commands (SET TO)

▶ **TABLE 12.5:** *Mixed-Type Functions*

FUNCTION	RESULT
MAX(<*exp 1*>, <*exp 2*>)	Greater of two values
MIN(<*exp 1*>, <*exp 2*>)	Lesser of two values

Expressions and Functions

Ch. **12**

► **TABLE 12.6:** *Numeric Functions*

FUNCTION	RESULT
ABS(*<expN>*)	Absolute value
CEILING(*<expN>*)	Round up away from zero
EXP(*<expN>*)	Raise e to the power
FLOAT(*<expN>*)	Convert number to floating point
FLOOR(*<expN>*)	Truncate to integer nearest 0
INT(*<expN>*)	Integer portion of decimal number
LOG(*<expN>*)	Natural logarithm
LOG10(*<expN>*)	Logarithm, base 10
MOD(*<dividend expN>*, *<divisor expN>*)	Remainder after division
RANDOM([*<expN>*])	Get random number
ROUND(*<expN 1>*, *<expN 2>*)	Numeric roundoff
SIGN(*<expN>*)	−1, 0, 1 for negative, zero, positive
SQRT(*<expN>*)	Square root

► **TABLE 12.7:** *String-Related Functions*

FUNCTION	RESULT
AT(*<search expC>* ...	Search for substring in string
CENTER(*<expC>* ...	Return centered string
DIFFERENCE(*<expC1>* ...	SOUNDEX difference between strings
EMPTY(*<exp>*)	Is string all blank?
ISALPHA(*<expC>* | *<memo field>*)	Is character alphabetic?
ISBLANK(*<exp>*)	Is string all blank?
ISCOLOR(*<expN>*)	Does computer do color?
ISLOWER(*<expC>* | *<memo field>*)	Is character lowercase letter?

▶ **TABLE 12.7:** *String-Related Functions (continued)*

FUNCTION	RESULT
ISUPPER(<*expC* > | <*memo field*>)	Is chararacter uppercase letter?
LEFT(<*expC*> ...	Return characters from left side of string
LEN(<*expC*> | <*memo field*>)	Length of string
LENNUM(<*expN*>)	Length of formatted number
LIKE(<*skeleton expC* > ...	Does string match skeleton?
LOWER(<*expC*> | <*memo field*>)	Convert to all lowercase
LTRIM(<*expC* > | <*memo field*>)	Trim leading blanks (left)
PROPER(<*expC*> | <*memo field*>)	Make SMITH into Smith
RAT(<*search expC*> ...	AT( ), from right to left
REPLICATE(<*expC*> ...	Repeat input string as specified
RIGHT(<*expC* > ...	Return characters from right side of string
RTRIM(<*expC*> ...	Trim trailing blanks (right)
SOUNDEX(<*expC*> ...	Return SOUNDEX value (for comparisons)
SPACE(<*expN*>)	Return blank string to specified length
STUFF(<*target expC*> ...	Put a substring into a string
SUBSTR(<*expC* > ...	Return a substring of a string
TRANSFORM(<*exp*>, <*picture expC*>)	Format with Picture specification
TRIM(<*expC* > | <*memo field*>)	Same as RTRIM( )
UPPER(<*expC* > | <*memo field*>)	Convert to all uppercase

Expressions and Functions

Ch. 12

▶ **TABLE 12.8:** *System-Related Functions*

FUNCTION	RESULT
FILE(<*filename expC* >)	Does file exist?
FUNIQUE(<*expC*>)	Create unique temp file name
RUN([<*is Windows expL1*> ...	Run DOS or Windows application

▶ **TABLE 12.9:** *Time-Related Functions*

FUNCTION	RESULT
ELAPSED(<*time expC 1*> ...	Time between two events
SECONDS( )	Seconds elapsed since midnight
TIME([<*exp*>])	Current time

▶ **TABLE 12.10:** *Trigonometric Functions*

FUNCTION	RESULT
ACOS(<*expN*>)	Arccosine of cosine
ASIN(<*expN*>)	Arcsine of sine
ATAN(<*expN*>)	Arctangent of tangent
ATN2(<*sine expN*> ...	Alternate form, arctangent
COS(<*expN*>)	Cosine of angle
DTOR(<*expN*>)	Degrees to radians
PI( )	Pi (3.1415 ...)
RTOD(<*expN*>)	Radians to degrees
SIN(<*expN*>)	Sine of angle
TAN(<*expN*>)	Tangent of angle

▶ **TABLE 12.11:** *Type-Conversion Functions*

FUNCTION	RESULT
ASC(<*expC*>)	Convert single character to ASCII number equivalent
CHR(<*expN*>)	Convert ASCII number (0–255) to equivalent character
CTOD(<*expC*>)	Convert character string to date
DMY(<*expD*>)	Convert date to *DD/MM/YYYY*-type format
DTOS(<*expD*>)	Convert date to string (month spelled-out)
MDY(<*expD*>)	Convert date to *MM/DD/YY*-type format
STR(<*expN*> ...	Convert number to character string
VAL(<*expC*>)	Convert string to number

- Mixed type
- Numeric
- String-related
- System-related
- Time-related
- Trigonometric
- Type-conversion

Tables 12.1 through 12.11 list the functions in these categories. The function's syntax is included in its entirety if it is simple, or truncated (with the truncated part replaced by ...) if it is more complex. The table also provides a brief summary of the intended use of each function.

Look through these tables to see which functions you might use, and then look up those functions in the descriptions that follow.

Expressions and Functions

▶ ▶
Ch.
12

▶▶ **W A R N I N G**

> You may find some differences between this listing and the on-line documentation. In case of differences, the safe approach is to test the alternatives in the Command window.

▶ Alphabetic Reference to Common Functions

The descriptions that follow include the use of the function, the function's syntax, and examples of the function in use (if examples clarify the use). The functions are listed in pure alphabetic order; they are not grouped in categories as they are in Tables 12.1 through 12.11.

For our examples, we've set decimals to four places. The syntax we've used has become standard in dBASE documentation, as well as in the documentation for other Xbase dialects. Functions are specified exactly as they should be typed, with these exceptions:

- *<item>*: Replace this with the suggested item. Do not type the angle brackets.

- [*item*]: The item is optional; do not include it if you do not need it. Do not type the square brackets.

- …: The preceding item may be repeated as often as you need. Do not type the ellipses.

- ¦: This means this item **or** that item. Use the item on the left or the item on the right. Use only one or the other. Do not type the ¦ symbol.

The expressions for the functions are specified by type:

- *<exp>*: Any dBASE expression
- *<expC >*: Character expression
- *<expN>*: Numeric expression
- *<expD>*: Date expression
- *<expL>*: Logical expression

Here's an example:

AT(*<search expC>*, *<target expC>* ¦ *<target memo field>*[, *<nth occurrence expN>*])

The AT function takes two or three arguments. The first is a search expression, for which any character expression is permitted. The second argument is separated from the first by a comma (as are all arguments). It is a target character expression or Memo field. The third argument is optional. If specified, it must be a numeric expression. Note that the second comma is inside the square brackets. If you don't include the third argument, don't include that comma (the second one).

ABS

The ABS function returns the absolute value of a number. If the number is positive, ABS returns the number. If the number is negative, ABS returns the number, stripped of the negative sign.

Syntax

ABS(*<expN>*)

Examples

? ABS(3.2)	Returns 3.2
? ABS(-27)	Returns 27

ACOS

The ACOS function returns the arccosine (or inverse cosine) of a number from 0 to 1. It returns its answer in radians. Use RTOD( ) to convert radians to degrees. Use DTOR( ) to convert degrees to radians.

Syntax

ACOS(*<expN>*)

Examples

? ACOS(1)	Returns 0
? ACOS(0)	Returns 1.5708
? RTOD(ACOS(0))	Returns 90

ALIAS

The ALIAS function returns the alias or name of the table in use in the current work area. It returns an empty string if no table is in use.

Syntax

ALIAS([*<alias>*])

Examples

```
* table in use: PEOPLE
? ALIAS( )                  Returns PEOPLE
* table in use: PEOPLE
ALIAS LIST1
? ALIAS( )                  Returns LIST1
```

ASC

The ASC function returns the number corresponding to a character in the ASCII character set.

Syntax

ASC(*<expC>*)

Examples

```
? ASC(" ")      Returns 32
? ASC("A")      Returns 65
```

ASIN

The ASIN function returns the arcsine (or inverse sine). It changes its argument, a sine, into an angle, in radians. Use RTOD to convert radians to degrees. Use DTOR to convert degrees to radians.

Syntax

ASIN(*<expN>*)

Examples

? ASIN(0)	Returns 0
? ASIN(SIN(DTOR(90)))	Returns 1.5708

AT

The AT function returns the location of a substring in a string or Memo field. With the optional third parameter, it returns the location of the *n*th occurrence of a string in a string or Memo field. It returns zero if the string, or specified occurrence of the string, is not found.

Syntax

AT(*<search expC>, <target expC>* | *<target memo field>*[, *<nth occurrence expN>*])

Examples

? AT('Smith','John Smith')	Returns 6
? AT('at', 'Cat in hat', 2)	Returns 9
? AT('x','abcde')	Returns 0

ATAN

The ATAN function returns the arctangent (or inverse tangent) of a number. Given the tangent of an angle, it returns the angle, in radians. Use RTOD to convert radians to degrees. Use DTOR to convert degrees to radians.

Syntax

ATAN(*<expN>*)

Examples

? ATAN(0)	Returns 0
? RTOD(ATAN(1))	Returns 45
? ATAN(TAN(DTOR(45)))	Returns 0.7854

Expressions and Functions

▶▶ Ch. **12**

ATN2

The ATN2 function returns an arctangent given a sine and cosine of an angle.

Syntax

ATN2(*<sine expN>*, *<cosine expN>*)

Examples

? ATN2(1, 1)	Returns 0.7854
? ATN2(1, 0)	Returns 1.5708
? ATN2(0, 1)	Returns 0

BINTYPE

The BINTYPE function returns the type of a binary field.

Syntax

BINTYPE([*<field name>*])

The types are as follows:

0 to 32K-1	Available for user definition
32K	.WAV
32K + 1	.BMP
32K + 2	.PCX
32K + 3	.TIF
32K + 4	.GIF
32K + 5	.EPS

BOF

The BOF function returns .T. if the active table is at the beginning of the file.

Syntax

BOF([<*alias*>])

BOOKMARK

The BOOKMARK function is used for SQL tables that do not have record numbers. It returns an identifier that you may subsequently use in a GO command, as if it were a record number.

Syntax

BOOKMARK( )

CATALOG

The CATALOG function returns the name of the currently open catalog, if any. It returns an empty string if no catalog is open.

Syntax

CATALOG( )

CDOW

The CDOW function returns the day of the week of a date argument as a character string.

Syntax

CDOW(<*expD*>)

Examples

? CDOW(DATE( ))	Returns "Monday" (if today is Monday)
? CDOW(DATE( )+2)	Returns "Wednesday"

CEILING

The CEILING function returns a number rounded up to the next highest integer.

Expressions and Functions

Ch.
12

Syntax

CEILING(<*expN*>)

Examples

? CEILING(1)   Returns 1

? CEILING(1.1)   Returns 2

? CEILING(-1.2)   Returns −1

CENTER

The CENTER function returns a text string resulting from the centering of an input string in a given number of characters. If the length of the result string is not supplied, 80 is implied. You can supply a pad character to be used in lieu of the space character for left and right side padding.

Syntax

CENTER(<*expC*> ¦ <*memo field*>[, <*lengthexpN*> [, <*padexpC*>]])

Examples

? CENTER('Title', 15)   Returns 'Title'

? CENTER('News!', 15, '*') Returns '*****News!*****'

CHR

The CHR function returns an ASCII character given a number in the range 0 to 255. This is the inverse of the ASC( ) function.

Syntax

CHR(<*expN*>)

Examples

? CHR(33)   Returns "!"

? CHR(65)   Returns "A"

CMONTH

The CMONTH function returns the month as a character string, given a date.

Syntax

CMONTH(<*expD*>)

Examples

? CMONTH(DATE( ))	Returns "June" (if the month is June)
? CMONTH(DATE( )+60	Returns "August"

COS

The COS function function returns the cosine of an angle, given in radians. Use DTOR to convert degrees to radians.

Syntax

COS(<*expN*>)

Examples

? COS(0)	Returns 1
? COS(DTOR(45))	Returns .7071

CTOD

The CTOD function converts a character string to a date.

Syntax

CTOD(<*expC*>)

Example

? CTOD("12/25/95")+365	Returns 12/24/96

Expressions and Functions

▶ ▶
Ch.
12

DATABASE

The DATABASE function returns the name of the currently open database or an empty string if no database is open.

▶▶ **N O T E**

.DBF and .DB files are not part of a database within the meaning of the DATABASE function. The DATABASE function applies to SQL databases.

Syntax

DATABASE( )

DATE

The DATE function returns today's date, as a date variable.

Syntax

DATE( )

DAY

The DAY function returns the number of the day in a date.

Syntax

DAY(*<expD>*)

Example

? DAY(CTOD("1/31/96"))   Returns 31

DBF

The DBF function returns the name of the table open in the current work area, or in a specified work area. It returns an empty string if no table is in use in the current or specified area.

Syntax

DBF([*<alias>*])

DELETED

The DELETED function returns .T. if the currently selected record is marked for deletion.

Syntax

DELETED([<*alias*>])

DESCENDING

The DESCENDING function returns .T. if the specified index is in descending sequence.

Syntax

DESCENDING([<*.mdx filename*>,] <*index position expN*> [, <*alias*>])

DIFFERENCE

The DIFFERENCE function returns the SOUNDEX difference between two strings. A difference of 4 is minimal; a difference of 0 is maximal. See the SOUNDEX function.

Syntax

DIFFERENCE(<*expC1*> ¦ <*memo field 1*>, <*expC2*> ¦ <*memo field 2*>)

Examples

```
? DIFFERENCE('Smith','Smythe')      Returns 4
? DIFFERENCE('Aardvark','Zebra')    Returns 1
```

DMY

The DMY function returns a string in *dd month yy* format, given a date. The *yy* portion is two or four digits, depending on the setting of CENTURY.

Syntax

DMY(<*expD*>)

Example

     ? DMY({12/31/95}+1)   Returns "1 January 96"

DOW

The DOW function returns a number representing the day of the week, given a date variable. Sunday is day 1, and Saturday is day 7.

 ▶▶ T I P

> To find weekends, take DOW(DATE-1). This command returns 1 through 5 for Monday through Friday, and 6 and 7 for Saturday and Sunday.

Syntax

     DOW(*<expD>*)

Example

     ? DOW(DATE( ))   Returns 2, which represents
                             Monday (if today is Monday)

DTOR

The DTOR function converts degrees to radians.

Syntax

     DTOR(*<expN>*)

Example

     ? DTOR(45)   Returns 0.7854

DTOS

The DTOS function converts a date to a string in the form *YYYYMMDD*. It always uses this format, which is guaranteed to sort dates correctly. DTOS is the function to use when you want to set up indexes on dates combined with other strings.

Syntax

DTOS(*<expD>*)

Example

? DTOS({12/31/95})   Returns "19951231"

ELAPSED

The ELAPSED function returns the time difference, in seconds, of two time strings in *HH:MM:SS* format. This time format is the one returned by the TIME function.

Syntax

ELAPSED(*<time expC 1>*, *<time expC 2>*)

EMPTY

The EMPTY function returns .T. if its argument (often a field) is all blank.

Syntax

EMPTY(*<exp>*)

EOF

The EOF function returns .T. if the current table's record pointer is at the end of the file.

Syntax

EOF([*<alias>*])

EXP

The EXP function returns 2.7183 (the base of the natural logarithm) raised to the specified power. It is the inverse of the LOG function.

Syntax

EXP(<*expN*>)

Examples

? EXP(1)	Returns 2.7183
? LOG(EXP(2))	Returns 1.000

FDECIMAL

The FDECIMAL function returns the number of decimal places in a given field in the current table, or in a table specified by its alias.

Syntax

FDECIMAL(<*field number expN*>[, <*alias*>])

FIELD

The FIELD function returns the name of a field specified by its number in the table structure. It uses the current table unless an optional table alias is specified.

Syntax

FIELD(<*field number expN*>[, <*alias*>])

Example

? FIELD(3)   Returns name of third field in current table

FILE

The FILE function tests for the existence of a file. It returns .T. if the file exists.

Syntax

FILE(<*filename expC*>)

Example

```
? FILE("\DBASEWIN\BIN\DBASEWIN.INI")    Returns .T. (for us)
```

FLDCOUNT

The FLDCOUNT function returns the number of fields in the current table or, if an alias is supplied, to the table specified by the alias.

Syntax

```
FLDCOUNT([<alias>])
```

FLDLIST

The FLDLIST function returns the expression given in a SET FIELDS TO command. (This is the command issued by a query to restrict the fields in a view of a table.)

Syntax

```
FLDLIST([<field number expN>])
```

FLENGTH

The FLENGTH function returns the length of a field, given its number in the current table, or, if an optional alias is specified, in a specified table.

Syntax

```
FLENGTH(<field number expN>[, <alias>])
```

FLOAT

The FLOAT function converts a Numeric data type to a Float data type.

Syntax

```
FLOAT(<expN>)
```

Example

```
? FLOAT(5)    Returns 5.0000 (with decimals set to four
              places)
```

FLOOR

The FLOOR function returns a number rounded down to the next lowest integer.

Syntax

FLOOR(<*expN*>)

Examples

? FLOOR(2)	Returns 2
? FLOOR(1.9)	Returns 1
? FLOOR(-1.5)	Returns -2

FOR

The FOR function returns the FOR clause used to specify an index (as in FOR state = 'CA').

Syntax

FOR([[<*.mdx filename*>,] <*index position expN*> [,<*alias*>]])

FOUND

The FOUND function returns .T. if the last FIND, SEEK, or LOCATE was successful.

Syntax

FOUND([<*alias*>])

Example

? SEEK 'Smith'	
? FOUND( )	Returns .T. if there is a 'Smith'

FUNIQUE

The FUNIQUE function returns the name of a new file. You can use FUNIQUE repeatedly to create new file names that are guaranteed not to already exist.

Syntax

FUNIQUE(*<expC>*)

<expC > is a DOS-type file name mask, such as ????????.TMP or TEMP????.DBF.

FV

The FV function calculates the future value of a stream of payments given a periodic interest rate and number of payments. The first payment is at time 0; the valuation is reported at time $n-1$.

Syntax

FV(*<payment expN>*, *<interest expN>*, *<term expN>*)

Example

```
? FV(100, 0.05, 10)     Returns 1257.79
```

IIF

The IIF function (immediate IF) evaluates a condition and picks one of two results, based on the condition. If the condition evaluates to .T., IIF picks the first result.

Syntax

IIF(*<expL>*, *<exp1>*, *<exp2>*)

Example

```
? IIF(test_grade > 90,     Result depends on
"Excellent!", "OK")        test_grade
```

INSPECT

The INSPECT function opens the Object Properties Inspector to examine the properties of an object, such as a form.

Expressions and Functions

Ch.
12

▶▶**T I P**

> Although INSPECT is never used in the contexts of our
> other expressions (index expressions, scope expressions,
> and so on), it is invaluable from the Command window.

Syntax

    INSPECT(<*object reference*>)

Examples

`?check_it = NEW my_form( )`	No result
`?INSPECT(check_it)`	Brings up Object Properties Inspector for your form

INT

The INT function chooses the integer part of a number. This rounds positive and negative numbers toward zero.

INT is commonly used for rounding by adding 0.5, as in

    INT(*amount*+0.5)

However, adding 0.5 and taking INT( ) rounds positive numbers correctly, but not negative numbers. To round negative values, you must subtract 0.5. This expression rounds negative numbers correctly:

    INT(*num* + IIF(*num* > 0, 0.5, -0.5))

▶▶**W A R N I N G**

> The examples describe mathematically correct
> rounding. Different business practices prescribe
> different methods for treating numbers that end
> exactly in .5.

Syntax

```
INT(<expN>)
```

Examples

? INT(1.49 + 0.5)	Returns 1
? INT(1.5 + 0.5)	Returns 2
? INT(-1.9)	Returns −1
? INT(-1.9 + 0.5)	Returns −1
? INT(-1.9 - 0.5)	Returns −2

ISALPHA

The ISALPHA function returns True if the first character of the argument string is *a* through *z* or *A* through *Z* (if you're using an English language driver). Non-English language drivers may include additional characters.

Syntax

```
ISALPHA(<expC> | <memo field >)
```

Examples

? ISALPHA('X')	Returns .T.
? ISALPHA('9')	Returns .F.
? ISALPHA(CHR(135))	Result depends on code page and language driver

ISBLANK

The ISBLANK function is a synonym for EMPTY. It returns .T. if its argument is all blank.

Syntax

```
ISBLANK(<exp >)
```

Expressions and Functions

Ch. 12

Examples

? ISBLANK("?")	Returns .T.
? ISBLANK("Smith")	Returns .F.

ISCOLOR

The ISCOLOR function returns .T. if the computer is capable of including color in its display.

Syntax

ISCOLOR( )

ISLOWER

The ISLOWER function returns .T. if the argument character is a lowercase alphabetic character. Non-English language drivers may include additional lowercase alphabetic characters.

Syntax

ISLOWER(<*expC*> | <*memo field*>)

Examples

? ISLOWER('a')	Returns .T.
? ISLOWER('A')	Returns .F.
? ISLOWER('9')	Returns .F.
? ISLOWER(CHR(135))	Result depends on code page and language driver

ISTABLE

The ISTABLE function is used to check if a table exists in an SQL database. It checks the currently open database, or, if one is specified, a named database. It returns .F. if no SQL database is open.

Syntax

ISTABLE(<*table name*> [, <*database name*>])

ISUPPER

The ISUPPER function returns .T. if the argument character is an uppercase alphabetic character. Non-English language drivers may include additional uppercase alphabetic characters.

Syntax

ISUPPER(*<expC>* ¦ *<memo field>*)

Examples

? ISUPPER('A')	Returns .T.
? ISUPPER('a')	Returns .F.
? ISUPPER('9')	Returns .F.
? ISUPPER(CHR(135))	Result depends on code page and language driver

KEY

The KEY function returns the key expression used to create the specified index. If no .MDX file name is specified, the selected table's production index is used. If no alias is specified, the current table is selected.

Syntax

KEY([*<.mdx filename>*,] *<index position expN>*[, *<alias>*])

KEYMATCH

The KEYMATCH function checks to see if an expression exists in an index. If nothing except the expression is specified, the current table's currently active index is used. The additional arguments let you specify an alternate index, an alternate index file, and an alternate table.

Syntax

KEYMATCH (*<exp>* [, *<index position expN1>* ¦?? [, *<.mdx filename>* ,] *<tag expN2>* [, *<alias>*]]])

LEFT

The LEFT function returns a specified number of characters from the left side of a character string.

Syntax

LEFT(*<expC>* ¦ *<memo field>*, *<length expN>*)

Example

? LEFT('Sample',3)   Returns 'Sam'

LEN

The LEN function returns the length, in characters, of a character expression.

Syntax

LEN(*<expC>* ¦ *<memo field>*)

Example

? LEN('Smith')   Returns 5

LENNUM

The LENNUM function returns the width, including leading decimal places, of a number formatted for output using the current default settings. The default output width for an integer is ten characters.

 ►►**TIP**

Use the STR function to gain more control over the output of numbers.

Syntax

LENNUM(*<expN>*)

LIKE

The LIKE function returns .T. if a skeleton expression with wildcard characters matches a target expression or Memo field.

Syntax

LIKE(*<skeleton expC>*, *<expC>* ¦ *<memo field>*)

Examples

? LIKE('a?c', 'abc')	Returns .T.
? LIKE('a*d', 'axxxxd')	Returns .T.
? LIKE('a*d', 'AxxxxD')	Returns .F. (LIKE is case-sensitive)
? LIKE('abc', 'a*c')	Returns .F. (* is a literal in target)

LOG

The LOG function returns the natural logarithm of its argument number. It is the inverse of the EXP function.

Syntax

LOG(*<expN >*)

Examples

? LOG(10)	Returns 2.3026
? LOG(1)	Returns 0.0000
? LOG(EXP(1))	Returns 1.0000

LOG10

The LOG10 function returns the log to the base 10 of its argument number.

Syntax

LOG10(*<expN>*)

Expressions and Functions

Ch.
12

Examples

| ? LOG10(10) | Returns 1.0000 |
| ? LOG10(100) | Returns 2.0000 |

LOOKUP

The LOOKUP function looks for a value in one column of a table. If it finds a match, it returns the value of a field in the row where it found the match.

Syntax

LOOKUP(<*return field 1*>, <*exp*>, <*lookup field 2* >)

Example

| ? LOOKUP(emp_id, 'Smith', last_name) | Returns emp_id of first 'Smith', or " if no 'Smith's' |

LOWER

The LOWER function changes all alphabetic characters in the argument expression into lowercase characters. This can be used to force case-insensitive searching and ordering.

Syntax

LOWER(<*expC*> ¦ <*memo field*>)

Example

```
?INDEX ON
LOWER(last_name)
```

| ?SEEK 'smith' | Finds any 'Smith', 'SMITH', 'smith', etc. |

LTRIM

The LTRIM function returns the argument string after removing any leading blanks.

Syntax

LTRIM(<*expC*> ¦ <*memo field*>)

Example

```
? LTRIM("?mith")        Returns "Smith"
```

LUPDATE

The LUPDATE function returns the date of the last update of the currently open table, or of one specified by an alias.

Syntax

```
LUPDATE([<alias>])
```

MAX

The MAX function returns the greater of two values. The input values most be of the same type (except that an N can be compared to an F). .T. is greater than .F. if you're comparing logical variables.

Syntax

```
MAX(<exp 1>, <exp 2 >)
```

Examples

```
? MAX(1.1*old_price, new_price)    Returns larger
                                   amount
? MAX({12/31/95},DATE( )}          Returns later date
```

MDX

The MDX function returns the name of the .MDX file that contains the specified index. If an alias is not supplied, the current table is used. Otherwise, the table specified by the alias is used.

Syntax

```
MDX(<index tag expN>[, <alias>])
```

MDY

The MDY function returns a text string, in the format *Month dd, yy*, for a date. The year values are either two or four digits, depending on the setting of CENTURY.

Expressions and Functions

Ch.
12

Syntax

MDY(<*expD*>)

►►**TIP**

MDY is one of numerous reasons why we prefer to set and leave CENTURY turned on. This is particularly true since the end of the century is rapidly approaching.

Example

? MDY({12/31/95})   With CENTURY off, returns "December 31, 95"; with CENTURY on, returns "December 31, 1995"

MIN

The MIN function returns the smaller of two values. The input values most be of the same type (except that an N can be compared to an F). .T. is greater than .F. if you're comparing logical variables.

Syntax

MIN(<*exp 1*>, <*exp 2* >)

Examples

? MIN(1.1*old_price, new_price)   Returns smaller amount

? MIN({12/31/95},DATE( )}   Returns earlier date

MOD

The MOD function returns the remainder after division. This is commonly used for finding remainders of integral arguments, although the function is not restricted to integral arguments.

Syntax

MOD(<*dividend expN*>, <*divisor expN*>)

Examples

? INT(DAY(my_date)/7)	Returns number of whole weeks in the month (4)
? MOD(DAY(my_date),7)	Returns 0 or 1 for February, 2 or 3 for other months
? MOD(6.4, 4.2)	Returns 2.2

MONTH

The MONTH function returns the number of the month, given a date. January is 1; December is 12.

Syntax

MONTH(*<expD>*)

Example

? MONTH({12/31/95})	Returns 12

ORDER

The ORDER function returns the name of the master index tag (.MDX or .NDX) in the currently active table, or in the table specified by the optional alias argument.

Syntax

ORDER([*<alias>*])

PAYMENT

The PAYMENT function returns the payment required to repay a given principal amount at a fixed interest rate over a given number of payments. The interest rate is the periodic rate. The *n* payments are made at time 0 through time *n*−1.

Syntax

PAYMENT(*<principal expN>*, *<interest expN>*, *<term expN>*)

Expressions and Functions

Ch. 12

Example

```
? PAYMENT(100000, .07/12, 30*12)
```
Returns 665.3025; amortizes a $100,000 mortgage at 5833%/month over 360 months

PI

The PI function returns the value of PI, the ratio of the circumference of a circle to its diameter (3.141596...). dBASE for Windows stores floating-point numbers to 16 decimal places.

Syntax

```
PI( )
```

PROPER

The PROPER function returns a character string with first letters in uppercase and other letters in lowercase. This is used, for example, to take a list of names in all capitals and convert them to uppercase and lowercase.

▶▶ **WARNING**

PROPER results aren't always proper. None of these will have the second capital letter: McPherson, LeBoeuf, DeVille. Doing human names requires human intelligence.

Syntax

```
PROPER(<expC> | <memo field>)
```

Examples

```
? PROPER("JOHN SMITH")
```
Returns "John Smith"

```
PROPER("Ms. Smith, MD")
```
Returns "Ms. Smith, Md"

```
PROPER("John Smith
III, PhD.")
```
Returns "John Smith Iii, Phd."

PV

The PV function returns the present value of a stream of constant payments at a fixed interest rate. The interest rate is the periodic interest rate. The n payments are made at time periods 0 through $n-1$. PV is the inverse of the PAYMENT function.

Syntax

PV(*<payment expN>*, *<interest expN>*, *<term expN>*)

Examples

? PAYMENT(100000, .07/12, 30*12)	Returns 665.3025
? PV(665.30, .07/12, 30*12)	Returns 99999.6250

RANDOM

The RANDOM function returns a random floating-point number between 0 and 1. If seeded with a positive number, RANDOM returns the identical number each time it is called. If RANDOM is called without an argument—RANDOM( )—it returns the value of RANDOM(0) the first time it is called. Subsequent calls without an argument use the previous value of RANDOM as an argument, creating an apparently random series. This series will be the same each time you run dBASE for Windows.

If RANDOM is seeded with a negative number, as in RANDOM(–1), it returns a value based on the precise state of the system clock, which approximates true randomness.

 ▶▶ T I P

> **Calling RANDOM without an argument is helpful in testing a calculation, because you know that the series of random numbers should be the same each time you run dBASE for Windows.**

Syntax

RANDOM([*<expN >*])

Ch.
12

RAT

The RAT function (reverse AT) finds the first occurrence of a sub-string in a string, searching from the right end toward the left.

Syntax

RAT(<*search expC*>, <*target expC*> ¦ <*target memo field* >)

Example

```
? RAT('at', 'Cat in Hat')
```
Returns 9 (using the AT function with the same arguments would return 2)

RECCOUNT

The RECCOUNT function returns the number of records actually in a table. If a table of 1000 records has 100 records deleted, and DE-LETED is on, the COUNT of records will return 900. RECCOUNT, on the other hand, will return 1000. Similarly setting a filter will affect the COUNT value, but not the value of RECCOUNT.

Syntax

RECCOUNT([<*alias*>])

RECNO

The RECNO function returns the number of the record pointed to by the record pointer in the currently active table, or, if an alias is speci-fied, in the specified table.

Syntax

RECNO([<*alias*>])

RECSIZE

The RECSIZE function returns the number of bytes in each record in the currently active table or, if an alias is specified, in the specified table.

RECCOUNT( )*RECSIZE( )+1000 gives a quick, though
imprecise, approximation of the size of a table on disk
(not including indexes or memo files). The 1000 is for
file overhead.

Syntax

    RECSIZE([<alias>])

RELATION

The RELATION function returns the key expression of a selected relation in the current table or, if an alias is specified, the specified table.

Syntax

    RELATION(<expN >[, <alias >])

REPLICATE

The REPLICATE function returns a character string that repeats the
argument string the specified number of times.

Syntax

    REPLICATE(<expC> ¦ <memo field>, <expN >)

Examples

    ? REPLICATE('*',10)   Returns '**********'
    ? REPLICATE('*--*', 4)   Returns '*--**--**--**--*'

RIGHT

The RIGHT function returns the specified number of characters from
the right side of a character string.

Ch.
12

Syntax

> RIGHT(*<expC>* ¦ *<memo field>*, *<expN>*)

Example

> ? RIGHT('Cat in Hat',3)   Returns 'Hat'

ROUND

The ROUND function rounds numbers to a specified number of decimal places.

Syntax

> ROUND(*<expN 1>*, *<expN 2 >*)

Examples

> ? ROUND(1.249, 1)   Returns 1.2000
>
> ? ROUND(1.250, 1)   Returns 1.3000
>
> ? ROUND(3.49, 0)   Returns 3.0000
>
> ? ROUND(3.5, 0)   Returns 4.000

RTOD

The RTOD function converts an angle specified in radians to an angle in degrees.

Syntax

> RTOD(*<expN>*)

Examples

> ? RTOD(1)   Returns 57.2958
>
> ? RTOD(PI( ))   Returns 180.0000

RTRIM

The RTRIM (right TRIM) function returns a string after removing trailing blanks from the argument character string.

Syntax

RTRIM(<*expC*> ¦ <*memo field* >)

Example

? RTRIM("Smith?)   Returns "Smith"

RUN

The RUN function runs a DOS or Microsoft Windows program or a DOS command. If the first parameter is .T., a Windows program is run. If it is .F. or omitted, a DOS program or command is run. The optional second logical parameter is ignored.

Syntax

RUN([<*is Windows expL1*>,]<*command expC*> [, <*expL2* >])

Examples

?RUN('chkdsk /f')   Runs DOS chkdsk /f
                                 command

?RUN(.T., '\windows\notepad.exe')   Runs Windows
                                 Notepad

SECONDS

The SECONDS function returns the number of seconds, to the nearest two-hundredths, elapsed since midnight. Because SECONDS returns a number, it is useful when you need to do calculations.

 ▶▶ **T I P**

> **The TIME function returns the same information as a**
> **character string. TIME is useful for reporting the time.**

Syntax

SECONDS( )

Expressions and Functions

▶▶

Ch.
12

SEEK

The SEEK function searches for the value of the expression in the current index in the current table, or, if the optional alias is specified, in the specified table. The type of expression must match the index expression.

Syntax

SEEK(<*expC*> ¦ <*expN*> ¦ <*expD*> [, <*alias*>])

Example

?SEEK('Smith')   Finds first 'Smith'
(if there is one)

SELECT

The SELECT function returns the next available work area number (where you can open an additional table without closing any open tables) if you omit the optional alias. If you include the alias, SELECT returns the work area number of the alias. You can have up to 225 work areas in each session.

►► **W A R N I N G**

While dBASE for Windows would be happy to let you open a hundred tables in each of an unlimited number of sessions, the DOS file handle limit seriously restricts you. We'll need a better operating system to exploit this capability.

Syntax

SELECT([<*alias expC or expN*>])

Examples

? SELECT( )   Returns number of next available
work area

? SELECT('people')   Returns number of work area for
People table

SET

The SET function returns the value of the current setting of the features listed in Table 12.12.

▶ **TABLE 12.12:** *Settings Reported by the SET Function*

SETTING	EFFECT IF ON
ALTERNATE	Echoes output to SET ALTERNATE TO device
AUTOSAVE	Automatic saving
BELL	Warning beeps
CARRY	Copy data from prior record on append
CATALOG	Add new files to active catalog
CENTURY	Use four-digit year format in dates
CONFIRM	Require keypress after typing last character in field
CONSOLE	Use results pane of Command window for output
COVERAGE	Do coverage analysis of running programs
CUA ENTER	Enter submits a form (if off, Enter completes a field)
CURRENCY	Position of currency symbol (left or right)
CURSOR	Show/hide cursor in dBASE IV-style applications
DELETED	Deleted records appear to be removed from tables
DELIMITERS	Mark start and stop of dBASE IV-style entry fields
DESIGN	Allow switching from Run mode to Design mode
DEVELOP-MENT	Check for more recent .PRG file before running .PRO file and other compiled programs (if off, always run .PRO file; no recompiles)
ECHO	Open the Debugger
ESCAPE	Pressing Esc interrupts a running program
EXACT	Matches are exact (if off, 'Smith' = 'S' is True)
EXCLUSIVE	All tables are opened for exclusive use
FIELDS	Fields are set (if off, SET FIELDS TO clauses are ignored)

Expressions and Functions

▶▶ Ch. **12**

▶ **TABLE 12.12:** *Settings Reported by the SET Function (continued)*

SETTING	EFFECT IF ON
FULLPATH	Functions that return file names include full drive and directory specifications
HEADINGS	Show column headings over commands such as AVERAGE and LIST
INTENSITY	Affect display in dBASE IV-style applications
IDCHECK	Check language driver (if off, suppresses language-driver checking)
LOCK	File locking (if off, suppresses file locking during read-only processing, such as in computing averages or sums)
MOUSE	Mouse use (if off, the mouse pointer is turned off, and mouse actions are ignored)
NEAR	Failed SEEKs stop at the next highest record (if off, failed SEEKs stop at the end of file)
PRINTER	Streaming output (such as from ? commands) is sent to the printer
SAFETY	Prompt before deleting records or overwriting files
SPACE	Put spaces between fields in output lists
STEP	Open the debugger
TALK	Echo results of commands to the Command window's results pane
TITLE	When CATALOG is on, added files are prompted for title information
UNIQUE	Only the first record matching a key value is included in an index

You can abbreviate the setting names to the first four characters. For example, CENTURY can be written as CENT, and SAFETY can be input as SAFE.

Syntax

> SET(*<expC>*)

Example

> ? SET("TALK")   Returns "OFF"
> (if the Talk setting is off)

SETTO

The SETTO function returns the values of the settings listed in Table 12.13, set by the SET TO command.

▶ **TABLE 12.13:** *Settings Reported by SETTO Function*

SETTING	REPORT
ALTERNATE	Device or file to receive output
BELL	Frequency and duration of bell tone
BLOCKSIZE	Size of index blocks, in units of 512 bytes
BORDER	Style of dBASE IV-type windows
CARRY	List of fields where data gets carried
CATALOG	Name of catalog file
COLOR	Color settings for dBASE IV-style applications
CURRENCY	Currency symbol
DATABASE	Name of the current SQL database
DATE	*MDY* (American style; other styles are available)
DBTYPE	Either DBASE or PARADOX
DECIMALS	Number of decimal places to display
DEFAULT	Default disk drive
DELIMITERS	Field delimiters character
DEVICE	One of screen, printer, or file *<filename>*

▶▶
Ch.
12

▶ **TABLE 12.13:** *Settings Reported by SETTO Function (continued)*

SETTING	REPORT
DIRECTORY	Current directory
DISPLAY	One of mono, color, ega, ega43, mono43, vga25, vga43, vga50
EDITOR	Default editor for program and text files
ERROR	Messages to precede/follow dBASE runtime error messages
FIELDS	Fields list specification
FILTER	Filter condition (only records matching the condition appear to be part of the table)
FORMAT	File name in dBASE IV-style applications
HELP	Help file name
IBLOCK	Size of index blocks, in multiples of 512 bytes
INDEX	One or more index files
KEY	Range of accepted values in master index
LIBRARY	Name of subroutine library file
MARGIN	Left margin of printed pages
MARK	Separator character in date displays
MBLOCK	Block size in memo files in units of 64 bytes
MEMOWIDTH	Display width for Memo fields
MESSAGE	Status bar message
ODOMETER	Units which will be displayed in the status bar as dBASE processes records
ORDER	Tag of the master index
PATH	Search path
PCOL	Next horizontal print position
POINT	Character separating the whole part from the decimal part of numbers

▶ **TABLE 12.13:** *Settings Reported by SETTO Function (continued)*

SETTING	REPORT
PRECISION	Number of decimal digits used in numeric comparisons
PRINTER	Device or file to receive printer output
PROCEDURE	Name of a file of subroutines
PROW	Printer's vertical position
REFRESH	Number of seconds between refreshing client screens with new file server data
RELATION	Relation(s) between tables
REPROCESS	Number of tries attempted to access a locked file or record before returning an error
SEPARATOR	Character used to separate the whole part of numbers into groups of three digits
SKIP	Alias list controlling the advancement of the record pointer with related tables
TIME	One of HH, HH:MM, HH.MM, HH:MM:SS, HH.MM.SS
TOPIC	Help topic
TYPEAHEAD	Length, in bytes, of the typeahead buffer
VIEW	Name of a QBE file
WP	Name of the editor used for Memo fields

  NOTE

> As alternatives to the American-style date (*MM/DD/YY*), of SET TO's DATE setting, there are other styles available, such as ANSI (*YY.MM.DD*), British (*DD/MM/YY*), German (*DD.MM.YY*), and USA (*MM - DD - YY*).

Syntax

> SETTO(*<expC>*)

Example

> ? SETTO('DBTYPE')   Returns "DBASE" or
>   "PARADOX"

SIGN

The SIGN function returns 1 for positive numbers, -1 for negative numbers, and 0 for zero.

Syntax

> SIGN(*<expN>*)

Examples

> ? SIGN(1.5)   Returns 1
>
> ? SIGN(0)   Returns 0
>
> ? SIGN(-1.5)   Returns −1

SIN

The SIN function returns the sine of an angle. The angle is in radians. Use DTOR to convert degrees to radians.

Syntax

> SIN(*<expN>*)

Examples

> ? SIN(1)   Returns 0.8415
>
> ? SIN(DTOR(45)) Returns 7071
>
> ? SIN(PI( )/2)   Returns 1.0000

SOUNDEX

The SOUNDEX function returns the SOUNDEX value of a character string. The SOUNDEX value is a character representation approximating the sound of the string. Comparing SOUNDEX values yields .T. if the sounds of the two strings are equal.

 ▶▶ **W A R N I N G**

> The SOUNDEX algorithm is far from perfect. "Alan"
> and "Allen" have equal SOUNDEX values. Unfortunately,
> the following also have equal SOUNDEX values:
> "Martin," "Morton," and "Martian."

Syntax

SOUNDEX(<*expC*> ¦ <*memo field*>)

Examples

? SOUNDEX("Smith")	Returns "S530"
? SOUNDEX("Smythe")	Returns "S530"

SPACE

The SPACE function returns a string of the specified number of spaces. This is useful in formatting outlines, for one example.

Syntax

SPACE(<*expN*>)

Example

? SPACE(4*indent_level)+outline_item

Indents an outline four spaces per indent level.

SQLEXEC

The SQLEXEC function executes a SQL statement in a SQL database. (See your SQL database documentation for its accepted SQL syntax.)

▶▶

Ch.
12

Syntax

> SQLEXEC(<*SQL statement*> [, <*Answer table*>])

SQRT

The SQRT function returns the square root of a nonnegative number.

Syntax

> SQRT(<*expN* >)

Examples

? SQRT(9)	Returns 3.0000
? SQRT(2)	Returns 1.4142

STR

The STR function returns a number in a character string. The length of the string and, optionally, the number of decimal places are given as arguments. The length is the total length, including decimals and the decimal point if the number of decimals is not zero. The default length is 10.

 ▶▶**WARNING**

> **Don't forget to allow space for the minus sign (–), if negative numbers are possible in your application.**

An optional fourth argument specifies the character used to pad the number on the left. (For instance, you might pad with "*" in a check-writing application.)

Syntax

> STR(<*expN*>[, <*length expN*>?? [, <*decimals expN*>[, <*expC*>]]])

Examples

? STR(4.5, 5, 2)	Returns "4.50"
? STR(4.5, 6, 1, "*")	Returns "***4.5"

STUFF

The STUFF function returns a string made by stuffing one string into another at a specified location, optionally overwriting bytes in the "stuffee" string.

Syntax

STUFF(*<target expC>* ¦ *<target memo field>*,?? *<start expN>*, *<quantity expN>*, *<replacement expC>*)

Examples

```
? STUFF("12345",4,0,"abc")
```
Returns "123abc45"

```
? STUFF("12345",4,1,"abc")
```
Returns "123abc5"

```
? STUFF("123abc5",4,3,"4")
```
Returns "12345"

SUBSTR

The SUBSTR function extracts a substring from a string. You supply the string, the starting location of the substring, and the length of the substring.

Syntax

SUBSTR(*<expC>* ¦ *<memo field>*,?? *<start expN>*[, *<length expN>*])

Example

```
? SUBSTR("Cat in Hat",5,2)
```
Returns "in"

TAG

The TAG function returns the name of a specified index tag in the current .MDX file for the current table. Optionally, if you specify an .MDX file name, the tag name in that .MDX file is returned. If you specify an optional alias, the tag name is returned for the table specified by that alias.

Syntax

TAG([*<.mdx filename expC>*,], *<index number expN>*[, *<alias>*])

Ch.
12

TAGCOUNT

The TAGCOUNT function returns the number of active indexes in the currently open table's open .MDX file. If you specify an .MDX file name, that file is used in lieu of the currently open one. If you specify an optional alias, the value is returned for the table specified by that alias.

Syntax

TAGCOUNT([<*.mdx filename*>[,<*alias*>]])

TAGNO

The TAGNO function function returns an index tag's number, given its name. Unless an optional alias is supplied, TAGNO applies to the table open in the current work area. Unless an optional .MDX file name is supplied, TAGNO applies to the current .MDX file.

Syntax

TAGNO([<*tag name expC*> [, <*.mdx filename*> [, <*alias*>]]])

TAN

The TAN function returns the tangent of an angle. The angle is given in radians. Use DTOR to convert degrees to radians.

Syntax

TAN(<*expN*>)

Examples

? TAN(0)	Returns 0
? TAN(DTOR(45))	Returns 1

TARGET

The TARGET function returns the name of the table linked by the specified relation number. If an optional alias is supplied, the value is returned for the work area specified by that alias. Otherwise, the value is returned for the table in the current work area.

Syntax

TARGET(<*expN*>[, <*alias*>])

TIME

The TIME function returns the time as a string in *HH:MM:SS* format unless an argument is supplied. If an argument is supplied, the time is returned in *HH:MM:SS.hh* format, where the *.hh* is in hundredths of a second. (DOS returns the time accurately to about two-hundredths of a second; in the form *HH:MM:SS.hh*, the last digit is provided, but it is only accurate plus or minus one-hundredth.)

  T I P

> **You can used ELAPSED to find the difference between two time strings.**

Syntax

    TIME([<exp>])

Examples

? TIME( )	Returns "09:57:42"
? TIME(0)	Returns "09:52:44.83"

TRANSFORM

The TRANSFORM function returns an input string formatted with a picture string. The formatting is the same as the formatting the Function property applies to an entry field.

Syntax

    TRANSFORM(<exp>, <picture expC>)

Example

    ? TRANSFORM   Returns '(123) 456-7890'
    ('1234567890',
    '@R(999) 999-9999')

Expressions and Functions

▶ ▶
Ch.
12

TRIM

The TRIM function returns a string after removing trailing blanks from the argument character string. This is the same as the RTRIM function

Syntax

TRIM(*<expC>* ¦ *<memo field>*)

Example

? TRIM("Smith?")   Returns "Smith"

UNIQUE

The UNIQUE function returns .T. if the indicated index was created with the UNIQUE option. If the optional alias is specified, the table open in that work area is used; otherwise, the table in the currently open work area is used. If the optional .MDX file name is supplied, that file is used; otherwise, the current .MDX file is used.

Syntax

UNIQUE([[*<.mdx filename>*,] *<index position expN>* [, *<alias>*]])

UPPER

The UPPER function returns a string formed by turning all lowercase letters in the input string into uppercase letters in the output string. As with LOWER, you can use UPPER to be sure that sorts and comparisons are not sensitive to case.

▶▶ **WARNING**

In the ASCII collating sequence, A–Z come before a–z. This means that 'Zebra' sorts before 'aardvark.'

Syntax

UPPER(*<expC>* ¦ *<memo field>*)

Example

```
?INDEX ON UPPER(last_name)
? UPPER('Zebra') >          Returns .T.
UPPER('aardvark')
```

VAL

The VAL function returns a number given a string representation of a number.

 ►► **W A R N I N G**

> **VAL will skip leading blanks, but otherwise it stops evaluating as soon as it sees a nonnumeric character.**

Syntax

```
VAL(<expC>)
```

Examples

? VAL("1234.5")	Returns 1234.5000
? VAL("-2")?	Returns -2.0000
? VAL("??)	Returns 3.0000
? VAL("123abcde")	Returns 123.0000
? VAL("abcde123")	Returns 0.0000

YEAR

The YEAR function returns the number corresponding to the year in a date input.

 ►► **N O T E**

> **YEAR returns the full numeric value of the year, such as 1995 from 12/31/95. The setting of CENTURY only changes the representation of the date when it is shown as a character string.**

Syntax

   YEAR(<*expD*>)

Examples

   ? YEAR({12/31/95})   Returns 1995

   ? YEAR({12/31/99}+1)   Returns 2000

▶ *Summary*

In this chapter, you've gotten a detailed breakdown of the operators and operands that make up dBASE for Windows expressions, and two organizations of the functions that make up a critical part of those expressions.

You reviewed the eight types of operands: constants, memory variables, fields, object properties, object references, subroutine references, function calls, and expressions.

You read about the six types of operators: arithmetic operators, date operators, string operators, logical operators, structure operators, and relational operators

As a special case, you looked at function calls, which are another way of combining operands with an operation.

You went on to learn about the functions available in dBASE for Windows. Although we eliminated the functions that are only useful to programmers, as well as the ones that are included just to support dBASE IV-style applications, there are plenty of other functions that you might find useful in dBASE for Windows expressions.

We divided these functions first into a categorical reference, so you could see the functions grouped by their uses.

We concluded with an alphabetical list, with syntax and examples, for convenient reference when you need to use these functions.

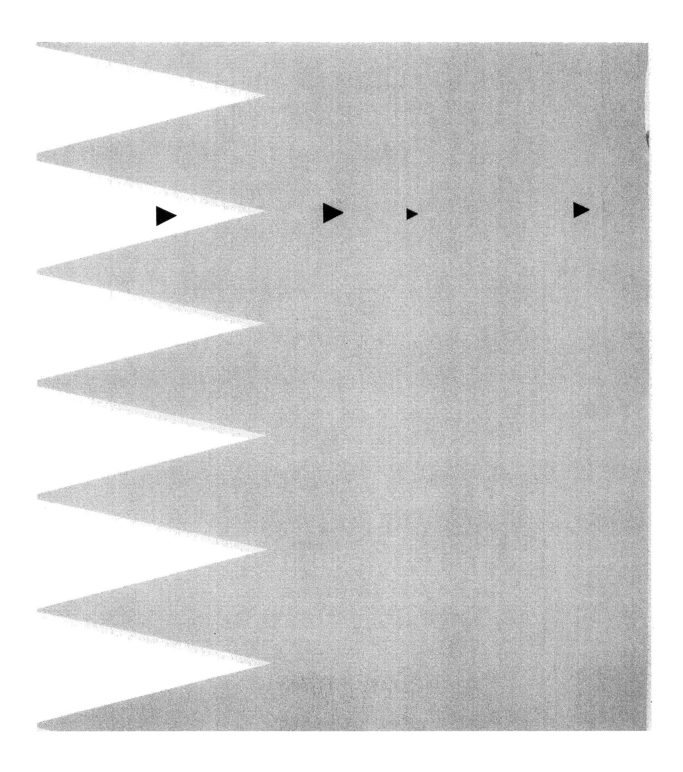

Using Command Window
Commands

▶▶ **T***he* commands covered in this chapter are the dBASE for Windows commands that are used in the Command window. dBASE 5 for Windows also includes dBASE IV compatibility commands, which are the ones you see in programs written before dBASE for Windows was available. We recommend that you avoid them. The dBASE IV compatibility commands are included in Appendix D, because sooner or later you will probably meet them in an old dBASE program. Also, you may see them in the dBASE for Windows on-line and printed documentation, which doesn't always tell you which commands to avoid.

We'll summarize the Command window commands by topic, and then provide an alphabetical reference.

 ▶▶**NOTE**

You'll find that dBASE for Windows's on-line documentation on each of these is extensive. The program documentation comes with lots of examples of how each command is used. We haven't tried to duplicate that here, since it would fill a book every bit as long as this one. You may find some differences between the syntax shown in this chapter and the on-line documentation. In case of differences, the safe approach is to test the alternatives in the Command window.

▶▶ *Commands versus Statements*

The two types of lines in dBASE for Windows program files, such as
.PRG, .WFM, and .QBE files, are commands and statements.

The commands all start with verbs, such as REPLACE, APPEND, and
SEEK, and they continue with the other information needed to perform the action. For example, this line holds a 20-percent-off sale:

    REPLACE ALL product->price WITH product->price*0.80

The language statements are used to structure applications and to control the order of execution of the commands. These statements are covered in the next chapter. As you will see, the dBASE for Windows
programming language is relatively small and simple.

▶▶ N O T E

**The dBASE for Windows documentation refers to both
statements and commands as *commands*. We think the
distinction helps you keep separate concepts separate.**

▶▶ *Commands Listed by Topic*

We have divided the dBASE for Windows commands into six categories:

- Data manipulation commands
- Data summary commands
- System related commands
- dBASE control commands
- Command window input/output commands
- Printer output commands

Table 13.1 lists the commands according to these categories.

► **TABLE 13.1:** *dBASE for Windows Commands*

DATA MANIPULATION COMMANDS	
APPEND AUTOMEM	INDEX
APPEND FROM	INSERT
APPEND FROM ARRAY	INSERT AUTOMEM
APPEND MEMO	JOIN
BLANK	LABEL FORM
BROWSE	LIST
CHANGE	LIST STRUCTURE
CONTINUE	LOCATE
CONVERT	MODIFY STRUCTURE
COPY	OPEN DATABASE
COPY BINARY	PACK
COPY FILE	RECALL
COPY INDEXES	REINDEX
COPY MEMO	RENAME TABLE
COPY STRUCTURE	REPLACE
COPY TABLE	REPLACE AUTOMEM
COPY TAG	REPLACE BINARY
COPY TO ARRAY	REPLACE FROM ARRAY
COPY TO STRUCTURE EXTENDED	REPLACE MEMO
CREATE	REPLACE MEMO FROM
CREATE FROM STRUCTURE EXTENDED	REPLACE OLE
DELETE	SEEK
DELETE TABLE	SKIP
EDIT	SORT

TABLE 13.1: *dBASE for Windows Commands (continued)*

DATA MANIPULATION COMMANDS (continued)

FIND	UPDATE
GENERATE	USE
IMPORT	ZAP

DATA SUMMARY COMMANDS

AVERAGE	SUM
CALCULATE	TOTAL
COUNT	

SYSTEM-RELATED COMMANDS

!	ERASE
CD	KEYBOARD
CLEAR TYPEAHEAD	LIST FILES
CLOSE ALTERNATE	MKDIR
CLOSE PRINTER	MODIFY FILE
DELETE FILE	RENAME
DIRECTORY	TYPE
DOS	

DBASE CONTROL COMMANDS

CANCEL	LOAD DLL
CLEAR AUTOMEM	MODIFY APPLICATION
CLEAR FIELDS	MODIFY COMMAND
CLEAR MEMORY	MODIFY FORM
CLEAR PROGRAM	MODIFY LABEL
CLEAR ALL	MODIFY QUERY
CLOSE ALL	MODIFY REPORT
CLOSE DATABASES	MODIFY VIEW
CLOSE FORMS	OPEN FORM

Command Windows Command

Ch
13

►► **TABLE 13.1:** *dBASE for Windows Commands (continued)*

DBASE CONTROL COMMANDS (continued)	
CLOSE INDEXES	PLAY SOUND
CLOSE TABLES	QUIT
CLOSE PROCEDURE	REDEFINE
COMPILE	REFRESH
CONTINUE	RELEASE
CREATE APPLICATION	RELEASE AUTOMEM
CREATE CATALOG	RELEASE DLL
CREATE FORM	RELEASE OBJECT
CREATE LABEL	REPORT FORM
CREATE QUERY	RESTORE
CREATE REPORT	RESTORE IMAGE
CREATE SESSION	RESUME
CREATE VIEW	RETRY
DEBUG	SAVE
DEFINE	SELECT
DELETE TAG	SET ... (all the SET commands)
DO	SHOW OBJECT
EXTERN	SLEEP
FLUSH	STORE
GO	STORE AUTOMEM
HELP	STORE MEMO
LIST COVERAGE	SUSPEND
LIST MEMORY	UNLOCK
LIST STATUS	WAIT

▶ **TABLE 13.1:** *dBASE for Windows Commands (continued)*

COMMAND WINDOW INPUT/OUTPUT COMMANDS	
?	DISPLAY FILES
??	DISPLAY MEMO
???	DISPLAY STATUS
CLEAR	DISPLAY STRUCTURE
DISPLAY	INPUT
DISPLAY COVERAGE	
PRINTER OUTPUT COMMANDS	
EJECT	EJECT PAGE

▶▶ *Alphabetical Reference to Commands*

The descriptions that follow include the use of the command, the command's syntax, and examples of the command's use (if examples clarify the use). The commands are listed in pure alphabetic order; they are not grouped in categories as they are in Table 13.1.

For an explanation of the format used for the command syntax, see the beginning of the alphabetical reference to functions in Chapter 12. We've used the same format here.

The ! Command

The ! command runs DOS commands and programs from the Command window.

Syntax

! *<DOS command>*

Example

!CHKDSK

The ? Command

The ? command lets you output the value of one or more expressions in the results pane of the Command window. The extensive formatting options are left over from the DOS versions, where ? output was a key part of reporting.

Syntax

```
? [<exp 1>
    [PICTURE <format expC>]
    [FUNCTION <function expC>]
    [AT <column expN>]
    [STYLE [<fontstyle expN>] [<fontstyle expC>] ]
    [,<exp 2>
    [PICTURE <format expC>]
    [FUNCTION <function expC>]
    [AT <column expN>]
    [STYLE [<fontstyle expN>] [<fontstyle expC>] ] ]...
  [,]
```

Example

```
? 'Send to results pane'
```

The ?? Command

The ?? command is identical to the ? command, except that the ? command precedes its output with a carriage return/line feed pair, putting you on a new line. The ?? command does not, so its output is appended to the output on the last line written.

Syntax

```
?? [<exp 1>
    [PICTURE <format expC>]
    [FUNCTION <function expC>]
    [AT <column expN>]
    [STYLE [<fontstyle expN>] [<fontstyle expC>] ]
    [,<exp 2>
    [PICTURE <format expC>]
    [FUNCTION <function expC>]
    [AT <column expN>]
    [STYLE [<fontstyle expN>] [<fontstyle expC>] ] ]   [,]
```

Examples

> ?? ' append to current line'

Here's an example of using ? and ?? in the Command window:

The ??? Command

The ??? command writes directly to a printer, bypassing the printer driver. In Microsoft Windows, this is totally unnecessary and bad programming practice. The command ??? may, however, come to your rescue in these cases:

- You have the printer manual, so you can look up printer control codes.
- You do *not* have an operable Microsoft Windows driver for the printer.
- You absolutely must print that report tonight. (We recommend putting on a fresh pot of coffee.)

Syntax

> ??? *<expC>*

Example

> ??? CHR(27)+'E'

CHR(27) is an Esc character.

The APPEND AUTOMEM Command

The automemory feature is used in programs to create a set of memory variables matching a table's fields. This lets the program have full control over the input process, prior to updating any data on disk. APPEND AUTOMEM is used when a valid new record has been entered. It adds the new record to the current table from the automemory variables.

Syntax

APPEND AUTOMEM

The APPEND FROM Command

APPEND FROM is used to add data in bulk to a table. It will read SDF (System Data Format, which are plain text files), Quattro Pro, dBASE III+, Paradox, and dBASE data files. The other options filter the incoming data (the FOR clause) and tune the efficiency (REINDEX). REINDEX turns the indexes off during the APPEND and does a full REINDEX after all the data has been appended. This is faster than indexing as you go for very large data sets.

Syntax

```
APPEND FROM <filename> | ? | <filename skeleton>
  [FOR <condition>]
  [[TYPE] SDF | WB1 | DBMEMO3 | PARADOX | DBASE |
    DELIMITED [WITH <char> | BLANK] ]
  [POSITION]
  [REINDEX]
```

Example

In producing this book, we used a dBASE program to grab the figure labels, preparing a list of figures. We used a table called TEXT with a single field, also called text. These commands read our ASCII text files into our dBASE table:

```
USE text EXCLUSIVE
ZAP
APPEND FROM chap13.txt SDF
```

The APPEND FROM ARRAY Command

Arrays are used as an alternative to memory variables. The disadvantage of arrays is that they lead to less readable programs. However, memory variables can lead to name conflicts. For example, your Customer table and your Product table might both have a field called NAME.

Syntax

```
APPEND FROM ARRAY <array name>
  [FIELDS <field list>]
  [FOR <condition>]
```

[REINDEX]

The APPEND MEMO Command

APPEND MEMO appends into Memo fields from text files.

Syntax

```
APPEND MEMO <memo field>
  FROM <filename> ¦ ? ¦ <filename skeleton>
  [OVERWRITE]
```

Example

```
APPEND MEMO notes FROM t.txt
```

The AVERAGE Command

AVERAGE computes the average value of one or more expressions (typically just field names representing Numeric or Float data types). The additional options let you compute the average for only a specified part of your records and store the results in memory variables or an array.

 ▶▶ T I P

> The AVERAGE command is also available through the Table Utilities menu (see Chapter 9). Try an average calculation and examine the command echoed to the Command window.

Syntax

```
AVERAGE
  [<exp list>]
  [<scope>]
  [FOR <condition 1>]
  [WHILE <condition 2>]
  [TO <memvar list> ¦ ARRAY <array name>]
```

The BLANK Command

The BLANK command writes blank values into your tables. A *blank* number, for example, is one that is not filled in. This is different from a zero value.

Syntax

```
BLANK
  [<scope>]
  [FOR <condition 1>]
  [WHILE <condition 2>]
  [FIELDS <field list> ¦ [LIKE <skeleton 1>] [EXCEPT <skeleton 2>]]
  [REINDEX]
```

Example

```
BLANK NEXT 5
```

The BROWSE Command

The BROWSE command lets a program present the user with a selective Table Records tool. From the Command window, you can use BROWSE to see the current table.

Launching a table with a left double-click (or by pressing F2) in the Navigator initiates a BROWSE. You can examine the command in the Command window after you use the Navigator. Note that the choices in the Table Properties dialog box (discussed in Chapter 9) set the multitude of parameters available for the BROWSE command.

Syntax

```
BROWSE
  [<browse name>]
  [<scope>]
  [FOR <condition 1>]
  [WHILE <condition 2>]
  [COLOR [<standard text>]
    [, [<enhanced text>]
    [, [<perimeter color>]
    [, [<background color>]]]]]
    [FIELDS <field 1> [<field option list 1>] ¦     <calculated field 1> =
    <exp 1> [<calculated field option list 1>]
    [, <field 2> [<field option list 2>] ¦
    <calculated field 2> = <exp 2> [<calculated field option list 2>] ...]]
  [FORMAT]
  [FREEZE <field 3>]
  [KEY <exp 3>[, <exp 4>]]
  [LOCK <expN 2>]
  [NOAPPEND]
```

```
[NODELETE]
[NOEDIT ¦ NOMODIFY]
[NOFOLLOW]
[NOINIT]
[NOMENU]
[NOORGANIZE]
[NORMAL]
[NOTOGGLE]
[NOWAIT]
[TITLE <expC 1>]
[WIDTH <expN 3>]
[WINDOW <window name>]
```

The *CALCULATE* Command

The CALCULATE command performs multiple calculations more efficiently than if you use multiple individual commands, such as COUNT and TOTAL. If you COUNT, dBASE for Windows examines each record once. If you then TOTAL, dBASE examines each record again. If you CALCULATE, you can do both these chores (and a lot more) in a single pass through the data.

  T I P

> **The CALCULATE command is also available through the Table Utilities menu (see Chapter 9). Try a calculation and examine the command echoed to the Command window.**

Syntax

```
CALCULATE <function list>
    [<scope>]
    [FOR <condition 1>]
    [WHILE <condition 2>]
    [TO <memvar list> ¦ ARRAY <array name>]
```

The *CANCEL* Command

The CANCEL command terminates a program. You will typically use this after program errors. For example, your program may halt with an error message. You can use the SUSPEND command so you can check things out in the Command window. When you find the problem, you can use CANCEL to terminate the program.

Syntax

    CANCEL

The CD Command

CD is the DOS CD (or CHDIR) command for changing directories. It is the same as setting the current directory in the Navigator. You can include a disk drive letter in the command.

Syntax

    CD [*<path>*]

Example

    CD D:\DBWORK

The CHANGE Command

CHANGE is a synonym for BROWSE. See the description of the BROWSE command for details.

Syntax

```
CHANGE
  [<edit name>]
  [<starting record expN 1> | <bookmark>]
  [<scope>]
  [FOR <condition 1>]
  [WHILE <condition 2>]
  [COLOR [<standard text>]
    [, [<enhanced text>]
    [, [<perimeter color>]
    [, <background color>]]]]
  [COLUMNAR]
  [COMPRESS]
  [FIELDS <field 1> [<field option list 1>] |   <calculated field 1> =
    <exp 1> [<calculated field option list 1>]
    [, <field 2> [<field option list 2>] |
    <calculated field 2> = <exp 2> [<calculated field option list 2>]
...]]
  [FORMAT]
```

```
[FREEZE <field 3>]
[KEY <exp 3>[, <exp 4>]]
[LOCK <expN 2>]
[NOAPPEND]
[NODELETE]
[NOEDIT ¦ NOMODIFY]
[NOFOLLOW]
[NOINIT]
[NORMAL]
[NOTOGGLE]
[NOWAIT]
[TITLE <expC 1>]
[WIDTH <expN 3>]
[WINDOW <window name>]
```

The CLEAR Command

CLEAR clears the Command window results pane. Unless you specify a character, it clears the pane to blanks.

Syntax

```
CLEAR [CHARACTER <expC>]
```

The CLEAR ALL Command

CLEAR ALL clears everything, except open PROCEDURE and LIBRARY files, in the current session. It closes tables, clears the results pane, releases memory variables, and more.

Syntax

```
CLEAR ALL
```

The CLEAR AUTOMEM Command

CLEAR AUTOMEM provides a blank set of automemory variables for use with commands such as APPEND AUTOMEM.

Syntax

```
CLEAR AUTOMEM
```

The CLEAR FIELDS Command

CLEAR FIELDS is a synonym for SET FIELDS TO. It removes any fields lists.

Syntax

    CLEAR FIELDS

The CLEAR MEMORY Command

CLEAR MEMORY releases all memory variables. If used from the Command window, it is the same as RELEASE ALL. It should not be used in programs.

Syntax

    CLEAR MEMORY

The CLEAR PROGRAM Command

When dBASE for Windows loads a program into memory, it does not automatically free that memory when the program terminates. It retains the compiled program so that it can be run again, without reloading. CLEAR PROGRAM forces dBASE to free the memory allocated to programs, except the memory for LIBRARY and PROCEDURE files.

Syntax

    CLEAR PROGRAM

The CLEAR TYPEAHEAD Command

dBASE for Windows allows you to set the length of the typeahead buffer (this buffer lets users type without waiting for the computer to process all their keystrokes). CLEAR TYPEAHEAD dumps any characters in the typeahead buffer, without processing them.

You cannot make constructive use of this command in the Command window, because everything you type in the Command window is entered through the typeahead buffer. Anything you've typed that you might want cleared has already been processed.

You can, however, use it in programs. Typically, this command is given when a program detects an error.

Syntax

> CLEAR TYPEAHEAD

The CLOSE ALL Command

The CLOSE ALL command closes all open databases and tables, as well as related files, such as index and memo files. CLOSE ALL also closes other open files, such as text files.

 ▶▶ **N O T E**

> **You'll need to use CLOSE ALL in the Command window when you want to create a report that does not use the current query or table choice.**

Syntax

> CLOSE ALL

The CLOSE ALTERNATE Command

The ALTERNATE file is a text file that has been set to receive output. CLOSE ALTERNATE closes that file.

Syntax

> CLOSE ALTERNATE

The CLOSE DATABASES Command

The CLOSE DATABASES command allows you to close the current database, a named database, or all databases. Unlike CLOSE ALL, CLOSE DATABASES does not affect open text files.

Syntax

> CLOSE DATABASES [<*database name*>][,<*database name*>]...

The CLOSE FORMS Command

The CLOSE FORMS command closes one or more forms.

Syntax

> CLOSE FORMS [<*form name list*>]

Example

> CLOSE FORMS my_form1, my_form3

The CLOSE INDEXES Command

The CLOSE INDEXES command closes all the .MDX and .NDX files in the current work area, except for the production .MDX file. CLOSE INDEXES does *not* close the production .MDX file.

Syntax

> CLOSE INDEXES

The CLOSE PRINTER Command

The CLOSE PRINTER command closes a file opened to receive printer output. This command does not affect the printer itself. It just closes files that were receiving printer output.

Syntax

> CLOSE PRINTER

The CLOSE PROCEDURE Command

The CLOSE PROCEDURE command closes a procedure file opened with a SET PROCEDURE TO command.

Syntax

> CLOSE PROCEDURE <*filename*>

The CLOSE TABLES Command

The CLOSE TABLES command closes all tables in all work areas or, in an SQL database, all tables in the open database.

Syntax

> CLOSE TABLES

The COMPILE Command

The COMPILE command invokes the dBASE for Windows built-in program compiler, without running the program. You can use COM-PILE to check a new program for syntax errors, without running that program.

 ▶▶ **N O T E**

If you run the program, it is automatically compiled when the source .PRG or .WFM file has been changed more recently than the compiled .PRO or .WFO file.

Syntax

COMPILE *<filename>* ¦ ? ¦ *<filename skeleton>*

The .PRG extension is implied. Other extensions, such as .QBE or .WFM, must be explicitly supplied.

Example

COMPILE tester

The CONTINUE Command

CONTINUE repeats the last LOCATE, beginning at the next record. When you LOCATE a particular record, dBASE for Windows stops at the first record it finds that matches your criteria. CONTINUE locates the next record matching your criteria. Used repeatedly, CONTINUE locates all the records that match your criteria.

Syntax

CONTINUE

The CONVERT Command

CONVERT updates a single-user table to multiuser status. The TO clause lets you fine-tune the update by setting the size of a multiuser field.

▶▶**T I P**

We recommend that you ignore the TO clause for CONVERT—potential disk space savings are slight—unless your files have more than a million records.

Syntax

CONVERT [TO <*expN*>]

The COPY Command

The COPY command lets you make a copy of your data into another table, or into a text file, Quattro Pro worksheet, dBASE III+ memo file, or other Paradox or dBASE file. The *scope*, FOR, and WHILE clauses let you select a portion of your data. The WITH PRODUCTION option copies the production .MDX file when your copy is to another dBASE table.

Syntax

COPY TO <*filename*> ¦ ?
  [<*scope*>]
  [FOR <*condition 1*>]
  [WHILE <*condition 2*>]
  [FIELDS <*field list*>]
  [[TYPE] SDF ¦ WB1 ¦ DBMEMO3 ¦ PARADOX ¦ DBASE ¦
    DELIMITED [WITH <*char*> ¦ BLANK]] ¦
  [[WITH] PRODUCTION]

Example

You can use a dBASE for Windows program to manipulate a text file. This is simple if you first read the text into a table. We use a table called Text with a single, wide field, also called TEXT. These commands will read, process, and write a text file.

USE text EXCLUSIVE
ZAP
APPEND FROM mytext.txt SDF

* run program(s) that manipulate the text in the file

COPY TO mytext.txt SDF

The COPY BINARY Command

The COPY BINARY command lets you copy a Binary field to a file. This lets you write file types such as .BMP, .PCX, and .WAV from your data. The ADDITIVE clause specifies that the field be added to the file. Without ADDITIVE, the file is overwritten.

Syntax

COPY BINARY *<field name>* TO *<filename>* ¦ ? [ADDITIVE]

Example

COPY BINARY bit_map TO my_pic.bmp

The COPY FILE Command

The COPY FILE command is similar to the DOS copy command. It copies one file to another. It does not copy multiple files. The ? and *<filename skeleton>* options open the Open File dialog box so that the user can pick a file.

Syntax

COPY FILE *<filename 1>* ¦ ? ¦ *<filename skeleton>* TO
<filename 2 > ¦ ? ¦ *<filename skeleton 2 >*

The COPY INDEXES Command

The COPY INDEXES command moves a list of .NDX files into a single .MDX file.

Syntax

COPY INDEXES *<.ndx filename list>* [TO *<.mdx filename>* ¦ ?]

The COPY MEMO Command

The COPY MEMO command lets you copy a memo field to an external text file. The ADDITIVE option lets you append to the external file.

Syntax

COPY MEMO *<memo field>* TO *<filename>* ¦ ? [ADDITIVE]

Example

Assume that you want a Memo field dumped to a temporary file, perhaps for transfer to a DOS word processor. You could use the COPY MEMO command like this:

```
COPY MEMO notes TO t.t
```

The COPY STRUCTURE Command

The COPY STRUCTURE command makes a copy of just the structure of the current table. You can select specific fields with the FIELDS clause, and also copy the index structure with the WITH PRODUCTION clause.

Syntax

```
COPY STRUCTURE TO <filename> | ?
  [[TYPE] PARADOX | DBASE]
  [FIELDS <field list>]
  [[WITH] PRODUCTION]
```

Example

These commands create an empty table that has the same fields as an active table.

```
USE active
COPY STRUCTURE TO empty
```

The COPY TABLE Command

COPY TABLE is like COPY FILE for tables. However, unlike COPY FILE, COPY TABLE will correctly copy index and memo files, along with the data table.

Syntax

```
COPY TABLE <source tablename> TO <target tablename>
  [[TYPE] DBASE | PARADOX ]
```

The COPY TAG Command

The COPY TAG command copies individual index tags from an .MDX file into an individual .NDX file.

▶▶ WARNING

> We don't recommend the use of single .NDX files. They date all the way back to 1981 and the beginning of dBASE, and they are not as good as today's .MDX files.

Syntax

COPY TAG <*tag name*> [OF .*mdx filename*] TO <.*ndx filename*>

The COPY TO ARRAY Command

The COPY TO ARRAY command makes a copy of all or a selected portion of your current table in an in-memory array.

Syntax

COPY TO ARRAY <*array name*>
 [<*scope*>]
 [FOR <*condition 1*>]
 [WHILE <*condition 2* >]
 [FIELDS <*field list* >]

The COPY TO STRUCTURE EXTENDED Command

The COPY TO STRUCTURE EXTENDED command creates a table that resembles the ones you edit when you use the Table Structure tool. Its contents are the structure of the current table. This file is then used by a CREATE FROM STRUCTURE EXTENDED command.

Syntax

COPY TO <*filename*> ¦ ? STRUCTURE EXTENDED
[[TYPE] PARADOX ¦ DBASE]

or

COPY STRUCTURE EXTENDED TO <*filename*> ¦ ?
[[TYPE] PARADOX ¦ DBASE]

The COUNT Command

The COUNT command counts the number of records in the current table, optionally counting just those that match your criteria. If SET

DELETED is off, records marked for deletion will be included in the count. If the TO clause is not specified, it reports its results in the Counted Records dialog box (see Chapter 9).

Syntax

```
COUNT
   [<scope>]
   [FOR <condition 1>]
   [WHILE <condition 2 >]
   [TO <memvar >]
```

The CREATE Command

The CREATE command opens the Table Structure tool, letting you create a new table. If you do not specify a file name, or you specify the ? option, it launches the Open File dialog box, so that you can choose a file.

▶▶ **T I P**

If you are already in the Command window, the CREATE commands can be quicker than the equivalent Navigator commands.

Syntax

```
CREATE [<filename> ¦ ? ]
   [[TYPE] PARADOX ¦ DBASE]
```

Example

```
CREATE new_tabl
```

The CREATE APPLICATION Command

The CREATE APPLICATION command is a synonym for CREATE FORM. It launches the Form Designer. If you do not specify a file name, it will open the Open File dialog box so you can select a file.

Syntax

```
CREATE APPLICATION [<filename> ¦ ? ¦ <filename skeleton>]
```

The **CREATE CATALOG** *Command*

The CREATE CATALOG command first launches the Open File dialog box if you do not specify an individual file name. It then creates a catalog file and launches the Catalog tool so you can work with the new catalog.

Syntax

```
CREATE CATALOG
    [<filename> | ? | <filename skeleton>]
```

The **CREATE FORM** *Command*

CREATE FORM launches the Form Designer. If you do not specify an individual file name, it will open the Open File dialog box so you can select a file.

Syntax

```
CREATE FORM [<filename> | ? | <filename skeleton>]
```

Example

```
CREATE FORM people_c
```

The **CREATE FROM STRUCTURE EXTENDED** *Command*

The CREATE FROM STRUCTURE EXTENDED command uses the data file created by a COPY TO STRUCTURE EXTENDED command to create a new table. If any of the fields are specified as indexed, the production .MDX file is also created.

  T I P

> **After you COPY TO STRUCTURE EXTENDED, the structure is in a normal .DBF file, which you can examine and modify with any of the normal Table tools. For an unmodified, exact copy, use COPY STRUCTURE.**

Syntax

```
CREATE <filename> ¦ ?
    STRUCTURE EXTENDED
    [[TYPE] PARADOX ¦ DBASE]
```

The CREATE LABEL Command

The CREATE LABEL command launches the Crystal Reports label design tool.

Syntax

```
CREATE LABEL [<filename> ¦ ? ¦ <filename skeleton>]
```

Example

```
CREATE LABEL orgs_c
```

The CREATE QUERY Command

The CREATE QUERY command launches the Query Designer. If you do not specify a file name, it first opens the Open File dialog box.

Syntax

```
CREATE QUERY <filename> ¦ ?
```

The CREATE REPORT Command

The CREATE REPORT command launches the Crystal Reports report design tool.

Syntax

```
CREATE REPORT [CROSSTAB] [<filename> ¦ ? ¦ <filename
skeleton>]
```

The CREATE SESSION Command

The CREATE SESSION command creates a new session. Each session behaves as if you had switched to a separate computer and started dBASE for Windows as another user. This lets you open the same table in multiple windows.

►►**N O T E**

> **You never explicitly close a session. Sessions are closed automatically by dBASE for Windows after the last open form or table in the session is closed.**

Syntax

CREATE SESSION

The **CREATE VIEW** Command

CREATE VIEW is a synonym for CREATE QUERY. It launches the Query Designer. If you do not specify a file name, it first opens the Open File dialog box.

Syntax

CREATE VIEW [*<filename>* ¦ ? ¦ *<filename skeleton>*]

The **DEBUG** Command

The DEBUG command launches the dBASE for Windows Debugger.

Syntax

DEBUG [*<filename>* ¦ ? ¦ *<filename skeleton>* ¦ *<procedure name>* ¦ *<UDF name>*
  [WITH *<parameter list>*]]

The **DEFINE** Command

The DEFINE command creates and assigns properties to new objects.

Syntax

DEFINE *<class name>* *<object name >*
  [OF *<container object>*]
  [FROM *<row, col>* TO *<row, col> >* ¦ *<AT <row, col>*]
  [PROPERTY *<stock property list >*]
  [CUSTOM *<custom property list >*]
  [WITH *<parameter list >*]

Example

```
DEFINE Pushbutton OK_button OF my_form ;
  PROPERTY;
    Top 13, Left 15, Height 2, Width 12, Text "OK"
```

The DELETE Command

The DELETE command lets you mark for deletion individual or groups of records in dBASE tables.

Syntax

```
DELETE
  [<scope>]
  [FOR <condition 1>]
  [WHILE <condition 2 >]
```

The DELETE FILE Command

The DELETE FILE command deletes an individual file. If you use the ? or *<filename skeleton>* options, it launches the Erase File dialog box.

Syntax

```
DELETE FILE <filename> ¦ ? ¦ <filename skeleton>
```

Example

```
DELETE FILE t.tmp
```

The DELETE TABLE Command

Like DELETE FILE, DELETE TABLE deletes a specified table or one selected with the Erase File dialog box. It takes care of deleting associated index and memo files, as well as the data table.

Syntax

```
DELETE TABLE <table name> ¦ ?
  [[TYPE] PARADOX ¦ DBASE ]
```

The DELETE TAG Command

The DELETE TAG command deletes one or more tags from .MDX files.

Syntax

```
DELETE TAG <tag name 1>
    [OF <filename 1> ¦ ? ¦ <filename skeleton 1>]
    [, <tag name 2 >
    [OF <filename 2 > ¦ ? ¦ <filename skeleton 2 >] ... ]
```

The DIR Command

The DIR (or DIRECTORY) command is similar to the DOS DIR command. If given without any arguments, it defaults to DIR *.DBF. DIR *.* must be explicitly specified.

Syntax

```
DIR ¦ DIRECTORY
    [ON <drive>[ON <drive>[:]]]
    [LIKE [<path>\] <filename> ¦ <filename skeleton>]
    [[<drive>:] [<path>\] [<filename> ¦ <filename skeleton>]]
```

Example

```
DIR *.*
```

The DISPLAY Command

The DISPLAY command displays one or more records in the Command window's results pane, unless you explicitly direct output to a file or to your printer. DISPLAY is a synonym for LIST, except that DISPLAY defaults to the current record; LIST defaults to all records.

Syntax

```
DISPLAY
    [<scope>]
    [FOR<condition 1>]
    [WHILE<condition 2>]
    [[FIELDS] <exp list>]
    [OFF]
    [TO FILE <filename> ¦ ? ¦ [TO PRINTER]]
```

Example

Here is an example of using a DISPLAY command in the Command window:

The DISPLAY COVERAGE Command

DISPLAY COVERAGE is used in programming to examine the results of program coverage—a detailed analysis of how much use each part of a program gets. This is used to tune a program for better performance.

Syntax

DISPLAY COVERAGE *<filename 1>* ¦ ? ¦ *<filename skeleton>*
[ALL]
[SUMMARY]
[TO FILE *<filename 2 >* ¦ ?] ¦ *<filename skeleton>* ¦ [TO PRINTER]

The DISPLAY FILES Command

DISPLAY FILES provides the same service as DIR. Like DIR, it defaults to *.DBF.

Syntax

DISPLAY FILES
[[LIKE] *<filename 1>* ¦ *<filename skeleton>*]
[ON *<drive>*]
[TO FILE *<filename 2>* ¦ ?] ¦ [TO PRINTER]

The DISPLAY MEMORY Command

The DISPLAY MEMORY command sends a long list, describing the contents of memory, to the Command window's results pane, to a file, or to the printer. You can use DISPLAY MEMORY to send the list to a .TXT file, and then use the text editor (MODI FILE starts it) to examine it.

Syntax

```
DISPLAY MEMORY [TO FILE <filename> | ? | <filename skeleton>
| PRINTER]
```

Example

```
DISPLAY MEMORY TO t.txt
```

The DISPLAY STATUS Command

Like DISPLAY MEMORY, DISPLAY STATUS sends an extensive
status report to the Command window's results pane. Again, you can use
DISPLAY STATUS to send the report to a .TXT file, and then use the
text editor to examine it.

Syntax

```
DISPLAY STATUS [TO FILE <filename> | ? | <filename skeleton> |
PRINTER]
```

The DISPLAY STRUCTURE Command

The DISPLAY STRUCTURE command shows the structure of a table in the results pane of the Command window or sends it to a file or
to the printer.

  T I P

> **For a better look at your structure, use MODI STRU to
> launch the Table Structure tool.**

Syntax

```
DISPLAY STRUCTURE
[IN <alias>]
[TO FILE <filename> | ? | <filename skeleton> | PRINTER]
```

The DO Command

The DO command runs a program (usually a .PRG file).

Syntax

DO *<filename>* ¦ *?* ¦ *<filename skeleton>* ¦ *<procedure name>* ¦
<UDF name> [WITH *<parameter list >*]

Examples

DO my_prog
DO my_prog WITH 100, .05, 30

The DOS Command

The DOS command runs a DOS session under dBASE for Windows.

Syntax

DOS

The EDIT Command

The EDIT command is a synonym for BROWSE. EDIT or BROWSE
instantly launches the Table Records tool. If you are in the Command window, using this command is quicker than returning to the Navigator.

Syntax

EDIT
  [*<starting record expN >* ¦ *<bookmark >*]
  [*<scope >*]
  [FOR *<condition 1 >*]
  [WHILE *<condition 2 >*]
  [COLOR [*<standard text >*] [, [*<enhanced text >*] [, *<border >*]]]
  [COLUMNAR]
  [COMPRESS]
  [FIELDS *<field 1>* [*<field option list 1 >*] ¦ *<calculated field 1>* =
    <exp 1> [*<calculated field option list 1 >*]
    [, *<field 2>* [*<field option list 2>*] ¦
    <calculated field 2> = *<exp 2>*
    [*<calculated field option list 2 >*]...]]
  [FORMAT]
  [FREEZE *<field 3 >*]
  [KEY *<exp 3>* [, *<exp 4 >*]]
  [LOCK *<expN >*]
  [NOAPPEND]
  [NOCLEAR]
  [NODELETE]

```
[NOEDIT | NOMODIFY]
[NOFOLLOW]
[NOINIT]
[NORMAL]
[NOTOGGLE]
[NOWAIT]
[TITLE <expC 1 >]
[WIDTH <expN >]
[WINDOW <window name >]
```

The EJECT Command

EJECT sends a form-feed to your printer.

Syntax

```
EJECT
```

The EJECT PAGE Command

The EJECT PAGE command sends a form-feed to your printer and calls any page handling set by an ON PAGE command.

Syntax

```
EJECT PAGE
```

The ERASE Command

The ERASE command erases a single file. Using the ? or *<filename skeleton>* option launches the Erase File dialog box.

 ▶▶ N O T E

> **ERASE *.tmp does *not* erase all files with the .TMP extension. It opens the Erase File dialog box so that you can choose a particular .TMP file to erase. To erase a group of files, run the DOS ERASE command with** `!ERASE *.tmp.`

Syntax

```
ERASE <filename> | ? | <filename skeleton>
```

The EXTERN Command

The EXTERN command is used in programs to gain full access to any routine in a .DLL file or another Microsoft Windows executable file, such as a Windows .EXE file. Routines in .DLL files include all of the Windows API (application programming interface). EXTERN lets advanced programmers interface directly with Windows and other libraries without using C or assembler code.

Syntax

EXTERN [CDECL] *<return type> <function name>*
([*<parameter type 1>*[*<parameter type 2 >*,...]])
[*<path >*] *<filename>*

The FIND Command

The FIND command is a form of SEEK that saves some typing in the Command window. You FIND Smith (no quotation marks around Smith), in lieu of SEEK "Smith".

Syntax

FIND *<search key literal>*

The FLUSH Command

FLUSH sends the contents of dBASE for Windows' internal data buffers to the operating system.

▶▶**WARNING**

FLUSH may not succeed in getting your critical data to disk. In a single-user setup, disk-buffering software may delay the actual writes to disk. On a network, considerable delays are possible. Unfortunately, there is no way for dBASE for Windows (or any database program) to tell our current operating systems, "Write it to disk, now!"

Syntax

FLUSH

The GENERATE Command

The GENERATE command adds random records to a table. This is useful for testing.

Syntax

GENERATE [*<expN >*]

Example

GENERATE 1000

The GO Command

The GO command moves the record pointer to either the BOTTOM, TOP, or a selected record number. SQL databases that do not have record numbers can use bookmarks instead.

Syntax

GO[TO] BOTTOM ¦ TOP ¦ *<bookmark >* ¦ [RECORD] *<expN>* [IN *<alias >*]

Examples

GO TOP
GO 300
GO BOTTOM

The HELP Command

The HELP command launches the dBASE for Windows Help program. If you supply a topic, the command launches Help's Search dialog box for that topic.

  T I P

> **Using the HELP command in the Command window is often quicker than using the Windows Help Search dialog box.**

Syntax

HELP [*<help topic >*]

Example

HELP class form

The IMPORT Command

The IMPORT command reads data into a table from another table or spreadsheet file.

Syntax

IMPORT FROM *<filename>* ¦ ?
  [[TYPE] WB1 ¦ WK1]
  [HEADING]

The INDEX Command

The INDEX command creates a new TAG in an .MDX file or a new .NDX file. You can index only unique values for a partial set of data and in ascending (the default) or descending sequence.

►►►**T I P**

If you have a large table, indexing on a small set of records makes access based on that index just as fast as if the table were small.

Syntax

INDEX ON *<key expC list >*
  TO *<.ndx filename>* ¦ ? ¦ *<.ndx filename skeleton>*
  [UNIQUE]

or

INDEX ON *<key expC list >*
  TAG *<tag name>* [OF *<.mdx filename>* ¦ ? ¦ *<.mdx filename skeleton >*]
  [FOR *<condition >*]
  [DESCENDING]
  [UNIQUE]

Example

INDEX ON date_order DESCENDING

The INPUT Command

INPUT dates to the earliest days of dBASE II and its mainframe predecessors. It is a *very* old-fashioned way of getting data from a user. It is still popular for use in beginning programming classes.

Syntax

INPUT [*<prompt expC >*] TO *<memvar >*

The INSERT Command

The INSERT command inserts a blank record after (or optionally before) the current record. If BLANK is not specified, INSERT launches the currently selected view to edit the new record.

 ▶▶ W A R N I N G

> **INSERT must physically move every record from the point of insertion to the end of the file. Always use APPEND [BLANK] except on tiny files.**

Syntax

INSERT [BLANK] [BEFORE] [NOWAIT]

The INSERT AUTOMEM Command

We include this command only because we want to warn you never to use it. While INSERT can be handy for working on small files from the Command window, INSERT AUTOMEM is only useful in a program. INSERT should never be used in programs. You should use APPENDs and use indexes to keep your data logically ordered.

Syntax

INSERT AUTOMEM [BEFORE]

The JOIN Command

The JOIN command performs a physical joining of two tables. Use it when you want to combine two tables into one (say, for export to a spreadsheet). For most work, SET RELATION achieves the same effect with much higher efficiency.

Syntax

JOIN WITH *<alias >* TO *<filename>* ¦ ? ¦ *<filename skeleton>*
[[TYPE] [PARADOX ¦ DBASE]]
FOR *<condition>*
[FIELDS *<field list >*]

The KEYBOARD Command

The KEYBOARD command puts one or more characters into the typeahead buffer, as if you had typed them.

 ▶▶ T I P

KEYBOARD commands can be used to provide macro facilities for starting any program that can be run from the keyboard. Put a single KEYBOARD command in a .PRG file, then DO that .PRG instead of typing.

Syntax

KEYBOARD *<expC>* [CLEAR]

Example

In a program, this command can be used instead of pressing Ctrl-F to find records, because CHR(6) is Ctrl-F:

KEYBOARD CHR(6)

The LABEL FORM Command

The LABEL FORM command uses a label design you have created with Crystal Reports (an .RPL file) to write mailing labels.

Syntax

LABEL FORM *<filename 1>* ¦ ? ¦ *<filename skeleton 1>*
[*<scope >*]
[FOR *<condition 1 >*]
[WHILE *<condition 2 >*]
[SAMPLE]
[TO FILE *<filename 2 >* ¦ ? ¦ *<filename skeleton 2 >* ¦ PRINTER]

Example

LABEL FORM phones_b

The LIST Command

The LIST command lists all, or selected, records to the results pane of the Command window, to a file, or to your printer. It is the same as DISPLAY, except that DISPLAY defaults to the current record; LIST defaults to all records. The OFF option eliminates record numbers from the listing.

Syntax

LIST
   [<*scope* >]
   [FOR <*condition 1* >]
   [WHILE <*condition 2* >]
   [[FIELDS] <*exp list* >]
   [OFF]
   [TO FILE <*filename*> ¦ ? ¦ <*filename skeleton*> ¦ PRINTER]

Example

Here's an example of using LIST in the Command window:

The LIST COVERAGE Command

LIST COVERAGE is used in programming to examine the results of program coverage—a detailed analysis of how much use each part of a program gets. This is used to tune a program for better performance.

Syntax

LIST COVERAGE
   [<*coverage filename*> ¦ ? ¦ <*coverage filename skeleton* >]
   [ALL]
   [SUMMARY]

    [TO FILE *<text filename>* ¦ ? ¦ *<text filename skeleton>* ¦
    [PRINTER]

The LIST FILES Command

LIST FILES provides the same service as DIR. Like DIR, it defaults to *.DBF.

Syntax

    LIST FILES
      [LIKE *<filename 1>* ¦ *<filename skeleton >*]
      [ON *<drive >*]
      [TO FILE *<filename 2 >* ¦ ? ¦ *<filename skeleton 2 >* ¦ PRINTER]

The LIST MEMORY Command

LIST MEMORY sends a long list, describing the contents of memory, to the Command window's results pane or to a file or the printer. You can use LIST MEMORY to send the list to a .TXT file, and then use the text editor (MODI FILE starts it) to examine it.

Syntax

    LIST MEMORY [TO FILE *<filename>* ¦ ? ¦ *<filename skeleton>* ¦
    PRINTER]

The LIST STATUS Command

Like LIST MEMORY, LIST STATUS sends an extensive status report to the Command window's results pane. Again, you can use LIST STATUS to send the report to a .TXT file, and then use the text editor to examine it.

Syntax

    LIST STATUS [TO FILE *<filename>* ¦ ? ¦ *<filename skeleton>* ¦
    PRINTER]

The LIST STRUCTURE Command

LIST STRUCTURE shows the structure of a table in the results pane of the Command window or sends it to a file or your printer.

▶▶ **T I P**

> **For a better look at your structure, use MODI STRU to launch the Table Structure tool.**

Syntax

```
LIST STRUCTURE
    [IN <alias >]
    [TO FILE <filename> ¦ ? <filename skeleton> ¦ PRINTER]
```

The LOAD DLL Command

LOAD DLL is used by programmers who have created .DLL files using a language other than dBASE. It lets dBASE programs access the routines written in the other language. Among other uses, it allows access to specialized Visual Basic controls.

Syntax

```
LOAD DLL [<path >] <DLL filename>
```

The LOCATE Command

LOCATE is used to search for a record based on criteria that may not be available in an index.

 ▶▶ **T I P**

> **LOCATE is many times slower than SEEK if you do not have an index. Add an index on any criteria for which you do frequent searches.**

Syntax

```
LOCATE
    [<scope >]
    [FOR <condition 1 >]
    [WHILE <condition 2 >]
```

Example

```
LOCATE FOR first_name = "Mary"
```

The MKDIR Command

The MKDIR command calls the DOS service of the same name.

Syntax

MD ¦ MKDIR *<directory>*

Example

MD new_subd

The MODIFY APPLICATION Command

MODIFY APPLICATION is a synonym for MODIFY FORM. It launches the Form Designer.

Syntax

MODIFY APPLICATION *<filename>* ¦ ? ¦ *<filename skeleton>*

The MODIFY COMMAND Command

MODIFY COMMAND starts the Program Editor. The default extension for the file is .PRG.

 ►►**TIP**

If you are working in the Command window, using MODI COMM from the Command window is much quicker than switching back to the Navigator for the same service.

Syntax

MODIFY COMMAND [*<filename>* ¦ ? ¦ *<filename skeleton >*]

MODIFY FILE starts the Text Editor. The default extension for the file is .TXT.

Syntax

MODIFY FILE [*<filename>* ¦ ? ¦ *<filename skeleton >*]

Example

MODIFY FILE dbasewin.ini

The MODIFY FORM Command

MODIFY FORM launches the Form Designer. If you are working in the Command window, use this command to work on your .WFM files.

Syntax

MODIFY FORM *<filename>* ¦ ? ¦ *<filename skeleton>*

The MODIFY LABEL Command

MODIFY LABEL launches the Crystal Reports label design tool.

Syntax

MODIFY LABEL *<filename>* ¦ ? ¦ *<filename skeleton>*

The MODIFY QUERY Command

MODIFY QUERY launches the Query Designer.

Syntax

MODIFY QUERY *<filename>* ¦ ? ¦ *<filename skeleton>*

The MODIFY REPORT Command

MODIFY REPORT launches the Crystal Reports report design tool.

Syntax

MODIFY REPORT *<filename>* ¦ ? ¦ *<filename skeleton>*

The MODIFY STRUCTURE Command

MODIFY STRUCTURE launches the Table Structure tool. It is the same as selecting the table in the Navigator and pressing Shift-F2 or right double-clicking.

Syntax

MODIFY STRUCTURE

The MODIFY VIEW Command

MODIFY VIEW is a synonym for MODIFY QUERY. It launches the Query Designer.

Syntax

MODIFY VIEW *<filename>* ¦ ? ¦ *<filename skeleton>*

The OPEN DATABASE Command

The OPEN DATABASE command opens an SQL database.

Syntax

OPEN DATABASE *<database name>*
   [LOGIN *<username>*/*<password >*]
   [WITH *<option string >*]

The OPEN FORM Command

The OPEN FORM command launches a dBASE for Windows form, such as the ones you create in the Form Designer. The ON clause specifies which object on the form receives focus.

Syntax

OPEN FORM *<form name 1>* [ON *<object name 1>*
   [*<form name 2>* [ON *<object name 2 >*] ...]]

Example

OPEN FORM my_form ON ok_button

The PACK Command

The PACK command physically removes deleted records from a table. For larger tables, it is generally part of regular maintenance procedures.

 ►►**TIP**

PACK is often used on network tables during weekend maintenance. A full backup should always be done before using the PACK command.

Syntax

PACK

The PLAY SOUND Command

The PLAY SOUND command plays a sound recorded in a .WAV file or stored in a Binary field.

Syntax

PLAY SOUND FILENAME *<filename>* | ? | *<filename skeleton>* | BINARY *<binary field>*

The QUIT Command

The QUIT command terminates your dBASE for Windows session. The WITH clause will return a code to the operating system. From DOS, the WITH return value becomes ERRORLEVEL in a DOS batch file.

Syntax

QUIT [WITH *<expN >*]

The RECALL Command

The RECALL command defaults to the current record. Any record that was deleted (with DELETE) may be recalled (the Delete flag is turned off) with RECALL prior to using PACK on a table. After using PACK, the data is physically gone.

Syntax

RECALL
  [*<scope >*]
  [FOR *<condition 1 >*]
  [WHILE *<condition 2 >*]

Examples

RECALL ALL
RECALL FOR Balance > 0

The REDEFINE Command

The REDEFINE command modifies definitions of objects, such as those made by a DEFINE command or a prior REDEFINE command, or through a tool such as the Form Designer.

Syntax

REDEFINE *<class name> <object name>*
  [OF *<container object >*]
  [FROM *<row, col>* TO *<row, col> >* ¦ *<*AT *<row, col >*]
  [PROPERTY *<stock property list >*]
  [CUSTOM *<custom property list >*]
  [WITH *<parameter list >*]

The REFRESH Command

REFRESH is used in multiuser situations. It causes dBASE for Windows to reread any data in its buffers. Any changes made by other users are read during a REFRESH.

 ►►**N O T E**

You operate as multiple users if you use multiple sessions, so you may need to REFRESH to keep all your windows current.

Syntax

REFRESH [*<alias >*]

The REINDEX Command

The REINDEX command rebuilds all open indexes for the table currently in use.

 ►►**W A R N I N G**

On a network, using REINDEX generates a storm of network traffic if your table is large. To avoid this, issue the REINDEX command in a dBASE for Windows session on the server itself.

Syntax

REINDEX

Example

A common maintenance procedure, generally run in the evening or over a weekend, is to back up the data in the table, and then issue these commands:

    PACK
    REINDEX

The RELEASE Command

The RELEASE command deletes memory variables and arrays, freeing the memory they took.

Syntax

    RELEASE <memvar list> ¦
        ALL [LIKE <memvar skeleton 1 >] [EXCEPT <memvar skeleton 2 >]

Example

    RELEASE ALL LIKE temp*

The RELEASE AUTOMEM Command

The RELEASE AUTOMEM command releases only the automemory (AUTOMEM) variables.

Syntax

    RELEASE AUTOMEM

The RELEASE DLL Command

RELEASE DLL releases a .DLL file previously loaded with a LOAD DLL command.

Syntax

    RELEASE DLL <DLL filename list>

The RELEASE OBJECT Command

RELEASE OBJECT deletes objects from memory, freeing the memory they took. If you release a Form, all objects on that form are automatically released before the Form object itself is released.

Syntax

RELEASE OBJECT <*object parent*>.<*object name*>

Example

RELEASE OBJECT Form.Pushbutton1

The RENAME Command

Similar to the DOS command of the same name, RENAME changes the name of a file.

Syntax

RENAME <*filename 1*> ¦ ? ¦ <*filename skeleton 1*> TO <*filename 2*> ¦ ? ¦ <*filename skeleton 2*>

Example

RENAME people.dbf TO people.sav

The RENAME TABLE Command

RENAME TABLE is an intelligent RENAME command, for use with tables. It takes care of the table name, as well as related index and memo files.

Syntax

RENAME <*old table name*> ¦ ? ¦ <*filename skeleton 1*> TO <*new table name*> ¦ ? ¦ <*filename skeleton 2*> [TYPE PARADOX ¦ DBASE]

Example

This command renames ORGS.DBF, ORGS.MDX, and ORGS.DBT:

RENAME TABLE orgs TO orgs_1

The REPLACE Command

A REPLACE command can update just the current record, a whole table, or part of a table.

> ▶▶ **T I P**
>
> **Using REPLACE from the Command window can do
> mass updates very easily. This is often quicker than
> using the Table menu Replace Records ...choice.**

Syntax

```
REPLACE
    <field 1> WITH <exp 1> [ADDITIVE]
    [, <field 2> WITH <exp 2> [ADDITIVE]...
    [<scope >]
    [FOR <condition 1 >]
    [WHILE <condition 2 >]
    [REINDEX]
```

Examples

```
REPLACE ALL Orgs_ID WITH RECNO()+1000
REPLACE last_name WITH "Smythe"
REPLACE ALL PRICE WITH PRICE * 0.80
```

The REPLACE AUTOMEM Command

The REPLACE AUTOMEM command transfers the values in your
automemory (AUTOMEM) variables into the equivalent fields in your
table's current record.

Syntax

```
REPLACE AUTOMEM
```

The REPLACE BINARY Command

The REPLACE BINARY command replaces a Binary field with a file.
This is used to load data such as .WAV, .BMP, and .PCX files.

Syntax

```
REPLACE BINARY <binary field name> FROM <filename> ¦ ? ¦
<filename skeleton> [TYPE <binary type user number >]
```

Example

```
REPLACE BINARY pic_field FROM my_pic.bmp
```

The REPLACE FROM ARRAY Command

The REPLACE FROM ARRAY command updates the current record, or a range of records, with data stored in a memory array.

Syntax

```
REPLACE FROM ARRAY <array name>
  [<scope >]
  [FOR <condition 1 >]
  [WHILE <condition 2 >]
  [FIELDS <field list >]
  [REINDEX]
```

The REPLACE MEMO Command

The REPLACE MEMO command is used when you have a memory array in which each line of the array is one line of text. This array will be written to the Memo field by a REPLACE MEMO command.

Syntax

```
REPLACE MEMO <memo field> WITH ARRAY <array name> [ADDITIVE]
```

The REPLACE MEMO FROM Command

The REPLACE MEMO FROM command lets you replace the contents of a Memo field with the contents of a file.

 ►► **N O T E**

> **Memo fields work, but Binary fields are the preferred method for storing binary data types, such as .WAV, .BMP, and .PCX files.**

Syntax

```
REPLACE MEMO <memo field> FROM <filename> ¦ ? ¦ <filename
skeleton> [ADDITIVE]
```

The REPLACE OLE Command

The REPLACE OLE command lets you put an OLE document in an OLE field (the default) or a link to an OLE document.

Command Windows Command

Ch.

13

Syntax

```
REPLACE OLE <OLE field name>
    <filename> ¦ ? ¦ <filename skeleton>
    [LINK [CLASS <class name >]]
```

The REPORT FORM Command

The REPORT FORM command provides data to a report format you
have defined in Crystal Reports. You can specify a regular report
(.RPT) or a cross-tab report (.RPC).

Syntax

```
REPORT FORM <filename 1> ¦ ? ¦ <filename skeleton 1>
    [<scope >] [FOR <condition 1 >] [WHILE <condition 2 >]
    [CROSSTAB]
    [HEADING <expC >]
    [NOEJECT]
    [PLAIN]
    [SUMMARY]
    [TO FILE <filename 2> ¦ ? ¦ <filename skeleton 2>
```

The RESTORE Command

RESTORE is used to restore data, such as memory variables, previously saved with a SAVE command.

Syntax

```
RESTORE FROM <filename> ¦ ? ¦ <filename skeleton> [ADDITIVE]
```

The RESTORE IMAGE FROM Command

The RESTORE IMAGE FROM command restores an image to your
screen or printer. It will get the image from a file or a Binary field. The
default type is .BMP.

Syntax

```
RESTORE IMAGE FROM
    <filename> ¦ ? ¦ <filename skeleton> ¦ BINARY <binary field>
    [TIMEOUT <expN >]
    [TO PRINTER]
    [[TYPE] PCX]
```

The RESUME Command

The RESUME command may be given after a SUSPEND command, to start a program at the point at which it was suspended. Typically, this command is issued in the Command window after an error, such as a file not being open, has been fixed.

Syntax

```
RESUME
```

The RETRY Command

The RETRY command attempts to access a record to which access was previously denied because another user had locked it.

Syntax

```
RETRY
```

The SAVE Command

The SAVE command stores one or more memory variables in a file. They can later be restored with a RESTORE command.

Syntax

```
SAVE TO <filename> | ? | <filename skeleton>
  [ALL]
  [LIKE <memvar skeleton 1 >]
  [EXCEPT <memvar skeleton 2 >]
```

Example

```
SAVE TO mem_file ALL LIKE *_saved_var
```

The SEEK Command

The SEEK command is similar to the FIND command. SEEK is usually preferred in programs. It locates values in the master index.

Syntax

```
SEEK <expC> | <expN> | <expD>
```

The SELECT Command

The SELECT command lets you choose any work area from 1 to 225, or name an area by an alias assigned to a table. Each work area can have one open table and as many related .MDX and .NDX files as needed. Each session can have up to 225 work areas.

 ▶▶ **W A R N I N G**

> dBASE for Windows has a virtually unlimited capacity for open tables and associated files. DOS does not. Your real limit on sessions and work areas will be your DOS files limit.

Syntax

SELECT <*alias*>

Examples

SELECT 2
SELECT orgs

The SET Command

The SET command launches the Desktop Properties multi-tab dialog box.

Syntax

SET

The SET ALTERNATE Command

The SET ALTERNATE command turns output to an alternate device or file ON. It routes output of the ?, ??, and dBASE IV-style output commands to this device or file.

Syntax

SET ALTERNATE ON ¦ OFF

The SET ALTERNATE TO Command

The SET ALTERNATE TO command sets a device or file to receive alternate output, when you SET ALTERNATE ON. If no file or device is specified, it closes the former alternate device or file.

Syntax

```
SET ALTERNATE TO [<filename> | ? | <filename skeleton>
[ADDITIVE]]
```

The SET AUTOSAVE Command

The SET AUTOSAVE command sets the autosave feature on or off. With AUTOSAVE ON, dBASE flushes its buffers to the operating system more frequently than with AUTOSAVE OFF. You can gain some safety at the cost of some speed. (With AUTOSAVE either ON or OFF, saving is automatic.)

Syntax

```
SET AUTOSAVE ON | OFF
```

The SET BELL Command

The SET BELL command sets the bell feature on or off. With BELL OFF, the beeps (when you fill a field completely, for instance) are turned off.

Syntax

```
SET BELL ON | OFF
```

The SET BELL TO Command

The SET BELL TO command lets you adjust the pitch and duration of the bell. The 256 setting is about middle C on the piano. Duration is measured in clock ticks; each tick occurs 18.2 times per second. One or two ticks makes a decent bell.

▶▶ **N O T E**

The word *bell* dates back to the dawn of dBASE, when there really was a bell in typical terminals.

Syntax

SET BELL TO [*<frequency expN>*, *<duration expN >*]

The SET BLOCKSIZE TO Command

The SET BLOCKSIZE TO command sets the size of blocks in index and memo files. The BLOCKSIZE is given in multiples of 512 bytes (1 is 512, 2 is 1024, and so on). The maximum BLOCKSIZE is 63.

Syntax

SET BLOCKSIZE TO *<expN>*

The SET CARRY Command

The SET CARRY command turns the CARRY property on or off. When ON, values for a newly appended record are carried forward from the previous record.

Syntax

SET CARRY ON ¦ OFF

The SET CARRY TO Command

The SET CARRY TO command allows the user to select the fields that participate in the CARRY.

Syntax

SET CARRY TO [*<field list>* [ADDITIVE]]

Example

SET CARRY TO City, State, Zip

The SET CATALOG Command

The SET CATALOG command turns cataloging on and off. When ON, files opened are automatically added to the current catalog.

Syntax

SET CATALOG ON ¦ OFF

The SET CATALOG TO Command

The SET CATALOG TO command opens a catalog file. Without a file name, it closes the current catalog. The ? option or using a skeleton calls the Open Catalog dialog box.

Syntax

SET CATALOG TO [*<filename>* ¦ ? ¦ *<filename skeleton >*]

The SET CENTURY Command

The SET CENTURY command, when ON, includes all four year digits in date displays.

Syntax

SET CENTURY ON ¦ OFF

Example

Here's an example of using the SET CENTURY command in the Command window:

The SET CONFIRM Command

The SET CONFIRM command controls the behavior of dBASE for Windows when you type the last character in a field. With CONFIRM ON, dBASE for Windows waits for you to press Tab or Enter to confirm that you have finished, which makes fixing errors very easy. With CONFIRM OFF, dBASE immediately moves to the next field. This behavior is better for high-volume data-entry work.

Syntax

SET CONFIRM ON ¦ OFF

The SET CONSOLE Command

The SET CONSOLE command, when ON, uses the results pane of the Command window for output from commands such as LIST and ?.

Syntax

    SET CONSOLE ON ¦ OFF

The SET COVERAGE Command

The SET COVERAGE command is used when you want an extended analysis of which portions of a program are used most often. This is useful when your program is not as fast as you would like and you want to know where you can gain the most speed.

Syntax

    SET COVERAGE ON ¦ OFF

The SET CUAENTER Command

The SET CUAENTER command controls the behavior of the Enter key. According to the CUA definition, pressing Enter submits a form (is the same as clicking OK). However, for much data-entry work, people are used to pressing Enter to complete a single field, which is the behavior when you set CUAENTER OFF.

Syntax

    SET CUAENTER ON ¦ OFF

The SET CURRENCY Command

The SET CURRENCY command specifies the side of a number for placement of the currency symbol.

Syntax

    SET CURRENCY LEFT ¦ RIGHT

The SET CURRENCY TO Command

The SET CURRENCY TO command specifies the symbol that is used for currency amounts.

Syntax

SET CURRENCY TO [<*expC* >]

The SET DATABASE Command

The SET DATABASE TO command selects a database in an SQL database environment.

Syntax

SET DATABASE TO [<*database name* >]

The SET DATE TO Command

The SET DATE [TO] command specifies the format used for the display of dates. The choices are as follows:

American	MM/DD/YY
ANSI	YY.MM.DD
British	DD/MM/YY
French	DD/MM/YY
German	DD.MM.YY
Italian	DD-MM-YY
Japanese	YY/MM/DD
USA	MM-DD-YY
MDY	MM/DD/YY
DMY	DD/MM/YY

 ►► N O T E

The YY form is used when CENTURY is OFF. YYYY is used when CENTURY is ON.

Syntax

SET DATE [TO]
    AMERICAN ¦ ANSI ¦ BRITISH ¦ FRENCH ¦ GERMAN ¦ ITALIAN
    ¦ JAPAN ¦ USA ¦ MDY ¦ DMY ¦ YMD

Example

SET DATE TO JAPAN

The SET DATE TO Command

The SET DATE TO command accepts a date as a character string and assigns its value to the system date. This is the same as using the DOS DATE command.

  ▶▶ N O T E

> **The SET DATE TO argument is a character string. The string "12/31/95" works, but {12/31/95} is not accepted.**

Syntax

SET DATE TO <*expC*>

Example

SET DATE TO "12/31/95"

The SET DBTYPE TO Command

The SET DBTYPE TO command selects .DB tables (Paradox) or .DBF tables (dBASE) as the default type for tables.

Syntax

SET DBTYPE TO [PARADOX ¦ DBASE]

The SET DECIMALS Command

The SET DECIMALS TO command specifies the number of decimals to display.

Syntax

SET DECIMALS TO [<*expN* >]

Example

Here's an example of using SET DECIMALS TO in the Command window:

The SET DEFAULT Command

The SET DEFAULT TO command selects a disk drive.

Syntax

SET DEFAULT TO [<*drive*>[:]]

Example

SET DEFAULT TO D:

The SET DELETED Command

When ON, SET DELETED treats deleted records as if they were physically deleted. When OFF, it treats deleted records as if they were only flagged for deletion. Pressing the default status is saved in DBASE WIN.INI and may be seen in the Desktop Properties dialog box.

Syntax

SET DELETED ON ¦ OFF

The SET DELIMITERS Command

When ON, SET DELIMITERS adds delimiter characters to older screen input/output (I/O) commands.

Syntax

SET DELIMITERS ON ¦ OFF

The SET DELIMITERS TO Command

The SET DELIMITERS TO command specifies the character to be used for delimiters when SET DELIMITERS is ON.

Command Windows Command

CH. 13

Syntax

SET DELIMITERS TO [<*expC*> ¦ DEFAULT]

The SET DESIGN Command

The SET DESIGN command, when ON, allows the use of Design mode. If OFF, only Run mode is permitted.

Syntax

SET DESIGN ON ¦ OFF

The SET DEVELOPMENT Command

The SET DEVELOPMENT command, if OFF, suppresses automatic recompilation of programs that have source forms more recent than their object forms. If SET DEVELOPMENT is ON, dBASE for Windows compares the date and time a .WFO file, for example, was last updated to the date and time of the corresponding .WFM file. If the .WFM file is more recent, it is recompiled.

 ▶▶ T I P

The date/time comparisons take very little time. Leave DEVELOPMENT ON whenever possible.

Syntax

SET DEVELOPMENT ON ¦ OFF

The SET DEVICE TO Command

The SET DEVICE TO command selects the destination for streaming output, such as output from the ? command.

Syntax

SET DEVICE TO SCREEN ¦ PRINTER ¦ FILE <*filename*> ¦ ? ¦ <*filename skeleton*>

The SET DIRECTORY TO Command

The SET DIRECTORY TO command specifies the current directory.

Syntax

SET DIRECTORY TO [<*path* >]

Example

SET DIRECTORY TO \DBWORK

The SET DISPLAY TO Command

The SET DISPLAY TO command selects a display type. This provides compatibility with older text-mode programs.

Syntax

SET DISPLAY TO MONO ¦ COLOR ¦ EGA25 ¦ EGA43 ¦ MONO 43 ¦ VGA25 ¦ VGA43 ¦ VGA50

The SET ECHO Command

The SET ECHO command is a synonym for DEBUG. (In older versions of dBASE, it echoed commands to the console, which was useful in debugging programs.)

Syntax

SET ECHO ON ¦ OFF

The SET EDITOR TO Command

The SET EDITOR TO command sets the editor used for text files to the specified executable file.

Syntax

SET EDITOR TO [<*expC* >]

The SET ERROR TO Command

The SET ERROR TO command specifies a string to precede, and, optionally, one to follow, run-time error messages from dBASE for Windows.

Syntax

SET ERROR TO [<*precedingexpC*>[, <*followingexpC* >]]

The SET ESCAPE Command

The SET ESCAPE command, if ON, lets you press the Esc key to interrupt a running program.

 ►►**W A R N I N G**

Never set ESCAPE OFF until you are absolutely sure that your program doesn't have any errors that could cause an infinite loop (such as forgetting to SKIP in a DO WHILE .NOT. EOF() loop).

Syntax

SET ESCAPE ON ¦ OFF

The SET EXACT Command

The SET EXACT command controls string comparisons. With EXACT OFF, *Smith* equals *S*. With EXACT ON, comparison is made to the length of the longer string. A longer string matches a shorter one only if the extra characters in the longer string are all space characters (blank).

Syntax

SET EXACT ON ¦ OFF

The SET EXCLUSIVE Command

The SET EXCLUSIVE command, if ON, opens all tables for exclusive use.

 ►►**W A R N I N G**

In Microsoft Windows your sessions are individual users of the table. Setting EXCLUSIVE ON will cause your forms to conflict if the users try to use the same table.

Syntax

SET EXCLUSIVE ON ¦ OFF

The SET FIELDS Command

The SET FIELDS command, if OFF, uses all the fields, not the fields specified in a SET FIELDS command. The SET FIELDS TO command automatically sets FIELDS ON.

Syntax

SET FIELDS ON ¦ OFF

The SET FIELDS TO Command

The SET FIELDS TO command establishes the list of fields that are active in subsequent data table commands.

Syntax

SET FIELDS TO [*<field list>* ¦ ALL [LIKE *<skeleton 1 >*] [EXCEPT *<skeleton 2 >*]]

Example

SET FIELDS TO Last_name, Full_name, City, Phone

The SET FILTER TO Command

The SET FILTER TO command establishes a condition that records must meet to appear in the table.

Syntax

SET FILTER TO [*<condition >*] ¦ [FILE *<filename>* ¦ ? ¦ *<filename skeleton >*]

Example

SET FILTER TO State = 'CA'

The SET FULLPATH Command

When ON, the SET FULLPATH command causes functions such as CATALOG() and MDX() to return a full path specification with the file name.

Syntax

SET FULLPATH ON ¦ OFF

The SET FUNCTION Command

The SET FUNCTION command causes the specified key to be equal to typing the character expression. If the last character in the expression is a semicolon, an Enter keypress is substituted for the semicolon.

Syntax

SET FUNCTION <*key* > TO <*expC*>

Example

SET FUNCTION F9 TO 'DO people.wfm;'

The SET HEADINGS Command

The SET HEADINGS command controls the use of default (field name) headings for commands such as DISPLAY and SUM. If ON, the headings are used.

Syntax

SET HEADINGS ON ¦ OFF

The SET HELP TO Command

The SET HELP TO command is used to change Help files. If you build a Help file for your own system (with a Help file builder, such as Borland's ForeHelp), you can activate it with this command.

Syntax

SET HELP TO [<*help filename*> ¦ ? ¦ <*help filename skeleton* >]

The SET IBLOCK TO Command

The SET IBLOCK TO command overrides the BLOCKSIZE setting for index blocks only. It sets the size of index blocks. The number given is the number of 512-byte blocks to allocate for each index blocks. The minimum is 2 (1024 bytes).

Syntax

SET IBLOCK TO <*expN*>

The SET INDEX TO Command

The SET INDEX TO command opens one or more index files or specifies the master index tag in an open index file.

Syntax

SET INDEX TO [*<filename list >* ¦ ? ¦ *<filename skeleton list >*]
[ORDER [TAG] *<filename 1>* ¦ *<tag name>* [OF
<filename 2> ¦ ? ¦ *<filename skeleton >*]]

Examples

SET INDEX TO TAG Last_name
SET INDEX TO special.mdx

The SET KEY Command

The SET KEY command sets a key to call a program file or subroutine in a program file.

Syntax

SET KEY *<expN>* ¦ *<expC>* TO [*<program name>* ¦ *<procedure name >*]

Examples

SET KEY "F2" TO open_it
SET KEY "F3" TO close_it

The SET KEY TO Command

The SET KEY TO command specifies a value or range of values for the master index.

Syntax

SET KEY TO [*<exp list 1>* ¦ RANGE *<exp 2>* [,] ¦ , *<exp 3>* ¦ *<exp 2 >*, *<exp 3 >* [LOW *<exp list 2>* [,]] [HIGH [,] *<exp list 3 >*]
[EXCLUDE]

Examples

These examples assume a master index on the STATE field:

SET KEY TO 'CA', 'NY'	California and New York
SET KEY TO RANGE ,'CA'	Start through California
SET KEY TO RANGE 'NY'	New York to end
SET KEY TO RANGE 'CA','NY'	California through New York

The SET LDCHECK Command

The SET LDCHECK command tells dBASE for Windows that you
do, or do not, want it to check that the language driver conforms to the
DOS code page.

▶▶ N O T E

**LDCHECK is a necessary check if you are preparing a
system to be used in multiple countries.**

Syntax

SET LDCHECK ON ¦ OFF

The SET LIBRARY TO Command

The SET LIBRARY TO command specifies a file of subroutines that
will be accessed by your other program files. The LIBRARY file is the
last place that dBASE for Windows will look for a subroutine that it
needs.

Syntax

SET LIBRARY TO [*<filename>* ¦ *?* ¦ *<filename skeleton >*]

The SET LOCK Command

The SET LOCK command affects the locking status of certain commands, such as SUM, that read values from a table. With LOCK ON, the table is locked, which prevents other users from accessing it but ensures that the returned value is correct as of the instant it is calculated. With LOCK OFF, another user can update a value just before or after the SUM command reads a record.

Syntax

SET LOCK ON ¦ OFF

The SET MARGIN TO Command

The SET MARGIN TO command sets the left margin for printed reports.

Syntax

SET MARGIN TO *<expN>*

The SET MARK TO Command

The SET MARK TO command sets the character used in formatting dates.

Syntax

SET MARK TO [*<expC >*]

Example

SET MARK TO '/'

The SET MBLOCK TO Command

The SET MBLOCK TO command sets the size of Memo field blocks. Its value is in units of 64 bytes each (1 is 64, 2 is 128, and so on).

►►**TIP**

Smaller memo blocks waste less disk space; larger ones run faster if you have large Memo fields. With today's disk-compression technology, the wasted space is for the most part insignificant, so opt for efficiency.

Syntax

SET MBLOCK TO *<expN>*

The SET MEMOWIDTH TO Command

The SET MEMOWIDTH TO command sets the display width for Memo fields.

Syntax

SET MEMOWIDTH TO [*<expN >*]

The SET MESSAGE TO Command

The SET MESSAGE TO command sets the message that is displayed on the left side of the status bar.

Syntax

SET MESSAGE TO [*<message expC >*]

The SET NEAR Command

The SET NEAR command determines the position of the record pointer after a SEEK command that does not find its target value. With NEAR OFF, the pointer is set at EOF (end of file). With NEAR ON, the record pointer stops at the first record after the SEEK value.

Syntax

SET NEAR ON ¦ OFF

The SET ODOMETER TO Command

The SET ODOMETER TO command controls the display of record counts in the status bar for commands such as APPEND and COPY. The odometer setting is the increment at which the odometer is updated.

Syntax

SET ODOMETER TO [<*expN* >]

Example

SET ODOMETER TO 100

Updates the status bar with every 100 records processed.

The SET ORDER TO Command

The SET ORDER TO command specifies an index tag in the production index, or selects a tag by number or specifies a new .MDX file for the master index and picks a tag in the new .MDX file.

Syntax

SET ORDER TO [<*index position expN* >] ¦
    [<.*ndx filename 1* >] [NOSAVE] ¦
    [TAG] <*tag name*> [OF <*filename*> ¦ ?] [NOSAVE]

Examples

SET ORDER TO 3

Uses the third tag

SET ORDER TO Last_name

The SET PATH TO Command

The SET PATH TO command sets one or more paths to search for files, or, with the path list omitted, turns off the former path settings.

Syntax

SET PATH TO [<*path list* >]

Examples

SET PATH TO D:\DBWORK, C:\GENERAL
SET PATH TO

The SET PCOL TO Command

The SET PCOL TO command sets the current printer column (horizontal position).

Syntax

    SET PCOL TO <expN>

The SET POINT TO Command

The SET POINT TO command specifies the character to use between the whole and fractional parts of a number.

Syntax

    SET POINT TO [<expC >]

The SET PRECISION TO Command

The SET PRECISION TO command sets the number of decimal places dBASE for Windows uses when it compares numbers. The range is 10–19.

Syntax

    SET PRECISION TO [<expN >]

The SET PRINTER Command

The SET PRINTER command turns files or devices that are receiving printer output on or off. (It does not turn the physical printer on or off.)

Syntax

    SET PRINTER ON ¦ OFF

The SET PRINTER TO Command

The SET PRINTER TO command establishes an alternate file of device for printer output.

Syntax

    SET PRINTER TO [[FILE] <filename> ¦ ? ¦ <filename skeleton >] ¦
    [<device >]

Example

SET PRINTER TO FILE print.tmp

The SET PROCEDURE TO Command

The SET PROCEDURE TO command establishes a file (usually a .PRG file) where dBASE for Windows will look for subroutines that it cannot find in its main program. The ADDITIVE clause adds the subroutines in the specified PROCEDURE file to any others that are already available. Without ADDITIVE, the PROCEDURE file replaces any other PROCEDURE files. When searching for subroutines, dBASE for Windows looks in PROCEDURE files before it looks in the LIBRARY file.

Syntax

SET PROCEDURE TO [*<filename>* ¦ ? ¦ *<filename skeleton >*] [ADDITIVE]

Example

SET PROCEDURE TO my_subrs.prg ADDITIVE

The SET PROW TO Command

The SET PROW TO command sets the printer's row (vertical position).

Syntax

SET PROW TO *<expN>*

The SET REFRESH TO Command

The SET REFRESH TO command specifies the number of seconds (0 to 3600) that elapse between dBASE for Windows refreshing client screens with data from the file server. Frequent refreshes ensure that each simultaneous user is looking at the same data, but they slow overall performance.

Syntax

SET REFRESH TO *<expN>*

The SET RELATION TO Command

The SET RELATION TO command establishes relationships between two or more tables. The Query Designer writes SET RELATION commands for you, based on a visual representation. Its output is a .QBE file, which includes SET RELATION commands. For more information about setting relations, refer to Chapter 5.

 ▶▶ **W A R N I N G**

> **Writing SET RELATION commands is tricky, at best, and terrifying, at worst. Running the Query Designer makes designing the relationships simple. When you save your work, dBASE for Windows does the hard work of writing SET RELATION commands.**

Syntax

SET RELATION TO
    [*<key exp list 1>* ¦ *<expN 1>*
    INTO *<child table alias 1>*
    [, *<key exp list 2>* ¦ *<expN 2>*
    INTO *<child table alias 2 >*] ...]
    [ADDITIVE]]

For dBASE for Windows tables only:

SET RELATION TO
    [*<key exp list 1>* ¦ *<expN 1>*
    INTO *<child table alias 1>*
    [CONSTRAIN]
    [INTEGRITY]
      [CASCADE ¦ RESTRICTED]]
    [, *<key exp list 2>* ¦ *<expN 2>*
        INTO *<child table alias 2 >*]
        [CONSTRAIN]
        [INTEGRITY]
        [CASCADE ¦ RESTRICTED]] ...]
    [ADDITIVE]

The SET REPROCESS TO Command

The SET REPROCESS TO command specifies the number of times dBASE for Windows will repeat an attempt to get access to a locked record or file before giving up and reporting a locking error. The default is 0; the maximum is 32000. A count of –1 tells dBASE to keep trying and never give up.

▶▶ **W A R N I N G**

Avoid large retry numbers. If someone else has locked a record or table, you can always try again yourself after dBASE for Windows gives you an error message. Never use –1, unless you want to "hang" your computer.

Syntax

SET REPROCESS TO <expN>

The SET SAFETY Command

When the SET SAFETY command is ON, it causes dBASE for Windows to prompt you before overwriting a file or deleting all the records in a table or other activities about which you might want to think twice.

▶▶ **W A R N I N G**

The only time to set SAFETY OFF is when you know that you are going to overwrite a scratch, temporary file, with another one. When your program turns it off, be sure it turns it back on again almost immediately.

Syntax

SET SAFETY ON ¦ OFF

Example

SET SAFETY OFF
SET ALTERNATE TO t.tmp
SET ALTERNATE ON

SET SAFETY ON

The SET SEPARATOR Command

The SET SEPARATOR command specifies the character that is used to separate the whole part of numbers into groups of three digits each.

Syntax

SET SEPARATOR TO [*<expC >*]

The SET SKIP TO Command

The SET SKIP TO command specifies the record pointer advancement order when you have two or more related tables. Although the SET SKIP command is much simpler than the SET RELATION command, if you use (as we recommend) the Query Designer to define your tables' relationships, your SET SKIP commands will be correctly written for you by the Query Designer. See the SET RELATION command for more on this subject.

Syntax

SET SKIP TO [*<alias 1>* [, *<alias 2 >*] ...]

The SET SPACE Command

The SET SPACE command, if set ON, has dBASE for Windows include a space between fields in an output field list in commands such as ? and ??.

Syntax

SET SPACE ON ¦ OFF

The SET STATUS Command

The SET STATUS command turns the status bar on or off.

Syntax

SET STATUS ON ¦ OFF

The SET STEP Command

The SET STEP command is a synonym for DEBUG. Earlier versions of dBASE, which lacked a real debugging tool, let you SET STEP ON, which meant running a program one line at a time, pausing after each command.

Syntax

```
SET STEP ON ¦ OFF
```

The SET TALK Command

The SET TALK command turns the echo of command results to the results pane of the Command window on or off.

Syntax

```
SET TALK ON ¦ OFF
```

The SET TIME TO Command

The SET TIME TO command is similar to the DOS TIME command. It sets the system time.

Syntax

```
SET TIME TO <expC>
```

Example

```
SET TIME TO "13:30:30"
```

The SET TITLE Command

When the SET TITLE command is ON, it asks dBASE to prompt you for title and comment information when CATALOG is ON. (This adds descriptive information to each file in the catalog.)

Syntax

```
SET TITLE ON ¦ OFF
```

The SET TOPIC TO Command

The SET TOPIC TO command specifies the current Help topic. This is not useful in the Command window, since the HELP command itself takes a topic parameter (for example, HELP CLASS BROWSE), but it can be useful in a program to control the results you get when you press F1.

Syntax

    SET TOPIC TO [<expC >]

Example

    SET TOPIC TO "CLASS BROWSE"

The SET TYPEAHEAD TO Command

The SET TYPEAHEAD TO command sets the size of the typeahead buffer. The range is 0–1600 characters.

Syntax

    SET TYPEAHEAD TO <expN>

The SET UNIQUE Command

When the SET UNIQUE command is ON, it suppresses entry of multiple records with identical key values in an index file. If it is OFF, every record is indexed. If ON, only the first record that has a key value is entered into the index. Subsequent records with the same value are not indexed.

Syntax

    SET UNIQUE ON | OFF

The SET VIEW Command

The SET VIEW command specifies a query file (.QBE) to be used as the current database view.

Syntax

    SET VIEW TO <filename> | ? | <filename skeleton>

Example

    SET VIEW TO phones_b.qbe

The SET WP TO Command

The SET WP TO command specifies the executable file to be used as the editor for Memo fields.

Syntax

```
SET WP TO [<expC >]
```

The SHOW OBJECT Command

The SHOW OBJECT command refreshes the display of an object on a form. If you changed a bitmap, you could refresh the display of an Image or Pushbutton object that used the bitmap.

Syntax

```
SHOW OBJECT <form name>.<object name>
```

The SKIP Command

The SKIP command moves the record pointer the specified number of records forward (backward if the number is negative). If you have multiple tables open, the IN *<alias>* clause lets you specify a table other than the one in the currently selected work area as the one to skip.

Syntax

```
SKIP [<expN >] [IN <alias >]
```

Examples

SKIP	Current table, defaults to 1
SKIP -1	Back up one
SKIP 5 IN orgs	5 forward in the Orgs table

The SLEEP Command

The SLEEP command causes dBASE for Windows to "go to sleep" (be inactive) for the specified number of seconds, or until the specified time on the specified date. If the date is omitted, the UNTIL time applies to today.

This command can be used to have dBASE wait a bit (for example, when a necessary table is locked), or it can be used to set up a program that should be run later (such as a backup process that you want to run after midnight).

Syntax

SLEEP *<seconds expN>* ¦ UNTIL *<time expC>* [, *<date expC >*]

Example

This example tells dBASE for Windows to get up late tomorrow morning:

SLEEP UNTIL "11:00:00", DATE()+1

The SORT Command

The SORT command sorts one table into another table. (Sorting is covered in Chapter 4.)

 ▶ ▶ T I P

> **Use the Table Utilities menu to sort a table. You should almost never need to put a SORT command into a program. If you do, use Table Utilities and copy the command it writes into the Command window.**

Syntax

SORT TO *<filename>* ¦ ? ¦ *<filename skeleton>*
[[TYPE] PARADOX ¦ DBASE]
ON *<field 1>* [/A ¦ /D [/C]]
[,*<field 2>* [/A ¦ /D [/C]] ...]
[*<scope >*]
[FOR *<condition 1 >*]
[WHILE *<condition 2 >*]
[ASCENDING ¦ DESCENDING]

The STORE Command

The STORE command is synonymous with the assignment statement. Both of these are the same:

STORE 123 TO x

```
x = 123
```

The STORE command is the handier form when you want to store one value into more than one memory variable or array element.

Syntax

STORE *<exp>* TO *<memvar list >* ¦ *<array element list >*

or

<memvar> ¦ *<array element>* = *<exp>*

Example

In this example, we initialize variables prior to doing a calculation:

STORE 0 TO qty_on_hand, sales_to_date, taxes_due

The STORE AUTOMEM Command

The STORE AUTOMEM command copies every field in the current record to a memory variable with the same name as the field. This lets you build forms that use the memory variables as DataLink properties.

Using fields, if you make changes and then decide to quit without saving (clicking a Cancel button, for example), your program must go to considerable trouble to undo the changes. If the form used memory variables, no additional work is needed.

Syntax

STORE AUTOMEM

The STORE MEMO Command

The STORE MEMO command puts a Memo field into an array. Each element of the array is filled with text from the Memo field, up to the length set with MEMOWIDTH.

Syntax

STORE MEMO *<memo field >* TO ARRAY *<array name>*

The SUM Command

The SUM command lets you sum one or more fields or expressions over part or all of a table, optionally storing the results to one or more memory variables or an array.

Syntax

```
SUM
  [<exp list >]
  [<scope >]
  [FOR <condition 1 >]
  [WHILE <condition 2 >]
  [TO <memvar list > ¦ ARRAY <array name >]
```

Example

```
SUM Price*Quantity TO M->sales
```

The SUSPEND Command

The SUSPEND command halts program execution and places you in the Command window. You place a SUSPEND command in a program when it is not working as you planned and you want to investigate the possible cause of an error.

You insert the SUSPEND command near your suspected problem area and then run the program. When it is suspended, you can use ? commands to examine your data, or type in the following program commands one at a time to see what is going wrong.

Syntax

```
SUSPEND
```

The TOTAL Command

The TOTAL command sums all records with matching key values from one table into a single record in a second table.

Syntax

```
TOTAL ON <key expC> TO <filename> ¦ ? ¦ <filename skeleton>
  [[TYPE] PARADOX ¦ DBASE]
  [<scope >]
  [FOR <condition 1 >]
  [WHILE <condition 2 >]
  [FIELDS <field list >]
```

Example

The following TOTAL command creates a new table, St_Tot, which will have one record for each value of the index "State" in the Custmers table. The St_Tot table will total each of the Numeric and Float fields from the Custmers table. The value in each will be the total of the records for each state in the Custmers table.

```
USE custmers ORDER state
TOTAL ON state TO st_tot
```

The TYPE Command

The TYPE command is analogous to the DOS TYPE command. It will display the contents of a text file in the Command window's results pane. The MORE clause is similar to the DOS more pipe; it pauses typing each time the results pane is filled with text. The NUMBER clause adds line numbers to the display. The TO clause lets you redirect output to a file or to the printer.

Syntax

```
TYPE <filename 1> | ? | <filename skeleton>
  [MORE]
  [NUMBER]
  [TO FILE <filename 2> | ? | PRINTER]
```

The UNLOCK Command

The UNLOCK command releases any file or record locks in the current work area and in tables related with SET RELATION commands to the current work area.

Syntax

```
UNLOCK [ALL | IN <alias >]
```

The UPDATE Command

The UPDATE command copies values from a specified table into the current table, based on matching index values.

Syntax

```
UPDATE ON <key exp> FROM <alias>
  REPLACE <field 1> WITH <exp 1>
```

```
[, <field 2> WITH <exp 2> ... ]
[RANDOM]
[REINDEX]
```

Example

Assume that you have an Invoic table and an Inv_Dtl table. The Inv_Dtl table contains multiple records for each Invoic record. The Inv_Dtl records contain a part ID, the quantity order, and the total cost for that part. Each invoice is related to one or more of these detail records. You could conveniently total the costs for each invoice with a TOTAL command:

```
USE inv_dtl ORDER Invoic_ID
TOTAL ON Invoic_ID TO temp
```

Then you could update your INVOIC file from the TEMP file you just created:

```
USE invoic ORDER Invoic_ID
UPDATE ON Invoic_ID FROM temp ;
    REPLACE tot_cost WITH temp->cost
```

The USE Command

The USE command opens a table. It defaults to a .DBF file unless one of the other types is specified. It will be opened in the current work area, unless the IN clause is used.

A dBASE for Windows table is automatically opened with the production index (the .MDX file that has the same name as the .DBF file) unless the INDEX clause is used to specify an alternate index.

No master index is used unless the ORDER clause is specified. The keyword TAG may be used if you find it more readable.

If you specify AGAIN, you can open a table that is also open in one or more other work areas.

The default alias name of a table is the table's name. With the ALIAS clause, you can specify an alternate name.

The AUTOMEM clause causes dBASE for Windows to create a set of memory variables whose names match the names of the fields in the table (see STORE AUTOMEM).

The EXCLUSIVE or SHARED clause overrides the setting of SET EXCLUSIVE.

NOSAVE opens the table for temporary use. It is deleted (along with related files) when it is closed.

NOUPDATE opens the table for read-only use.

Syntax

```
USE
  [<filename 1> | ? | <filename skeleton 1>
  [[TYPE] PARADOX | DBASE] | [DATABASE <database name >]
  [IN <alias >]
  [INDEX <index name list> | <? list> | <index name skeleton
  list >]
  [ORDER [TAG] <.ndx filename> |
      <tag name>[OF <.mdx filename >]]
  [AGAIN]
  [ALIAS <alias name >]
  [AUTOMEM]
  [EXCLUSIVE | SHARED]
  [NOSAVE]
  [NOUPDATE]]
```

Example

Assume your system is for many stores, and you have a table for each store's sales. Your program could say:

```
USE store_1 ALIAS sales
DO my_prog

USE store_2 ALIAS sales
DO my_prog
```

Your my_prog routine would be programmed to use a Sales table and would work for any .DBF name.

The WAIT Command

The WAIT command can be used to pause output displayed in the Command window's results pane or program execution. The optional prompt replaces the default "Press any key to continue" message. The TO clause provides a memory variable to record the key pressed to continue.

Syntax

WAIT [<*prompt expC* >] [TO <*memvar* >]

Example

```
USE my_table
DO WHILE .NOT. EOF()
   LIST NEXT 10
   WAIT "Press Y to continue" TO key_pressed
   IF UPPER(key_pressed) <> 'Y'
     EXIT
   ENDIF
ENDDO
```

The ZAP Command

The ZAP command deletes every record in a table. (It is much faster than the equivalent DELETE ALL and PACK.) The ZAP command displays the Zap Records dialog box, which asks you if you want to delete every record in the table, unless SAFETY is off. The operation requires exclusive use of the table.

Syntax

ZAP

Example

```
USE scratch EXCLUSIVE
SET SAFETY OFF
ZAP
SET SAFETY ON
```

►► Summary

We divided all dBASE for Windows commands into two categories: programming statements and commands. The commands are lines that start with a verb, such as:

```
USE
LIST
SUM
```

The statements are the lines that control the execution of commands, and are covered separately in Chapter 14.

From the total set of commands, we placed those that are provided to support dBASE IV and older programs in Appendix D. In this chapter, we covered the commands that are used in the Command window and dBASE for Windows programs.

We divided the remaining commands into six categories. We listed the commands in each of these categories, and then gave you an alphabetical list showing the syntax and explaining the use of each command.

In the next chapter, we'll complete Part 4 with an overview of the programming statements.

Basics of Programming Statements

▶ ▶ *n* Chapter 12 we looked at dBASE for Windows expressions and functions. In Chapter 13 you met the Command window commands. The commands give you tremendous data-manipulation power, and the expressions let you specify indexes, data scopes, and more.

Although you don't need to be a dBASE for Windows programmer to handle your databases, you'll want to be able to put together simple programs to handle events, as you've already been doing in the Form Designer.

So far, you've let the Procedure Editor handle the details for you. In this chapter, you'll learn to use the basic dBASE for Windows program statements. These are program lines that provide structure and control, making decisions on which commands to execute at what times. Let's skip ahead a bit to look at a simple example:

```
IF total_sales <= slow
   REPLACE ALL product->price WITH product->price*0.9
ENDIF
```

The IF statement is one of the block statements. It controls *conditional* execution—one or more commands will be executed if the condition following the word IF evaluates to True. Here, we assume that a variable, *total_sales*, has been calculated, and another variable, *slow*, has been assigned some level of sales that we don't like.

If our sales have been slow, we'll do an across-the-board 10 percent price cut. (This is an example of dBASE programming, not an example of smart retail practice.)

As you can see, these statements are almost self-explanatory. The IF/ENDIF block does just what you might guess. The other good news about dBASE statements is that there aren't very many of them, so you won't have trouble keeping track of all of them.

We'll start with the block statements that you'll use frequently in the Form Designer's Procedure Editor. There are only four blocks to learn. After we're done with blocks, we'll show you the rest, so that you'll be able to read the output from the Form Designer and the Query Designer. But bear in mind that the block statements are the ones you'll need for your mental tool kit. The others are for reference, not daily use.

 ▶▶ **N O T E**

> **You may notice that our syntax is not always the syntax that you'll find in the software's language reference or in the on-line documentation. We think that ours is the most accurate documentation available at this time. Of course, we expect that the on-line documentation will be corrected and updated, so it should eventually become the best source.**

▶▶ *Block Statements*

When you use the Procedure Editor in the Form Designer, you'll be developing a single subroutine. Within any routine, the basic order of execution is sequential: the first command is executed, then the second, and so on.

The dBASE for Windows block statements let you vary this in two ways. First, you may wish to execute one or more commands conditionally, as you saw in the example in this chapter's introduction.

The other type of nonsequential operation is called *looping*. If you wanted to perform some operation on each of a dozen items, you could write the logic a dozen times. This is tedious, and gets unreasonable when a dozen items grow to hundreds or thousands of items. Looping lets you write the logic once and apply it to as many items as needed.

Let's start with the conditional statement blocks.

► Conditional Execution

There are two conditional execution blocks. The basic IF can be used for any conditional need, but the DO CASE is much easier to write when it applies. We'll begin with IF.

IF

The IF block begins with an IF statement and ends with an ENDIF. You've seen it used to execute a single command. Any number of commands can be placed between the IF and the ENDIF. They are all executed if the IF condition is True. None are executed if the IF condition is False.

The IF block can also contain an ELSE statement, which divides the block into two parts. Commands in the first part are executed if the IF condition is True. Commands in the second part are executed if the IF condition is False.

The syntax of the IF/ELSE command is:

```
IF <condition expL>
    <statements>
  [ELSEIF <condition expL>
    <statements>]...
   [ELSE
    <statements>]
ENDIF
```

This is an example:

```
IF total_sales <= slow

    REPLACE ALL product->price WITH product->price*0.9
    LIST OFF ALL product->name, product->price

ELSE

    REPLACE FOR produce->price > 100 ;
       product->price WITH product->price*1.05
    LIST OFF FOR product->price > 100 ;
       product->name, product->price

ENDIF
```

In this example, all product prices are reduced by 10 percent, and a new price list is printed when *total_sales* is bad. If *total_sales* is greater than *slow*, the products priced over 100 are increased by 5 percent, and a new list of just those product prices is printed.

We've shown two common uses of "white space" (blank lines and spaces within lines). We've indented the commands inside the IF block, and we've set them off with blank lines. Both of these improve the readability of the block. White space has no effect on the execution of the program and has very little effect on the program's size (a blank line adds two bytes to the file size). Use white space generously.

 ▶▶ **T I P**

> **Always write the entire block statement before you begin to fill in the details. Write the IF and ENDIF lines, with the ELSE if you want one, for example. Then go back and put the commands in between the IF and ENDIF.**

DO CASE

In some situations, you want to implement a variety of rules, covering different possibilities. For these, you could write lots of IF blocks:

```
IF total_sales <= slow

    REPLACE ALL product->price WITH product->price*0.9

ENDIF

IF total_sales > slow .AND. ;
    total_sales <= OK

    REPLACE ALL product->price WITH product->price*0.95

ENDIF

IF total_sales > OK .AND. ;
    total_sales <= fast

    REPLACE ALL product->price WITH product->price*1.05
```

```
ENDIF

IF total_sales > fast

    REPLACE ALL product->price WITH product->price*1.1

ENDIF
```

Although this type of programming works, it isn't much fun to type, and it's error-prone. The DO CASE block does a better job. Here's the same example:

```
DO CASE
    CASE total_sales <= slow
        REPLACE ALL product->price WITH product->price*0.9

    CASE total_sales <= OK
        REPLACE ALL product->price WITH product->price*0.95

    CASE total_sales <= fast
        REPLACE ALL product->price WITH product->price*1.05

    OTHERWISE
        REPLACE ALL product->price WITH product->price*1.1

ENDCASE
```

In a DO CASE block, each CASE is evaluated until one is True. The first one that is True is executed and that completes the block. If none are True, the optional OTHERWISE statement does just what it looks like: it heads a block of commands that execute if none of the CASEs is True.

As you can see in this example, this form simplifies the relational expressions. The second case here, for example says:

```
CASE total_sales <= OK
```

The comparable IF test was:

```
IF total_sales > slow .AND. ;
    total_sales <= OK
```

The CASE is simpler because the test immediately before was:

```
CASE total_sales <= slow
```

If *total_sales* was less than or equal to *slow*, the previous CASE would
have been True, its command(s) executed, and the DO CASE terminated. A DO CASE only gets to the second CASE if the first one isn't
True. It only gets to the third CASE if both the first and second ones
are False, and so on.

The syntax for the DO CASE command is:

```
DO CASE
  [CASE <condition expL>
    <statements>]...
  [OTHERWISE
    <statements>]
ENDCASE
```

▶ Looping

There are three looping blocks in dBASE for Windows. They are the
FOR, the DO WHILE, and the DO UNTIL loops. FOR loops are
used when you can count a specific number of repetitions. DO WHILE
and DO UNTIL loops are used when you want to keep looping as long
as some condition is True.

FOR

FOR loops were introduced into the Xbase family from BASIC. The
Clipper compiler adopted them, and they were later copied by FoxPro.
The DOS and Windows 5.0 products are the first to bring FOR loops
into dBASE. We're glad to have them.

The syntax of the FOR command is:

```
FOR <memvar> = <start expN> TO <end expN> [STEP <step expN>]
    <statements>
  [LOOP | EXIT
    <statements>]...
ENDFOR | NEXT
```

There is nothing that the FOR loop can do that the DO WHILE loop
can't handle. But since they are more limited, they can get their job
done more efficiently than DO WHILE.

Here's a sample FOR loop that writes the numbers 1 through 10 into
the Command window's results pane:

```
FOR i = 1 TO 10
  ? i
ENDFOR
```

BASIC's FOR loop is terminated with the NEXT statement. dBASE also allows NEXT as a synonym for ENDFOR. We like ENDFOR because all the other blocks are terminated with an END statement.

By adding the optional STEP clause, you can have the FOR loop work backward, and by units other than 1. Here's one that counts backward from 10 to 1 by halves:

```
FOR i = 10 TO 1 STEP -0.5
  ? i
ENDFOR
```

You can try a simple FOR loop in the Command window, entering it on a single line. Here's how:

```
FOR i = 1 TO 10; ? i; ENDFOR
```

 ▶▶ **N O T E**

> To enter a block command in the Command window, you must put it all on a single line. Use the semicolon to separate the components.

DO WHILE and DO UNTIL

The DO WHILE and DO UNTIL loops are very general. The most common use is to process each record in a table:

```
GO TOP
DO WHILE .NOT. EOF()
  * process the record here
  SKIP
ENDDO
```

You could also write:

```
GO TOP
DO
  * process the record here
  SKIP
UNTIL EOF()
```

The GO TOP command forces the record pointer to the top of the table. The SKIP command advances the pointer by one record. The comment "* process the record here" shows where you would place whatever commands or calculations you would like to do.

You can think of the flow of control in the DO WHILE as starting at the logical expression following the DO WHILE. If it evaluates to True, control passes to the commands inside the DO WHILE. The ENDDO transfers control back to the top, where this repeats.

```
DO WHILE <condition expL>
    <statements>
  [LOOP | EXIT
    <statements>]...
ENDDO
```

The DO UNTIL construct always executes the enclosed commands once. At the UNTIL statement, the logical expression is tested. If it is False, control passes back up to the top of the loop, and the commands in the loop are repeated until the UNTIL expression is True. The syntax is:

```
DO
MS   <statements>
  [LOOP | EXIT
    <statements>]...
  UNTIL <condition expL>
```

Use DO WHILE unless you want to be sure your commands get executed at least once. In that case, use DO UNTIL.

The DO WHILE construct tests its condition at the top, so it can execute zero or more times. The DO UNTIL tests at the bottom, so it executes one or more times.

In fact, the second version or our example may have a bug.

```
GO TOP
DO
  * process the record here
  SKIP
UNTIL EOF()
```

This code will probably fail if the table is empty. The DO WHILE version will correctly handle an empty table (by doing nothing).

▸▸ **W A R N I N G**

> If you had a dollar for every time a dBASE session was "hung" because someone forgot the SKIP command in a DO WHILE .NOT. EOF(), you would be very rich. If you omit the SKIP, the DO WHILE loop will execute forever (or until you reboot your computer).

LOOP and EXIT

There are two statements that apply inside DO WHILE, DO UNTIL, and FOR loops: LOOP and EXIT. They are usually found inside IF/ENDIF blocks. LOOP transfers control back to the beginning of the loop. EXIT terminates execution of the loop.

Here's an example, with comments in lieu of logic:

```
GO TOP
DO WHILE .NOT. EOF()

    IF && the current record isn't of interest
       SKIP && to the next record
       LOOP && back to the beginning
    ENDIF

    * This is the logic that applies to
    * the right sort of record.

    IF && the current record is the last one of interest
       EXIT && we're done
    ENDIF

    SKIP
ENDDO
```

Although LOOP can occur anywhere in a DO WHILE or FOR loop, it is most common at the top. You know that only some records get special treatment, so you SKIP and LOOP back to the top for the records that you don't want to process.

Similarly, the EXIT statement can be placed anywhere in a DO WHILE, DO UNTIL, or FOR loop, but it is most common near the end. You check for some condition that tells you that you have processed all the records you are interested in.

Combined, these give you the general capability that FOR and WHILE clauses do on commands. LOOPing back to the top if the record doesn't meet a condition is like executing a command FOR that condition. EXITing when a record doesn't meet a condition is like executing WHILE that condition is True.

LOOP and EXIT control the innermost loop in which they occur.

▶ Nesting

The example of LOOP and EXIT statements in the previous section used *nesting*, which is including one block statement within another. There is no limit to the level or kind of nesting that you can do. When you nest block statements, it is particularly important to keep using progressively more indentation levels, or you could easily fall into crossed-block conditions.

Here's the right way:

```
FOR i = 1 TO 5 && loop over 5 work areas

   GO TOP
   DO WHILE .NOT. EOF()

      * do some interesting calculations

      IF && last record of interest?
        EXIT
      ENDIF

      SKIP

   ENDDO

ENDFOR
```

You can use a block statement anywhere that you can use a simple command. What you cannot do is cross them up like this:

```
FOR i = 1 TO 5 && loop over 5 work areas

   GO TOP
   DO WHILE .NOT. EOF()

      * do some interesting calculations

      IF && last record of interest?
         EXIT
ENDFOR && Error!

   ENDDO && Error!

      ENDIF && Error!
```

The last block statement you started must be completed before any prior block statement can be completed. If you start a FOR and then a DO WHILE, you must complete the DO WHILE before you complete the FOR. If you start other block statements inside the DO WHILE, they must all be completed before you finish the DO WHILE.

This is where you'll see that the indentation custom is vitally important. The errors in our example above were fairly obvious. But suppose we weren't in the habit of using white space so generously. Is this example correct?

```
FOR i = 1 TO 5 && loop over 5 work areas
GO TOP
DO WHILE .NOT. EOF()
* do some interesting calculations
IF && last record of interest?
EXIT
SKIP
ENDDO
ENDIF
ENDFOR
```

It's not correct, and dBASE's compiler will tell you so. The good news is that these mistakes are caught when the program is compiled, so it won't start executing and then get into a thorough tangle.

►► *Intra-file Program Structure*

Within a program file, you can have a mainline and multiple subroutines. When you are in the Procedure Editor in the Form Designer, you are working on a subroutine.

A subroutine begins when you declare it, and it ends at the end of the file or class, or when another subroutine is declared.

► *Subroutine Declarations*

The two types of subroutines that you can declare in dBASE for Windows are PROCEDURE and FUNCTION. The PROCEDURE subroutine does not return a value; the FUNCTION subroutine does return a value. (See Chapter 12 for a discussion of the dBASE for Windows built-in functions.)

We should point out that the above rule can be broken, if you like. FUNCTIONs *must* return values, but PROCEDUREs may be used just like functions. We don't use PROCEDUREs to return values, though, just so that it's easier for us to read our own programs.

The PROCEDURE Statement

A PROCEDURE begins with a PROCEDURE statement. The documentation suggests that a PROCEDURE ends with an optional RETURN statement, but this is not true. RETURN statements are covered a little later. As you'll see, they can be used anywhere.

The syntax for the PROCEDURE command is

```
PROCEDURE <procedure name>[(<parameter list>)]
   [PARAMETERS <parameter list>]
   [[<statements>] RETURN <return exp>]...
```

Here's a simple procedure that prints a full name when first and last names are in the open table:

```
PROCEDURE say_full_name

? RTRIM(first_name)+' '+RTRIM(last_name)

* end of say_full_name
```

When your program does a procedure or function, it temporarily halts and passes control to the subroutine. The subroutine executes its statement, and then returns control to the calling routine. The calling routine resumes executing after the call to the subroutine.

When a PROCEDURE ends (at the end of the file, the class, or when another subroutine is declared), it passes control back to the routine that called it. A RETURN statement can be used to make this explicit. Here's the same example with an explicit RETURN:

```
PROCEDURE say_full_name

? RTRIM(first_name)+' '+RTRIM(last_name)

RETURN && end of say_full_name
```

The syntax of the RETURN command is:

```
RETURN [<return exp> ¦ TO MASTER ¦ TO <routine name> ]
```

Sometimes we use RETURNs, and sometimes we don't. It makes no difference in the program. We always use a comment that identifies the end of the procedure and names the procedure that is ending. In the above examples, this may seem a little redundant. But many procedures grow over time as you add more logic. When the end of the procedure is not on the same page or screen as the start, you'll see that this is a valuable habit.

FUNCTION

The other type of subroutine is the function, declared with the FUNCTION statement. As we noted earlier, FUNCTIONs must return values.

The syntax of the FUNCTION command is:

```
FUNCTION <function name>[(<parameter list>)]
  [PARAMETERS <parameter list>]
  [ [<statements>]
  RETURN <return exp>]...
```

Here is a function that prepares a full name from first and last names, but returns it to the calling program instead of displaying it on the screen:

```
FUNCTION make_full_name
LOCAL s
```

```
s = RTRIM(first_name)+' '+RTRIM(last_name)

RETURN s

* end of make_full_name
```

Functions written this way can be used just like the dBASE for Windows built-in functions. They are used as parts of expressions, just as you see RTRIM used in this function. Here's an example of code that uses that make_full_name( ) function above:

```
* List employees:
USE emps
LIST ALL emp_id, make_full_name()
```

Note that you need the parentheses. These identify the item as a subroutine call.

▶ *Other Subroutine Statements*

The subroutines above did not have parameters, which sometimes is the case in running code. Frequently, however, functions have parameters.

RETURN statements may mark the end of procedures and functions, but they have other uses, too. These are covered here.

Including Parameters

In a very confusing bit of terminology, you pass *arguments* to functions, and the functions receive *parameters*, which are the same values that you called *arguments* when you were thinking about calling the function.

The syntax of the PARAMETERS command is:

```
PARAMETERS <parameter list>
```

Here is a mainline and function for calculating the cubic volume of cartons:

```
? 'Little one: ' + STR( carton_volume(2, 3, 4) )
? 'Big one: ' + STR( carton_volume(20, 30, 40) )

FUNCTION carton_volume
PARAMETERS height, length, width

RETURN height * length * width
```

```
* end of carton_volume
```

This code will report:

Little one:	24
Big one:	24000

The call carton_volume(2, 3, 4) is said to *pass the arguments* 2, 3, and 4 to the carton_volume function. In turn, the carton_volume function is said to *receive the parameters* height, length, and width. In this case, height is 2, length is 3, and width is 4.

Parameters may be specified by enclosing them in parentheses in the function declaration line. Here's the same example, with this alternate form:

```
? 'Little one: ' + STR( carton_volume(2, 3, 4) )
? 'Big one: ' + STR( carton_volume(20, 30, 40) )

FUNCTION carton_volume(height, length, width)

RETURN height * length * width

* end of carton_volume
```

There is a subtle difference between these forms that is unimportant if your function, such as this one, does not call other functions you have written. If you start writing functions that call your other functions, you'll want to carefully consider the different scoping.

RETURN

RETURN statements can be used anywhere in a dBASE for Windows program. Their primary use is to RETURN values from functions, or to specify the RETURN of control to the calling routine in procedures. You have seen both of these uses in the examples above.

Here we'll show some of their other uses. First, multiple RETURNs may be used. A typical case is to check for an error condition and RETURN immediately:

```
PROCEDURE long_complicated_proc

IF EOF() && can't do this at EOF()
```

```
    RETURN
ENDIF

* long, complicated set
* of statements here

RETURN && end of long_complicated_proc
```

Functions can also RETURN from different points in the function. Here's an example that returns an adjective describing business conditions:

```
* logic here calculates "unemp_rate"

? "Unemployment is "+unemp_descrip(unemp_rate)

FUNCTION unemp_descrip(urate)

DO CASE
    CASE urate < .02
        RETURN "dangerously low"

    CASE urate < .04
        RETURN "low"

    CASE urate < .06
        RETURN "moderate"

    OTHERWISE
        RETURN "high"

ENDCASE

* end of unemp_descrip
```

Note that some software-engineering theorists recommend that each subroutine have exactly one RETURN point. We disapprove of the indiscriminate use of RETURNs, but think that both the examples above are good examples of well-written, readable, and maintainable code.

▶▶ **W A R N I N G**

You should avoid burying a RETURN someplace in the middle of a complex function that looks like it returns a value from the end. If you have a nonobvious RETURN, put a comment at the end of the routine that says, "* under such and such conditions, there's a RETURN taken 25 lines above." Keep your RETURNs obvious.

DO

You've seen that your functions can be called by including them in expressions, just like the dBASE built-in functions. You call a procedure with the DO statement, giving a command as you would for any other dBASE command:

```
* start of SAY_HI.PRG

DO hello

* end of mainline

PROCEDURE hello
? "Hello, world!"
* end of hello

* end of SAY_HI.PRG
```

The above example is a complete program illustrating the DO command. The DO keyword can be eliminated if you use parentheses following the subroutine name, as in this example:

```
* start of SAY_HI.PRG

hello()

* end of mainline

PROCEDURE hello
? "Hello, world!"
* end of hello
```

```
* end of SAY_HI.PRG
```

In both cases, the subroutine you DO could be either a procedure or a function, but we think that calling functions this way (the value they return will be discarded) doesn't make much sense.

In both cases, parameters can be included with the call. Here's an example showing both ways:

```
* start of SAY_HI.PRG

DO hello WITH "DO/WITH form"
hello("parentheses form")

* end of mainline

PROCEDURE hello(string_to_report)
? string_to_report
* end of hello

* end of SAY_HI.PRG
```

Both calls to hello( ) report their respective argument strings. There is no difference in the compiled code that is produced for these two methods.

 ►►**T I P**

> **Adopt a consistent method of calling subroutines and stick with it. We like to use DO *<procname>* when there are no arguments and we use the form with parentheses when there are arguments (saves typing).**

ON

In addition to explicitly calling your subroutine, you can use an ON command to notify dBASE for Windows that there is a condition to watch for and that your subroutine should be called when it occurs. The ON KEY and ON ERROR commands are two ON commands.

ON KEY is used to assign a dBASE command (a DO command or any other) to respond to a specific keystroke. The ON ERROR command assigns a dBASE command (almost always a DO command, but it could be any other) to execute in response to an error.

The primary use for ON KEY is to respond to an extended set of function keys (F1 is assigned to Help, automatically). ON ERROR's primary use is to gracefully handle multiuser situations, such as attempting to write to a record locked by another user.

The syntax of the ON commands is:

ON ERROR [*<command>*]

ON ESCAPE [*<command>*]

ON KEY [LABEL *<key label>*] [*<command>*]

ON NETERROR [*<command>*]

ON PAGE [AT LINE *<expN>* *<command>*]

ON READERROR [*<command>*]

ON SELECTION FORM *<form name>* [*<expFP>* ¦ *<expCB>*]

▸ CLASS Blocks

Building your own classes is best left to major programming efforts, and we would like to say that they are beyond the scope of this book. But we can't say that.

The problem is that if you have generated your first Form Designer form, you have built your first class using CLASS blocks. That's precisely what a form is—a customized class inheriting the Form class's properties and adding the details specific to your form.

If you look at the generated .WFM file, it starts like this:

```
** END HEADER -- do not remove this line*
* Generated on 07/05/94
*
LOCAL f
f = NEW OBJECTSFORM()
f.Open()

CLASS OBJECTSFORM OF FORM
```

As discuss in Chapter 15, your commands and comments can precede the ** END HEADER line. The Two-Way-Tool capability requires this line. It lets the Form Designer know where its code starts and your code stops.

The next three lines after the comment establish a LOCAL variable (LOCALs are covered later in this chapter, in the section about variable declarations) and creates a NEW instance of your class. The third line launches the form.

The CLASS OBJECTSFORM OF FORM begins a CLASS/END-CLASS block. The OF FORM tells dBASE for Windows that your OBJECTSFORM class should inherit all the properties (including data, event handlers, and methods) of the Form class.

The CLASS block has this structure:

```
CLASS
    * constructor code
    * method 1
    * method 2
    * ...
ENDCLASS
```

The *constructor code* is the part that runs when you create a member of your class. It will define the text labels, entry fields, pushbuttons, comboboxes, and whatever else builds your form.

The *methods* are subroutines that are specific to your class. For example, you could have an OnResize method that adjusted your form's components sizes when the user resizes the form. This is important when you remember that you could have many sorts of forms which all have their own OnResize methods.

As with the other blocks, you can have as many CLASS blocks as you like, and other blocks can nest inside the CLASS blocks. CLASS blocks themselves cannot be nested, however.

The syntax of the CLASS command is:

```
CLASS <class name> [(parameters)] [CUSTOM]
PARAMETERS [(parameters)]
[OF <base class name>] [(parameters)]
[<constructor code>]
[<member functions>]
ENDCLASS
```

►► *Inter-file Program Structure*

Two commands, SET PROCEDURE and SET LIBRARY, give you access to classes and subroutines spread over multiple files. Additionally, the DO command will also let you run code in a separate file.

► *The SET PROCEDURE Command*

The SET PROCEDURE command informs dBASE for Windows that your subroutines and classes may be found in a separate file. This example lets your program use code in the MY_LIB.PRG file:

```
SET PROCEDURE TO my_lib
```

The procedure file does not need to be in your current working directory. (Normally, you move your procedure files to a separate directory when all their programs are fully debugged.) This example uses a procedure file in another directory:

```
SET PROCEDURE TO \dbwork\lib\my_lib
```

These examples opened a single file as *the* procedure file. You may want to have more than one open. In this case, use the ADDITIVE keyword:

```
SET PROCEDURE TO my_lib
SET PROCEDURE TO another_lib ADDITIVE
```

 ►►**T I P**

> **We always include the ADDITIVE keyword. If no other procedure files are open, it has no effect. Other routines elsewhere may be depending on open procedure files, so you want to be sure you don't inadvertently close them.**

You may close all open procedure files with the simplest form of the SET PROCEDURE command:

```
SET PROCEDURE TO
```

Without a parameter, all open procedure files are closed.

▶ *The SET LIBRARY Command*

The LIBRARY file is a special case of a PROCEDURE file. You get exactly one library file, and it has a special place (last) in the search order. It has the same capabilities as the PROCEDURE file, except that it does not accept the ADDITIVE keyword.

Over time, you may find that you have created several subroutines that you use in different systems. These should be placed in your library file.

To open a library file:

    SET LIBRARY TO my_lib

To open a library file in another directory:

    SET LIBRARY TO \dbwork\lib\my_lib

To close the library file:

    SET LIBRARY TO

▶ *The DO Command*

We have used DO to call a subroutine in the same file as itself. DO has much more power than that. First, the file name alone is the name of the code that comes before any subroutine or class declaration. It can be used as a subroutine. Here's an example, where the main routine calls another file as a subroutine. We'll start with the main routine:

    * Start of MAIN.PRG

    DO banger

    * end of MAIN.PRG

This is the subroutine file:

    * Start of BANGER.PRG

    ? 'BIIGGG BBBBAAAAANNNNNNGGGGGGG!!!!!!!!'

    * end of BANGER.PRG

Running the mainline will get the big bang from BANGER.PRG. Both MAIN and BANGER could also have additional subroutines and classes.

Programming Statements

Ch. 14

This means, of course, that you could have two subroutines with the same name. How does dBASE decide which to use? The answer is that it knows by the search order.

The Search Order

dBASE for Windows searches for a subroutine in a specific order. First, it looks in the file where the subroutine (procedure or function) is called. All this searching stops as soon as dBASE finds the subroutine it's looking for. If it finds it in the current file, it looks no further.

If it can't find the subroutine in the current file, dBASE looks in any other running files. In the previous example, MAIN.PRG called BANGER.PRG. If BANGER called another subroutine, dBASE would look in BANGER first, then in MAIN.

Next, dBASE looks in any PROCEDURE files (files opened with SET PROCEDURE commands). It examines PROCEDURE files in the order they were opened with SET PROCEDURE commands.

If it still hasn't found the routine, dBASE looks in your LIBRARY file (if you have SET LIBRARY to a file). This means that your LIBRARY file has last priority, which is useful. If your LIBRARY file has a routine that you want to modify for just one application, put the modified version in a PROCEDURE file opened in that application. Your other applications will still access the standard LIBRARY version.

Finally, dBASE looks for a program file (.PRG extension) whose name matches the subroutine's name. It looks first in the current directory, and then follows your search path, if you've specified one.

And there's one more detail. dBASE looks for a .PRG and a .PRO file. The .PRO file is the compiled version of the .PRG file. If it finds both, it compares their time/date stamps. If the .PRG file has been modified (changed after the .PRO file was created), dBASE recompiles the .PRG file to create a new .PRO file. If dBASE can't find the .PRG file, it will use the .PRO file as is. If it finds a .PRG file but not a .PRO file, it will compile to .PRO and then use that .PRO.

Shortening the Search

If you specify a path with the DO command, dBASE assumes that you want to run the .PRG file you specified. In our big bang example, we could have written:

    DO \dbwork\banger

In this form, there is no search. dBASE compares the .PRG file to the .PRO file, recompiles if necessary, and runs the program.

 ►►N O T E

> **You can also put subroutines in classes. See a dBASE programming book for details.**

►► *Variable Declarations*

The final class of dBASE for Windows statements we'll consider is the group of variable declarations. In dBASE, these declarations restrict the scope of the variable.

► *LOCAL Variables*

LOCAL variables are new with dBASE for Windows 5.0. For experienced programmers, LOCALs will be by far the most popular data declarations.

The syntax of the LOCAL command is:

    LOCAL <memvar list>

This example declares three LOCAL variables:

    LOCAL i, j, summary_total

LOCAL variables exist just in the subroutine in which they are declared. No other routine can see them. (This means that no other routine can inadvertently change them.) Every subroutine you have could use the same name, but if the variables are LOCAL, they never conflict.

LOCAL variables are created when the subroutine begins, and they are discarded when the subroutine ends.

▶ STATIC Variables

STATIC variables are permanent. They are created when the subroutine that declares them starts for the first time. They are discarded when the whole program terminates.

The syntax of the STATIC command is:

    STATIC <memvar list>

The declaration statement can assign a value:

    STATIC x, y, z
    STATIC background_color = 'N/W'

The STATIC declaration can mix assignments freely within its variable list. For instance:

    STATIC x=1, y, z=.T.

STATIC variables are used when you want persistent values. You might use one to keep a session-wide total of records added to a file, or to store color specifications and other system settings.

▶ PRIVATE Variables

PRIVATE data is not in the least PRIVATE. Like a LOCAL, a PRIVATE variable is created by the subroutine that declares it and is discarded when that subroutine terminates. But it is visible to that subroutine and every subroutine called by it.

This is useful only when you have a specific reason for letting a lower-level routine modify a value in the current routine. Software-engineering theorists claim that this should never be done. We almost never use PRIVATEs anymore.

In the early days (before dBASE 5.0) the only scopes you could declare were PUBLIC and PRIVATE. Declaring a variable PRIVATE prevented that variable from inadvertently changing a value in a higher-level routine. So it provided a bit of privacy to the routines above it, but had no privacy with respect to routines that it called, which may not have always declared their variables PRIVATE.

The syntax of the PRIVATE command is:

    PRIVATE <memvar list> | ALL

```
[LIKE <memvar skeleton 1>]
[EXCEPT <memvar skeleton 2>]
```

▶ *PUBLIC Variables*

PUBLIC data is available to every routine in the system. Importantly, the lifetime of a PUBLIC is the life of your dBASE session, not just the program that creates the variable.

The syntax of the PUBLIC command is:

```
PUBLIC <memvar list> ¦
    ARRAY <array name 1>"["<expN list 1>"]"
    [, <array name 2>"["<expN list 2>"]"]...
```

Let's look at an example:

```
PUBLIC myform
myform = NEW Form()
myform.Open()
```

When you run this code, you create a PUBLIC variable, assign a reference to a new default form to it, and then open the form. When your form is opened, your program is completed. By making *myform* a PUBLIC variable, you have it still available in the Command window, or to other programs.

In the Command window you could say, for example:

```
INSPECT(myform)
```

If *myform* were not PUBLIC, that INSPECT( ) function would only report that the variable *myform* was undefined. It would have been discarded when the program terminated.

Programming Statements

Ch.
14

▶ *DECLARE Declarations*

Arrays are created with DECLARE declarations. An array is a named, sized collection of memory variables.

The syntax of the DECLARE command is:

```
DECLARE <array name 1>"["<expN list 1>"]"
    [,<array name 2>"["<expN list 2>"]"...]
```

These are declarations of one- and two-dimensional arrays:

```
DECLARE names[10]
DECLARE square[5, 5]
DECLARE small[50], medium[500], large[5000]
```

These arrays are then used to store data. For example:

```
DECLARE names[10]

names[1] = "Tom"
names[2] = "Dick"
names[3] = "Harry"
```

▶▶ Adding Comments

As you've seen in this and previous chapters, you can (and should) use comments generously in your program code. There are several ways you can put comments into a dBASE program:

```
&& <comment>
```

```
* <comment>
```

```
NOTE <comment>
```

▶▶ Other Statements

Some other statements you may use are PRINTJOB and SCAN. The TEXT statement is used in earlier versions of dBASE.

▶ The PRINTJOB Command

The PRINTJOB block can be used to program the printer directly, without using Crystal Reports. Its syntax is:

```
PRINTJOB
  <commands>
ENDPRINTJOB
```

▶ *The SCAN Command*

SCAN provides an alternative to the DO WHILE or DO/UNTIL loops. Its syntax is:

```
SCAN... [WHILE <condition 2>]
     [<statements>]
    [LOOP ¦ EXIT
       <statements>]...
ENDSCAN
```

▶ *The TEXT Command*

The TEXT command is a block statement that is primarily used in dBASE IV and older programs. Its syntax is:

```
TEXT
     <text characters>
ENDTEXT
```

The TEXT block could contain a block of text from one to many lines long. This would be output to the output device. One application of the TEXT block was to write the body of form letters. With dBASE for Windows, the same function is provided by the text capability of Crystal Reports (see Chapter 11.)

▶▶ *Summary*

In this chapter, you've studied the commands that give the program structure. We call these commands *statements*.

You met the block statements. The conditional blocks are the IF/ELSE/ENDIF test and the DO CASE/CASE/OTHERWISE/ ENDCASE switch. The looping blocks are FOR/ENDFOR, DO WHILE/ENDDO, and DO/UNTIL. The loops can include LOOP and EXIT statements.

You also learned that all the block statements can be nested, and that indenting your code is a good way of making it clear and avoiding errors.

Programming Statements

Ch.
14

After the block statements, you looked at the structures that are used within a program file. These include the FUNCTION and PROCE-DURE subroutine declarations. Other statements used in subroutines are PARAMETERS, RETURN, DO, and ON.

You also studied the CLASS/ENDCLASS blocks. These are always written by the Form Designer when it saves your designs.

You went on to examine the inter-file structure statements, including SET PROCEDURE, SET LIBRARY, and DO. You learned that a program could be used as a subroutine by another program. We discussed the order in which dBASE searches your files for subroutines, and learned to control the one it picks if you have more than one with the same name.

Finally, you met all the variable declaration statements. These are LOCAL, STATIC, PRIVATE, PUBLIC, and DECLARE.

This concludes Part 4. In Part 5, we'll delve into the Form Designer and its associated tools, such as the Menu Designer and the Procedure Editor.

www.ingramcontent.com/pod-product-compliance
Lightning Source LLC
Chambersburg PA
CBHW080128060326
40689CB00018B/3720